best over salads.

PRICE: $36.99 (3559/wi   )

500 BEST-EVER SALADS

500 BEST-EVER SALADS

Presenting every kind of salad, from appetizers and side dishes to impressive main courses, with meat, fish and vegetarian options, and more than 500 colour photographs

CONSULTANT EDITOR: JULIA CANNING

LORENZ BOOKS

This edition is published by Lorenz Books, an imprint of Anness Publishing Ltd, Hermes House, 88–89 Blackfriars Road, London SE1 8HA; tel. 020 7401 2077; fax 020 7633 9499

www.lorenzbooks.com; www.annesspublishing.com

If you like the images in this book and would like to investigate using them for publishing, promotions or advertising, please visit our website www.practicalpictures.com for more information.

UK agent: The Manning Partnership Ltd; tel. 01225 478444; fax 01225 478440; sales@manning-partnership.co.uk

UK distributor: Grantham Book Services Ltd; tel. 01476 541080; fax 01476 541061; orders@gbs.tbs-ltd.co.uk

North American agent/distributor: National Book Network; tel. 301 459 3366; fax 301 429 5746; www.nbnbooks.com

Australian agent/distributor: Pan Macmillan Australia; tel. 1300 135 113; fax 1300 135 103; customer.service@macmillan.com.au

New Zealand agent/distributor: David Bateman Ltd; tel. (09) 415 7664; fax (09) 415 8892

ETHICAL TRADING POLICY
At Anness Publishing we believe that business should be conducted in an ethical and ecologically sustainable way, with respect for the environment and a proper regard to the replacement of the natural resources we employ.
As a publisher, we use a lot of wood pulp to make high-quality paper for printing, and that wood commonly comes from spruce trees. We are therefore currently growing more than 500,000 trees in two Scottish forest plantations near Aberdeen – Berrymoss (130 hectares/320 acres) and West Touxhill (125 hectares/305 acres). The forests we manage contain twice the number of trees employed each year in paper-making for our books.
Because of this ongoing ecological investment programme, you, as our customer, can have the pleasure and reassurance of knowing that a tree is being cultivated on your behalf to naturally replace the materials used to make the book you are holding.
Our forestry programme is run in accordance with the UK Woodland Assurance Scheme (UKWAS) and will be certified by the internationally recognized Forest Stewardship Council (FSC). The FSC is a non-government organization dedicated to promoting responsible management of the world's forests. Certification ensures forests are managed in an environmentally sustainable and socially responsible basis. For further information about this scheme, go to www.annesspublishing.com/trees

© Anness Publishing Ltd 2007

A CIP catalogue record for this book is available from the British Library.

Publisher: Joanna Lorenz
Editorial Director: Helen Sudell
Project Editor: Rosie Gordon
Copy-editor: Julia Canning
Jacket Design: Nigel Partridge
Production Controller: Don Campaniello

Notes

Bracketed terms are intended for American readers.

For all recipes, quantities are given in both metric and imperial measures and, where appropriate, in standard cups and spoons. Follow one set of measures, but not a mixture, because they are not interchangeable.

Standard spoon and cup measures are level.
1 tsp = 5ml, 1 tbsp = 15ml, 1 cup = 250ml/8fl oz

Australian standard tablespoons are 20ml.
Australian readers should use 3 tsp in place of 1 tbsp for measuring small quantities.

American pints are 16fl oz/2 cups. American readers should use 20fl oz/2.5 cups in place of 1 pint when measuring liquids.

Electric oven temperatures in this book are for conventional ovens. When using a fan oven, the temperature will probably need to be reduced by about 10–20°C/20–40°F. Since ovens vary, you should check with your manufacturer's instruction book for guidance.

The nutritional analysis given for each recipe is calculated per portion (i.e. serving or item), unless otherwise stated. If the recipe gives a range, such as Serves 4–6, then the nutritional analysis will be for the smaller portion size, i.e. 6 servings. Measurements for sodium do not include salt added to taste.

Medium (US large) eggs are used unless otherwise stated.

Main front cover image shows Sautéed Herb Salad with Chilli & Preserved Lemon – for recipe, see page 92.

Contents

Salads are the perfect choice for contemporary meals. Quick, easy and inevitably composed of the freshest ingredients, they provide the healthy answer to the eternal question of what to serve for lunch or supper. There's a salad for every season and every occasion, from snacks through light lunches to casual suppers and formal dinners. Just how varied these fresh and colourful dishes are is obvious from this selection of five hundred favourites. Within these pages you'll find simple tapas, appetizers and starters, side salads and substantial platters based on fish and shellfish, meat or poultry. Many of the recipes are meat or fish-free, but there's also a chapter of dedicated dishes that cooks can serve with confidence to vegetarian guests. Fruit salads make great desserts but are also ideal for breakfast, especially now that many people prefer a lighter option.

Because salads are almost inevitably based on fresh produce, they are more ingredient-driven than other dishes. It is no use planning to serve a superb salad, only to discover that the central ingredient is out of season, or looks limp and unappetizing after a long journey from some foreign field. It makes sense, therefore, to abandon the usual practice of basing a meal around specific recipes before going shopping. Instead, check out what's freshest and best, and then plan your menu. Farm shops and farmers' markets are a great source of seasonal vegetables and fruits, or you may belong to a box scheme, and have a regular delivery of freshly pulled or picked produce. You may even grow your own. You don't have to own an vegetable garden to have a regular supply of fresh vegetables – seed manufacturers increasingly offer packs that are perfect for growing in pots. The range is quite extensive and includes salad leaves, rocket (arugula), chillies, bush courgettes (zucchini), dwarf beans, spring onions, carrots, sweet (bell) peppers, herbs of every description and tomatoes, especially tumblers.

This book is organised so that like vegetables are grouped together in various categories, so whatever is in season, whether it be Jersey potatoes, fat fennel bulbs, glossy mizuna leaves or baby broad (fava) beans, you'll find it easy to locate a suitable recipe. In fact, you'll be spoiled for choice, since there are several different suggestions for every ingredient.

Every country has its own favourite salad and it is fascinating to see how many ways there are of presenting the same ingredient. Take something as simple as a tomato, for

instance. In Italy it might be sliced with mozzarella cheese and basil, or mixed with bread and anchovies to make panzanella. A Jewish cook might combine tomatoes and peppers, while in Turkey and Greece, feta cheese and black olives are popular additions. Moroccan and French cooks like tomatoes and tuna, while a favourite Mexican treatment is to use tomatoes in all sorts of salsas, sometimes with the chillies that are so common in that country, but also with oranges and chives, coriander (cilantro) or other fresh herbs. Tomato salads can also include grains, like couscous or bulgur wheat, and are great blended with pasta or rice.

Warm salads are becoming increasingly popular, and this book contains a superb selection. Try Braised Artichokes with Fresh Peas, Roast Mediterranean Vegetables with Pecorino, or Warm Hazelnut and Pistachio Salad. Among the more unusual offerings are Baked Sweet Potato Salad and Stir-fried Pineapple Salad with Ginger and Chilli.

The golden rule when making a salad is not to toss in everything but the kitchen sink, but rather to choose a few ingredients with complementary or contrasting textures and compatible flavours. Vegetables or fruits will provide plenty of colour, but you can also add edible flowers such as nasturtiums,

marigolds or borage to enliven green leaves. Use herbs with discretion; rocket gives green salads a lovely peppery flavour, but tastes best when balanced with milder green leaves or with a sweet fruit such as pears or figs. Parsley, dill, mint and basil all make good additions when matched with other flavours.

Occasionally, a recipe will suggest marinating meat or fish, or steeping in a dressing to allow flavours to blend, but it is more usual to add a dressing just before serving. Salad servers can be used for mixing, but many cooks prefer to use clean hands, since they are softer and less likely to bruise delicate leaves. Use only enough dressing to gloss the ingredients, enhancing their flavour without being too dominant.

The recipes in this book come with carefully selected dressings, but by mixing and matching, you can create new and different combinations, giving you even more choice when serving these versatile dishes. With practice, you will instinctively know the flavours and textures that work together.

Finally, all of these recipes have been analysed by a nutritionist, and the energy, fat, carbohydrate and protein count, and levels of fibre, calcium and sodium, are detailed under each entry. This information enables you to plan meals that are delicious and nutritious.

Saffron Dip

Serve this mild dip with crudités – it's especially good with cauliflower.

Makes about 220ml/ 7½fl oz/1 cup

15ml/1 tbsp boiling water

small pinch of saffron threads
200g/7oz/scant 1 cup
   fromage frais
10 fresh chives
10 fresh basil leaves
5ml/1 tsp paprika
salt and ground black pepper

1 Infuse the saffron strands in the freshly boiled water for 3 minutes.

2 Beat the fromage frais until smooth and soft, then stir in the saffron infusion.

3 Using scissors, snip the chives into the dip. Tear the basil leaves into small pieces and stir them in.

4 Season with salt and freshly ground black pepper to taste and serve immediately.

French Dressing

French vinaigrette is the most widely used salad dressing.

Makes about 120ml/4fl oz/ ½ cup

90ml/6 tbsp extra-virgin olive oil
15ml/1 tbsp white wine vinegar
5ml/1 tsp French mustard

1 Place the extra-virgin olive oil and white wine vinegar in a clean screw-top jar.

2 Add the mustard and sugar.

3 Replace the lid and shake well.

Creamy Raspberry Dressing

This tangy dressing goes very well with asparagus instead of hollandaise sauce.

Makes about 100ml/3fl oz/ ⅓ cup

30ml/2 tbsp raspberry vinegar
2.5ml/½ tsp salt
5ml/1 tsp Dijon mustard
60ml/4 tbsp crème fraîche or
   natural (plain) yogurt
ground white pepper

1 Mix the vinegar and salt in a bowl and stir with a fork until the salt is dissolved.

2 Stir in the mustard, crème fraîche or yogurt and add pepper to taste.

French Herb Dressing

The delicate scents and flavours of fresh herbs combine especially well in a French dressing. Use just one herb or a selection. Toss with a simple green salad and serve with good cheese, fresh bread and wine.

Makes about 120ml/ 4fl oz/½ cup

60ml/4 tbsp extra-virgin olive oil
30ml/2 tbsp groundnut or
   sunflower oil
15ml/1 tbsp lemon juice
60ml/4 tbsp finely chopped
   fresh herbs
pinch of caster (superfine) sugar

1 Place the olive oil and groundnut or sunflower oil in a clean screw-top jar.

2 Add the lemon juice, chopped fresh herbs and sugar. Replace the lid and shake well.

Thousand Island Dressing

This creamy dressing is great with green salads and grated carrot, hot potato, pasta and rice salads.

Makes about 120ml/ 4fl oz/½ cup

60ml/4 tbsp sunflower oil
15ml/1 tbsp orange juice
15ml/1 tbsp lemon juice
10ml/2 tsp grated (shredded)
   lemon rind
15ml/1 tbsp finely chopped onion

5ml/1 tsp paprika
5ml/1 tsp Worcestershire sauce
15ml/1 tbsp finely chopped
   fresh parsley
salt and ground black pepper

1 Put all the ingredients into a screw-top jar and season to taste.

2 Replace the lid and shake well.

Blue Cheese & Chive Dressing

Blue cheese dressings have a strong, robust flavour and are well suited to winter salad leaves such as escarole, chicory and radicchio.

Makes about 350ml/ 12fl oz/1½ cups
75g/3oz blue cheese (Stilton, Bleu d'Auvergne or Gorgonzola)
150ml/¼ pint/⅔ cup natural (plain) yogurt
45ml/3 tbsp olive oil
30ml/2 tbsp lemon juice
15ml/1 tbsp chopped fresh chives
ground black pepper

1 Remove the rind from the cheese and combine with a third of the yogurt in a bowl.

2 Add the remainder of the yogurt, the olive oil and the lemon juice.

3 Stir in the chopped chives and season to taste with ground black pepper.

Coriander Dressing & Marinade

This simple dressing has a pleasing bite, and works well as a dressing for leaves or as a marinade for chicken.

Makes about 475ml/ 16fl oz/2 cups
120ml/4floz/½ cup lemon juice
30ml/2 tbsp wholegrain mustard
250ml/8fl oz/1 cup olive oil
75ml/5 tbsp sesame oil
5ml/1 tsp coriander seeds, crushed

1 Mix all the ingredients together in a bowl. Chill the dressing until you are ready to serve.

2 If desired, pour over chicken pieces and leave, covered, in the refrigerator overnight, until you are ready to cook them.

Yogurt Dressing

This is a less rich version of a classic mayonnaise and is much easier to make.

Makes about 210ml/ 7fl oz/scant 1 cup
150 ml/¼ pint/⅔ cup natural (plain) yogurt
30ml/2 tbsp mayonnaise

30ml/2 tbsp milk
15ml/1 tbsp chopped fresh parsley
15ml/1 tbsp chopped fresh chives

1 Put all the ingredients together in a bowl.

2 Season to taste and mix well.

Mayonnaise

For consistent results, ensure that both egg yolks and oil are at room temperature before combining. Home-made mayonnaise is made with raw egg yolks and may therefore be considered unsuitable for young children, pregnant mothers and the elderly.

Makes about 300 ml/½ pint/1¼ cups
2 egg yolks
5ml/1 tsp French mustard
150ml/¼ pint/⅔ cup extra-virgin olive oil
150ml/¼ pint/⅔ cup groundnut or sunflower oil
10ml/2 tsp white wine vinegar
salt and ground black pepper

1 Place the egg yolks and mustard in a food processor and blend smoothly.

2 Add the olive oil a little at a time while the processor is running. When the mixture is thick, add the groundnut or sunflower oil in a slow, steady stream.

3 Add the vinegar and season to taste with salt and pepper.

Garlic Mayonnaise

Use ready-made mayonnaise to save time, and blanch the garlic in boiling water if you prefer a milder flavour.

Makes about 300 ml/½ pint/1¼ cups
2 egg yolks
5ml/1 tsp French mustard

150ml/¼ pint/⅔ cup extra-virgin olive oil
150ml/¼ pint/⅔ cup groundnut or sunflower oil
10ml/2 tsp white wine vinegar (or lemon juice or warm water)
2–4 garlic cloves
salt and ground black pepper

1 Make the mayonnaise as above. Then crush the garlic with the blade of a knife and stir it in.

Basil & Lemon Mayonnaise

This luxurious dressing is flavoured with lemon juice and two types of basil. Serve with all kinds of leafy salads, crudités or coleslaws. It is also good with baked potatoes or as a delicious dip for French fries. The dressing will keep in an airtight jar for up to a week in the fridge.

**Makes about 300ml/
½ pint/1 ¼ cups**
2 large egg yolks
15ml/1 tbsp lemon juice
*150ml/¼ pint/⅔ cup extra-virgin
    olive oil*
*150ml/¼ pint/⅔ cup
    sunflower oil*
4 garlic cloves
handful of fresh green basil
handful of fresh opal basil
salt and ground black pepper

1 Place the egg yolks and lemon juice in a blender or food processor and mix them briefly until lightly blended.

2 In a jug, stir together both oils. With the machine running, pour in the oil very slowly, a drop at a time at first, increasing to a thin drizzle.

3 Once half of the oil has been added, and the dressing has successfully emulsified, the remaining oil can be incorporated more quickly. Continue processing until a thick, creamy mayonnaise has formed.

4 Peel and crush the garlic cloves and add to the mayonnaise.

5 Alternatively, place the peeled cloves on a chopping board and sprinkle with salt, then flatten them with the heel of a heavy-bladed knife and chop the flesh. Flatten the garlic again to make a coarse purée. Add to the mayonnaise.

6 Remove the basil stalks and tear both types of leaves into small pieces. Stir into the mayonnaise.

7 Add salt and pepper to taste, then transfer the mayonnaise to a serving dish. Cover and chill until ready to serve.

Hollandaise Sauce

The classic sauce for warm salads, and particularly good with fresh asparagus or artichokes.

15ml/1 tbsp cold water
15–30ml/1–2 tbsp lemon juice
½ tsp salt
cayenne pepper

Serves 6
*¾ cup unsalted butter, cut
    into pieces*
3 egg yolks

1 Clarify the butter by melting it in a small saucepan over a low heat; do not boil. Skim off any foam with a perforated spoon.

2 In a small heavy saucepan or in the top of a double boiler, combine the egg yolks, water, 15ml/1 tbsp of the lemon juice, salt and pepper, and whisk for 1 minute.

3 Place the pan over a very low heat or place the double boiler top over barely simmering water and whisk constantly until the egg yolk mixture begins to thicken and the whisk leaves tracks on the base of the pan. Remove from heat.

4 Whisk in the clarified butter, drop by drop, until the sauce begins to thicken, then pour it in a little more quickly, making sure that the butter is absorbed before adding any more.

5 When you reach the milky solids at the bottom of the clarified butter, stop pouring. Season to taste with salt and cayenne and a little more lemon juice if wished. If the sauce seems too sharp, add a little more butter.

> **Cook's Tips**
> • *The sauce has a similar consistency to mayonnaise. To make it thinner, add 15–30ml/1–2 tbsp single (light) cream and serve immediately.*
> • *The sauce will keep for up to 1 week. When ready to use, reheat it gently in a bowl over simmering water, whisking constantly to retain the smooth consistency.*

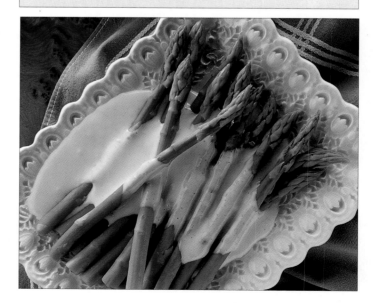

Creamy dips

1 Creamy black olive dip
Stir a little black olive paste into a carton of extra-thick double cream until smooth and well blended. Add salt, ground black pepper and a squeeze of lemon juice to taste. Serve chilled.

2 Crème fraîche dressing with spring onions
Finely chop a bunch of spring onions (scallions) and stir into a carton of crème fraîche. Add a dash of chilli sauce, a squeeze of lime juice, and salt and ground black pepper.

3 Greek-style yogurt and mustard dip
Mix a small carton of creamy, Greek-style (US strained plain) yogurt with 5–10ml/1–2 tsp wholegrain mustard.

4 Herb mayonnaise
Liven up ready-made mayonnaise with a handful of chopped fresh herbs.

5 Sundried tomato dip
Stir 15–30ml/1–2 tbsp sun-dried tomato paste into a carton of Greek-style yogurt. Season to taste with salt and ground pepper.

6 Spiced yogurt dressing
Stir a little curry paste and mango chutney into a carton of natural (plain) yogurt.

7 Passata and horseradish dip
Bring a little tang to a small carton or bottle of passata (strained tomatoes) with some horseradish sauce or 5–10ml/1–2 tsp creamed horseradish and salt and pepper to taste. Serve with lightly-cooked vegetables.

8 Pesto dip
For a simple, speedy, Italian-style dip, stir 15ml/1 tbsp ready-made red or green pesto into a carton of soured cream. Serve with crisp crudités or wedges of oven-roasted Mediterranean vegetables, such as peppers, courgettes and onions, for a delicious starter.

9 Soft cheese and chive dip
Mix a tub of soft cheese with 30–45ml/2–3 tbsp snipped fresh chives and season to taste with salt and black pepper. If the dip is too thick, stir in a little milk to soften it.

Thousand Island Dip

A great dip to have with shellfish on skewers.

Serves 4
4 sun-dried tomatoes in oil
4 plum tomatoes, or
  2 beefsteak tomatoes
150g/5oz/⅔ cup mild soft cheese,
  or marscapone or fromage frais
60ml/4 tbsp mayonnaise
30ml/2 tbsp tomato
  purée (paste)
30ml/2 tbsp chopped
  fresh parsley
1 lemon
Tabasco sauce, to taste
5ml/1 tsp Worcestershire or
  soy sauce
salt and ground black pepper

1 Drain the sun-dried tomatoes on kitchen paper. Chop finely.

2 Cut a cross in the base of each fresh tomato. Plunge into freshly boiled water for 30 seconds. Lift out with slotted spoon and place in a bowl of cold water. Drain, remove the skin, halve the tomatoes and discard the seeds. Chop the flesh finely.

3 Beat the soft cheese, mayonnaise and tomato purée together. Stir in the parsley and sun-dried tomatoes, then the fresh tomatoes. Grate (shred) the lemon rind finely and add to the dip. Squeeze and add lemon juice and Tabasco sauce to taste, then chill until you are ready to serve.

Hummus

A garlicky chickpea dip, ideal with crudités.

Serves 4
400g/4oz can chickpeas, drained
2 garlic cloves
30ml/2 tbsp tahini paste
60ml/4 tbsp olive oil
juice of 1 lemon
2.5ml/½ tsp cayenne pepper
15ml/1 tbsp sesame seeds
sea salt

1 Rinse the chickpeas and whizz in a food blender or processor with the garlic, tahini and a good pinch of salt until smooth. As you blend, slowly pour in the oil and lemon juice.

2 Stir in the cayenne pepper and salt to taste. Add cold water if the mixure is too thick.

3 Lightly toast the sesame seeds in a non-stick frying pan (skillet), then sprinkle them over the finished hummus.

Guacamole

Serve with tortilla chips or crudités.

Serves 4
2 ripe avocados
2 tomatoes, peeled, seeded
  and chopped
6 spring onions (scallions)
30ml/2 tbsp fresh lime juice
15ml/1 tsbp chopped fresh
  coriander (cilantro)
salt and ground black pepper
fresh coriander (cilantro) sprigs
  to garnish

1 Mash the ingredients together with a fork and add salt and pepper to taste. Garnish with sprigs of coriander.

Raw Vegetable Platter

This colourful array of vegetables makes an enticing appetizer when served with a creamy dip – choose a dip with bags of flavour for the best effect.

Serves 6–8
225g/8oz fresh baby corn cobs
175–225g/6–8oz thin
  asparagus, trimmed

2 red and 2 yellow (bell) peppers,
  seeded and sliced lengthwise
1 chicory (Belgian endive) head,
  trimmed and leaves separated
1 small bunch radishes with small
  leaves
175g/6oz cherry tomatoes
12 quails' eggs, boiled for
  3 minutes, drained, refreshed
  and peeled
aïoli or tapenade, to serve

1 Bring a large pan of water to the boil, add the baby corn cobs and trimmed asparagus and bring back to the boil. Blanch for 1–2 minutes, then drain and cool quickly under cold running water or dip in a bowl of iced water. Drain well.

2 Arrange the corn cobs, asparagus, chicory leaves, radishes and tomatoes on a serving plate together with the quails' eggs.

3 Cover with a damp dish towel until ready to serve. Serve with aïoli or tapenade for dipping.

Cook's Tips
• To make tapenade, place 175g/6oz/1½ cups pitted black olives, 50g/2oz drained anchovy fillets and 30ml/2 tbsp capers in a food processor with 120ml/4fl oz/½ cup olive oil and the finely grated rind of 1 lemon. Lightly process to blend, then season with black pepper and a little more oil if very dry.
• To make a herby aïoli, beat together 2 egg yolks, 5ml/1 tsp Dijon mustard and 10ml/2 tsp white wine vinegar. Gradually blend in 250m/8fl oz/1 cup olive oil, a trickle at a time, whisking well after each addition, until thick and smooth. Season with salt and pepper to taste, then stir in 45ml/3 tbsp chopped mixed fresh herbs, and 4–5 crushed garlic cloves.

Tomato & Cucumber Salad

Refreshing cucumber slices are coated with a delicious minty cream, then combined with colourful tomatoes to make a tangy salad starter with a difference.

Serves 4–6
1 medium cucumber, peeled and
  thinly sliced

30ml/2 tbsp white wine vinegar
5–6 ice cubes
90ml/6 tbsp crème fraîche or
  soured cream
30ml/2 tbsp chopped fresh mint
4 or 5 ripe tomatoes, sliced
salt and ground black pepper
fresh mint sprig, to garnish

1 Place the cucumber in a bowl, sprinkle with a little salt and 15 ml/1 tbsp of the vinegar and toss with the ice cubes. Chill for 1 hour to crisp, then rinse, drain and pat dry.

2 Return the cucumber to the bowl, add the cream, pepper and mint and stir to mix well.

3 Arrange the tomato slices on a serving plate, sprinkle with the remaining vinegar and spoon the cucumber slices into the centre. Serve garnished with a mint sprig.

Cook's Tip
This is delicious served as part of a tapas medley. Try serving with tapas dishes such as salted almonds and marinated olives.
• For salted almonds, mix 1.5ml/¼ tsp cayenne pepper and 30ml/2 tbsp sea salt in a bowl. Melt 25g/1oz/2 tbsp butter with 60ml/4 tbsp olive oil in a frying pan. Add 200g/7oz/1¾ cups blanched almonds and fry for 5 minutes until golden. Toss in the salt mixture to coat, then leave to cool before serving.
• For marinated olives, crush 2.5ml/½ tsp each coriander and fennel seeds in a mortar with a pestle. Work in 2 garlic cloves, then add 5ml/1 tsp each chopped fresh rosemary and parsley, with 15ml/1 tbsp sherry vinegar and 30ml/2 tbsp olive oil. Put 115g/4oz/⅔ cup each black and green olives in a small bowl and pour over the marinade. Cover and chill for up to 1 week.

Caesar Salad

This famous salad of crisp lettuce tossed with a fresh egg dressing and crunchy croûtons is always popular.

Serves 4
2 large garlic cloves, halved
45ml/3 tbsp extra-virgin olive oil
4 slices wholemeal (whole-wheat) bread
1 small romaine or 2 Little Gem (Bibb) lettuces

50g/2oz piece of Parmesan cheese, shaved or coarsely grated (shredded)

For the dressing
1 egg
10ml/2 tsp French mustard
5ml/1 tsp Worcestershire sauce
30ml/2 tbsp fresh lemon juice
30ml/2 tbsp extra-virgin olive oil
salt and ground black pepper

1 Preheat the oven to 190°C/375°F/Gas 5. Rub the inside of a salad bowl with one of the half cloves of garlic.

2 Heat the oil gently with the remaining garlic in a frying pan for 5 minutes, then remove and discard the garlic.

3 Remove the crusts from the bread and cut the bread into small cubes. Toss these in the garlic-flavoured oil, making sure they are well coated. Spread out the bread cubes on a baking sheet and bake for about 10 minutes, until crisp. Remove from the oven, then leave to cool.

4 Separate the lettuce leaves, wash and dry them and arrange in a shallow salad bowl. Chill until ready to serve.

5 To make the dressing, bring a small pan of water to the boil, lower the egg into the water and boil for 1 minute only. Crack it into a bowl. Use a teaspoon to scoop out and discard any softly set egg white. Using a balloon whisk, beat in the French mustard, Worcestershire sauce, lemon juice and olive oil, then season with salt and pepper to taste.

6 Sprinkle the Parmesan over the salad and then drizzle the dressing over. Scatter with the croûtons. Take the salad to the table, toss lightly and serve immediately.

Olives with Moroccan Lemon Marinades

Preserved and fresh lemons provide their own distinct qualities to these appetizers. Start preparations a week in advance to allow the flavours to develop.

Serves 6–8
450g/1lb/2⅔ cups whole olives

For the piquant marinade
45ml/3 tbsp chopped fresh coriander (cilantro)
45ml/3 tbsp chopped fresh parsley
1 garlic clove, finely chopped

good pinch of cayenne pepper
good pinch of ground cumin
30–45ml/2–3 tbsp olive oil
30–45ml/2–3 tbsp lemon juice

For the spicy marinade
60ml/4 tbsp chopped fresh coriander (cilantro)
60ml/4 tbsp chopped fresh parsley
1 garlic clove, finely chopped
5ml/1 tsp grated (shredded) fresh root ginger
1 red chilli, seeded and sliced
¼ preserved lemon, cut into strips

1 Using the flat side of a large knife blade, crack the olives, hard enough to break the flesh, but taking care not to crack the pits. Place the olives in a bowl of cold water, cover and leave overnight in a cool place to remove the excess brine. The next day, drain them thoroughly and divide among two sterilized screw-top jars.

2 To make the piquant marinade, mix the coriander, parsley and garlic together in a bowl. Add the cayenne pepper and cumin and 30ml/2 tbsp of the olive oil and lemon juice. Add the olives from one jar, mix well and return to the jar. Add more olive oil and lemon juice to cover if necessary. Seal.

3 To make the spicy marinade, mix together the coriander, parsley, garlic, ginger, chilli and preserved lemon. Add the olives from the second jar, mix well and return to the jar. Seal.

4 Store the olives in the refrigerator for at least 1 week before using, shaking the jars occasionally.

Caesar salad: Energy 261kcal/1083kJ; Protein 9.2g; Carbohydrate 11.5g, of which sugars 1.5g; Fat 20.1g, of which saturates 5g; Cholesterol 60mg; Calcium 190mg; Fibre 1.9g; Sodium 305mg
Olives with lemon mariandes: Energy 78kcal/320kJ; Protein 1.1g; Carbohydrate 0.7g, of which sugars 0.4g; Fat 7.9g, of which saturates 1.2g; Cholesterol 0mg; Calcium 55mg; Fibre 2g; Sodium 1017mg

Avocado Salad

In India, avocados are called butter fruit, reflecting their subtle taste. This delicate dish makes a good appetizer.

Serves 4

2 avocados
75ml/5 tbsp/⅓ cup natural (plain) yogurt, beaten
115g/4oz cottage cheese with chives
1 garlic clove, crushed
2 green chillies, finely chopped
a little lemon juice
a few lettuce leaves, shredded (a mixture will make a good display)
salt and ground black pepper
paprika and fresh mint leaves, to garnish

1 Cut the avocados in half lengthwise and remove the stones (pits). Gently scoop out the flesh, reserving the skins. Cut the flesh into small cubes.

2 In a bowl, mix the yogurt, cottage cheese, garlic, chillies and salt and pepper and fold in the avocado cubes. Chill.

3 Rub the avocado skins with some lemon juice to prevent discolouration and line each cavity with some shredded lettuce. Top with the chilled avocado mixture, garnish with the paprika and mint leaves and serve immediately.

Variation
Try combining avocado with tropical fruit to make an unusual starter. Halve, stone (pit) and peel 2 avocados, then cut into thick slices. Peel a papaya, cut in half and scoop out the seeds. Set aside 5ml/1tsp seeds and cut the papaya flesh into thick slices. Peel 1 large sweet orange and cut into segments, removing the membranes. Make a dressing by mixing 50ml/2fl oz/¼ cup olive oil with 30ml/2 tbsp fresh lime juice and salt and pepper. Stir in the reserved papaya seeds. Arrange alternate slices of fruit and avocado on individual plates. Top with a little rocket and scatter over thinly sliced red onion rings. Spoon on the dressing and serve immediately.

Avocado, Orange & Almond Salad

A wonderful combination of creamy avocado with fresh-tasting oranges and tomatoes, this salad is bursting with authentic Spanish flavours. Serve with chunks of rustic bread, flavoured with sun-dried tomato, for a great starter

Serves 4

2–3 oranges
2 ripe tomatoes
2 small avocados
60ml/4 tbsp extra-virgin olive oil
30ml/2 tbsp lemon juice
15ml/1 tbsp chopped parsley
small onion rings
25g/1oz/¼ cup split, toasted almonds
10–12 black olives
salt and ground black pepper

1 Peel the oranges and slice them into thick rounds. Make a cut in the top of the tomatoes, then plunge them into boiling water for 30 seconds. Lift out with a slotted spoon and refresh in cold water. Peel away the skins, cut the tomatoes into quarters, remove the seeds and chop roughly.

2 Cut the avocados in half, remove the stones (pits) and carefully peel away the skin. Cut into chunks.

3 Mix together the olive oil, lemon juice and parsley. Season with salt and pepper, then toss the avocado and tomatoes in half of the dressing.

4 Arrange the sliced oranges on a plate and scatter with the onion rings. Drizzle with the remaining dressing. Spoon the avocados, tomatoes, almonds and olives on top of the oranges and serve immediately.

Cook's Tip
Spanish onions are perfect for this dish as they are sweet and mild, and pleasant to eat raw, but they are very large. Slice them and use just the small central rings for salads, keeping the large outer rings for frying.

Avocado salad: Energy 160kcal/662kJ; Protein 6.2g; Carbohydrate 3.5g, of which sugars 2.6g; Fat 13.4g, of which saturates 3.4g; Cholesterol 4mg; Calcium 81mg; Fibre 2.2g; Sodium 124mg
Avocado, orange & almond salad: Energy 286kcal/1183kJ; Protein 3.5g; Carbohydrate 7.3g, of which sugars 6.4g; Fat 27.1g, of which saturates 4.4g; Cholesterol 0mg; Calcium 70mg; Fibre 4.4g; Sodium 575mg

Guacamole Salsa in Red Leaves

This lovely, light, summery starter looks especially attractive when it is arranged in individual cups of radicchio leaves.

Serves 4
2 tomatoes
15ml/1 tbsp grated onion
1 garlic clove, crushed
1 green chilli, halved, seeded and chopped
2 ripe avocados

30 ml/2 tbsp olive oil
2.5ml/½ tsp ground cumin
30ml/2 tbsp chopped fresh coriander (cilantro) or parsley
juice of 1 lime
radicchio leaves
salt and ground black pepper
fresh coriander (cilantro) sprigs, to garnish
crusty garlic bread and lime wedges, to serve

1 Using a sharp knife, slash a small cross on the top of the tomatoes, then plunge into a bowl of boiling water for 30 seconds. Refresh in cold water and peel away the skins. Remove the core of each tomato and chop the flesh.

2 Put the tomato flesh into a bowl together with the onion, garlic and chilli. Halve the avocados, remove the stones (pits), then scoop the flesh into the bowl, mashing it with a fork.

3 Add the oil, cumin, coriander or parsley and lime juice. Mix well together and season with salt and pepper to taste.

4 Lay the radicchio leaves on a platter and spoon in the salsa. Serve garnished with coriander sprigs and accompanied by garlic bread and lime wedges.

Cook's Tip
Garlic bread is ideal with this starter. Cut a French loaf into 2.5cm/1in slices, without cutting right through the base. Cream about 115g/4oz butter until soft, then beat in 2–3 crushed garlic cloves. Spread the butter between the slices. Wrap in foil and bake at 180°C/350°F/Gas 4 for about 15 minutes.

Lamb's Lettuce & Beetroot

This salad makes a colourful and unusual starter – the delicate flavour of the lamb's lettuce is perfect with the earthiness of the beetroot. For extra texture, sprinkle with chopped walnuts.

Serves 4
150–175g/5–6oz/3–4 cups lamb's lettuce (corn salad), washed and roots trimmed
250g/9oz/3 or 4 small fresh beetroot (beets), cooked, peeled and diced
30ml/2 tbsp chopped fresh parsley

For the vinaigrette
30–45ml/2–3 tbsp white wine vinegar or lemon juice
20ml/4 tsp Dijon mustard
2 garlic cloves, finely chopped
2.5ml/½ tsp sugar
120ml/4fl oz/½ cup sunflower or grapeseed oil
120ml/4fl oz/½ cup crème fraîche or double (heavy) cream
salt and ground black pepper

1 First make the vinaigrette. Mix the vinegar or lemon juice, mustard, garlic and sugar in a small bowl. Season with salt and pepper, then slowly whisk in the oil until the sauce thickens.

2 Lightly beat the crème fraîche or double cream to lighten it slightly, then whisk it into the dressing.

3 Toss the lettuce with a little of the vinaigrette and arrange on a serving plate or in a bowl.

4 Spoon the beetroot into the centre of the lettuce and drizzle over the remaining vinaigrette.

5 Sprinkle with chopped parsley and serve immediately.

Cook's Tip
To cook fresh beetroot (beet), place unpeeled in a roasting pan with 1cm/½in water and roast in a medium oven for about an hour until tender. Allow to cool slightly before peeling.

Guacamole salsa: Energy 189kcal/783kJ; Protein 2.4g; Carbohydrate 4.2g, of which sugars 3.2g; Fat 18.1g, of which saturates 3.5g; Cholesterol 0mg; Calcium 50mg; Fibre 3.8g; Sodium 14mg
Lamb's lettuce & beetroot: Energy 329kcal/1360kJ; Protein 2.7g; Carbohydrate 7.5g, of which sugars 6.9g; Fat 32.3g, of which saturates 10.5g; Cholesterol 34mg; Calcium 64mg; Fibre 2g; Sodium 200mg

Egg-stuffed Tomatoes

Tomato & Bread Salad

This simple dish looks elegant and is incredibly easy to assemble. The herb-flavoured mayonnaise is the perfect foil to the egg and tomato. Served with lots of warmed baguette, it makes a lovely appetizer or quick, light lunch dish.

Serves 4

175ml/6fl oz/³⁄₄ cup mayonnaise
30ml/2 tbsp chopped fresh chives
30ml/2 tbsp chopped fresh basil
30ml/2 tbsp chopped
   fresh parsley
4 hard-boiled (hard-cooked) eggs
4 ripe tomatoes
salt and ground black pepper
salad leaves, to serve

1 Mix together the mayonnaise and herbs in a small bowl, transfer to a small serving dish and set aside.

2 Using an egg slicer or sharp knife, cut the eggs into thin slices, taking care to keep the slices intact.

3 Make deep cuts to within 1cm/½in of the base of each tomato. (There should be the same number of cuts in each tomato as there are slices of egg.)

4 Fan open the tomatoes and sprinkle with salt, then insert an egg slice into each slit. Place each stuffed tomato on a plate with a few salad leaves and season with salt and pepper. Serve accompanied by the herb mayonnaise.

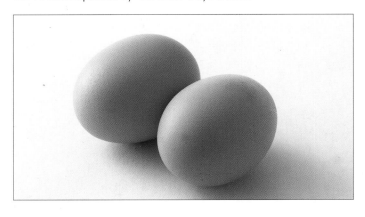

This rustic salad, which originally hails from Italy, is a convenient way of using up bread that is a few days old. It is easy to make, but the success of the dish depends on the quality of the tomatoes – they must be ripe and flavourful.

Serves 4

400g/14oz stale white or brown
   bread or rolls
4 large tomatoes
1 large red onion or 6 spring
   onions (scallions)
a few fresh basil leaves, to garnish

For the dressing
60ml/4 tbsp extra-virgin olive oil
30ml/2 tbsp white wine vinegar
salt and ground black pepper

1 Cut the bread or rolls into thick slices. Place in a shallow bowl and soak with cold water. Leave for at least 30 minutes.

2 Cut the tomatoes into chunks and place in a bowl. Finely slice the onion or spring onions and add to the tomatoes.

3 Squeeze as much water out of the bread as possible and add it to the vegetables.

4 To make the dressing, whisk the olive oil with the vinegar, then season with salt and pepper.

5 Pour the dressing over the salad and mix well. Garnish with basil leaves. Allow to stand in a cool place for at least 2 hours.

> **Cook's Tip**
> *Tomatoes left to ripen on the vine will have the best flavour so try to buy "vine-ripened" varieties. Luckily, these are now widely available in supermarkets and more flavourful varieties are now becoming easier to find. However, nothing can beat the taste of home-grown, organic tomatoes. You can use any type of tomato for this dish – halved cherry tomatoes will look attractive or use Italian plum tomatoes for an authentic touch.*

Egg-stuffed tomatoes: Energy 309kcal/1276kJ; Protein 7.6g; Carbohydrate 3.6g, of which sugars 3.4g; Fat 29.6g, of which saturates 5.2g; Cholesterol 214mg; Calcium 62mg; Fibre 1.5g; Sodium 223mg
Tomato & bread salad: Energy 354kcal/1496kJ; Protein 9.4g; Carbohydrate 52.9g, of which sugars 6.1g; Fat 13.3g, of which saturates 1.7g; Cholesterol 0mg; Calcium 123mg; Fibre 2.7g; Sodium 530mg

Mango, Tomato & Red Onion Salad

The firm texture of under-ripe mango blends well with the tomato and gives this starter a tropical touch.

Serves 4
1 firm under-ripe mango
2 large tomatoes or 1 beef
   tomato, sliced
1/2 red onion, sliced into rings
1/2 cucumber, peeled and
   thinly sliced

For the dressing
30ml/2 tbsp sunflower or
   vegetable oil
15ml/1 tbsp lemon juice
1 garlic clove, crushed
2.5ml/1/2 tsp hot pepper sauce
salt and ground black pepper
snipped chives, to garnish

1 Have the mango lengthwise, cutting either side of the stone (pit). Cut the flesh into slices and peel the skin away.

2 Arrange the mango, tomato, onion and cucumber on a large serving plate.

3 To make the dressing, blend the oil, lemon juice, garlic, pepper sauce and seasoning in a blender or food processor, or place in a small screw-top jar and shake vigorously.

4 Pour the dressing over the salad and serve garnished with snipped chives.

Sun-Dried Tomato & Pepper Salad

This appetizer is very new-wave – a modern Mediterranean dish that bridges the gap between Middle-Eastern and contemporary European styles. It is good served with slices of very fresh bread or wedges of flat bread.

Serves 4–6
10–15 sun-dried tomatoes
60–75ml/4–5 tbsp olive oil
3 yellow (bell) peppers, cut into
   bitesize pieces

6 garlic cloves, chopped
400g/14oz can chopped
   tomatoes
5ml/1 tsp fresh thyme leaves,
   or more to taste
large pinch of sugar
15ml/1 tbsp balsamic vinegar
2–3 capers, rinsed and drained
15ml/1 tbsp chopped fresh
   parsley, or more to taste
salt and ground black pepper
fresh thyme, to garnish

1 Put the sun-dried tomatoes in a bowl and pour over boiling water to cover. Leave to stand for at least 30 minutes until plumped up and juicy, then drain and cut the tomatoes into halves or quarters.

2 Heat the olive oil in a pan, add the peppers and cook for 5–7 minutes until lightly browned but not too soft.

3 Add half the garlic, the tomatoes, thyme and sugar and cook over a high heat, stirring occasionally, until the mixture is reduced to a thick paste. Season with salt and pepper to taste. Stir in the sun-dried tomatoes, balsamic vinegar, capers and the remaining chopped garlic. Leave to cool to room temperature.

4 Serve the salad at room temperature, heaped into a serving bowl and sprinkled with parsley. Garnish with thyme.

Cook's Tip
Do not waste the tomato-flavoured soaking liquid – it can be used to add flavour to soups or sauces.

Mango, tomato & red onion salad:: Energy 89kcal/369kJ; Protein 1.1g; Carbohydrate 8.6g, of which sugars 7.9g; Fat 5.8g, of which saturates 0.8g; Cholesterol 0mg; Calcium 17mg; Fibre 1.9g; Sodium 7mg
Sun-dried tomato & pepper salad: Energy 125kcal/520kJ; Protein 2.7g; Carbohydrate 11g, of which sugars 9.6g; Fat 8.1g, of which saturates 1.2g; Cholesterol 0mg; Calcium 34mg; Fibre 3.2g; Sodium 33mg

Roasted Tomatoes & Mozzarella with Basil Oil

The basil oil needs to be made just before serving to retain its fresh colour.

Serves 4
olive oil, for brushing
6 large plum tomatoes
350g/12oz fresh mozzarella
    cheese, cut into 8–12 slices
fresh basil leaves, to garnish

For the basil oil
25 fresh basil leaves
60ml/4 tbsp extra-virgin olive oil
1 garlic clove, crushed

For the salad
90g/3¹/₂ oz/4 cups salad leaves
50g/2oz/2 cups mixed salad
    herbs, such as coriander
    (cilantro), basil and
    rocket (arugula)
25g/1oz/3 tbsp pumpkin seeds
25g/1oz/3 tbsp sunflower seeds
60ml/4 tbsp extra-virgin olive oil
15ml/1 tbsp balsamic vinegar
2.5ml/¹/₂ tsp Dijon mustard

1 Preheat the oven to 200°C/400°F/Gas 6 and oil a baking sheet. Cut the tomatoes in half lengthwise and remove the seeds. Place skin-side down on a baking sheet and roast for 20 minutes or until the tomatoes are tender.

2 Meanwhile, make the basil oil. Place the basil leaves, olive oil and garlic in a food processor and process until smooth. Transfer to a bowl and chill.

3 Put the salad leaves and herbs in a large bowl and toss lightly to mix. Toast the pumpkin and sunflower seeds in a dry frying pan over a medium heat for 2 minutes until golden, tossing frequently. Allow to cool before sprinkling over the salad.

4 Whisk together the oil, vinegar and mustard, then pour the dressing over the salad and toss until the leaves are well coated.

5 For each serving, place the tomato halves on top of two or three slices of mozzarella and drizzle over the basil oil. Season well. Garnish with basil leaves and serve with the salad.

Spiced Aubergine & Tomato Salad

Packed with Middle-Eastern ingredients, this lovely salad would be perfect to serve before a main course of chargrilled meats or fish. Simply serve with warm pitta bread and your guests will be more than satisfied.

Serves 4
2 small aubergines
    (eggplants), sliced
75ml/5 tbsp olive oil
60ml/4 tbsp red wine vinegar
2 garlic cloves, crushed
15ml/1 tbsp lemon juice
2.5ml/¹/₂ tsp ground cumin
2.5ml/¹/₂ tsp ground coriander
7 well-flavoured tomatoes
¹/₂ cucumber
30ml/2 tbsp natural (plain) yogurt
salt and ground black pepper
chopped flat leaf parsley,
    to garnish

1 Preheat the grill (broiler). Brush all the aubergine slices lightly with some of the oil and cook under a high heat, turning once, until golden and tender. Cut each slice into quarters.

2 In a bowl, mix together the remaining oil, vinegar, garlic, lemon juice, cumin and coriander. Season with salt and pepper, and mix thoroughly. Add the warm aubergines, stir well and chill for at least 2 hours.

3 Slice or quarter the tomatoes and slice the cucumber finely. Add both cucumber and tomato to the aubergine mixture.

4 Transfer the aubergine mixture to a serving dish and spoon the natural yogurt over the top. Sprinkle with chopped flat leaf parsley and serve immediately.

Variation
An equally delicious warm salad can be made by dicing the aubergines and frying them in olive oil with 1 chopped onion and 2 crushed garlic cloves. Then stir in 5–10ml/1–2 tsp mild curry powder and 3 chopped tomatoes. Cook until soft, then serve with natural (plain) yogurt.

Roasted tomatoes & mozzarella: Energy 525kcal/2174kJ; Protein 20.2g; Carbohydrate 7g, of which sugars 4.8g; Fat 46.4g, of which saturates 15.9g; Cholesterol 51mg; Calcium 371mg; Fibre 2.8g; Sodium 381mg
Spiced aubergine & tomato salad: Energy 174kcal/722kJ; Protein 2.6g; Carbohydrate 8.1g, of which sugars 7.6g; Fat 14.8g, of which saturates 2.3g; Cholesterol 0mg; Calcium 47mg; Fibre 4g; Sodium 28mg

Spanish Salad with Capers & Olives

Make this refreshing salad in the summer when tomatoes are at their sweetest and full of flavour. Serve with warm ciabatta or walnut bread.

Serves 4
4 tomatoes
$^1/_2$ cucumber
I bunch spring onions (scallions), trimmed and chopped
I bunch watercress
8 stuffed olives
30ml/2 tbsp drained capers

For the dressing
30ml/2 tbsp red wine vinegar
5ml/I tsp paprika
2.5ml/$^1/_2$ tsp ground cumin
I garlic clove, crushed
75ml/5 tbsp extra-virgin olive oil
salt and ground black pepper

I Using a sharp knife, make a small cross on the top of the tomatoes, then plunge into a bowl of boiling water for 30 seconds. Peel, then finely dice the flesh. Put in a salad bowl.

2 Peel the cucumber, dice finely and add to the tomatoes. Add half the spring onions to the salad bowl and mix lightly. Break the watercress into sprigs. Add to the tomato mixture, with the olives and capers.

3 To make the dressing, mix the wine vinegar, paprika, cumin and garlic in a bowl. Whisk in the oil and add salt and pepper to taste. Pour over the salad and toss lightly. Serve immediately with the remaining spring onions.

Chicory Salad with Roquefort

The distinctive flavour and creamy richness of Roquefort cheese perfectly complements the slightly bitter taste of the salad leaves in this palate-tingling starter. Warmed French bread makes the ideal accompaniment.

Serves 4
30ml/2 tbsp red wine vinegar
5ml/I tsp Dijon mustard
60ml/2fl oz/$^1/_4$ cup walnut oil
15–30ml/I–2 tbsp sunflower oil
2 chicory (Belgian endive) heads, white or red
I celery heart or 4 celery sticks, peeled and cut into julienne strips
75g/3oz/I cup walnut halves, lightly toasted
30ml/2 tbsp chopped fresh parsley
115g/4oz Roquefort cheese, crumbled
fresh parsley sprigs, to garnish

I Whisk together the vinegar and mustard in a small bowl, then whisk in salt and pepper to taste. Slowly whisk in the walnut oil, then the sunflower oil.

2 Divide the chicory heads into leaves and arrange decoratively on individual plates. Sprinkle over the celery julienne strips, walnut halves and chopped parsley.

3 Crumble equal amounts of Roquefort cheese over each serving and drizzle a little vinaigrette over each. Garnish with parsley sprigs and serve immediately.

Cook's Tip
Roquefort is a rich, blue cheese with a soft, crumbly texture and quite a sharp flavour. Good for salads or cooking, it is made in the village of Roquefort in France and is produced from ewe's milk. The good sheep-grazing land and limestone caves in this district contribute to giving the cheese its unique flavour. Roquefort is widely available in larger supermarkets, but if you have difficulty in finding it, you could use another well-flavoured blue cheese, such as Gorgonzola or Stilton.

Spanish salad with capers & olives: Energy 172kcal/712kJ; Protein 2.5g; Carbohydrate 5g, of which sugars 4.3g; Fat 16g, of which saturates 2.4g; Cholesterol 0mg; Calcium 71mg; Fibre 2.2g; Sodium 305mg
Chicory salad with roquefort: Energy 361kcal/1488kJ; Protein 9.4g; Carbohydrate 1.5g, of which sugars 1.3g; Fat 35.3g, of which saturates 7.9g; Cholesterol 22mg; Calcium 204mg; Fibre 1.8g; Sodium 423mg

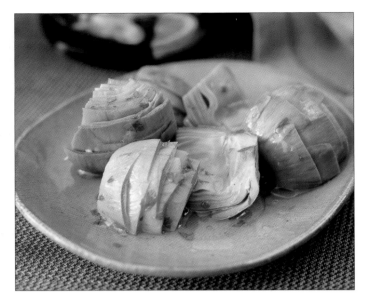

Globe Artichoke Salad

This salad first course is a great way to make the most of artichokes. It is equally good served hot or cold.

Serves 4
4 artichokes
juice of 1 lemon

900ml/1½ pints/3¾ cups
   home-made vegetable stock
   and water mixed
2 garlic cloves, chopped
1 small bunch parsley
6 whole peppercorns
15ml/1 tbsp olive oil, plus
   extra for drizzling

1 To prepare the artichokes, trim the stalks of the artichokes close to the base, cut the very tips off the leaves and then divide them into quarters. Remove the inedible hairy choke (the central part), carefully scraping the hairs away from the heart at the base of the artichoke.

2 Squeeze a little of the lemon juice over the cut surfaces of the artichokes to prevent discolouration.

3 Put the artichokes into a pan and cover with the stock and water, garlic, parsley, peppercorns and olive oil. Cover with a lid and cook gently for 1 hour, or until the artichokes are tender. They are ready when the leaves come away easily when pulled. Remove the artichokes with a slotted spoon. Boil the cooking liquid hard to reduce by half, then strain.

4 To serve, arrange the artichokes in small serving dishes and pour over the reduced juices. Drizzle over a little extra olive oil and lemon juice. Provide finger bowls and a bowl for the leaves.

5 To eat, pull a leaf away from the artichoke and scrape the fleshy part at the base with your teeth. Discard the remainder of the leaves and then eat the heart at the base.

> **Variation**
> If you can find tiny purple artichokes with tapered leaves, they can be cooked and eaten whole as the chokes are very tender.

Leek Salad with Anchovies, Eggs & Parsley

Chopped hard-boiled eggs and cooked leeks are a classic combination in French-style salads. This one makes a good first course.

Serves 4
675g/1½lb thin or baby leeks,
   trimmed
2 large or 3 medium eggs
50g/2oz good-quality anchovy
   fillets in olive oil, drained
15g/½oz flat leaf parsley,
   chopped

a few black olives, pitted
salt and ground black pepper

For the dressing
5ml/1 tsp Dijon mustard
15ml/1 tbsp tarragon vinegar
75ml/5 tbsp olive oil
30ml/2 tbsp double
   (heavy) cream
1 small shallot, very
   finely chopped
pinch of caster (superfine) sugar
   (optional)

1 Boil the leeks for 3–4 minutes. Drain, plunge into cold water, then drain again. Squeeze out the excess water, then pat dry.

2 Place the eggs in a pan of cold water, bring to the boil and cook for 6–7 minutes. Drain, plunge into cold water, then shell and chop the eggs.

3 To make the dressing, whisk the mustard with the vinegar. Gradually whisk in the oil, followed by the cream. Stir in the shallot, then season to taste with salt, pepper and a pinch of caster sugar, if liked.

4 Arrange the leeks and anchovies on a serving platter, pour over the dressing and scatter the egg, parsley and olives on top.

> **Cook's Tip**
> Make sure the leeks are well drained and squeezed of excess water or they will dilute the dressing and spoil the flavour.

Globe artichoke salad: Energy 59Kcal/245kJ; Protein 0.7g; Carbohydrate 7.8g, of which sugars 7.3g; Fat 3.1g, of which saturates 0.5g; Cholesterol 0mg; Calcium 25mg; Fibre 2.4g; Sodium 61mg
Leek salad: Energy 265kcal/1099kJ; Protein 9.4g; Carbohydrate 6.3g, of which sugars 4.8g; Fat 22.7g, of which saturates 5.6g; Cholesterol 113mg; Calcium 107mg; Fibre 4.1g; Sodium 533mg

Leek & Grilled Pepper Salad with Goat's Cheese

This is a perfect dish for entertaining, as the salad actually benefits from being made in advance.

Serves 6
675g/1½ lb young leeks
15ml/1 tbsp olive oil
2 large red (bell) peppers, halved
    and seeded
few fresh thyme sprigs, chopped
4 x 1cm/½in slices goat's cheese
75g/3oz/1½ cups fine dry
    white breadcrumbs

vegetable oil, for shallow frying
45ml/3 tbsp chopped fresh flat
    leaf parsley
salt and ground black pepper

For the dressing
75ml/5 tbsp extra-virgin olive oil
1 small garlic clove,
    finely chopped
5ml/1 tsp Dijon mustard
15ml/1 tbsp red wine vinegar

1 Preheat the grill (broiler). Bring a pan of lightly salted water to the boil and cook the leeks for 3–4 minutes. Drain, cut into 10cm/4in lengths and place in a bowl. Add the olive oil, toss to coat, then season to taste. Place the leeks on a grill rack and grill (broil) for 3–4 minutes on each side.

2 Set the leeks aside. Place the peppers on the grill rack, skin side up, and grill until blackened and blistered. Place them in a bowl, cover with crumpled kitchen paper and leave for 10 minutes. Rub off the skin and cut the flesh into strips. Place in a bowl and add the leeks, thyme and a little pepper.

3 To make the dressing, shake all the ingredients together in a screw-top jar, adding salt and pepper to taste. Pour the dressing over the leek mixture, cover and chill for several hours.

4 Roll the cheese slices in the breadcrumbs, pressing them in so that the cheese is well coated. Chill the cheese for 1 hour. Heat a little oil and fry the cheese until golden on both sides. Drain and cool, then cut into bitesize pieces. Toss the cheese and parsley into the salad and serve at room temperature.

Grilled Leek & Fennel Salad with Spicy Tomato Dressing

This is an excellent salad for the early autumn, when leeks are at their best and tomatoes are full of flavour.

Serves 6
675g/1½lb leeks
2 large fennel bulbs
120ml/4fl oz/½ cup olive oil
2 shallots, chopped
150ml/¼ pint/⅔ cup dry white
    wine or white vermouth

5ml/1 tsp fennel seeds, crushed
6 fresh thyme sprigs
2–3 bay leaves
pinch of dried red chilli flakes
350g/12oz tomatoes, peeled,
    seeded and diced
5ml/1 tsp sun-dried tomato paste
    (optional)
good pinch of sugar (optional)
75g/3oz/¾ cup small black olives
salt and ground black pepper

1 Cook the leeks in boiling salted water for 4–5 minutes. Using a slotted spoon, place them in a colander to drain and cool. Then cut into 7.5cm/3in lengths. Reserve the cooking water.

2 Trim and slice the fennel. Keep the tops for a garnish. Cook the fennel in the reserved water for about 5 minutes, drain, then toss with 30ml/2 tbsp of olive oil. Season to taste.

3 On a ridged cast iron griddle, grill (broil) the vegetables until tinged deep brown, then place them in a large shallow dish.

4 Heat the remaining oil, the shallots, white wine or vermouth, crushed fennel seeds, thyme, bay leaves and chilli flakes in a large pan and bring to the boil over a medium heat. Lower the heat and simmer for 10 minutes.

5 Add the diced tomoes and cook briskly until the consistency of the dressing has thickened. Add the tomato paste and adjust the seasoning, adding a pinch of sugar if you like.

6 Toss the fennel and leeks in the dressing and chill. Bring the salad back to room temperature and garnish it with fennel fronds and olives before serving. Season with black pepper.

Grilled leek & fennel salad: Energy 193kcal/800kJ; Protein 2.8g; Carbohydrate 6.7g, of which sugars 5.9g; Fat 14.7g, of which saturates 2.2g; Cholesterol 0mg; Calcium 53mg; Fibre 4.6g; Sodium 297mg
Leek & grilled pepper salad: Energy 265kcal/1100kJ; Protein 5.7g; Carbohydrate 17g, of which sugars 6.5g; Fat 19.7g, of which saturates 3.9g; Cholesterol 8mg; Calcium 60mg; Fibre 3.7g; Sodium 174mg

Grilled Leek & Courgette Salad with Feta & Mint

Bursting with tangy flavours, this makes a delicious summery starter. Try to find genuine ewe's milk feta for the best flavour and texture.

Serves 6
12 slender, baby leeks
6 small courgettes (zucchini)
90ml/6 tbsp extra-virgin olive oil
finely shredded rind and juice
  of ½ lemon
1–2 garlic cloves, finely chopped
½ fresh red chilli, seeded
  and diced
pinch of caster (superfine)
  sugar (optional)
50g/2oz/½ cup black olives,
  pitted and roughly chopped
30ml/2 tbsp chopped fresh mint
150g/5oz feta cheese, sliced
  or crumbled
salt and ground black pepper
fresh mint leaves, to garnish

1 Bring a large pan of salted water to the boil. Add the leeks and cook for 2–3 minutes. Drain, refresh under cold water, then squeeze out excess water and leave to drain.

2 Cut the courgettes in half lengthwise. Place in a colander, adding 5ml/1 tsp salt to the layers, and leave to drain for 45 minutes. Rinse and dry thoroughly on kitchen paper.

3 Preheat the grill (broiler). Toss the leeks and courgettes in 30ml/2 tbsp of the oil. Grill (broil) the leeks for 2–3 minutes on each side and the courgettes for about 5 minutes on each side. Cut the leeks into serving pieces and place them in a shallow dish with the courgettes.

4 Place the remaining oil in a small bowl and whisk in the lemon rind, 15ml/1 tbsp of the lemon juice, the garlic, chilli and a pinch of sugar, if using. Season to taste with salt and pepper. Add more lemon juice to taste.

5 Pour the dressing over the leeks and courgettes. Stir in the olives and mint, then set aside to marinate for a few hours, turning once or twice. Just before serving, spoon the salad on to individual serving plates, add the feta and garnish with mint.

Grilled Spring Onions & Asparagus with Parma Ham

This is a good choice of first course at the beginning of summer, when both spring onions and asparagus are at their best. The slight smokiness of the grilled vegetables goes very well with the sweetness of the air-dried ham.

Serves 4–6
2 bunches (about 24) plump
  spring onions (scallions)
500g/1¼lb asparagus
45–60ml/3–4 tbsp olive oil
sea salt and ground black pepper
20ml/4 tsp balsamic vinegar
8–12 slices Parma or San
  Daniele ham
50g/2oz Pecorino cheese
extra-virgin olive oil, to serve

1 Trim the root, outer skin and the top off the spring onions. Cut off and discard the woody ends of the asparagus. Use a vegetable peeler to peel the bottom 7.5cm/3in of the spears.

2 Preheat the grill (broiler). Toss the spring onions and asparagus in 30ml/2 tbsp of the oil. Place on two baking sheets and season with salt and pepper.

3 Grill (broil) the asparagus for 5 minutes on each side, until just tender when tested with the tip of a sharp knife. Protect the tips with foil if they seem to char too much.

4 Grill the spring onions for about 3–4 minutes on each side, until tinged with brown. Brush the vegetables with more oil as you turn them.

5 Arrange the vegetables on individual plates. Season with pepper and drizzle over the vinegar. Lay 2–3 slices of ham on each plate and shave the Pecorino over the top.

> **Cook's Tip**
> *If more convenient, the trimmed and peeled asparagus spears can be roasted at 200°C/400°F/Gas 6 for 15 minutes.*

Leek & courgette salad: Energy 197kcal/812kJ; Protein 6.2g; Carbohydrate 3.4g, of which sugars 2.9g; Fat 17.6g, of which saturates 5.3g; Cholesterol 18mg; Calcium 140mg; Fibre 2.6g; Sodium 552mg.
Grilled spring onions with parma ham: Energy 109kcal/450kJ; Protein 8g; Carbohydrate 2.9g, of which sugars 2.8g; Fat 7.3g, of which saturates 1.4g; Cholesterol 15mg; Calcium 47mg; Fibre 1.9g; Sodium 312mg

Salad of Puréed Aubergines

In the heat of high summer, this Middle-Eastern dish makes a surprisingly refreshing appetizer. To be strictly authentic, the aubergines should be grilled over charcoal.

Serves 4

3 large aubergines (eggplants), about 900g/2lb total weight
15ml/1 tbsp roughly chopped onion
2 garlic cloves, crushed
juice of ½ lemon, or a little more
90–105ml/6–7 tbsp extra-virgin olive oil
1 ripe tomato, peeled, seeded and finely diced
salt and ground black pepper
finely chopped fresh flat leaf parsley, to garnish
chicory (Belgian endive) leaves and black and green olives, to serve

1 Preheat the oven to 180°C/350°F/Gas 4. Prick the aubergines with a fork and lay them directly on the oven shelves. Roast for 1 hour, or until soft, turning them over twice.

2 When the aubergines are cool enough to handle, cut them in half. Spoon the flesh into a food processor and add the onion, garlic and lemon juice. Season with salt and ground black pepper and process until smooth.

3 With the motor running, drizzle in the olive oil through the feeder tube, until the mixture forms a smooth paste. Taste the mixture and adjust the seasoning.

4 Spoon the mixture into a bowl and stir in the diced tomato.

5 Cover and chill for 1 hour before serving. Garnish with chopped fresh flat leaf parsley and serve with fresh, washed chicory leaves to scoop up the purée and bowls of olives.

> **Cook's Tip**
> You can chargrill the aubergines instead of using the oven. Prick them and grill over a low to medium heat for at least 1 hour.

Grilled Onion & Aubergine Salad with Garlic & Tahini Dressing

This is a deliciously smoky salad that balances sweet and sharp flavours. It makes a substantial starter, served with hot pitta bread.

Serves 6

3 aubergines (eggplants), cut into 1cm/½ in thick slices
675g/1½lb onions, thickly sliced
75–90ml/5–6 tbsp olive oil
45ml/3 tbsp roughly chopped flat leaf parsley
45ml/3 tbsp pine nuts, toasted
salt and ground black pepper

For the dressing
2 garlic cloves, crushed
150ml/¼ pint/⅔ cup light tahini paste
juice of 1–2 lemons
45–60ml/3–4 tbsp water

1 Place the aubergines on a rack or in a colander and sprinkle generously with salt. Leave to drain for 45–60 minutes, then rinse under cold running water and pat dry with kitchen paper.

2 Preheat the grill (broiler). Thread the onions on to skewers or place them in an oiled wire grill (broiler) cage.

3 Brush the aubergines and onions with about 45ml/3 tbsp of the oil and grill (broil) for 6–8 minutes on each side. Brush with more oil, if necessary, when you turn the vegetables. The vegetables should be browned and soft.

4 Arrange the grilled vegetables on a serving dish and season with salt and black pepper to taste. Sprinkle with the remaining oil if they seem dry.

5 To make the dressing, crush the garlic in a mortar with a pinch of salt and gradually work in the tahini. Gradually work in the juice of 1 lemon, then the water. Taste and add more lemon juice if necessary. Thin with more water to make it fairly runny.

6 Drizzle the dressing over the salad and leave for 30–60 minutes, then sprinkle with the chopped parsley and pine nuts. Serve immediately at room temperature, not chilled.

Puréed aubergines: Energy 190Kcal/788kJ; Protein 2.3g; Carbohydrate 6.7g, of which sugars 5.9g; Fat 17.5g, of which saturates 2.6g; Cholesterol 0mg; Calcium 28mg; Fibre 4.9g; Sodium 7mg
Grilled onion & aubergine salad: Energy 294kcal/1216kJ; Protein 7.2g; Carbohydrate 11.8g, of which sugars 8.6g; Fat 24.6g, of which saturates 3.5g; Cholesterol 0mg; Calcium 224mg; Fibre 6g; Sodium 13mg

Nutty Salad

An unusual combination of nuts, pasta shells and colourful vegetables, this substantial salad makes an interesting starter. The creamy spiced dressing gives the dish a hot tangy bite.

Serves 4
1 onion, cut into 12 rings
115g/4oz/³/₄ cup canned red
   kidney beans, drained
1 courgette (zucchini), sliced
1 yellow courgette, sliced
50g/2oz pasta shells, cooked
50g/2oz/¹/₂ cup cashew nuts

25g/1oz/¹/₄ cup peanuts
lime wedges and fresh coriander
   (cilantro) sprigs, to garnish

For the dressing
120ml/4 fl oz/¹/₂ cup fromage
   frais or crème fraîche
30ml/2 tbsp natural (plain) yogurt
1 green chilli, chopped
15ml/1 tbsp chopped fresh
   coriander (cilantro)
2.5ml/¹/₂ tsp salt
2.5ml/¹/₂ tsp crushed black
   peppercorns
2.5ml/¹/₂ tsp crushed dried red
   chillies
15ml/1 tbsp lemon juice

1 Arrange the onion rings, red kidney beans, green and yellow courgette slices and pasta shells in a salad dish, ready for serving. Sprinkle the cashew nuts and peanuts over the top.

2 To make the dressing, place the fromage frais in a separate bowl with the yogurt, green chilli, coriander and salt. Beat well together with a fork.

3 Sprinkle the crushed black peppercorns, red chillies and lemon juice over the dressing.

4 Garnish the salad with the lime wedges and coriander sprigs and serve the dressing separately or poured over the salad.

Cook's Tips
• For wholesome finger food at a party, try serving the salad stuffed into mini pitta breads. Omit the beans, if you like.
• Toast the nuts in a dry frying pan (skillet) for extra crunch.

Marinated Mushrooms

This Spanish dish makes a refreshing alternative to the ever-popular mushrooms fried in garlic. .

Serves 4
30ml/2 tbsp extra virgin olive oil
1 small onion, very finely chopped
1 garlic clove, finely chopped

15ml/1 tbsp tomato
   purée (paste)
50ml/2fl oz/¹/₄ cup
   amontillado sherry
50ml/2fl oz/¹/₄ cup water
2 cloves
225g/8oz/3 cups button (white)
   mushrooms, trimmed
salt and ground black pepper
chopped fresh parsley, to garnish

1 Heat the oil in a pan. Add the onion and garlic and cook until soft. Stir in the tomato purée, sherry, water and the cloves and season with salt and black pepper.

2 Bring to the boil, cover and simmer gently for 45 minutes, adding more water if the mixture becomes too dry.

3 Add the mushrooms to the pan, then cover and allow to simmer for about 5 minutes. Remove from the heat and allow to cool, still covered.

4 Chill the mushrooms in the refrigerator overnight so that they take on the flavours. Serve the salad cold, sprinkled with the chopped parsley.

Nutty salad: Energy 236kcal/980kJ; Protein 9.2g; Carbohydrate 15.1g, of which sugars 6.1g; Fat 15.8g, of which saturates 4.3g; Cholesterol 3mg; Calcium 102mg; Fibre 3.5g; Sodium 167mg
Marinated mushrooms: Energy 80kcal/329kJ; Protein 1.4g; Carbohydrate 2.1g, of which sugars 1.7g; Fat 5.8g, of which saturates 0.9g; Cholesterol 0mg; Calcium 9mg; Fibre 0.9g; Sodium 14mg

Avocado & Pink Grapefruit Salad

Minted Melon & Grapefruit Cocktail

A refreshing and attractive citrus and avocado salad, ideal as a light first course.

Serves 8
mixed red and green lettuce
  or other salad leaves
2 sweet pink grapefruit
1 large or 2 small avocados,
  peeled, stoned (pitted)
  and cubed

For the dressing
90ml/6 tbsp extra-virgin olive oil
30ml/2 tbsp red wine vinegar
1 garlic clove, crushed
5ml/1 tsp Dijon mustard
salt and ground black pepper

For the caramelized peel
4 oranges
50g/2oz/¼ cup caster
  (superfine) sugar
60ml/4 tbsp cold water

1 To make the caramelized peel, using a vegetable peeler, carefully remove the rind from the oranges in thin strips and reserve the fruit. Scrape away the white pith from the underside of the rind with a small, sharp knife, and cut the rind into fine shreds.

2 Put the sugar and water in a small pan and heat gently until the sugar has dissolved. Add the shreds of orange rind, increase the heat and boil steadily for 5 minutes, or until the rind is tender. Using two forks, remove the orange rind from the syrup and spread it out on a wire rack to dry. Reserve the cooking syrup to add to the dressing.

3 Wash and dry the lettuce or other salad leaves and tear or chop them into bitesize pieces. Using a sharp knife, remove the pith from the oranges and the pith and peel from the grapefruit. Hold the citrus fruits over a bowl and cut out each segment leaving the membrane behind. Squeeze the remaining juice from the membrane into the bowl.

4 Put all the dressing ingredients into a screw-top jar and shake well. Add the reserved syrup and adjust the seasoning to taste. Arrange the salad ingredients on plates with the cubed avocado. Spoon over the dressing and sprinkle with the caramelized peel. Serve immediately.

Melon is always a popular starter. Here the flavour is complemented by the clean taste of citrus fruit and a simple dressing.

Serves 4
1 small Galia melon, about
  1kg/2¼lb
2 pink grapefruits
1 yellow grapefruit

5ml/1 tsp Dijon mustard
5ml/1 tsp raspberry or
  sherry vinegar
5ml/1 tsp clear honey
15ml/1 tbsp chopped fresh mint
fresh mint sprigs, to garnish

1 Cut the melon in half and, using a teaspoon, scoop out and discard the seeds. Use a melon baller, to scoop out the flesh.

2 Using a sharp knife, peel all three grapefruit and cut away all the white pith. Remove the segments by cutting between the membranes, holding the fruit over a bowl to catch any juice.

3 Whisk the mustard, vinegar, honey, chopped mint and grapefruit juice together in a mixing bowl. Add the melon balls and grapefruit segments and mix well. Chill for 30 minutes.

4 Ladle the salad into four individual dishes, garnish each one with a sprig of fresh mint and serve immediately.

Avocado & pink grapefruit salad: Energy 151kcal/624kJ; Protein 1.1g; Carbohydrate 5.6g, of which sugars 5.1g; Fat 13.9g, of which saturates 2.4g; Cholesterol 0mg; Calcium 24mg; Fibre 1.9g; Sodium 12mg
Minted melon & grapefruit cocktail: Energy 101kcal/429kJ; Protein 2.3g; Carbohydrate 23.2g, of which sugars 23.2g; Fat 0.5g, of which saturates 0g; Cholesterol 0mg; Calcium 61mg; Fibre 2.6g; Sodium 118mg

Pear & Parmesan Salad with Poppy Seed Dressing

This is a good starter when pears are at their seasonal best. Drizzle them with a poppy-seed dressing and top them with shavings of Parmesan cheese.

Serves 4

4 just-ripe dessert pears
50g/2oz piece of
    Parmesan cheese
watercress, to garnish
water biscuits (crackers) or rye
    bread, to serve (optional)

For the dressing

30ml/2 tbsp cider vinegar or
    white wine vinegar
2.5ml/½ tsp soft light
    brown sugar
good pinch of dried thyme
30ml/2 tbsp extra-virgin olive oil
15ml/1 tbsp sunflower oil
15ml/1 tbsp poppy seeds
salt and ground black pepper

1 Cut the pears into quarters and remove the cores. Peel the pears if you wish, although they look more attractive (and have more fibre) unpeeled.

2 Cut each pear quarter in half lengthwise and arrange them on four small serving plates.

3 To make the dressing, mix the vinegar, sugar and thyme in a bowl. Gradually whisk in the olive oil, then the sunflower oil. Season with salt and pepper, then add the poppy seeds.

4 Trickle the dressing over the pears. Shave Parmesan over the top and garnish with watercress. Serve with water biscuits or thinly sliced rye bread, if you like.

Variation
Blue cheese and pears have a natural affinity. Stilton, Dolcelatte, Gorgonzola or Danish Blue (Danablu) can be used instead of Parmesan. Allow about 200g/7oz and cut into cubes.

Rocket & Grilled Goat's Cheese Salad

Simple and delicious – peppery leaves topped with grilled cheese croûtons.

Serves 4

15ml/1 tbsp extra-virgin olive oil
15ml/1 tbsp sunflower oil
4 slices French bread
225g/8oz cylinder-shaped
    goat's cheese
generous handfuls of rocket
    (arugula) leaves

115g/4oz frisée leaves
salt and ground black pepper

For the sauce

45ml/3 tbsp apricot jam
60ml/4 tbsp white wine
5ml/1 tsp Dijon mustard

For the dressing

45ml/3 tbsp walnut oil
15ml/1 tbsp lemon juice

1 Fry the slices of French bread in olive oil, on one side only, until lightly golden. Transfer to a plate lined with kitchen paper.

2 To make the sauce, heat the jam in a small pan until warm but not boiling. Sieve into a clean pan, to remove the pieces of fruit, then stir in the white wine and mustard. Heat gently and keep warm until ready to serve.

3 Blend the walnut oil and lemon juice and season with a little salt and pepper.

4 Preheat the grill (broiler) a few minutes before serving. Cut the goat's cheese into 50g/2oz rounds and place each piece on a slice of bread, toasted side down. Grill until the cheese melts.

5 Toss the rocket and curly endive leaves in walnut dressing and arrange on individual plates. Top with cheese croûtons and pour over a little of the apricot dressing, then serve.

Cook's Tip
Look for small goat's cheese logs that can be cut into halves.

Pear & parmesan salad: Energy 240kcal/996kJ; Protein 6.1g; Carbohydrate 16.4g, of which sugars 15.7g; Fat 17g, of which saturates 4.2g; Cholesterol 13mg; Calcium 171mg; Fibre 3.5g; Sodium 141mg
Rocket & grilled goat's cheese salad: Energy 453kcal/1890kJ; Protein 15.9g; Carbohydrate 31.7g, of which sugars 10.4g; Fat 29.3g, of which saturates 11.7g; Cholesterol 52mg; Calcium 139mg; Fibre 1.4g; Sodium 592mg

Broad Bean & Feta Salad

Tomato & Feta Cheese Salad

This recipe is loosely based on a typical medley of fresh-tasting Greek salad ingredients – broad beans, tomatoes and feta cheese. It is lovely as a starter, served warm or cold and accompanied by pitta bread.

Serves 4–6
900g/2lb broad (fava) beans, shelled, or 350g/12oz shelled frozen beans

60ml/4 tbsp olive oil
175g/6oz plum tomatoes, halved, or quartered if large
4 garlic cloves, crushed
115g/4oz/1 cup firm feta cheese, cut into chunks
45ml/3 tbsp chopped fresh dill
12 black olives
salt and ground black pepper
chopped fresh dill, to garnish

1 Cook the fresh or frozen broad beans in boiling, salted water until just tender. Drain and set aside.

2 Meanwhile, heat the oil in a heavy-based frying pan (skillet) and add the tomatoes and garlic. Cook until the tomatoes are beginning to colour.

3 Add the feta cheese to the pan and toss the ingredients together for 1 minute. Mix with the drained beans, chopped dill, and black olives. Season with salt and pepper to taste and serve garnished with chopped dill.

Sweet, sun-ripened tomatoes are rarely more delicious than when served with feta cheese and olive oil. Serve with warm pitta bread to complete the Greek character of the dish.

Serves 4
900g/2lb tomatoes
200g/7oz feta cheese
120ml/4fl oz/½ cup olive oil
12 black olives
4 fresh basil sprigs
ground black pepper

1 Remove any tough cores from the tomatoes, using a small, sharp knife.

2 Slice the tomatoes thickly and arrange them attractively in a shallow serving dish.

3 Crumble the feta cheese over the tomatoes and sprinkle with the olive oil. Scatter the black olives and basil sprigs over the salad and season to taste with black pepper.

4 Serve the salad at room temperature.

Cook's Tip
Feta cheese has a strong flavour and can be salty. The least salty variety is imported from Greece and Turkey.

Broad bean & feta salad: Energy 175kcal/727kJ; Protein 8.3g; Carbohydrate 8.8g, of which sugars 2.2g; Fat 12g, of which saturates 3.8g; Cholesterol 13mg; Calcium 121mg; Fibre 4.7g; Sodium 342mg
Tomato & feta salad: Energy 369kcal/1528kJ; Protein 9.6g; Carbohydrate 7.7g, of which sugars 7.7g; Fat 33.5g, of which saturates 10.4g; Cholesterol 35mg; Calcium 211mg; Fibre 3g; Sodium 1303mg

French Goat's Cheese Salad

Here is the French salad and cheese course all on one plate. Serve as a satisfying starter or even as a light lunch. The tangy flavour of goat's cheese contrasts wonderfully with the mild salad leaves.

Serves 4
200g/7oz bag prepared mixed salad leaves

4 back bacon rashers (strips)
115g/4oz goat's cheese
16 thin slices crusty white bread

For the dressing
60ml/4 tbsp olive oil
15ml/1 tbsp tarragon vinegar
10ml/2 tsp walnut oil
5ml/1 tsp Dijon mustard
5ml/1 tsp wholegrain mustard

1 Preheat the grill (broiler) to a medium heat. Rinse and dry the salad leaves, then arrange them in four individual bowls. Place the ingredients for the dressing in a screw-top jar, shake together well and reserve.

2 Lay the bacon rashers on a board, then stretch them with the back of a knife and cut each one into four. Roll each piece up and grill (broil) for 2–3 minutes.

3 Slice the goat's cheese into eight and halve each slice. Top each slice of bread with a piece of goat's cheese and place under the grill. Turn over the bacon and continue cooking with the toasts until the cheese is golden and bubbling.

4 Arrange the bacon rolls and toasts on top of the prepared salad leaves, shake the dressing well and pour a little dressing over each one. Serve immediately.

Cook's Tip
If you prefer, just slice the goat's cheese and place it on toasted crusty white bread. Or use wholemeal (whole-wheat) toast for a deliciously nutty flavour. Vegetarians can replace the bacon rolls with halved cherry tomatoes for an alternative juicy flavour.

Watermelon & Feta Salad with Mixed Seeds & Olives

The combination of sweet watermelon with salty feta cheese is refreshing and flavoursome. The salad may be served plain and light, on a leafy base, or with a herbed dressing drizzled over. It is perfect served as an appetizer or as part of a summery mezze spread.

Serves 4
4 slices watermelon, chilled
130g/4½ oz feta cheese, preferably sheep's milk feta, cut into bitesize pieces
handful of mixed seeds, such as pumpkin seeds and sunflower seeds, lightly toasted
10–15 black olives

1 Cut the rind off the watermelon and remove and discard as many seeds as possible. The sweetest and juiciest part is right in the core, and you may want to cut off any whiter flesh just under the skin.

2 Cut the flesh into triangular chunks and place in a salad bowl. Add the feta cheese, mixed seeds and black olives and mix gently to combine.

3 Cover and chill the salad for 30 minutes before serving.

Goat's cheese salad: Energy 667kcal/2806kJ; Protein 24.5g; Carbohydrate 85.6g, of which sugars 5.4g; Fat 27.8g, of which saturates 9g; Cholesterol 40mg; Calcium 240mg; Fibre 4.1g; Sodium 1483mg
Watermelon & feta salad: Energy 203Kcal/849kJ; Protein 7.8g; Carbohydrate 16.2g, of which sugars 14.8g; Fat 12.4g, of which saturates 5.2g; Cholesterol 23mg; Calcium 148mg; Fibre 1.1g; Sodium 754mg

Rocket, Pear & Parmesan Salad

Pears with Cashel Blue Cream & Walnuts

For a sophisticated start to an elaborate meal, try this simple salad of honey-rich pears, fresh Parmesan and aromatic rocket leaves.

10ml/2 tsp lemon juice
45ml/3 tbsp hazelnut or
   walnut oil
115g/4oz rocket (arugula) leaves
75g/3oz piece Parmesan cheese
ground black pepper

Serves 4

3 ripe pears, such as Williams or
   Packhams

1 Peel and core the pears and slice thickly. Moisten with lemon juice to keep the flesh white.

2 Combine the hazelnut or walnut oil with the pears. Add the rocket leaves and toss together.

3 Turn the salad out on to four individual plates and top with shavings of Parmesan cheese. Season with pepper and serve.

Cook's Tip
Buy a chunk of fresh Parmesan and shave strips off the side, using a vegetable peeler. The distinctive flavour is quite strong. Store the rest of the Parmesan uncovered in the refrigerator.

The Irish cheese Cashel Blue is the perfect partner to ripe, juicy pears – and it is now widely available from specialist cheese suppliers.

6 ripe pears
15ml/1 tbsp lemon juice
mixed salad leaves, such as frisée,
   oakleaf lettuce and radicchio
6 cherry tomatoes
sea salt and ground black pepper
walnut halves and sprigs of fresh
   flat leaf parsley, to garnish

Serves 6

115g/4oz fresh cream cheese
75g/3oz Cashel Blue cheese
30–45ml/2–3 tbsp single
   (light) cream
115g/4oz/1 cup roughly
   chopped walnuts

For the dressing
juice of 1 lemon
a little finely grated lemon rind
pinch of caster (superfine) sugar

1 Mash the cream cheese and Cashel Blue cheese together in a mixing bowl with a good grinding of black pepper, then blend in the cream to make a smooth mixture. Add 25g/1oz/¼ cup chopped walnuts and mix to distribute evenly. Cover and chill.

2 Peel and halve the pears and scoop out the core. Put them into a bowl of water with the lemon juice to prevent them from browning. To make the dressing, whisk the lemon juice, lemon rind, caster sugar and olive oil together in a bowl and season with salt and pepper to taste.

3 Arrange a bed of salad leaves on six plates – shallow soup plates are ideal – add a tomato to each and sprinkle over the remaining chopped walnuts.

4 Drain the pears well and pat dry with kitchen paper, then turn them in the prepared dressing and arrange, hollow side up, on the salad leaves. Divide the Cashel Blue mixture between the six halved pears and spoon the rest of the dressing over the top. Garnish each pear with a walnut half and a sprig of parsley.

Rocket, pear & parmesan salad: Energy 210kcal/875kJ; Protein 8.6g; Carbohydrate 11.4g, of which sugars 11.4g; Fat 14.8g, of which saturates 4.7g; Cholesterol 19mg; Calcium 286mg; Fibre 2.9g; Sodium 222mg
Pears with cashel blue: Energy 331Kcal/1373kJ; Protein 6.7g; Carbohydrate 16.3g, of which sugars 16.1g; Fat 27g, of which saturates 9.8g; Cholesterol 30mg; Calcium 120mg; Fibre 4.1g; Sodium 219mg

Pear & Blue Cheese Salad

This salad is very quick to assemble, making it just the thing for an impromptu gathering. The key to success is to use pears that are just ripe and a blue cheese with lots of bite.

Serves 4

4 ripe pears
115g/4oz blue cheese
15ml/1 tbsp balsamic vinegar
30ml/2 tbsp olive oil
salt and ground black pepper

1 Cut the pears into quarters and remove the cores. Thinly slice each pear quarter and arrange on a serving platter.

2 Cut the cheese into bitesize pieces, or crumble roughly, and scatter over the pears. Whisk the oil and vinegar together and drizzle over the pears. Season with salt and pepper and serve.

Cook's Tips
• Rich, dark balsamic vinegar has an intense yet mellow flavour. It is produced in Modena in the north of Italy and is widely available in most supermarkets.
• A mature Stilton, with it slightly crumbly texture, would make an excellent choice for this dish. Look for a piece where the veins of blue are evenly spread throughout the cheese. Other suitable cheeses would be Roquefort or Gorgonzola.

Watercress Salad with Pear & Dunsyre Blue Dressing

A refreshing light salad, this starter combines lovely peppery watercress, soft juicy pears and a tart dressing. Dunsyre Blue has a wonderfully sharp flavour with a crumbly texture.

Serves 4

25g/1oz Dunsyre Blue cheese
30ml/2 tbsp walnut oil
15ml/1 tbsp lemon juice
2 bunches watercress, thoroughly washed and trimmed
2 ripe pears
salt and ground black pepper

1 Crumble the Dunsyre Blue into a bowl, then mash into the walnut oil, using a fork.

2 Whisk in the lemon juice to create a thickish mixture. If you need to thicken it further, add a little more cheese. Season to taste with salt and ground black pepper.

3 Arrange a pile of watercress on the side of four plates.

4 Peel and slice the two pears then place the pear slices to the side of the watercress, allowing half a pear per person. You can also put the pear slices on top of the watercress, if you prefer. Drizzle the dressing over the salad. The salad is best served immediately at room temperature.

Cook's Tips
• Choose ripe Comice or similar pears that are soft and juicy.
• If you want to get things ready in advance, peel and slice the pears then rub with some lemon juice; this will stop them discolouring so quickly.

Variation
For a milder, tangy dressing use Dolcelatte cheese instead.

Pear & blue cheese salad: Energy 208kcal/865kJ; Protein 6.4g; Carbohydrate 15g, of which sugars 15g; Fat 14g, of which saturates 6.3g; Cholesterol 22mg; Calcium 157mg; Fibre 3.3g; Sodium 355mg
Watercress salad: Energy 106Kcal/442kJ; Protein 2.3g; Carbohydrate 7.6g, of which sugars 7.6g; Fat 7.6g, of which saturates 1.8g; Cholesterol 5mg; Calcium 81mg; Fibre 2g; Sodium 91mg

Mozzarella, Tomato & Basil Salad

Jicama, Chilli & Lime Salad

This very popular first course salad is considered rather patriotic in Italy, as its three ingredients are the colours of the national flag. It is divine with a glass of chilled Pinot Grigio and warmed ciabatta bread.

Serves 4

4 large tomatoes
225g/8oz/2 cups mozzarella
* cheese, from cow or*
* buffalo milk*
8–10 fresh basil leaves
60ml/4 tbsp extra-virgin olive oil
salt and ground black pepper

1 Using a sharp knife, slice the tomatoes and mozzarella into thick even rounds.

2 Arrange the tomatoes and cheese in overlapping slices on a serving dish. Decorate with basil leaves.

3 Sprinkle the salad with olive oil and a little salt. Serve the salad at room temperature once it has had a few minutes to take on the flavour of the olive oil. Pass the black pepper around separately.

Cook's Tip
In Italy, the most sought-after mozzarella is made from the milk of water buffalo as it has a far superior texture.

A very tasty, crisp vegetable, the jicama is sometimes called the Mexican potato. Unlike potato, however, it can be eaten raw and here it is transformed into a zingy salad appetizer to serve with drinks.

Serves 4

1 jicama
2.5ml/½ tsp salt
2 fresh serrano chillies
2 limes

1 Peel the jicama with a potato peeler or knife, then cut it into 2cm/¾in cubes. Put the cubes in a large bowl, add the salt and toss well to coat.

2 Cut the chillies in half, scrape out the seeds with a sharp knife, then cut the flesh into fine strips. Grate one of the limes thinly, removing only the coloured part of the skin, then cut the lime in half and squeeze the juice.

3 Add the chillies, lime rind and juice to the jicama and mix thoroughly to ensure that all the jicama cubes are coated. Cut the other lime into wedges.

4 Cover the salad and chill for at least 1 hour before serving with lime wedges. If the salad is to be served as an appetizer with drinks, transfer the jicama cubes to little bowls and offer them with cocktail sticks for spearing.

Cook's Tips
• Look for jicama in Oriental supermarkets, as it is widely used in Chinese cooking. It goes by several names and you may find it labelled as either yam bean or Chinese turnip.
• Take care when handling fresh chillies as the juice can burn sensitive skin. Wear rubber gloves to protect your hands or wash your hands very thoroughly after preparation. Be careful also not to touch your eyes when preparing chillies as the juices can cause unpleasant stinging.

Mozzarella, tomato & basil salad: Energy 261kcal/1080kJ; Protein 11.2g; Carbohydrate 3.1g, of which sugars 3.1g; Fat 22.7g, of which saturates 9.4g; Cholesterol 33mg; Calcium 211mg; Fibre 1g; Sodium 231mg
Jicama, chilli & lime salad: Energy 6kcal/26kJ; Protein 0.4g; Carbohydrate 0.8g, of which sugars 0.8g; Fat 0.2g, of which saturates 0g; Cholesterol 0mg; Calcium 32mg; Fibre 0.8g; Sodium 45mg

Stuffed Vine Leaves with Rice

Start a meal on a sunny note with these traditional Greek delicacies.

Serves 4–6
50 fresh or 225g/8oz preserved vine leaves
175g/6oz/scant 1 cup long grain rice
350g/12oz onions, very finely diced
4–5 spring onions (scallions), green and white parts, thinly sliced

30ml/2 tbsp pine nuts, toasted
60ml/4 tbsp finely chopped fresh dill
45ml/3 tbsp finely chopped fresh mint
30ml/2 tbsp finely chopped fresh flat leaf parsley
150ml/¼ pint/⅔ cup extra-virgin olive oil
juice of 1 lemon
450ml/¾ pint/scant 2 cups hot water
salt and ground black pepper
4–6 lemon wedges, to serve

1 If using fresh leaves, blanch them briefly in batches in a pan of boiling water, then lift out with a slotted spoon after a few seconds and drain in a colander. They should just be wilted to make them pliable; not cooked. Preserved leaves can be extremely salty and must be rinsed well before being immersed in a bowl of hot water. Leave the vine leaves in the water for 4–5 minutes, then drain, rinse and drain again.

2 Put the rice in a large bowl. Add the onions, spring onions, pine nuts, dill, mint and parsley. Mix well, then stir in half the olive oil and half the lemon juice. Season with salt and pepper.

3 Line the bottom of a wide pan with 2–3 of the vine leaves. Spread another vine leaf out on a board, veined side up, and place 15ml/1 tsp of the stuffing near the stalk end. Fold the two opposite sides of the leaf over the stuffing and then roll up tightly from the stalk end. Make more rolls in the same way and pack them tightly together in circles in the pan.

4 Mix the remaining oil and lemon juice and pour over the rolls. Invert a small plate on top to hold in place. Carefully pour in the hot water, cover tightly and simmer gently for 1 hour. Serve hot or at room temperature with lemon wedges.

Zahlouk with Pale Courgette & Cauliflower Salad

Serve Zahlouk, a delicious, spicy aubergine and tomato appetizer, with plenty of flat bread for scooping it up.

Serves 4
For the zahlouk
3 large aubergines (eggplants), peeled and cubed
3–4 large tomatoes, peeled and chopped to a pulp
5ml/1 tsp sugar
3–4 garlic cloves, crushed
60ml/4 tbsp olive oil
juice of 1 lemon
scant 5ml/1 tsp harissa
5ml/1 tsp cumin seeds, roasted and ground
small bunch flat leaf parsley, chopped
salt and ground black pepper

For the courgette and cauliflower salad
60ml/4 tbsp olive oil
2–3 small courgettes (zucchini), thickly sliced
1 cauliflower, broken into florets
juice of 1 lemon
2–3 garlic cloves, crushed
small bunch parsley, finely chopped

1 To make the zahlouk, boil the aubergines in salted water for about 15 minutes, until they are very soft. Drain and squeeze out the excess water, then chop and mash them with a fork.

2 Put the pulped tomatoes in a pan, stir in the sugar and cook over a gentle heat until they are reduced to a thick sauce. Add the mashed aubergines. Stir in the garlic, olive oil, lemon juice, harissa, cumin and parsley until well mixed. Season to taste.

3 To make the courgette and cauliflower salad, heat about half the olive oil in a heavy pan and brown the courgettes on both sides. Drain on kitchen paper.

4 Meanwhile, steam the cauliflower over boiling water for 7–10 minutes until tender. While the cauliflower is still warm, mash it lightly in a bowl and mix in the remaining olive oil, half the lemon juice and the garlic. Add the courgettes and parsley with the remaining lemon juice and season to taste. Serve the salad at room temperature, with the zahlouk.

Stuffed vine leaves: Energy 339kcal/1407kJ; Protein 5.8g; Carbohydrate 32.2g, of which sugars 7.3g; Fat 20.9g, of which saturates 2.7g; Cholesterol 0mg; Calcium 95mg; Fibre 3.4g; Sodium 14mg
Zahlouk: Energy 296kcal/1225kJ; Protein 7.5g; Carbohydrate 12.7g, of which sugars 10.4g; Fat 24.3g, of which saturates 3.7g; Cholesterol 0mg; Calcium 90mg; Fibre 6.9g; Sodium 23mg

Creamy Cucumber & Walnut Appetizer

In this Bulgarian salad, diced cucumber is bathed in a luscious garlicky yogurt dressing and topped with chopped walnuts for a delicious contrast in texture and flavour. Serve with chunks of rustic bread as a fresh-tasting alternative to a meat or fish pâté.

Serves 6

1 large cucumber
3–5 garlic cloves, finely chopped
250ml/8fl oz/1 cup soured cream or 120ml/4fl oz/½ cup Greek (US strained plain) yogurt mixed with 120ml/4fl oz/ ½ cup double (heavy) cream
250ml/8fl oz/1 cup yogurt, preferably thick Greek yogurt
2–3 large pinches of dried dill or 30–45ml/2–3 tbsp chopped fresh dill
45–60ml/3–4 tbsp chopped walnuts
salt
sprig of dill, to garnish (optional)

1 Do not peel the cucumber. Using a sharp knife, dice it finely and place in a large mixing bowl.

2 Add the garlic, soured cream or yogurt and cream, yogurt and dill and season with salt. Mix together, then cover and chill.

3 To serve, pile the mixture into a bowl and sprinkle with walnuts. Garnish with dill, if you like.

> **Cook's Tip**
> When made with very thick Greek yogurt, this appetizer can be shaped into balls and served on salad leaves.

> **Variation**
> For a Greek version, to serve as part of a mezze, add chopped fresh mint instead of dill, omit the walnuts and serve with olives and pitta bread.

Mint & Parsley Tahini Salad

The almost dry flavour of tahini marries wonderfully with the fresh herbs and subtle spices in this refreshing appetizer.

Serves 4–6

115g/4oz/½ cup tahini paste
3 garlic cloves, chopped
½ bunch (about 20g/¾oz) fresh mint, chopped
½ bunch (about 20g/¾oz) fresh coriander (cilantro), chopped
½ bunch (about 20g/¾oz) fresh flat leaf parsley, chopped
juice of ½ lemon, or to taste
pinch of ground cumin
pinch of ground turmeric
pinch of ground cardamom seeds
cayenne pepper, to taste
salt

To serve
extra-virgin olive oil
warmed pitta bread
black olives
raw vegetable sticks, such as carrots, cucumber, celery and cauliflower

1 Combine the tahini with the chopped garlic, fresh herbs and lemon juice in a bowl. Taste and add a little more lemon juice, if you like. Stir in a little water if the mixture seems too dense and thick. Alternatively, place the ingredients in a food processor. Process briefly, then stir in a little water if required.

2 Stir in the cumin, turmeric and cardamom to taste, then season with salt and cayenne pepper.

3 To serve, spoon into a shallow bowl or onto plates and drizzle with olive oil. Serve with warmed pitta bread, olives and raw vegetables.

> **Cook's Tip**
> Tahini is a creamy-textured, oily paste made from ground sesame seeds. Popular in Middle-Eastern cooking, it is used to give a nutty flavour to dishes. It is widely available from wholefood shops and delicatessens, as well as from some supermarkets. Tahini paste is an integral flavouring in the famous chickpea dip, hummus.

Cucumber & walnut appetizer: Energy 167kcal/688kJ; Protein 4.9g; Carbohydrate 5.7g, of which sugars 5.6g; Fat 14g, of which saturates 5.8g; Cholesterol 26mg; Calcium 148mg; Fibre 0.9g; Sodium 56mg
Mint & parsley tahini salad: Energy 121kcal/500kJ; Protein 4g; Carbohydrate 0.5g, of which sugars 0.4g; Fat 11.5g, of which saturates 1.6g; Cholesterol 0mg; Calcium 157mg; Fibre 2.2g; Sodium 8mg

Prawn Cocktail

There is no nicer starter than a good, fresh prawn cocktail – and nothing nastier than one in which soggy prawns swim in a thin, vinegary sauce embedded in limp lettuce. This recipe shows just how good a prawn cocktail can be.

Serves 6
60ml/4 tbsp double (heavy) cream, lightly whipped
60ml/4 tbsp mayonnaise, preferably home-made
60ml/4 tbsp tomato ketchup
5–10ml/1–2 tsp Worcestershire sauce
juice of 1 lemon
1/2 cos or romaine lettuce or other very crisp lettuce
450g/1lb cooked peeled prawns (shrimp)
salt, ground black pepper and paprika
6 large whole cooked prawns (shrimp) in the shell, to garnish (optional)
thinly sliced, buttered brown bread and lemon wedges, to serve

1 Place the lightly whipped cream, mayonnaise and tomato ketchup in a small bowl and whisk lightly to combine. Add Worcestershire sauce to taste, then whisk in enough of the lemon juice to make a really tangy sauce.

2 Finely shred the lettuce and use to fill six individual glasses one-third full.

3 Stir the prawns into the sauce, then check the seasoning and spoon the prawn mixture generously over the lettuce.

4 If you like, drape a whole cooked prawn over the edge of each glass and sprinkle each of the cocktails with ground black pepper and/or paprika. Serve immediately, with thinly sliced brown bread and lemon wedges.

Cook's Tip
Partly peeled prawns make a pretty garnish. To prepare, carefully peel the body shell from the prawns and leave the tail "fan" for decoration.

Prawn & Vegetable Crostini

Use bottled carciofini (tiny artichoke hearts preserved in olive oil) for this simple Italian starter, which can be prepared very quickly.

Serves 4
450g/1lb whole cooked prawns (shrimp), in the shell
4 thick slices of ciabatta, cut diagonally across
3 garlic cloves, peeled and 2 garlic cloves halved lengthwise
60ml/4 tbsp extra virgin olive oil
200g/7oz/2 cups small button mushrooms, trimmed
12 bottled carciofini, drained
60ml/4 tbsp chopped flat leaf parsley
salt and ground black pepper

1 Peel the prawns and remove the heads. Rub the ciabatta slices on both sides with the cut sides of the halved garlic cloves, drizzle with a little of the olive oil and toast in the oven or grill (broil) until lightly browned. Keep hot.

2 Finely chop the remaining garlic. Heat the remaining oil in a frying pan and gently fry the chopped garlic until golden, but do not allow it to brown.

3 Add the mushrooms and stir to coat with oil. Season with salt and pepper and fry for about 2–3 minutes. Gently stir in the drained carciofini, then add the chopped flat leaf parsley.

4 Adjust the seasoning, then stir in the prawns and cook briefly to warm through.

5 Pile the prawn mixture on top of the toasted ciabatta slices, pouring over any remaining cooking juices from the pan.

Cook's Tip
Don't use frozen peeled prawns in this recipe: freshly cooked prawns in their shells are infinitely nicer.

Prawn cocktail: Energy 190kcal/792kJ; Protein 13.8g; Carbohydrate 3.7g, of which sugars 3.6g; Fat 13.5g, of which saturates 4.6g; Cholesterol 167mg; Calcium 74mg; Fibre 0.2g; Sodium 373mg
Prawn & vegetable crostini: Energy 264kcal/1104kJ; Protein 23.7g; Carbohydrate 13.6g, of which sugars 1.2g; Fat 13.1g, of which saturates 1.9g; Cholesterol 219mg; Calcium 152mg; Fibre 1.9g; Sodium 356mg

Piquant Prawn Salad

The fish sauce dressing adds a superb flavour to the noodles and prawns. This delicious salad can be enjoyed warm or cold.

Serves 6

200g/7oz rice vermicelli
8 baby corn cobs, halved
150g/5oz mangetouts
  (snow peas)
15ml/1 tbsp vegetable oil
2 garlic cloves, finely chopped
2.5cm/1in piece fresh root ginger,
  peeled and finely chopped
1 fresh red or green chilli, seeded
  and finely chopped

450g/1lb raw peeled tiger prawns
  (jumbo shrimp)
4 spring onions (scallions), very
  thinly sliced
15ml/1 tbsp sesame seeds, toasted
1 lemon grass stalk, thinly shredded

For the dressing

15ml/1 tbsp chopped fresh chives
15ml/1 tbsp Thai fish sauce
5ml/1 tsp soy sauce
45ml/3 tbsp groundnut
  (peanut) oil
5ml/1 tsp sesame oil
30ml/2 tbsp rice vinegar

1 Put the rice vermicelli in a wide heatproof bowl, pour over boiling water to cover and leave to soak for 10 minutes. Drain, refresh under cold water and drain well again. Transfer to a large serving bowl and set aside until required.

2 Boil or steam the corn cobs and mangetouts for about 3 minutes until just tender. Refresh under cold water and drain.

3 To make the dressing, put all the ingredients in a screw-top jar, close tightly and shake vigorously to combine. Set aside.

4 Heat the oil in a large frying pan or wok. Add the garlic, ginger and red or green chilli and cook for 1 minute. Add the tiger prawns and toss over the heat for about 3 minutes, until they have just turned pink. Stir in the spring onions, corn cobs, mangetouts and sesame seeds, and toss lightly to mix.

5 Turn the contents of the pan or wok over the rice vermicelli. Pour the dressing on top and toss well. Sprinkle with shredded lemon grass and serve, or chill for 1 hour before serving.

Prawns with Tomatoes & Feta

Prawns baked in a rich tomato sauce and topped with tangy feta cheese make a luxurious first course, bursting with sunny flavours. Serve with plenty of crusty bread for mopping up the delectable sauce.

Serves 6

75ml/5 tbsp extra-virgin olive oil
1 onion, chopped
½ red (bell) pepper, seeded
  and cubed

675g/1½lb ripe tomatoes, peeled
  and roughly chopped
generous pinch of sugar
2.5ml/½ tsp dried oregano
450g/1lb peeled (but with the tail
  shells intact) raw tiger or king
  prawns (jumbo shrimp), thawed
  if frozen
30ml/2 tbsp finely chopped fresh
  flat leaf parsley
75g/3oz feta cheese, cubed
salt and ground black pepper
fresh green salad, to serve

1 Preheat the oven to 180°C/350°F/Gas 4.

2 Heat the oil in a frying pan over a low to medium heat, add the onion and sauté gently for a few minutes until translucent.

3 Add the cubed red pepper and cook, stirring occasionally, for a further 2–3 minutes.

4 Stir in the chopped tomatoes, sugar and oregano, then season with salt and pepper to taste.

5 Cook gently over a low heat for about 15 minutes, stirring occasionally, until the sauce reduces slightly and thickens.

6 Stir the prawns and parsley into the tomato sauce, transfer to a baking dish and spread evenly. Sprinkle the cheese cubes on top, then bake for 30 minutes. Serve hot with a crisp, fresh green salad.

Cook's Tip
Use crayfish tails or mixed seafood if you can't find king prawns.

Piquant prawn salad: Energy 298kcal/1240kJ; Protein 18.8g; Carbohydrate 28.1g, of which sugars 1.6g; Fat 12.1g, of which saturates 2g; Cholesterol 146mg; Calcium 102mg; Fibre 1.4g; Sodium 587mg
Prawns with tomatoes & feta: Energy 183kcal/760kJ; Protein 12.1g; Carbohydrate 5.8g, of which sugars 5.5g; Fat 12.5g, of which saturates 3.2g; Cholesterol 106mg; Calcium 113mg; Fibre 2g; Sodium 289mg

Ceviche

Prawn, Avocado & Citrus Salad

This is a fruity first course of marinated fresh fish. Take care in choosing the fish for this dish; it must be as fresh as possible and served on the day it is made, since it is "cooked" by the action of the citrus juices, rather than by heating.

Serves 6
350g/12oz medium cooked prawns (shrimp)
350g/12oz scallops, removed from their shells, with the corals intact
175g/6oz tomatoes

1 mango, about 175g/6oz
1 red onion, finely chopped
350g/12oz salmon fillet
1 fresh red chilli, seeded and chopped
12 limes
30ml/2 tbsp caster (superfine) sugar
2 pink grapefruit
3 oranges
salt and ground black pepper

1 Set aside two prawns for the garnish. Peel the remaining prawns and cut the scallops into 1cm/½in dice.

2 Dice the tomatoes and add to the chopped scallops and prawns. Peel the mango, cut the flesh from the stone (pit) and dice. Add to the bowl with the red onion. Mix well.

3 Skin the salmon, then remove any pin bones with a pair of tweezers. Cut the fish into small pieces and mix with the tomato, mango and onion. Add the chilli and mix well.

4 Squeeze the juice from 8 limes and add it to the tomato mixture with the sugar and a little salt and pepper. Stir, cover and leave to marinate in a cool place for 3 hours.

5 Peel the grapefruit, oranges and remaining limes and cut out the segments from between the membranes. Drain off as much excess lime juice as possible from the fish mixture and mix the fruit segments into the marinated ingredients. Season to taste and serve, garnished with the reserved prawns.

For a refreshing start to a meal this elegant, citrus-flavoured prawn dish is hard to beat. The sharp tang of the fruit complements the succulence of the prawns and creamy texture of the avocado to perfection.

Serves 6
15ml/1 tbsp fresh lemon juice
15ml/1 tbsp fresh lime juice
15ml/1 tbsp clear honey
45ml/3 tbsp olive oil

30–45ml/2–3 tbsp walnut oil
30ml/2 tbsp chopped fresh chives
450g/1lb large cooked prawns (shrimp), shelled and deveined
1 avocado, peeled, stoned (pitted) and cut into tiny dice
1 pink grapefruit, peeled and segmented
1 large navel orange, peeled and segmented
30ml/2 tbsp toasted pine nuts (optional)
salt and ground black pepper
baby salad leaves, to serve

1 Blend the lemon and lime juices, with the honey and salt and pepper in a small bowl.

2 Slowly whisk in the olive oil, then the walnut oil to make a creamy sauce. Stir in the chopped chives.

3 Arrange the prawns with the avocado pieces, grapefruit and orange segments on individual plates. Drizzle over the dressing and sprinkle with the toasted pine nuts, if using. Serve immediately, with salad leaves.

Ceviche: Energy 290kcal/1224kJ; Protein 37.5g; Carbohydrate 18.5g, of which sugars 16.2g; Fat 7.9g, of which saturates 1.5g; Cholesterol 170mg; Calcium 135mg; Fibre 3.3g; Sodium 251mg
Prawn, avocado & citrus salad: Energy 194kcal/806kJ; Protein 14g; Carbohydrate 5.7g, of which sugars 5.5g; Fat 12.9g, of which saturates 1.9g; Cholesterol 146mg; Calcium 77mg; Fibre 1.3g; Sodium 146mg

Asparagus & Langoustine Salad

For a really extravagant treat, you could make this attractive salad with medallions of lobster. For a less expensive version, use large prawns, allowing six per serving.

Serves 4
16 langoustines
16 fresh asparagus spears, trimmed
2 carrots
30ml/2 tbsp extra-virgin olive oil
1 garlic clove, peeled
15ml/1 tbsp chopped fresh tarragon
4 fresh tarragon sprigs and some chopped, to garnish

For the dressing
30ml/2 tbsp tarragon vinegar
120ml/4fl oz/½ cup olive oil
salt and ground black pepper

1 Shell the langoustines and keep the discarded parts for stock. Set aside.

2 Steam the asparagus over boiling salted water until just tender, but still a little crisp. Refresh under cold water, drain and place in a shallow dish.

3 Peel the carrots and cut into fine julienne shreds. Cook in a pan of lightly salted boiling water for about 3 minutes, until tender but still crunchy. Drain, refresh under cold water and drain again. Place in the dish with the asparagus.

4 To make the dressing, whisk the tarragon vinegar with the oil, then season with salt and pepper to taste. Pour over the vegetables and leave to marinate.

5 Heat the oil with the garlic in a frying pan until very hot. Add the langoustines and cook quickly until just heated through. Discard the garlic.

6 Cut the asparagus spears in half and arrange on four individual plates with the carrots. Drizzle over the dressing left in the dish and top each portion with four langoustine tails. Garnish with the tarragon sprigs and sprinkle over the chopped tarragon. Serve immediately.

Surtido de Pescado

This pretty salad is a lesson from the Spanish on how to enjoy and make the most of preserved fish. Ideal as a last-minute party starter, it can be made predominantly from storecupboard items. For the best results try to use Spanish canned fish.

Serves 4
6 eggs
cos or romaine lettuce leaves
75–90ml/5–6 tbsp mayonnaise
90g/3½oz jar Avruga herring roe, Eurocaviar grey mullet roe or undyed (or black) lumpfish roe
2 × 115g/4oz cans sardines in oil
2 × 115g/4oz cans mackerel fillets in oil
2 × 150g/5oz jars cockles (small clams) in brine, drained
2 × 115g/4oz cans mussels or scallops in tomato sauce
fresh flat leaf parsley or dill sprigs, to garnish

1 Put the eggs in a pan with enough water to cover and bring to the boil. Turn down the heat and simmer for 10 minutes. Drain immediately, then cover with cold water and set aside until completely cool. Peel the eggs and slice in half.

2 Arrange the lettuce leaves on a large serving platter, with the tips pointing outwards. (You may need to break off the bottom end of each leaf if the leaves are large).

3 Place 5ml/1 tsp of mayonnaise on the flat side of each halved egg and top with a spoonful of fish roe. Carefully arrange in the centre of the dish.

4 Arrange the sardines and mackerel fillets at four points on the plate. Spoon the pickled cockles into two of the gaps, opposite each other, and the mussels in sauce in the remaining gaps. Garnish with parsley or dill and chill until needed.

> **Cook's Tip**
> Smoked salmon, kippers (smoked herrings) and rollmops (pickled herring fillets) can also be included on the platter.

Asparagus & langoustine salad: Energy 320Kcal/1323kJ; Protein 16.3g; Carbohydrate 4g, of which sugars 3.8g; Fat 26.6g, of which saturates 3.9g; Cholesterol 146mg; Calcium 93mg; Fibre 2.3g; Sodium 150mg
Surtido de pescado: Energy 622kcal/2592kJ; Protein 56.9g; Carbohydrate 2.5g, of which sugars 0.7g; Fat 43.1g, of which saturates 8.9g; Cholesterol 506mg; Calcium 454mg; Fibre 0.2g; Sodium 1257mg

Marinated Herrings

Sweet-and-sour and lightly spiced, this classic dish needs to be prepared well in advance to allow for the marinating time.

Serves 4–6
2–3 herrings, filleted

1 onion, sliced
juice of 1½ lemons
30ml/2 tbsp white wine vinegar
25ml/1½ tbsp sugar
10–15 black peppercorns
10–15 allspice berries
1.5ml/¼ tsp mustard seeds
3 bay leaves, torn
salt

1 Soak the herrings in cold water for 5 minutes, then drain. Pour over water to cover and soak for 2–3 hours, then drain. Again, pour over water to cover and leave to soak overnight.

2 Hold the soaked herrings under cold running water and rinse very well, both inside and out.

3 Cut each fish into bitesize pieces, then place the pieces in a glass bowl or shallow dish.

4 Sprinkle the onion over the fish, then add the lemon juice, vinegar, sugar, peppercorns, allspice, mustard seeds, bay leaves and salt. Add enough water to just cover.

5 Cover and chill for 2 days to allow the flavours to blend.

Black Olive, Tomato & Sardine Salad

Flavourful sardines, sweet red onion and tasty olives all combine to make a lively starter, packed with Mediterranean flavours.

Serves 4
8 large firm ripe tomatoes
1 large red onion
60m/4 tbsp white wine vinegar

90ml/6 tbsp extra-virgin olive oil
12–16 small sardines, cooked
75g/3oz/¾ cup pitted black olives, well drained
salt and ground black pepper
45ml/3 tbsp chopped fresh parsley, to garnish

1 Slice the tomatoes into 5mm/¼in slices. Slice the red onion thinly.

2 Arrange the tomatoes on individual plates, overlapping the slices, then top with the red onion.

3 Mix together the wine vinegar and olive oil and season with salt and pepper. Spoon over each plate of salad.

4 Top each salad with 3–4 sardines and a few black olives. Sprinkle the chopped parsley over the top of the each serving and serve immediately.

Cook's Tip
For the best flavour, it is worth using a good-quality extra-virgin oil for the dressing. You may not need all the vinegar as the juice from the tomatoes will contribute some acidity.

Variation
For a vegetarian version, you can replace the sardines with 4–6 shelled and halved hard-boiled (hard-cooked) eggs.

Marinated herrings: Energy 94kcal/393kJ; Protein 7.7g; Carbohydrate 3.4g, of which sugars 3.2g; Fat 5.6g, of which saturates 1.4g; Cholesterol 21mg; Calcium 29mg; Fibre 0.1g; Sodium 52mg.
Black olive, tomato & sardine salad: Energy 281kcal/1167kJ; Protein 11.7g; Carbohydrate 5.8g, of which sugars 5.5g; Fat 23.6g, of which saturates 4.2g; Cholesterol 0mg; Calcium 68mg; Fibre 2.3g; Sodium 496mg

Smoked Trout Salad

Horseradish is as good a partner to smoked trout as it is to roast beef. In this recipe it is mixed with yogurt, mustard powder, oil and vinegar to make a deliciously piquant light salad dressing that complements the smoked trout perfectly.

Serves 4

1 oakleaf or other red lettuce
225g/8oz small tomatoes, cut into thin wedges
1/2 cucumber, peeled and thinly sliced

4 smoked trout fillets, about 200g/7oz each, skinned and flaked

For the dressing
pinch of mustard powder
15–20ml/3–4 tsp white wine vinegar
30ml/2 tbsp extra-virgin olive oil
100ml/3 1/2fl oz/scant 1/2 cup natural (plain) yogurt
about 30ml/2 tbsp grated fresh or bottled horseradish
pinch of caster (superfine) sugar

1 To make the dressing, mix the mustard powder and white wine vinegar in a bowl, then gradually whisk in the olive oil, yogurt, horseradish and sugar. Set aside for 30 minutes to allow all the flavours to develop.

2 Place the lettuce leaves in a large bowl. Stir the dressing again, then pour half of it over the leaves and toss them lightly.

3 Arrange the lettuce on four individual plates with the tomatoes, cucumber and trout. Spoon over the remaining dressing and serve immediately.

Cook's Tip
Horseradish is a root belonging to the same family as turnip and mustard. It has a strong, pungent flavour that is released when the root is cut. If you cannot find the fresh version, the bottled variety will work just as well. This piquant dressing is also delicious with smoked mackerel.

Smoked Salmon Salad with Dill

The delicate texture and flavour of smoked salmon contrasts beautifully with crisp, fresh-tasting fennel and cucumber. Perfect with thinly sliced brown bread.

Serves 4

225g/8oz smoked salmon, thinly sliced
1 fennel bulb, thinly sliced

1 medium cucumber, seeded and cut into julienne strips
30ml/2 tbsp fresh lemon juice
120ml/4fl oz/1/2 cup extra-virgin olive oil
30ml/2 tbsp fresh chopped dill, plus a few sprigs for garnishing
ground black pepper
caviar or lumpfish roe, to garnish (optional)

1 Arrange the salmon slices on four individual plates. Decoratively arrange the slices of fennel on top, then sprinkle over the cucumber julienne strips.

2 Mix the lemon juice with pepper to taste in a small bowl. Gradually whisk in the olive oil to make a creamy vinaigrette. Stir in the chopped dill.

3 Spoon a little vinaigrette over the fennel and cucumber.

4 Drizzle the remaining vinaigrette over the smoked salmon and garnish with sprigs of dill.

5 Top each salad with a spoonful of caviar, if you like.

Variation
Smoked salmon and caviar are perfect ingredients for canapés. You can use this recipe "in miniature" to make beautiful and delicious bitesize appetizers to hand around at a party. Spread small discs of brown bread (or blinis) with cream cheese. Top these with julienne strips of cucumber. Roll small strips of the salmon into rosettes. After dressing the rosettes, place them on top of the cucumber. Top each canapé with a small amount of caviar.

Smoked trout salad: Energy 318kcal/1331kJ; Protein 41.2g; Carbohydrate 6.2g, of which sugars 6g; Fat 14.4g, of which saturates 1.1g; Cholesterol 1mg; Calcium 91mg; Fibre 1.4g; Sodium 208mg
Smoked salmon salad: Energy 258kcal/1070kJ; Protein 15.1g; Carbohydrate 1.2g, of which sugars 1.1g; Fat 21.5g, of which saturates 3.1g; Cholesterol 20mg; Calcium 46mg; Fibre 1.4g; Sodium 1065mg

Carpaccio with Rocket

Invented in Venice, carpaccio is named in honour of the Renaissance painter. In this sophisticated Italian dish, raw beef is lightly dressed with lemon juice and olive oil, and it is traditionally served with shavings of Parmesan cheese. Use very fresh meat of the best quality and ask the butcher to slice it very thinly.

Serves 4

1 garlic clove, peeled and cut
   in half
1½ lemons
50ml/2fl oz/¼ cup extra-virgin
   olive oil
2 bunches rocket (arugula)
4 very thin slices of beef fillet
115g/4oz Parmesan cheese,
   shaved
salt and ground black pepper

1 Rub the cut side of the garlic over the inside of a bowl. Squeeze the lemons into the bowl, then whisk in the olive oil. Season with salt and black pepper, then leave to stand for at least 15 minutes.

2 Carefully wash the rocket and tear off any thick stalks. Spin or pat dry with kitchen paper. Arrange the rocket around the edge of a serving platter or divide among four individual plates.

3 Place the sliced beef in the centre of the platter and pour the dressing over, ensuring that the meat gets an even covering.

4 Arrange the Parmesan shavings on top of the meat slices and serve immediately.

> **Variation**
> *You can also serve meaty fish, such as tuna, in the same way. Place a tuna steak between sheets of clear film (plastic wrap) and pound with a rolling pin. Then roll it up tightly and wrap in clear film. Place in the freezer for about 4 hours until firm. Unwrap and, using a very sharp knife, cut the fish crossways into very thin slices. Serve in the same way.*

Prosciutto Salad with an Avocado Fan

Avocados are at their most elegant when sliced thinly and fanned on a plate. Served with air-cured ham and a few salad leaves, they make a stunning starter.

Serves 4

3 avocados
150g/5oz prosciutto
75–115g/3–4oz rocket (arugula)

24 marinated black
   olives, drained

For the dressing
15ml/1 tbsp balsamic vinegar
5ml/1 tsp lemon juice
5ml/1 tsp prepared
   English mustard
5ml/1 tsp sugar
75 ml/5 tbsp extra-virgin olive oil
salt and ground black pepper

1 To make the dressing, combine the balsamic vinegar, lemon juice, mustard and sugar in a bowl. Whisk in the olive oil, season to taste with salt and pepper and set aside.

2 Cut two of the avocados in half. Remove the stones (pits) and skins, then cut the flesh into 1cm/½in thick slices. Toss with half the dressing. Divide the prosciutto, avocado slices and rocket between four individual plates. Sprinkle the olives and the remaining dressing over the top.

3 Halve, stone and peel the remaining avocado. Slice each half lengthwise into eighths. Gently draw a cannelle knife across the quarters at 1cm/½in intervals to create regular stripes.

4 Make four cuts lengthwise down each avocado eighth, leaving 1cm/½in intact at the end. Carefully fan out the slices and arrange on the side of each plate.

Melon & Parma Ham Salad

This classic starter is given a delicious new twist with the addition of a fragrant strawberry salsa.

Serves 4

1 large melon (cantaloupe,
   Galia or Charentais)
175g/6oz Parma ham, thinly
   sliced

For the salsa
225g/8oz strawberries, hulled
5ml/1 tsp caster (superfine) sugar
30ml/2tbsp groundnut oil
15ml/1 tbsp orange juice
2.5ml/½ tsp finely grated
   orange rind
2.5ml/½ tsp grated fresh
   root ginger
salt and ground black pepper

1 Halve the melon and remove the seeds. Cut the rind away, then slice the melon flesh thickly. Chill until ready to serve.

2 To make the salsa, dice the strawberries. Place in a small mixing bowl with the sugar and crush lightly to release the juices. Add the oil, orange juice and rind and ginger. Season with salt and a generous twist of black pepper.

3 Arrange the melon slices on a serving plate and lay the ham over the top. Serve the salsa separately in a small bowl.

Carpaccio with rocket: Energy 244kcal/1013kJ; Protein 17.3g; Carbohydrate 0.1g, of which sugars 0.1g; Fat 19.4g, of which saturates 7.9g; Cholesterol 44mg; Calcium 384mg; Fibre 0.4g; Sodium 336mg
Prosciutto salad: Energy 341kcal/1407kJ; Protein 9.1g; Carbohydrate 3.2g, of which sugars 2.1g; Fat 32.4g, of which saturates 5.9g; Cholesterol 22mg; Calcium 59mg; Fibre 3.7g; Sodium 1043mg
Melon & Parma ham salad: Energy 173kcal/725kJ; Protein 9.8g; Carbohydrate 18.2g, of which sugars 18.2g; Fat 7.3g, of which saturates 1.1g; Cholesterol 25mg; Calcium 45mg; Fibre 1.6g; Sodium 606mg

Thai Fruit & Vegetable Salad

A cooling, refreshing salad served with a coconut dipping sauce that has a slight kick.

Serves 4–6

1 small pineapple
1 small mango, peeled and sliced
1 green apple, cored and sliced
6 lychees, peeled and stoned (pitted)
115g/4oz green beans, trimmed and halved
1 red onion, sliced
1 small cucumber, cut into short fingers
115g/4oz/1/2 cup beansprouts
2 spring onions (scallions), sliced
1 ripe tomato, quartered
225g/8oz cos or iceberg lettuce leaves

For the coconut dipping sauce

30ml/2 tbsp coconut cream
30ml/2 tbsp sugar
75ml/5 tbsp/1/3 cup boiling water
1.5ml/1/4 tsp chilli sauce
15ml/1 tbsp Thai fish sauce
juice of 1 lime

1 To make the coconut dipping sauce, put the coconut cream, sugar and boiling water in a screw-top jar. Add the chilli and fish sauces and lime juice and shake.

2 Trim both ends of the pineapple with a serrated knife, then cut away the outer skin. Remove the central core with an apple corer. Alternatively, cut the pineapple into quarters down the middle and remove the core with a knife. Roughly chop the pineapple and set aside with the other fruits.

3 Bring a small pan of salted water to the boil and cook the beans for 3–4 minutes. Refresh under cold running water and set aside. To serve, arrange the fruits and vegetables in small heaps in a wide, shallow bowl. Serve the coconut sauce separately as a dip.

> **Cook's Tip**
> To make coconut cream for the sauce, dissolve 75g/3oz of the solid creamed coconut in 100ml/3½fl oz/½ cup hot water.

Sweet Cucumber Cooler

This sweet dipping sauce is good served with Thai bites.

Makes 120ml/4fl oz/½ cup

1/4 small cucumber, thinly sliced
75ml/5 tbsp water
30ml/2 tbsp sugar
2.5ml/1/2 tsp salt
15ml/1 tbsp rice or white wine vinegar
2 shallots or 1 small red onion,

1 With a sharp knife, cut the cucumber slices into quarters.

2 Measure the water, sugar, salt and vinegar into a stainless steel or enamel pan, bring to the boil and simmer for less than 1 minute until the sugar has dissolved. Allow to cool. Add the cucumber and shallots. Serve at room temperature.

Hot Peanut Sauce & Oriental Salad

Serve crisp salad vegetables with a hot peanut sauce for a tasty Oriental appetizer.

Serves 4–6

a selection of crisp vegetables, such as beansprouts, shredded Chinese cabbage, cucumber sticks, spring onions (scallions), red (bell) pepper strips, to serve

For the peanut sauce

150g/5oz raw peanuts
15ml/1 tbsp vegetable oil
2 shallots, finely chopped
1 garlic clove, crushed
1–2 small chillies, finely chopped
30ml/2 tbsp tamarind sauce
120ml/4fl oz/1/2 cup canned coconut milk
15ml/1 tbsp clear honey

1 Dry-fry the peanuts in a wok, tossing them all the time to prevent burning. Turn the peanuts out onto a clean dish towel and rub vigorously to remove the papery skins. Place the peanuts in a food processor and blend for 2 minutes.

2 Heat the oil in a wok and soften the shallots, garlic and chillies. Add the tamarind sauce, coconut milk and honey. Simmer briefly, add to the peanuts and process to form a thick sauce. Turn into a bowl and serve with crisp salad vegetables.

Thai fruit & vegetable salad: Energy 131kcal/555kJ; Protein 2.6g; Carbohydrate 22.5g, of which sugars 21.7g; Fat 4.1g, of which saturates 3.1g; Cholesterol 0mg; Calcium 49mg; Fibre 3.2g; Sodium 8mg
Cucumber cooler: Energy 147kcal/624kJ; Protein 1.4g; Carbohydrate 37.2g, of which sugars 35.8g; Fat 0.2g, of which saturates 0g; Cholesterol 0mg; Calcium 44mg; Fibre 1.3g; Sodium 6mg
Oriental salad Energy 201kcal/838kJ; Protein 7.4g; Carbohydrate 12.8g, of which sugars 10.9g; Fat 13.7g, of which saturates 2.5g; Cholesterol 0mg; Calcium 28mg; Fibre 2.9g; Sodium 108mg

Wild Rocket & Cos Lettuce Salad with Herbs

This leafy Greek-style salad combines cos lettuce, which is native to Greece, with peppery rocket and fresh herbs, producing a clean-tasting side dish. If cos lettuce is not available, romaine lettuce can be used with just as much success.

Serves 4

a large handful of rocket
   (arugula) leaves
2 cos or romaine lettuce hearts
3 or 4 fresh flat leaf parsley
   sprigs, coarsely chopped
30–45ml/2–3 tbsp finely
   chopped fresh dill
75ml/5 tbsp extra-virgin olive oil
15–30ml/1–2 tbsp lemon juice
salt

1 If the rocket leaves are young and tender they can be left whole, but older ones should be trimmed of thick stalks and then sliced coarsely. Discard any tough stalks.

2 Slice the cos or romaine lettuce hearts into thin ribbons and place these in a bowl, then add the rocket and the chopped fresh parsley and dill.

3 To make the dressing, whisk the extra-virgin olive oil and lemon juice with salt to taste in a bowl until the mixture emulsifies and thickens.

4 Just before serving, pour the dressing over the salad and toss lightly to coat the ingredients well. Serve immediately.

Cook's Tips
• It is important to balance the bitterness of the rocket and the sweetness of the cos or romaine lettuce, and the best way to find this out is by taste.
• If you want to make the salad a little more substantial, try adding shavings of Parmesan cheese, canned anchovy fillets or steamed asparagus spears.

Mixed Green Leaf & Herb Salad

Bursting with fresh, herby flavours, this attractive salad makes an ideal side dish to serve with grilled meat or fish. You can vary the herbs according to taste and season. Try adding edible flowers, such as nasturtiums, for a splash of colour.

Serves 4

15g/½oz/½ cup mixed fresh
   herbs, such as chervil, tarragon
   (use sparingly), dill, basil,
   marjoram (use sparingly), flat
leaf parsley, mint, sorrel, fennel
   and coriander (cilantro)
350g/12oz mixed salad leaves,
   such as rocket (arugula),
   radicchio, chicory (Belgian
   endive), watercress, frisée, baby
   spinach, oakleaf lettuce
   and dandelion

For the dressing
50ml/2fl oz/¼ cup extra-virgin
   olive oil
15ml/1 tbsp cider vinegar
salt and ground black pepper

1 Wash and dry the herbs and salad leaves in a salad spinner, or use two clean, dry dish towels to pat them dry.

2 To make the dressing, whisk together the olive oil and cider vinegar in a small bowl and season with salt and pepper.

3 Place the mixed herbs and salad leaves in a large salad bowl. Just before serving, pour over the dressing and toss thoroughly with your hands to mix well. Serve immediately.

Cook's Tip
Try to get the herb and salad leaves as dry as possible otherwise the dressing will not coat properly.

Variation
To make a more substantial salad for a light lunch or supper, add baby broad (fava) beans, cooked, sliced artichoke hearts and quartered hard-boiled (hard-cooked) eggs.

Wild rocket & cos lettuce salad: Energy 135kcal/554kJ; Protein 0.6g; Carbohydrate 1.3g, of which sugars 1.3g; Fat 14.1g, of which saturates 2.1g; Cholesterol 0mg; Calcium 21mg; Fibre 0.7g; Sodium 2mg
Mixed green leaf & herb salad: Energy 88kcal/362kJ; Protein 0.8g; Carbohydrate 1.6g, of which sugars 1.6g; Fat 8.7g, of which saturates 1.3g; Cholesterol 0mg; Calcium 32mg; Fibre 1g; Sodium 4mg

Rocket & Coriander Salad

A quick and easy side salad, packed with peppery flavour.

Serves 4

115g/4oz rocket (arugula)
115g/4oz young spinach leaves
1 large bunch fresh coriander (cilantro), about 25g/1oz
2–3 fresh parsley sprigs

For the dressing

1 garlic clove, crushed
45ml/3 tbsp olive oil
10ml/2 tsp white wine vinegar
pinch of paprika
cayenne pepper
salt

1 Place the rocket and spinach leaves in a salad bowl. Chop the coriander and parsley and scatter them over the top.

2 Whisk together the garlic, olive oil, vinegar and paprika in a small bowl, adding cayenne pepper and salt to taste. Pour the dressing over the salad and serve immediately.

Garlicky Green Salad with Raspberry Dressing

Adding a splash of raspberry vinegar to the dressing enlivens a simple green salad, turning it into a sophisticated side dish.

Serves 4

45ml/3 tbsp olive oil
2 garlic cloves, finely sliced
4 handfuls of green salad leaves
15ml/1 tbsp raspberry vinegar
salt and ground black pepper

1 Heat the oil in a small pan and add the garlic. Fry gently for 1–2 minutes, or until just golden: do not burn the garlic. Remove the garlic with a slotted spoon and drain on kitchen paper. Pour the oil into a small bowl.

2 Arrange the salad leaves in a serving bowl. Whisk the vinegar into the reserved oil and season with salt and pepper. Pour the dressing over the salad, toss and sprinkle with the fried garlic.

Mixed Leaf & Herb Salad with Toasted Seeds

This simple salad is the perfect antidote to a rich, heavy meal as it contains fresh herbs that can aid the digestion.

Serves 4

115g/4oz/4 cups mixed salad leaves
50g/2oz/2 cups mixed salad herbs, such as coriander (cilantro), parsley, basil and rocket

25g/1oz/2 tbsp pumpkin seeds
25g/1oz/2 tbsp sunflower seeds

For the dressing

60ml/4 tbsp extra-virgin olive oil
15ml/1 tbsp balsamic vinegar
2.5ml/½ tsp Dijon mustard
salt and ground black pepper

1 Start by making the dressing. Combine the olive oil, balsamic vinegar and mustard in a screw-top jar. Add salt and pepper to taste. Close the jar tightly, then shake the dressing vigorously.

2 Place the salad and herb leaves in a large salad bowl and toss lightly together.

3 Toast the pumpkin and sunflower seeds in a dry frying pan over a medium heat for 2 minutes, until golden, tossing frequently to prevent them from burning. Allow the seeds to cool slightly before sprinkling over the salad.

4 Pour the dressing over the salad and toss gently with your hands until the leaves are well coated. Serve immediately.

Variations
• Balsamic vinegar adds a rich, sweet taste to the dressing, but red or white wine vinegar could be used instead.
• A few nasturtium flowers would look very pretty in this salad, as would borage flowers.

Rocket & coriander Salad: Energy 68kcal/280kJ; Protein 2g; Carbohydrate 1.3g, of which sugars 1.2g; Fat 6.1g, of which saturates 0.9g; Cholesterol 0mg; Calcium 123mg; Fibre 1.8g; Sodium 85mg
Garlicky green salad: Energy 78kcal/320kJ; Protein 0.2g; Carbohydrate 0.4g, of which sugars 0.4g; Fat 8.4g, of which saturates 1.2g; Cholesterol 0mg; Calcium 7mg; Fibre 0.2g; Sodium 1mg
Mixed lead & herb salad: Energy 178kcal/737kJ; Protein 2.9g; Carbohydrate 3.1g, or which sugars, 1g; Fat: 17.2g, or which saturates 2.2g; Cholesterol 0mg; Caclium 26mg; Fibre 1.1g; Sodium 20mg

Lettuce & Herb Salad

Shops now sell many different types of lettuce leaves all year, so try to use a mixture. Pre-packed bags of mixed baby lettuce leaves are a convenient option.

Serves 4
½ cucumber
mixed lettuce leaves
1 bunch watercress, about
  115g/4oz
1 chicory (Belgian endive)
  head, sliced
45ml/3 tbsp chopped fresh herbs
  such as parsley, thyme,
  tarragon, chives, chervil

For the dressing
15ml/1 tbsp white wine vinegar
5ml/1 tsp Dijon mustard
75ml/5 tbsp extra-virgin olive oil
salt and ground black pepper

1 To make the dressing, mix the vinegar and mustard together, then whisk in the oil, seasoning with salt and pepper to taste.

2 Peel the cucumber, if liked, then halve it lengthwise and scoop out the seeds. Thinly slice the flesh. Tear the lettuce leaves into bitesize pieces.

3 Either toss the cucumber, lettuce, watercress, chicory and herbs together in a bowl, or arrange them in the bowl in layers.

4 Stir the dressing, then pour over the salad and toss lightly to coat well. Serve immediately.

Flower Garden Salad

Dress a colourful mixture of salad leaves with good olive oil and freshly squeezed lemon juice, then top it with crispy bread crostini.

Serves 4–6
3 thick slices day-old bread, such
  as ciabatta
120ml/4fl oz/½ cup extra-virgin
  olive oil
1 garlic clove, halved
½ small cos or romaine lettuce
½ small oakleaf lettuce
25g/1oz rocket (arugula) leaves
25g/1oz fresh flat leaf parsley
a small handful of young
  dandelion leaves
juice of 1 lemon
a few nasturtium leaves
  and flowers
pansy and pot marigold flowers
sea salt flakes and ground
  black pepper

1 Cut the slices of bread into 1cm/½in cubes.

2 Heat half the oil gently in a frying pan and fry the bread cubes in it, tossing them until they are well coated and lightly browned. Remove and cool.

3 Rub the inside of a large salad bowl with the cut sides of the garlic clove, then discard. Pour the remaining oil into the bottom of the bowl.

4 Tear all the salad leaves into bitesize pieces and pile them into the bowl with the oil. Season with salt and pepper. Cover and chill until you are ready to serve the salad.

5 To serve, toss the leaves in the oil at the bottom of the bowl, then sprinkle with the lemon juice and toss again. Scatter the crostini and the flowers over the top and serve immediately.

Cook's Tip
It's fun to grow your own edible flowers for salads – you can even cultivate them in a box on a window sill. If you grow your own, you can be sure that they are totally organic.

Lettuce & herb salad: Energy 1483kcal/6098kJ; Protein 0.6g; Carbohydrate 1.7g, of which sugars 1.1g; Fat 164g, of which saturates 23.5g; Cholesterol 0mg; Calcium 19mg; Fibre 0.6g; Sodium 39mg
Flower garden salad: Energy 174kcal/722kJ; Protein 2.4g; Carbohydrate 11.3g, of which sugars 1.5g; Fat 13.5g, of which saturates 2g; Cholesterol 0mg; Calcium 38mg; Fibre 0.9g; Sodium 109mg

Apple & Celeriac Salad

Celeriac, despite its coarse appearance, has a sweet and subtle flavour. Traditionally par-boiled in lemony water, in this salad it is served raw, allowing its unique taste and texture to come through.

Serves 3–4

675g/1½lb celeriac, peeled
10–15ml/2–3 tsp lemon juice
5ml/1 tsp walnut oil (optional)
1 apple
45ml/3 tbsp mayonnaise
10ml/2 tsp Dijon mustard
15ml/1 tbsp chopped
   fresh parsley
salt and ground black pepper

1 Using a food processor or coarse cheese grater, shred the celeriac. Alternatively, cut it into very thin julienne strips. See the cook's tip below.

2 Place the prepared celeriac in a bowl and sprinkle with the lemon juice and the walnut oil, if using. Stir well to mix.

3 Peel the apple if you like. Cut the apple into quarters and remove the core. Slice the apple quarters thinly crossways and toss together with the celeriac.

4 Whisk together the mayonnaise, mustard and parsley, seasoning with salt and pepper to taste.

5 Add the dressing to the celeriac mixture and stir well. Chill the salad for several hours until ready to serve.

Cook's Tip
Celeriac browns very quickly. If you are grating or slicing it by hand, you will need to add lemon juice frequently to prevent discolouration. One way to do this is to grate the celariac over a bowl of lemony water. If you are hand cutting julienne strips, have a bowl of lemony water beside you and drop the strips in as you go. Drain the celeriac and squeeze out excess water when you have finished.

Chicory, Fruit & Nut Salad

The mildly bitter taste of the attractive white chicory leaves combines wonderfully well with sweet fruit, and is especially delicious when complemented by a creamy curry sauce.

Serves 4

45ml/3 tbsp mayonnaise
15ml/1 tbsp Greek (US strained
   plain) yogurt
15ml/1 tbsp mild curry paste
90ml/6 tbsp single (light) cream
½ iceberg lettuce
2 chicory (Belgian endive) heads
50g/2oz/½ cup cashew nuts
50g/2oz/1¼ cups flaked coconut
2 red apples
75g/3oz/⅓ cup currants

1 Mix the mayonnaise, yogurt, curry paste and single cream in a small bowl. Cover and chill until required.

2 Tear the lettuce into pieces and put into a mixing bowl.

3 Cut the root end off each head of chicory, separate the leaves and add them to the lettuce. Preheat the grill (broiler).

4 Grill (broil) the cashew nuts for 2 minutes, until golden. Transfer to a bowl and set aside. Spread out the coconut on a baking sheet. Grill for 1 minute, until golden.

5 Quarter the apples and cut out the cores. Slice the apples and add them to the lettuce with the toasted coconut and cashew nuts and the currants.

6 Spoon the dressing over the salad, toss lightly and serve.

Cook's Tips
• Watch the coconut flakes and cashew nuts with great care when they are under the grill, as they brown very fast.
• This lightly spiced salad is excellent served as a side dish to perk up plainly grilled chicken or lamb chops.

Apple & celeriac salad: Energy 99kcal/410kJ; Protein 1.2g; Carbohydrate 3.5g, of which sugars 3.4g; Fat 9.1g, of which saturates 1.3g; Cholesterol 8mg; Calcium 73mg; Fibre 2.1g; Sodium 226mg
Chicory, fruit & nut salad: Energy 319kcal/1327kJ; Protein 5.1g; Carbohydrate 20.9g, of which sugars 18.2g; Fat 24.5g, of which saturates 9.3g; Cholesterol 21mg; Calcium 84mg; Fibre 3.4g; Sodium 120mg

Fresh Spinach & Avocado Salad

Young, tender spinach leaves make a change from lettuce. They are delicious served with avocado, cherry tomatoes and radishes in an unusual tofu sauce.

Serves 2–3
1 large avocado
juice of 1 lime
225g/8oz baby spinach leaves
115g/4oz cherry tomatoes
4 spring onions (scallions), sliced
½ cucumber
50g/2oz radishes, sliced

For the dressing
115g/4oz soft silken tofu
45ml/3 tbsp milk
10ml/2 tsp mustard
2.5ml/½ tsp white wine vinegar
cayenne pepper
salt and ground black pepper
radish roses and fresh herb sprigs, to garnish

1 Cut the avocado in half, remove the stone (pit) and strip off the skin. Cut the flesh into slices. Transfer to a plate, drizzle over the lime juice and set aside.

2 Put the baby spinach leaves in a mixing bowl. Cut the larger cherry tomatoes in half and add all the tomatoes to the mixing bowl with the spring onions. Cut the cucumber into chunks and add to the bowl with the sliced radishes.

3 To make the dressing, put the tofu, milk, mustard, vinegar and a pinch of cayenne in a food processor or blender. Add salt and pepper to taste. Process for 30 seconds, until smooth. Scrape the dressing into a bowl and add a little extra milk if you like a thinner dressing.

4 Sprinkle the dressing with a little extra cayenne and garnish with radish roses and herb sprigs. Transfer the avocado with the spinach salad to a serving dish and serve with the dressing.

Cook's Tip
Use soft silken tofu rather than the firm block variety. It can be found in most supermarkets in long-life cartons.

Spinach & Mushroom Salad

This nutritious salad goes well with strongly flavoured dishes. If served alone as a light lunch, it could be dressed with a French vinaigrette and served with warm, crusty French bread.

Serves 4
10 baby corn cobs
2 tomatoes
115g/4oz/1½ cups mushrooms
1 onion cut into rings
20 small spinach leaves
25g/1oz salad cress (optional)
salt and ground black pepper

1 Halve the baby corn cobs lengthwise and slice the tomatoes.

2 Trim the mushrooms and cut them into thin slices.

3 Arrange all the salad ingredients attractively in a large bowl. Season with salt and pepper and serve.

Radish, Mango & Apple Salad

Clean, crisp tastes and mellow flavours make this salad a good choice at any time, although it is at its best with fresh garden radishes in early summer.

Serves 4
10–15 radishes
1 eating apple
2 celery stalks, thinly sliced
1 small ripe mango
fresh dill sprigs, to garnish

For the dressing
120ml/4fl oz/½ cup crème fraîche
10ml/2 tsp creamed horseradish
15ml/1 tbsp chopped fresh dill
salt and ground black pepper

1 To make the dressing, mix the crème fraîche with the creamed horseradish and dill in a small bowl. Season with a little salt and pepper.

2 Top and tail the radishes, then slice them thinly. Place in a large bowl. Cut the apple into quarters, remove the cores from each wedge, then slice the flesh thinly and add it to the bowl with the thinly sliced celery.

3 Cut through the mango lengthwise either side of the stone (pit). Leaving the skin on each section, cross hatch the flesh, then bend it back so that the cubes stand proud of the skin. Slice them off with a small knife and add them to the bowl.

4 Pour the dressing over the vegetables and fruit and stir gently to coat. When ready to serve, spoon the salad into a salad bowl and garnish with the dill.

Cook's Tip
Radishes are members of the mustard family and may be red or white, round or elongated. They vary considerably in their strength of flavour; small, slender French radishes are especially mild and sweet. Whatever type you are buying, look for small, firm, brightly coloured specimens, with no sign of limpness.

Spinach & avocado salad: Energy 137kcal/566kJ; Protein 7.5g; Carbohydrate 5.5g, of which sugars 4.7g; Fat 9.4g, of which saturates 1.9g; Cholesterol 1mg; Calcium 364mg; Fibre 3.6g; Sodium 221mg
Spinach and mushroom salad: Energy 21kcal/89kJ; Protein 2g; Carbohydrate 2.4g, of which sugars 2.2g; Fat 0.5g, of which saturates 0.1g; Cholesterol 0mg; Calcium 29mg; Fibre 1.5g; Sodium 309mg
Radish, mango and apple salad: Energy 77kcal/324kJ; Protein 1.4g; Carbohydrate 7.6g, of which sugars 7g; Fat 4.9g, of which saturates 3.1g; Cholesterol 0mg; Calcium 44mg; Fibre 1.4g; Sodium 46mg

Marinated Cucumber Salad

This wonderfully cooling salad makes a welcome addition to a summery cold spread. The cider marinade imparts a delicious flavour to the sliced cucumber, and the dill topping is the perfect finishing touch.

Serves 4-6

2 cucumbers
15ml/1 tbsp salt
90g/3½oz/½ cup sugar
175ml/6fl oz/¾ cup dry cider
15ml/1 tbsp cider vinegar
45ml/3 tbsp chopped fresh dill
ground black pepper

1 Slice the cucumbers thinly and place them in a colander, sprinkling salt between each layer. Put the colander over a bowl and leave to drain for 1 hour.

2 Thoroughly rinse the cucumber under cold running water to remove excess salt, then pat dry with kitchen paper.

3 Gently heat the sugar, cider and vinegar in a pan, until the sugar has dissolved. Remove from the heat and leave to cool. Put the cucumber slices in a bowl, pour over the cider mixture and leave to marinate for 2 hours.

4 Drain the cucumber and sprinkle with the chopped dill and black pepper to taste. Mix well and transfer to a serving dish. Chill until ready to serve.

Tofu & Cucumber Salad

A nutritious and refreshing salad with a hot, sweet-and-sour dressing, this is ideal for buffets.

Serves 4–6

1 small cucumber
115g/4oz square tofu
oil, for frying
115g/4oz/½ cup beansprouts
salt
celery leaves, to garnish

For the dressing

1 small onion, grated (shredded)
2 garlic cloves, crushed
5–7.5ml/1–1½ tsp chilli sauce
30–45ml/2–3 tbsp dark soy sauce
15–30ml/1–2 tbsp rice wine vinegar
10ml/2 tsp dark brown sugar

1 Cut the cucumber into neat cubes. Place in a colander and sprinkle with salt to extract excess liquid. Put the colander over a bowl and leave to drain for 1 hour, while you prepare the remaining ingredients.

2 Cut the tofu into cubes. Heat a little oil in a pan and fry the tofu on both sides until golden brown. Drain on kitchen paper.

3 To make the dressing, place the onion, garlic and chilli sauce in a screw-top jar. Close the jar tightly, then shake vigorously to mix. Add the soy sauce, vinegar and sugar with salt to taste. Shake the jar again until the ingredients are well combined.

4 Just before serving, rinse the cucumber under cold running water. Drain and thoroughly pat dry with kitchen paper.

5 Toss the cucumber, tofu and beansprouts together in a serving bowl and pour over the dressing. Garnish with celery leaves and serve the salad immediately.

Cook's Tip
Tofu is made from soya beans and is a good source of protein for vegetarians. It is bland tasting so needs a flavourful dressing.

Marinated cucumber salad: Energy 79kcal/335kJ; Protein 0.8g; Carbohydrate 17.7g, of which sugars 17.6g; Fat 0.2g, of which saturates 0g; Cholesterol 0mg; Calcium 39mg; Fibre 0.8g; Sodium 8mg
Tofu & cucumber salad: Energy 52kcal/215kJ; Protein 2.6g; Carbohydrate 4.3g, of which sugars 3.6g; Fat 2.8g, of which saturates 0.3g; Cholesterol 0mg; Calcium 109mg; Fibre 0.5g; Sodium 537mg

Cucumber & Tomato Salad

Yogurt cools the dressing for this salad; fresh chilli hots it up. The combination works very well and is delicious with cold meat and crusty French bread.

Serves 4
450g/1lb firm ripe tomatoes
1/2 cucumber
1 onion
1 small hot chilli, seeded and chopped and snipped chives, to garnish

For the dressing
60ml/4 tbsp olive oil
90ml/6 tbsp thick Greek (US strained plain) yogurt
30ml/2 tbsp chopped fresh parsley or snipped chives
2.5ml/ 1/2 tsp white wine vinegar
salt and ground black pepper

1 Peel the tomatoes by first cutting a cross in the base of each tomato. Place in a bowl and cover with boiling water for 30 seconds, or until the skin starts to curl back from the crosses. Drain, plunge into cold water and drain again. Peel, cut the tomatoes into quarters, seed and chop.

2 Chop the cucumber and onion into pieces that are the same size as the tomatoes and put them all in a bowl.

3 To make the dressing, whisk together the oil, yogurt, parsley or chives and vinegar in a bowl and season to taste with salt and pepper. Pour over the salad and toss together. Sprinkle with black pepper and the chopped chilli and chives to garnish.

> **Cook's Tip**
> As a light snack, this salad is delicious served with Tomato Toasts. To make the toasts, cut a French loaf diagonally into thin slices. Mix together a crushed garlic clove, a peeled and chopped tomato and 30ml/2 tbsp olive oil. Season with salt and pepper, then spread evenly on the bread and bake at 220°C/425°F/Gas 7 for 10 minutes.

Cucumber & Dill Salad

Aromatic dill is a particularly useful herb to use with salads. Here, its aniseed flavour is partnered with fresh-tasting cucumber in a soured cream dressing.

Serves 4
2 cucumbers
5ml/1 tsp salt
5 fresh dill sprigs
15ml/1 tbsp white wine vinegar
150ml/1/4 pint/2/3 cup soured cream

1 Use a cannelle knife (zester) to peel away strips of rind from along the length of the cucumbers, creating a striped effect. Slice thinly.

2 Put the slices in a colander and sprinkle with salt. Place the colander over a bowl and leave for to drain for 1 hour.

3 Rinse well under cold running water, then pat dry with kitchen paper.

4 Finely chop about 45ml/3 tbsp fresh dill, setting aside one sprig for the garnish. Put the slices of cucumber in a bowl, add the chopped dill and combine the ingredients together, either mixing with your hands or with a fork.

5 In another bowl, stir the vinegar into the soured cream and season the mixture with pepper.

6 Pour the soured cream over the cucumber and chill for 1 hour before turning into a serving dish. Garnish with the reserved sprig of dill, and serve immediately.

> **Cook's Tips**
> • Salting the cucumber draws out some of the moisture, thereby making it firmer. Make sure you rinse it thoroughly before using or the salad will be too salty.
> • A cannelle knife is easy to use and is also useful for creating an attractive edge to lemon slices.

Yogurt Salad

Raitas cool the effect of hot curries. Cucumber and mint raita is most common, but why not try this variation?

Serves 4
350ml/12fl oz/1½ cups natural (plain) yogurt
75g/3oz seedless grapes, washed and dried
50g/2oz shelled walnuts
2 firm bananas
5ml/1 tsp sugar
5ml/1 tsp freshly ground cumin seeds
salt
2.5ml/½ tsp freshly roasted cumin seeds, chilli powder or paprika, to garnish

1 Place the yogurt in a chilled bowl and add the grapes and walnuts. Slice the bananas directly into the bowl and fold in gently before the bananas turn brown.

2 Add the sugar, salt and ground cumin, and gently mix together. Chill, and just before serving, sprinkle over the cumin seeds, chilli powder or paprika.

Variation
Try using roughly chopped pecan nuts or roasted hazelnuts instead of walnuts, and adding chopped apple with the grapes.

Turkish Tomato Salad

This classic salad is a wonderful combination of textures and flavours. The saltiness of the cheese is perfectly balanced by the refreshing salad vegetables.

Serves 4
1 cos or romaine lettuce heart
1 green (bell) pepper
1 red (bell) pepper
½ cucumber
4 tomatoes
1 red onion
225g/8oz feta cheese, crumbled
black olives, to garnish

For the dressing
45ml/3 tbsp extra-virgin olive oil
45ml/3 tbsp lemon juice
1 garlic clove, crushed
15ml/1 tbsp chopped fresh parsley
15ml/1 tbsp chopped fresh mint
salt and ground black pepper

1 Chop the lettuce into bitesize pieces. Quarter the peppers, remove the cores and seeds, then cut the flesh into thin strips. Chop the cucumber and slice or chop the tomatoes. Cut the onion in half, then slice finely.

2 Place the chopped lettuce, peppers, cucumber, tomatoes and onion in a large bowl. Sprinkle the feta over the top and toss together lightly.

3 To make the dressing, blend together the extra-virgin olive oil, lemon juice and garlic in a small bowl or a screw-top jar. Stir in the freshly chopped parsley and mint, and season with salt and pepper to taste.

4 Pour the dressing over the salad, toss lightly with your hands until well coated, then garnish with a few black olives.

Variations
• *The feta cheese can be substituted with a firm goat's cheese very successfully.*
• *Try adding croûtons for a contrast in texture – simply cut cubes from day-old bread and fry in olive oil.*

Yogurt salad: Energy 189kcal/792kJ; Protein 6.9g; Carbohydrate 20.5g, of which sugars 19.5g; Fat 9.6g, of which saturates 1.2g; Cholesterol 1mg; Calcium 184mg; Fibre 1g; Sodium 74mg
Turkish tomato salad: Energy 276kcal/1146kJ; Protein 11.2g; Carbohydrate 12.1g, of which sugars 11.4g; Fat 20.6g, of which saturates 9.1g; Cholesterol 39mg; Calcium 246mg; Fibre 3.4g; Sodium 827mg

Tomato Salad

This easy-to-make salad is a particularly good foil to hot curries, with its refreshing ingredients and crunchy texture.

Serves 4–6
2 limes
2.5ml/½ tsp sugar
2 onions, finely chopped

4 firm tomatoes, finely chopped
½ cucumber, finely chopped
I green chilli, finely chopped
a few fresh coriander (cilantro)
　leaves, chopped
salt and ground black pepper
a few fresh coriander (cilantro)
　and mint leaves, to garnish

1 Squeeze the limes into a small bowl and add the sugar with salt and pepper to taste. Leave to rest until the sugar and salt have dissolved. Mix well.

2 Add the onions, tomatoes, cucumber, chilli and the fresh coriander leaves. Chill until ready to serve. Garnish with fresh coriander and mint before serving.

Cook's Tip
Chillies can vary in strength so add a little at a time, according to taste. If you prefer a milder salad, omit the chilli altogether and add extra chopped fresh mint.

Persian Salad With Tomatoes

This easy-to-make salad is versatile enough to accompany almost any main course dish, but is especially good with chargrilled meat and rice dishes.

Serves 4
4 tomatoes
½ cucumber
I cos or romaine lettuce heart
I onion, finely chopped

For the dressing
30ml/2 tbsp olive oil
juice of I lemon
I garlic clove, crushed
salt and ground black pepper

1 Peel the tomatoes by first cutting a cross in the base of each tomato. Place in a bowl and cover with boiling water for 30 seconds, or until the skin starts to curl back from the crosses. Drain, plunge into cold water and drain again. Peel, cut the tomatoes into quarters. Remove the seeds, if you like, and dice the flesh.

2 Cut the cucumber into cubes, removing the skin first if you like. Tear the lettuce into pieces.

3 Place the tomatoes, cucumber, onion and lettuce in a large salad bowl and toss lightly together.

4 To make the dressing, pour the olive oil into a small bowl. Add the lemon juice and garlic and season with salt and pepper. Whisk together well. Alternatively, combine the dressing ingredients in a screw-top jar, close tightly and shake vigorously.

5 Pour the dressing over the salad and toss lightly to mix. Sprinkle with black pepper before serving.

Variation
Use lime juice for this dressing – it will add a deliciously aromatic flavour and it will be slightly sweeter too.

Tomato salad: Energy 30kcal/124kJ; Protein 1.2g; Carbohydrate 5.6g, of which sugars 4.8g; Fat 0.4g, of which saturates 0.1g; Cholesterol 0mg; Calcium 33mg; Fibre 1.7g; Sodium 10mg
Persian salad: Energy 74kcal/307kJ; Protein 1.2g; Carbohydrate 4g, of which sugars 3.9g; Fat 6g, of which saturates 0.9g; Cholesterol 0mg; Calcium 25mg; Fibre 1.5g; Sodium 10mg

Tomato, Savory & Green Bean Salad

Savory and beans could have been invented for each other. This salad mixes them with ripe tomatoes, and is superb with cold meats.

Serves 4
450g/1lb green beans
1kg/2¼lb ripe tomatoes
3 spring onions (scallions),
 roughly sliced
15ml/1 tbsp pine nuts, toasted
4 fresh savory sprigs

For the dressing
30ml/2 tbsp extra-virgin olive oil
juice of 1 lime
75g/3oz Dolcelatte cheese
1 garlic clove, peeled and crushed
salt and ground black pepper

1 To make the dressing, place all the dressing ingredients in the bowl of a food processor, seasoning with salt and pepper to taste. Process to form a smooth dressing and leave to stand.

2 Top and tail the green beans, then boil in salted water until they are just cooked. Drain the beans and rinse under running cold water until completely cooled. Drain well and transfer to a salad bowl.

3 Slice the tomatoes or, if they are fairly small, quarter them. Add to the green beans, together with the spring onions, and toss together.

4 Pour the dressing onto the salad, toss once more, then sprinkle the pine nuts and savory sprigs over the top and serve.

Cook's Tip
Summer savory has a delicious peppery taste. It is particularly good for enhancing the flavour of beans and peas. The winter variety is sharper and better in dishes such as stuffings.

Chopped Egg & Onions

This tasty dish is a traditional Jewish version of egg mayonnaise. Some say that the recipe goes back to Egyptian times. It is delicious as a side salad to cold chicken or salmon, or as part of a summery spread, served with crackers for scooping it up.

Serves 4–6
8–10 eggs
6–8 spring onions (scallions)
 and/or 1 yellow or white onion,
 very finely chopped, plus extra
 to garnish
60–90ml/4–6 tbsp mayonnaise
 or rendered chicken fat
mild French wholegrain mustard,
 to taste (optional)
15ml/1 tbsp chopped
 fresh parsley
salt and ground black pepper
rye toasts or crackers, to serve

1 Put the eggs in a large pan and cover with cold water. When the water comes to the boil, reduce the heat and simmer over a low heat for 10 minutes.

2 Hold the eggs under cold running water, then remove the shells, pat the eggs dry and chop roughly.

3 Place the chopped eggs in a large bowl, add the onions, season generously with salt and pepper and mix well. Add enough mayonnaise or chicken fat to bind the mixture together.

4 Stir in the mustard, if using, and the chopped parsley, or sprinkle the parsley on top to garnish. Chill before serving with rye toasts or crackers.

Cook's Tips
• The amount of mayonnaise or chicken fat required will depend on how much onion you use in the dish.
• This salad is wonderful piled onto toast or used as a sandwich or bagel filling. Add thinly sliced tomato, cucumber and lettuce leaves or watercress sprigs.

Tomato, savory & bean salad: Energy 211kcal/877kJ; Protein 8.4g; Carbohydrate 11.7g, of which sugars 10.7g; Fat 14.8g, of which saturates 4.9g; Cholesterol 14mg; Calcium 153mg; Fibre 5.2g; Sodium 252mg
Chopped egg & onions: Energy 197kcal/816kJ; Protein 11g; Carbohydrate 0.7g, of which sugars 0.6g; Fat 17g, of which saturates 3.7g; Cholesterol 325mg; Calcium 69mg; Fibre 0.6g; Sodium 165mg

Mushroom Salad

This simple refreshing salad is often served as part of a selection of vegetable salads, or crudités. Leaving it to stand before serving brings out the inherent sweetness of the mushrooms.

Serves 4
175g/6oz white mushrooms, trimmed
grated (shredded) rind and juice of 1½ lemons
about 30–45ml/2–3 tbsp crème fraîche or soured cream
salt and white pepper
15ml/1 tbsp chopped fresh chives, to garnish

1 Slice the mushrooms thinly and place in a bowl.

2 Add the lemon rind and juice and the cream, adding a little more cream if needed.

3 Stir gently to mix, then season with salt and pepper.

4 Leave the salad to stand for at least 1 hour to allow the flavours to develop. Stir occasionally.

5 Sprinkle the salad with chopped chives before serving.

Variations
•Add colour and a nutty flavour by sustituting all or half of the white mushrooms with chestnut mushrooms, which are widely available.
•If you prefer, toss the mushrooms in a little vinaigrette – simply make the vinaigrette by whisking 60ml/4 tbsp walnut oil or extra-virgin olive oil into the lemon juice.
•This salad has a freshness and texture that make it the perfect accompaniment to chilli con carne. Use lime, rather than lemon juice, to complement the chillies. Serve the creamy mushrooms on top of shredded iceberg lettuce, with a hunk of warm crusty bread and a hearty bowl of chilli, for the perfect winter supper.

Salad of Fresh Ceps

Mushrooms can make a marvellous salad, especially if you are able to obtain fresh ceps or porcini. Any wild or cultivated mushrooms can be used: remove the stems from shiitake mushrooms.

Serves 4
350g/12oz fresh ceps, thinly sliced
175g/6oz mixed salad leaves, preferably including batavia, young spinach and frisée
50g/2oz/½ cup broken walnut pieces, toasted
50g/2oz piece Parmesan cheese
salt and ground black pepper

For the dressing
2 egg yolks
2.5ml/½ tsp French mustard
75ml/5 tbsp groundnut oil
45ml/3 tbsp walnut oil
30ml/2 tbsp lemon juice
30ml/2 tbsp chopped fresh parsley
pinch of caster (superfine) sugar

1 To make the dressing, place the egg yolks in a screw-top jar with the mustard, groundnut and walnut oils, lemon juice, parsley and sugar. Close the jar tightly and shake well.

2 Place the mushrooms in a large mixing bowl and pour over the dressing. Toss to coat, then set aside for 10–15 minutes to allow the flavours to mingle.

3 Add the salad leaves to the mushrooms and toss lightly. Season with plenty of salt and pepper.

4 Divide the salad among four large plates. Sprinkle each portion with the toasted walnuts and shavings of Parmesan cheese. Serve immediately.

Cook's Tip
The dressing for this salad uses raw egg yolk. Be sure to use only the freshest eggs from a reputable supplier. Expectant mothers, young children and the elderly are advised to avoid raw egg yolks. The dressing can be made without the egg yolks.

Mushroom salad: Energy 22kcal/93kJ; Protein 1.1g; Carbohydrate 0.6g, of which sugars 0.5g; Fat 1.8g, of which saturates 1g; Cholesterol 5mg; Calcium 17mg; Fibre 0.7g; Sodium 7mg
Salad of fresh ceps: :Energy 388kcal/ 603kJ; Protein 10.1g; Carbohydrate 1.5g, of which sugars 1.3g; Fat 38g, of which saturates 6.8g; Cholesterol 113mg; Calcium 191mg; Fibre 1.8g; Sodium 147mg

Turnip Salad in Soured Cream

This tangy salad partners cheese dishes extremely well, and it makes an interesting addition to a selection of salads. Only very young, tender turnips should be used.

Serves 4

2–4 young, tender turnips, peeled
¼–½ onion, finely chopped
2–3 drops white wine vinegar, or
  to taste
60–90ml/4–6 tbsp soured cream
salt and ground black pepper
chopped fresh parsley or paprika,
  to garnish

1 Thinly slice or coarsely grate (shred) the turnips. Alternatively, thinly slice half the turnips and grate the remaining half. Place in a serving bowl.

2 Add the onion, vinegar and salt and pepper to taste. Toss together then stir in the soured cream.

3 Serve chilled, garnished with a sprinkling of parsley or paprika.

Variations
• Crème fraîche can be used instead of the sour cream.
• When young turnips are not available, try using the dressing with sliced radishes instead, and replace the onion with spring onions (scallions) or snipped chives.

Gingered Carrot Salad

This fresh and zesty salad is ideal served as an accompaniment to simple grilled chicken or fish. Fresh root ginger goes perfectly with sweet carrots, and the tiny black poppy seeds not only add taste and texture, but also look stunning against the bright orange of the carrots.

Serves 4

350g/12oz carrots
30ml/2 tbsp garlic-infused olive oil
2.5cm/1in piece of fresh root
  ginger, peeled and grated
  (shredded)
15ml/1 tbsp poppy seeds
salt and ground black pepper

1 Peel the carrots and cut them into fine matchsticks. Put them in a bowl and stir in the oil and grated ginger. Cover and chill for at least 30 minutes, to allow the flavours to develop fully.

2 Season the salad with salt and pepper to taste. Stir in the poppy seeds just before serving.

Cook's Tips
• Some food processors have an attachment that can be used to cut the carrots into batons, which makes quick work of the preparation, but even cutting them by hand doesn't take long.
• It is best to use organic carrots for the best flavour, or at least carrots with their green tops still attached.
• You can always use another type of flavoured oil, such as chilli oil, or even use extra-virgin olive oil and add a little chopped fresh coriander (cilantro) or chives to the salad.

Variation
To make a parsnip and sesame seed salad, replace the carrots with parsnips and blanch in boiling salted water for 1 minute before combining with the oil and ginger. Replace the poppy seeds with the same quantity of sesame seeds.

Turnip salad: Energy 48kcal/198kJ; Protein 1.1g; Carbohydrate 4.1g, of which sugars 3.7g; Fat 3.2g, of which saturates 1.9g; Cholesterol 9mg; Calcium 42mg; Fibre 1.4g; Sodium 14mg
Gingered carrot salad: Energy 103kcal/424kJ; Protein 1.2g; Carbohydrate 7g, of which sugars 6.5g; Fat 7.9g, of which saturates 1.2g; Cholesterol 0mg; Calcium 47mg; Fibre 2.4g; Sodium 23mg

Romanian Pepper Salad

This is traditionally made
with long sweet peppers.

Serves 4
8 long green and/or orange
   peppers, halved and seeded
1 garlic clove, crushed

60ml/4 tbsp wine vinegar
75ml/5 tbsp olive oil
4 tomatoes, sliced
1 red onion, thinly sliced
salt and ground black pepper
fresh coriander (cilantro) sprigs,
   to garnish

1 Grill (broil) the peppers, skin-side up, until the skins have
blistered and charred. Transfer to a bowl and cover with
crumpled kitchen paper. Cool slightly, then remove the skins
and cut each piece in half lengthwise.

2 Mix the garlic and vinegar in a bowl, then whisk in the olive
oil. Arrange the peppers, tomatoes and onion on four serving
plates and pour over the garlic dressing. Season to taste with
salt and pepper and serve, garnished with coriander sprigs.

Simple Pepper Salad

Succulent grilled peppers
make a lovely salad.

Serves 4
4 large (bell) peppers, halved and
   seeded
60ml/4 tbsp olive oil

1 onion, thinly sliced
2 garlic cloves, crushed
4 tomatoes, peeled and chopped
pinch of sugar
5ml/1 tsp lemon juice
salt and ground black pepper

1 Grill (broil) the peppers, skin-side up, until the skins have
blistered and charred. Put in a bowl and cover with crumpled
kitchen paper. Cool slightly, then remove skins and slice thinly.

2 Heat the oil and fry the onion and garlic until softened. Add
the peppers and tomatoes and fry for 10 minutes more.
Remove from the heat, stir in the sugar and lemon juice and
season. Leave to cool and serve at room temperature.

Chargrilled Pepper Salad

The simple addition of fresh
basil and coriander to this
pepper and pasta salad give
it loads of flavour. A lemon
and pesto dressing brings all
the flavours together making
this an ideal side dish for a
summery al fresco meal.

Serves 4
1 large red (bell) pepper
1 large green (bell) pepper
250g/9oz/2¼ cups dried fusilli
   tricolore pasta

1 handful fresh basil leaves,
   roughly torn
1 handful fresh coriander
   (cilantro) leaves, roughly torn
1 garlic clove
salt and ground black pepper

For the dressing
30ml/2 tbsp pesto
juice of ½ lemon
60ml/4 tbsp extra-virgin olive oil

1 Put the peppers under a hot grill (broiler) and grill (broil) for
about 10 minutes, turning frequently, until the skins have
blistered and charred. Transfer to a bowl, cover with crumpled
kitchen paper and set aside until cool.

2 Meanwhile, bring a large pan of salted water to the boil. Add
the pasta and cook according to the instructions on the packet.

3 Whisk all the dressing ingredients together in a large mixing
bowl. Drain the cooked pasta and add to the bowl of dressing.
Toss well to mix and set aside to cool.

4 Rinse the cooled peppers under cold running water. Peel off
the skins. Cut the peppers in half, remove the cores and seeds,
then pat dry on kitchen paper. Chop and add to the pasta

5 Stir the basil and parsley into the pasta and toss well to mix,
then taste and adjust the seasoning, if necessary.

Cook's Tip
Fusilli tricolore are small, red, white and green pasta spirals.

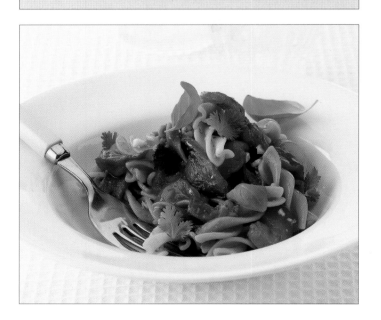

Romanian pepper salad: Energy 203kcal/841kJ; Protein 2.5g; Carbohydrate 16g, of which sugars 15g; Fat 14.7g, of which saturates 2.2g; Cholesterol 0mg; Calcium 23mg; Fibre 3.9g; Sodium 11mg
Simple pepper salad: Energy 161kcal/670kJ; Protein 2.1g; Carbohydrate 12.3g, of which sugars 11.6g; Fat 11.8g, of which saturates 1.8g; Cholesterol 0mg; Calcium 21mg; Fibre 3.2g; Sodium 15mg
Chargrilled pepper salad: Energy 481kcal/2025kJ; Protein 13.2g; Carbohydrate 70.8g, of which sugars 8.5g; Fat 18.1g, of which saturates 3.2g; Cholesterol 4mg; Calcium 99mg; Fibre 4.6g; Sodium 51mg

Roasted Pepper & Tomato Salad

A lovely, colourful dish that is designed to be eaten at room temperature. It is delicious with salamis and savoury flans.

Serves 4
3 red (bell) peppers
6 large plum tomatoes
2.5ml/¹/₂ tsp dried red
 chilli flakes
1 red onion, finely sliced
3 garlic cloves, finely chopped
grated (shredded) rind and juice
 of 1 lemon
45ml/3 tbsp chopped fresh
 flat leaf parsley
30ml/2 tbsp extra-virgin olive oil
salt and ground black pepper
black and green olives and extra
 chopped flat leaf parsley,
 to garnish

1 Preheat the oven to 220°C/425°F/Gas 7. Place the peppers on a baking sheet and roast, turning occasionally, for 10 minutes or until the skins are almost blackened. Add the tomatoes to the baking sheet and bake for a further 5 minutes.

2 Place the peppers in a strong polythene bag, close the top loosely, trapping in the steam. Set aside, with the tomatoes, until cool enough to handle.

3 Carefully remove the skins from the peppers. Remove the core and seeds, then chop the peppers and tomatoes roughly and place in a mixing bowl.

4 Add the chilli flakes, onion, garlic and lemon rind and juice. Sprinkle over the parsley. Mix and transfer to a serving dish.

5 Sprinkle with a little salt and black pepper, drizzle over the olive oil and scatter the olives and extra parsley over the top. Serve at room temperature.

Cook's Tip
Roasting or grilling (broiling) the peppers brings out their sweet flavour and makes them meltingly soft. This cooking process also loosens the pepper skins, making them easy to remove.

Roasted Red Peppers with Feta, Capers & Preserved Lemons

A delightful burst of piquant fruit gives these sumptuous roast peppers a typically Moroccan flavour. Capers and feta cheese give added flavour to a dish that is quite delicious with kebabs and barbecued meats, as well as with mezze dishes.

Serves 4
4 fleshy, red (bell) peppers
200g/7oz feta cheese, crumbled
30–45ml/2–3 tbsp olive oil or
 argan oil
30ml/2 tbsp capers
peel of 1 preserved lemon, cut
 into small pieces
salt

1 Put the peppers under a hot grill (broiler) and grill (broil) for about 10 minutes, turning frequently, until until the skins have blistered and charred.

2 Transfer the peppers to a bowl, cover with crumpled kitchen paper and leave to cool slightly. Strip off the pepper skins, then remove the stalks and seeds. Slice the flesh and arrange on a serving plate.

3 Add the crumbled feta and pour over the olive or argan oil. Scatter the capers and preserved lemon over the top and sprinkle with a little salt, if required, and serve.

Cook's Tips
• *To make preserved lemons, scrub and quarter lemons almost through to the base, then rub the cut sides with salt. Pack tightly into a large sterilized jar. Half fill the jar with more salt, adding some bay leaves, peppercorns and cinnamon, if you like. Cover completely with lemon juice. Cover with a lid and store for 2 weeks, shaking the jar daily. Add a little olive oil to seal and use within 1–6 months, washing off the salt before use.*
• *Instead of grilling the peppers, you can roast them in a hot oven. Alternatively, thread them onto metal skewers and hold over a gas flame, turning constantly, until charred.*

Aubergine, Lemon & Caper Salad

This cooked vegetable relish is delicious served as an accompaniment to cold meats or with pasta.

Serves 4
1 large aubergine (eggplant), about 675g/1½lb
60ml/4 tbsp olive oil
grated (shredded) rind and juice of 1 lemon
30ml/2 tbsp capers, rinsed
12 pitted green olives
30ml/2 tbsp chopped fresh flat leaf parsley
salt and ground black pepper

1 Cut the aubergine into 2.5cm/1in cubes. Heat the olive oil in a large frying pan and cook the aubergine cubes over a medium heat for about 10 minutes, tossing regularly, until golden and soft. You may need to do this in two batches. Drain on kitchen paper and sprinkle with a little salt.

2 Place the aubergine cubes in a large serving bowl. Toss with the lemon rind and juice, capers, olives and chopped parsley, Season well with salt and pepper. Serve at room temperature.

> **Cook's Tip**
> *This will taste even better when made the day before. It will store, covered, in the refrigerator for up to 4 days.*

Spiced Aubergine Salad

The delicate flavours of aubergine, tomatoes and cucumber are lightly spiced with cumin and coriander in this fresh-tasting salad. Topped with refreshing yogurt, this salad is the ideal accompaniment to grilled fish or a rice dish.

Serves 4
2 small aubergines (eggplants), sliced
75ml/5 tbsp extra-virgin olive oil
50ml/2fl oz/¼ cup red wine vinegar
2 garlic cloves, crushed
15ml/1 tbsp lemon juice
2.5ml/½ tsp ground cumin
2.5ml/½ tsp ground coriander
½ cucumber, thinly sliced
2 well-flavoured tomatoes, thinly sliced
30ml/2 tbsp natural (plain) yogurt
salt and ground black pepper
chopped fresh flat leaf parsley, to garnish

1 Preheat the grill (broiler). Lightly brush the aubergine slices with olive oil and cook under a high heat, turning once, until golden and tender.

2 When the aubergine slices are done, transfer them to a chopping board and cut them into quarters.

3 Mix together the remaining oil, the vinegar, garlic, lemon juice, cumin and coriander. Season with salt and pepper to taste and mix thoroughly.

4 Add the warm aubergines, stir well and chill for at least 2 hours. Add the cucumber and tomatoes. Transfer to a serving dish and spoon the yogurt on top. Sprinkle with parsley and serve immediately.

> **Cook's Tip**
> *Cook the aubergines on a ridged cast-iron griddle pan, if you prefer. Heat the griddle pan and cook the aubergine slices for 6-8 minutes on each side, brushing with more oil as necessary.*

Aubergine, lemon & caper salad: Energy 141kcal/585kJ; Protein 2g; Carbohydrate 4.1g, of which sugars 3.7g; Fat 13.2g, of which saturates 2g; Cholesterol 0mg; Calcium 50mg; Fibre 4.4g; Sodium 289mg
Spiced aubergine salad: Energy 161kcal/669kJ; Protein 2.3g; Carbohydrate 5.8g, of which sugars 5.5g; Fat 14.6g, of which saturates 2.2g; Cholesterol 0mg; Calcium 37mg; Fibre 3.7g; Sodium 15mg

Baby Leeks in Red Wine with Aromatics

Coriander seeds and oregano lend a Greek flavour to this dish of braised leeks. Serve it as part of a mixed hors d'oeuvre or as a partner for baked white fish fillets.

Serves 6
12 baby leeks or 6 thick leeks
15ml/1 tbsp coriander seeds, lightly crushed
5cm/2in piece cinnamon stick
120ml/4fl oz/½ cup olive oil
3 fresh bay leaves
2 strips pared orange rind
5–6 fresh or dried oregano sprigs
5ml/1 tsp caster (superfine) sugar
150ml/¼ pint/⅔ cup fruity red wine
10ml/2 tsp balsamic or sherry vinegar
30ml/2 tbsp coarsely chopped fresh oregano or marjoram
salt and ground black pepper

1 Leave baby leeks whole, but cut thick ones into even 5–7cm/2–3in lengths.

2 Cook the coriander seeds and cinnamon in a large pan over a medium heat for 2–3 minutes, until the spices are fragrant.

3 Stir in the oil, bay leaves, orange rind, oregano, sugar, wine and vinegar. Bring to the boil and simmer for 5 minutes.

4 Add the leeks. Bring back to the boil, reduce the heat and cover the pan. Cook gently for 5 minutes. Uncover and simmer gently for another 5–8 minutes, until the leeks are just tender when tested with the tip of a sharp knife.

5 Using a slotted spoon, transfer the leeks to a serving dish.

6 Boil the juices until they reduce to about 75–90ml/5–6 tsp. Add salt and pepper to taste and pour the reduced juices over the leeks.

7 Leave to cool, so that the flavours develop fully before serving.

Little Onions with Coriander, Wine & Olive Oil

Packed with Mediterranean flavours, this delicious chilled dish of baby onions bathed in a piquant wine dressing makes a versatile side salad.

Serves 6
105ml/7 tbsp olive oil
675g/1½ lb small onions, peeled
150ml/¼ pint/⅔ cup dry white wine
2 bay leaves
2 garlic cloves, bruised
1–2 small dried red chillies
15ml/1 tbsp coriander seeds, toasted and lightly crushed
2.5ml/½ tsp sugar
a few fresh thyme sprigs
30ml/2 tbsp currants
10ml/2 tsp chopped fresh oregano or marjoram
5ml/1 tsp grated (shredded) lemon rind
15ml/1 tbsp chopped fresh flat leaf parsley
30–45ml/2–3 tbsp pine nuts, lightly toasted
salt and ground black pepper

1 Place 30ml/2 tbsp of the olive oil in a wide pan. Add the onions, place over a medium heat and cook gently for about 5 minutes, or until the onions begin to colour. Using a slotted spoon, transfer the onions to a dish and set aside.

2 Add the remaining oil to the pan, then stir in the wine, bay leaves, garlic, chillies, coriander seeds, sugar and thyme.

3 Bring to the boil and cook briskly for 5 minutes. Return the onions to the pan. Add the currants, reduce the heat and cook gently for 15–20 minutes, or until the onions are tender but not falling apart.

4 Using a slotted spoon, transfer the onions to a serving dish, then boil the liquid vigorously until it reduces considerably. Season with salt and pepper to taste, then pour the cooking liquid over the onions.

5 Scatter the chopped oregano or marjoram over the onions in the dish, then cool and chill. Just before serving, stir in the grated lemon rind, chopped parsley and toasted pine nuts.

Baby leeks: Energy 239kcal/998kJ; Protein 2.3g; Carbohydrate 7.6g, of which sugars 3g; Fat 20.5g, of which saturates 2.8g; Cholesterol 0mg; Calcium 83mg; Fibre 3.2g; Sodium 4mg
Onions with coriander, wine & olive oil: Energy 227kcal/935kJ; Protein 2.5g; Carbohydrate 9.8g, of which sugars 7.2g; Fat 18.2g, of which saturates 2.2g; Cholesterol 0mg; Calcium 37mg; Fibre 1.9g; Sodium 5mg

Beetroot with Fresh Mint

For adding a splash of colour to a cold spread, this ruby red salad is hard to beat. The simple mint and balsamic dressing really brings out the earthy flavour of beetroot.

Serves 4

4–6 raw beetroot (beets)
5–10ml/1–2 tsp sugar
15–30ml/1–2 tbsp balsamic
    vinegar
juice of 1/2 lemon
30ml/2 tbsp extra-virgin olive oil
1 bunch fresh mint, leaves
    stripped and thinly sliced
salt

1 Trim off the tops of the leafy stalks down to about 2.5cm/1in of the beetroot. Wash the beetroot but do not peel. Cook in boiling water for 1–2 hours, depending on the size: small ones will be tender after about 1 hour. Drain the beetroot, then cool and peel. Slice or cut into even dice with a sharp knife.

2 Put the cooked beetroot in a bowl. Add the sugar, balsamic vinegar, lemon juice, olive oil and a pinch of salt and toss together to combine.

3 Add half the thinly sliced fresh mint to the salad and toss lightly until well combined. Place the salad in the refrigerator and chill for about 1 hour. Serve garnished with the remaining thinly sliced mint leaves.

Beetroot Salad with Oranges

An unusual and delicious combination of sweet beetroot, zesty orange and warm cinnamon, this fragrant dish provides a lovely burst of colour in a summer buffet spread.

Serves 4–6

675g/1 1/2lb raw beetroot (beet)
1 orange
30ml/2 tbsp orange flower water
15ml/1 tbsp sugar
5ml/1 tsp ground cinnamon
salt and ground black pepper

1 Trim off the tops of the leafy stalks down to about 2.5cm/1in of the beetroot. Wash the beetroot but do not peel. Cook in boiling water for 1–2 hours, depending on the size: small ones will be tender after about 1 hour.

2 Meanwhile, prepare the orange. Cut a slice off the top and bottom of the orange. Place, upright, on a board and cut off the peel, working downwards with a sharp knife and taking care to remove all the bitter white pith. Turn the orange onto its side and cut into slices.

3 Drain the beetroot and leave to stand until cool enough to handle. Peel the beetroot, then cut into quarters. Cut the quarters into slices.

4 Arrange the beetroot on a plate with the orange slices, or toss them together in a bowl.

5 Gently heat the orange flower water with the sugar, stir in the cinnamon and season with salt and pepper to taste. Pour over the beetroot and orange salad and chill in the refrigerator for at least 1 hour before serving.

Cook's Tips
If you cannot find fresh beetroot (beets), or you are short of time, this salad can be successfully made with ready-cooked vacuum-packed beetroot, but pickled beetroot is not suitable as it has a vinegary flavour.

Beetroot with fresh mint: Energy 90kcal/378kJ; Protein 1.7g; Carbohydrate 8.9g, of which sugars 8.3g; Fat 5.6g, of which saturates 0.8g; Cholesterol 0mg; Calcium 21mg; Fibre 1.9g; Sodium 66mg
Beetroot salad with oranges: Energy 58kcal/247kJ; Protein 2.2g; Carbohydrate 12.9g, of which sugars 12.2g; Fat 0.1g, of which saturates 0g; Cholesterol 0mg; Calcium 33mg; Fibre 2.5g; Sodium 75mg

Beetroot & Red Onion Salad

This salad looks especially attractive when it is made with a mixture of red and yellow beetroot.

Serves 6
500g/1¼lb small raw
  beetroot (beet)
75ml/5 tbsp water
60ml/4 tbsp olive oil
90g/3½ oz/scant 1 cup
  walnut halves
5ml/1 tsp caster (superfine)
  sugar, plus a little extra for
  the dressing
30ml/2 tbsp walnut oil

15ml/1 tbsp sherry vinegar
5ml/1 tsp soy sauce
5ml/1 tsp grated (shredded)
  orange rind
2.5ml/½ tsp ground roasted
  coriander seeds
5–10ml/1–2 tsp orange juice
1 red onion, halved and very
  thinly sliced
15–30ml/1–2 tbsp chopped
  fresh fennel
75g/3oz watercress or
  mizuna leaves
handful of beetroot (beet)
  leaves (optional)
salt and ground black pepper

1 Preheat the oven to 180°C/350°F/Gas 4. Place the beetroot in an ovenproof dish in a single layer and add the water. Cover tightly and roast for 1–1½ hours, or until they are just tender.

2 Cool, then peel the beetroot. Slice or cut them into strips and toss with 15ml/1 tbsp of the olive oil in a bowl. Set aside.

3 Heat 15ml/1 tbsp of the remaining olive oil in a small frying pan. Fry the walnuts until starting to brown. Add the sugar and cook, stirring, until starting to caramelize. Season with pepper and 2.5ml/½ tsp salt, then turn them onto a plate to cool.

4 In a bowl, whisk together the remaining olive oil, the walnut oil, sherry vinegar, soy sauce, orange rind and coriander seeds. Season with salt and pepper and add a pinch of caster sugar. Whisk in orange juice to taste.

5 Separate the onion slices and add them to the beetroot. Pour over the dressing and toss well. Just before serving, toss with the fennel, watercress and beetroot leaves, if using. Transfer to individual plates and sprinkle with the caramelized nuts.

Apple & Beetroot Salad with Red Leaves

Bitter salad leaves are complemented by sweet-flavoured apples and juicy beetroot in this side salad.

Serves 4
50g/2oz/⅓ cup whole
  unblanched almonds
2 red apples, cored and diced
juice of ½ lemon

115g/4oz/4 cups red salad
  leaves, such as lollo rosso,
  oakleaf and radicchio
200g/7oz pre-cooked beetroot
  (beet) in natural juice, sliced

For the dressing
30ml/2 tbsp olive oil
15ml/1 tbsp walnut oil
15ml/1 tbsp red or white
  wine vinegar
salt and ground black pepper

1 Toast the almonds in a dry frying pan for 2–3 minutes until golden brown, tossing frequently to prevent them burning

2 Meanwhile, make the dressing. Put the olive and walnut oils, vinegar and salt and pepper in a bowl or screw-top jar. Stir or shake thoroughly to combine.

3 Toss the apples in lemon juice to prevent them browning, then place in a large bowl and add the salad leaves, beetroot and almonds. Pour over the dressing and toss gently to disperse the ingredients evenly.

Cook's Tips
• Try to use fresh, raw beetroot (beet) if it is available. Cooking fresh beetroot is surprisingly easy – the important thing is not to puncture the skin before cooking, otherwise the bright red juice will leak out. To prepare fresh beetroot, trim off most of the leafy stalks, then wash and cook the unpeeled roots in boiling water for 1–2 hours, depending on size.
• Red fruits and vegetables have high levels of vitamins C and E and beta carotene.

Beetroot & red onion salad: Energy 238kcal/986kJ; Protein 3.8g; Carbohydrate 8g, of which sugars 7.4g; Fat 21.4g, of which saturates 2.2g; Cholesterol 0mg; Calcium 36mg; Fibre 2.3g; Sodium 116mg
Apple & beetroot salad: Energy 216kcal/895kJ; Protein 4.1g; Carbohydrate 9.5g, of which sugars 8.8g; Fat 18.2g, of which saturates 1.9g; Cholesterol 0mg; Calcium 54mg; Fibre 2.7g; Sodium 58mg

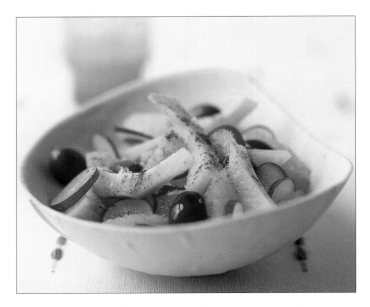

Beetroot with Lemon Dressing

Fresh beetroot has a lovely, sweet, earthy flavour which is beautifully enhanced with this simple lemon dressing. The subtle taste of freshly cooked beetroot is a far cry from commercially sold pickled beetroot.

Serves 4
450g/1lb raw beetroot (beets)
grated (shredded) rind and juice
    of ½ lemon
about 150ml/¼ pint/⅔ cup
    extra-virgin olive oil (or a
    mixture of olive and sunflower
    oil, blended to taste)
sea salt and ground black pepper
chopped fresh chives, to
    garnish

1 Trim off the tops of the leafy stalks down to about 2.5cm/1in of the beetroot. Wash the beetroot but do not peel.

2 Cook in boiling water for 1–2 hours, depending on the size; small ones will be tender after about 1 hour.

3 Drain the beetroot and, when cool enough to handle, remove the skin, which will come away easily. Leave until completely cool.

4 Peel when cool and slice into wedges into a bowl. Add the lemon rind and juice, and the oil; season to taste. Mix the dressing in gently and serve.

Artichoke Heart & Orange Salad

Fresh artichoke hearts are combined with citrus fruit, radishes and black olives to create a colourful salad that will please the eye and refresh the palate – perfect to serve alongside, or after, a spicy dish.

Serves 4
1 lemon, halved
4 artichoke hearts
4 Seville (Temple) oranges
6 red radishes, finely sliced
12 kalamata olives
30–45ml/2–3 tbsp olive oil
salt
2.5ml/½ tsp paprika, to serve

1 Squeeze the juice from ½ lemon and pour into a pan. Add the artichoke hearts and plenty of water to cover. Bring to the boil, then reduce the heat and simmer gently for about 15 minutes until just tender.

2 Drain and refresh the hearts under cold running water, then drain again. Slice the artichoke hearts thickly and place them in a mixing bowl.

3 Peel the oranges with a sharp knife, cutting off all the pith. Cut between the membranes to remove the segments of fruit. Discard any pips and add the segments to the artichoke hearts.

4 Add the radishes and olives, drizzle with the olive oil and the juice from the remaining ½ lemon, and carefully mix together. Season with salt, sprinkle with a little paprika and serve.

Cook's Tips
• To prepare the artichoke hearts for cooking, remove the leaves from whole fresh artichokes. Cut off the stems, scoop out the choke and hairy bits, and immerse them in water mixed with a squeeze of lemon juice.
• When fresh artichokes are not readily available, opt for the frozen hearts that can be found in some supermarkets.
• You can use sweet or sour Seville oranges for this dish. When Sevilles are out of season, use any large, juicy variety.

Beetroot with lemon dressing: Energy 265kcal/1097kJ; Protein 1.9g; Carbohydrate 8.6g, of which sugars 7.9g; Fat 25.1g, of which saturates 3.6g; Cholesterol 0mg; Calcium 23mg; Fibre 2.2g; Sodium 74mg
Artichoke heart & orange salad: Energy 243kcal/1007kJ; Protein 2.1g; Carbohydrate 12g, of which sugars 12g; Fat 21.1g, of which saturates 3g; Cholesterol 0mg; Calcium 112mg; Fibre 3.6g; Sodium 83mg

Squash à la Grecque

Chickpea Salad

This recipe, usually made with mushrooms, also works well with patty pan squash. Make sure that you cook the baby squash until they are quite tender, so they absorb the delicious flavours of the marinade.

Serves 4
175g/6oz patty pan squash
250ml/8fl oz/1 cup white wine
juice of 2 lemons

1 fresh thyme sprig
1 bay leaf
small bunch fresh chervil,
   roughly chopped
1.5ml/¼ tsp crushed coriander
   seeds
1.5ml/¼ tsp crushed black
   peppercorns
75ml/5 tbsp olive oil
150ml/¼ pint/⅔ cup water
bay leaves, to garnish

1 Blanch the patty pan squash in boiling water for 3 minutes, then refresh them in cold water.

2 Place the wine, lemon juice, thyme sprig, bay leaf, chervil, coriander seeds, black peppercorns and oil in a pan. Add the water, cover and simmer for 10 minutes.

3 Add the patty pan squash and cook for 10 minutes until they are tender. Using a slotted spoon, transfer the cooked squash to a serving dish.

4 Reduce the liquid in the pan by boiling vigorously for 10 minutes, then strain and pour over the squash. Leave to cool to allow the flavours to be absorbed. Serve the squash cold, garnished with bay leaves.

> **Cook's Tip**
> *Patty pan squashes are a type of summer squash, and have thin skins and tender flesh. They are treated rather like courgettes (zucchini), which are also a member of the squash family. Winter squashes, such as butternut squash, have much harder skins and are not suitable for this recipe.*

Topped with hard-boiled eggs, this substantial salad is good with smoked fish.

Serves 4–6
2 x 400g/14oz cans chickpeas, or
   300g/11oz/2 cups cooked
   chickpeas
6 spring onions (scallions),
   chopped
2 tomatoes, diced
1 small red onion, finely chopped

12 black olives, pitted and halved
15ml/1 tbsp capers, drained
30ml/2 tbsp finely chopped fresh
   parsley or mint leaves
4 hard-boiled (hard-cooked) eggs,
   cut into quarters, to garnish

For the dressing
75ml/5 tbsp olive oil
45ml/3 tbsp wine vinegar
salt and ground black pepper

1 Rinse the chickpeas under cold running water. Drain and place in a serving bowl. Add the spring onions, tomatoes, red onion, olives, capers and parsley or mint.

2 To make the dressing, whisk all the ingredients together in a small bowl. Add to the salad, toss and serve with the eggs.

> **Variation**
> *Other types of canned cooked beans may be substituted in this salad, such as cannellini or borlotti beans.*

Squash à la grecque: Energy 171kcal/704kJ; Protein 0.4g; Carbohydrate 1.4g, of which sugars 1.1g; Fat 13.8g, of which saturates 2g; Cholesterol 0mg; Calcium 18mg; Fibre 0.5g; Sodium 3mg
Chickpea salad: Energy 305kcal/1275kJ; Protein 14.4g; Carbohydrate 23.5g, of which sugars 2.4g; Fat 17.8g, of which saturates 2.9g; Cholesterol 127mg; Calcium 90mg; Fibre 6.3g; Sodium 531mg

Butter Bean, Tomato & Red Onion Salad

This quick and easy salad can be assembled ahead of time, making it ideal for entertaining. It is particularly useful for eating al fresco and is delicious as an accompaniment to meat cooked on a barbecue.

Serves 4

2 x 400g/14oz cans butter
   (lima) beans
4 plum tomatoes,
   roughly chopped
1 red onion, finely sliced
45ml/3 tbsp herb-infused olive oil
salt and ground black pepper

1 Drain the beans and rinse under cold running water. Drain well and mix with the tomatoes and onion in a large bowl. Season with salt and pepper to taste and stir in the herb-infused olive oil. Transfer to a serving dish.

2 Cover the bowl with clear film (plastic wrap) and chill for 20 minutes before serving.

Variation
To make a wholesome version of the Italian salad Panzanella, tear half a loaf of ciabatta into bitesize pieces and stir into the salad. Leave to stand for 20 minutes before serving.

Peppery Bean Salad

This pretty salad uses canned beans for speed and convenience. Hot pepper sauce gives a bit of a kick.

Serves 4–6

425g/15oz can red kidney beans
425g/15oz can black-eyed beans
425g/15oz can chickpeas
¼ red (bell) pepper
¼ green (bell) pepper
6 radishes
15ml/1 tbsp chopped spring
   onion (scallion), plus extra sliced
   to garnish

For the dressing
5ml/1 tsp ground cumin
15ml/1 tbsp tomato ketchup
30ml/2 tbsp olive oil
15ml/1 tbsp white wine vinegar
1 garlic clove, crushed
2.5ml/½ tsp hot pepper sauce

1 Drain the red kidney beans, black-eyed beans and chickpeas and rinse under cold running water. Shake off the excess water and turn them into a large bowl.

2 Core, seed and chop the red and green peppers. Trim the radishes and slice thinly. Add the peppers, radishes and spring onion to the beans.

3 Mix together the cumin, ketchup, oil, vinegar and garlic in a small bowl. Add a little salt and hot pepper sauce to taste and stir again thoroughly.

4 Pour the dressing over the salad and toss to mix well. Chill the salad for at least 1 hour before serving, garnished with the sliced spring onion.

Variations
• To make a tasty tuna salad, make up the dressing without the cumin. Drain a 200g/7oz can tuna, flake the flesh and stir into the bean salad. Add some lightly cooked, halved green beans, hard-boiled (hard-cooked) egg and tomato quarters.
• For extra flavour and colour, stir in a handful of pitted black olives and a handful of chopped fresh parsley.

Bean, tomato & red onion salad: Energy 251kcal/1055kJ; Protein 12.7g; Carbohydrate 30.3g, of which sugars 6.2g; Fat 9.6g, of which saturates 1.5g; Cholesterol 0mg; Calcium 41mg; Fibre 10.4g; Sodium 850mg
Peppery bean salad: Energy 249kcal/1051kJ; Protein 15.6g; Carbohydrate 37g, of which sugars 8.5g; Fat 5.3g, of which saturates 0.7g; Cholesterol 0mg; Calcium 162mg; Fibre 12.5g; Sodium 826mg

White Bean & Celery Salad

This simple bean salad is a delicious alternative to the potato salad that seems to appear on every salad menu. If you do not have time to soak and cook dried beans, use canned ones.

Serves 4

450g/1lb dried white beans (haricot, cannellini, navy or butter (lima) beans) or 3 x 400g/14oz cans white beans

1 litre/1¾ pints/4 cups vegetable stock
3 celery sticks, cut into 1cm/½in strips
120ml/4fl oz/½ cup French dressing
45ml/3 tbsp chopped fresh parsley
salt and ground black pepper

1 If you are using dried beans, cover them with plenty of cold water and soak for at least 4 hours. Discard the soaking water, then place the beans in a heavy pan. Cover with water.

2 Bring to the boil and simmer without a lid for 1½ hours, or until the skins are broken. Cooked beans will squash readily between a thumb and forefinger. Drain the beans. If using canned beans, drain and rinse.

3 Place the cooked beans in a large pan. Add the vegetable stock and celery, bring to the boil, cover and simmer for 15 minutes. Drain thoroughly. Moisten the beans with the French dressing and leave to cool.

4 Add the chopped parsley and mix. Season to taste with salt and pepper, transfer to a salad bowl and serve.

Cook's Tip
To make a French dressing, whisk 90ml/6tbsp extra-virgin olive oil with about 15ml/1 tbsp each white wine vinegar and balsamic vinegar, 5ml/1 tsp French mustard, a little sugar and salt and pepper to taste. Vary the vinegar quantity to taste.

Pepper & Cucumber Salad

Generous quantities of fresh herbs transform familiar ingredients into a wonderful, fresh-tasting side salad.

Serves 4
1 yellow or red (bell) pepper
1 large cucumber
4–5 tomatoes
1 bunch spring onions (scallions)

30ml/2 tbsp fresh parsley
30ml/2 tbsp fresh mint
30ml/2 tbsp fresh coriander (cilantro)
2 pitta breads, to serve

For the dressing
2 garlic cloves, crushed
75ml/5 tbsp olive oil
juice of 2 lemons
salt and ground black pepper

1 Halve, seed and core the pepper, then slice. Roughly chop the cucumber and tomatoes. Place in a large salad bowl.

2 Trim and slice the spring onions. Add to the cucumber, tomatoes and pepper. Finely chop the parsley, mint and coriander and add to the bowl. If you have plenty of herbs, you can add as much as you like.

3 To make the dressing, blend the garlic with the olive oil and lemon juice in a bowl, then season to taste with salt and pepper. Pour the dressing over the salad and toss lightly to mix.

4 Toast the pitta breads in a toaster or under a hot grill (broiler) until crisp and serve alongside the salad.

White bean & celery salad: Energy 496kcal/2082kJ; Protein 25.1g; Carbohydrate 49.9g, of which sugars 3.1g; Fat 16.5g, of which saturates 3.2g; Cholesterol 0mg; Calcium 125mg; Fibre 17.9g; Sodium 313mg
Pepper & cucumber salad: Energy 159kcal/656kJ; Protein 1.8g; Carbohydrate 5.8g, of which sugars 5.6g; Fat 14.4g, of which saturates 2.1g; Cholesterol 0mg; Calcium 46mg; Fibre 2.4g; Sodium 13mg

Greek Salad

This classic salad is a wonderful combination of textures and flavours. The saltiness of the cheese is perfectly balanced by the refreshing salad vegetables.

Serves 4
1 cos lettuce heart
1 green pepper
1 red pepper
1/2 cucumber
4 tomatoes
1 red onion
225 g/8 oz/2 cups feta
 cheese, crumbled
black olives, to garnish

For the dressing
45 ml/3 tbsp olive oil
45 ml/3 tbsp lemon juice
1 garlic clove, crushed
15 ml/1 tbsp chopped
 fresh parsley
15 ml/1 tbsp chopped fresh mint
salt and ground black pepper

1 Chop the lettuce into bite-size pieces. Seed the peppers, remove the cores and cut the flesh into thin strips.

2 Chop the cucumber and slice or chop the tomatoes. Cut the onion in half, then slice finely.

3 Place the chopped lettuce, peppers, cucumber, tomatoes and onion in a large bowl. Scatter the feta over the top and toss together lightly. Don't worry if the feta breaks up a little, but don't let it disintegrate.

4 To make the dressing, blend together the olive oil, lemon juice and garlic in a small bowl. Stir in the chopped parsley and mint and season with salt and pepper to taste.

5 Pour the dressing over the salad and toss lightly. Garnish with a handful of black olives and serve immediately.

Variation
If you find raw peppers a little indigestible, roast or grill (broil) them first. Cook until charred, then cover with kitchen paper and, when cooled, remove the skin and seeds, then slice.

Assorted Seaweed Salad

Seaweed is a nutritions, alkaline food, which is rich in fibre. Its flavours are a great complement to oriental fish and tofu dishes.

Serves 4
5g/1/8oz each dried wakame,
 dried arame and dried
 hjiki seaweeds
about 130g/41/2oz fresh
 enokitake mushrooms
50ml/1 tbsp rice vinegar
6.5ml/11/4 tsp salt
2 spring onions (scallions)
 a few ice cubes
1/2 cucumber, cut lengthwise
250g/9oz mixed salad leaves

For the dressing
60ml/4 tbsp rice vinegar
7.5ml/11/2 tsp toasted sesame oil
15ml/1 tbsp shoyu
15ml/1 tbsp water with a pinch
 of dashi powder
2.5cm/1in piece fresh root ginger,
 finely grated (shredded)

1 Soak the dried wakame seaweed for 10 minutes in one bowl of water and, in a seperate bowl of water, soak the dried arame and hijiki seaweeds together for 30 minutes.

2 Trim the hard end of the enokitake mushroom stalks, then cut the bunch in half and separate the stems.

3 Cook the wakame and enokitake in boiling water for 2 minutes, then add the arame and hijiki for a few seconds. Immediately remove from the heat. Drain in a sieve (strainer) and sprinkle with the vinegar and salt while still warm. Chill.

4 Slice the spring onions (scallions) into thin, 4cm/11/2in long strips, then soak the strips in a bowl of cold water with a few ice cubes added to make them curl up. Drain. Slice the cucumber into thin half-moon shapes.

5 Mix the dressing ingredients together. Arrange the mixed salad leaves with the cucumber on top, then add the seaweed and enokitake mixutre.

6 Decorate the salad with spring onion curls and serve with the dressing.

Greek salad: Energy 225kcal/935kJ; Protein 11.2g; Carbohydrate 11.8g, of which sugars 11.1g; Fat 15.1g, of which saturates 8.3g; Cholesterol 39mg; Calcium 249mg; Fibre 3.4g; Sodium 827mg
Assorted seaweed salad: Energy 26Kcal/107kJ; Protein 1.5g; Carbohydrate 2.2g, of which sugars 2g; Fat 1.3g, of which saturates 0.2g; Cholesterol 0mg; Calcium 28mg; Fibre 1.2g; Sodium 272mg

Cabbage Salad with Lemon Dressing & Black Olives

During the winter in Greece, this *lahano salata* frequently appears on the meal table. Traditionally made with compact creamy-coloured "white" cabbage, it has a lovely crisp texture.

Serves 4
1 white cabbage
12 black olives

For the dressing
75–90ml/5–6 tbsp extra-virgin olive oil
30ml/2 tbsp lemon juice
1 garlic clove, crushed
30ml/2 tbsp finely chopped fresh flat leaf parsley
salt

1 Cut the cabbage in quarters, discard the outer leaves and trim off any thick, hard stems as well as the hard base.

2 Lay each quarter in turn on its side and cut long, very thin slices until you reach the central core, which should be discarded. Place the cabbage in a bowl and stir in the olives.

3 To make the dressing, whisk the extra-virgin olive oil, lemon juice, garlic, chopped parsley and salt together in a bowl until well blended.

4 Pour the dressing over the cabbage and olives, and toss the salad until evenly coated. Serve immediately.

Cook's Tip
The key to a perfect cabbage salad is to choose a very fresh, crisp cabbage and shred it as finely as possible; use a large, very sharp knife.

Variation
Add shredded raw carrot and toasted pine nuts for variety.

Fruit & Nut Coleslaw

A delicious and nutritious mixture of crunchy vegetables, fruit and nuts, tossed together in a mayonnaise dressing.

Serves 6
225g/8oz white cabbage
1 large carrot
175g/6oz/ ¾ cup ready-to-eat dried apricots
50g/2oz/ ½ cup walnuts
50g/2oz/ ½ cup hazelnuts
115g/4oz/ ⅔ cup raisins
30ml/2 tbsp chopped fresh parsley
105ml/7 tbsp mayonnaise
75ml/5 tbsp natural (plain) yogurt
salt and ground black pepper
fresh chives, to garnish

1 Finely shred the cabbage and coarsely grate (shred) the carrot. Place both in a large mixing bowl.

2 Roughly chop the dried apricots, walnuts and hazelnuts. Stir them into the cabbage and carrot mixture with the raisins and chopped parsley.

3 In a separate bowl, mix together the mayonnaise and yogurt and season to taste with salt and pepper.

4 Add the mayonnaise mixture to the cabbage mixture and toss together to mix. Cover and set aside in a cool place for at least 30 minutes before serving, to allow the flavours to mingle. Garnish with a few fresh chives and serve.

Variations
• *For a salad that is lower in fat, use low-fat natural (plain) yogurt and reduced-calorie mayonnaise.*
• *Instead of walnuts and hazelnuts, use flaked almonds and chopped pistachios.*
• *Omit the dried apricots and add a cored and chopped, unpeeled eating apple.*
• *Substitute other dried fruit or a mixture for the apricots – try nectarines, peaches or prunes.*

Cabbage salad: Energy 307kcal/1269kJ; Protein 3.9g; Carbohydrate 12.8g, of which sugars 12.5g; Fat 26.9g, of which saturates 3.8g; Cholesterol 0mg; Calcium 145mg; Fibre 5.8g; Sodium 21mg
Fruit & nut coleslaw: Energy 309kcal/1285kJ; Protein 4.3g; Carbohydrate 19.1g, of which sugars 18.8g; Fat 24.5g, of which saturates 2.9g; Cholesterol 13mg; Calcium 72mg; Fibre 2.5g; Sodium 103mg

Carrot, Raisin & Apricot Coleslaw

A tasty variation on classic coleslaw, this colourful salad combines cabbage, carrots and two kinds of dried fruit in a yogurt dressing.

Serves 6
350g/12oz/3 cups white cabbage
225g/8oz/1½ cups carrots
1 red onion, finely sliced
3 celery sticks, sliced
175g/6oz/generous 1 cup raisins

75g/3oz/½ cup dried apricots, chopped

For the dressing
120ml/4fl oz/½ cup mayonnaise
90ml/6 tbsp natural (plain) yogurt
30ml/2 tbsp chopped fresh mixed herbs
salt and ground black pepper

1 Finely shred the cabbage and coarsely grate (shred) the carrots. Place both in a large mixing bowl.

2 Add the onion, celery, raisins and apricots to the cabbage and carrots and mix well.

3 In a small bowl, mix together the mayonnaise and yogurt, then stir in the chopped fresh mixed herbs. Season with salt and pepper to taste.

4 Add the mayonnaise dressing to the coleslaw ingredients and toss together to mix. Cover and chill before serving.

Coleslaw with Pesto Mayonnaise

Basil-flavoured pesto gives this coleslaw a deliciously different taste.

Serves 4–6
1 small or ½ medium white cabbage
3–4 carrots, grated
4 spring onions (scallions), finely sliced
25–40g/1–1½oz/¼–⅓ cup pine nuts

15ml/1 tbsp chopped or torn fresh mixed herbs such as parsley, basil and chervil

For the pesto mayonnaise
1 egg yolk
about 10ml/2tsp lemon juice
200ml/7fl oz/scant 1 cup sunflower oil
10ml/2 tsp pesto
60ml/4 tbsp natural (plain) yogurt
salt and ground black pepper

1 To make the mayonnaise, place the egg yolk in a blender or food processor and process with the lemon juice. With the machine running, very slowly add the oil, pouring it more quickly as the mayonnaise emulsifies.

2 Season to taste with salt and pepper and a little more lemon juice if necessary. (Alternatively, make the mayonnaise by hand using a balloon whisk.) Spoon 75ml/5 tbsp of the mayonnaise into a bowl and stir in the pesto and yogurt, beating well to make a fairly thin dressing.

3 Remove the outer leaves of the cabbage and discard. Using a food processor or a sharp knife, thinly slice the cabbage and place in a large salad bowl.

4 Add the carrots and spring onions, together with the pine nuts and herbs, mixing thoroughly with your hands. Stir the pesto dressing into the salad or serve separately in a small dish.

Cook's Tip
If you are short of time, you can use ready-made mayonnaise with just as much success. Add the dressing just before serving to keep the cabbage crisp.

Carrot, raisin & apricot coleslaw: Energy 263kcal/1099kJ; Protein 3g; Carbohydrate 29.4g, of which sugars 28.8g; Fat 15.7g, of which saturates 2.4g; Cholesterol 15mg; Calcium 92mg; Fibre 3.2g; Sodium 143mg
Coleslaw with pesto mayonnaise: Energy 292kcal/1202kJ; Protein 2.7g; Carbohydrate 5.1g, of which sugars 5g; Fat 29g, of which saturates 3.5g; Cholesterol 34mg; Calcium 61mg; Fibre 1.8g; Sodium 17mg

Fennel Coleslaw

Another variation on traditional coleslaw in which the aniseed flavour of fennel plays a major role.

Serves 4
175g/6oz fennel
2 spring onions (scallions)
175g/6oz white cabbage
115g/4oz celery
175g/6oz carrots
50g/2oz/scant ½ cup sultanas (golden raisins)
2.5ml/½ tsp caraway seeds (optional)
15ml/1 tbsp chopped fresh parsley
45ml/3 tbsp extra-virgin olive oil
5ml/1 tsp lemon juice
strips of spring onion (scallion), to garnish

1 Using a sharp knife, cut the fennel and spring onions into thin slices. Place in a serving bowl.

2 Slice the cabbage and celery finely and cut the carrots into fine strips. Add to the fennel and spring onions in the serving bowl. Add the sultanas and caraway seeds, if using, and toss lightly to mix through.

3 Stir in the chopped parsley, olive oil and lemon juice and mix all the ingredients very thoroughly.

4 Cover and chill for 3 hours to allow the flavours to mingle. Serve garnished with strips of spring onion.

Curried Red Cabbage Slaw

A variation on a Jewish favourite, this spicy coleslaw is excellent for adding flavour and colour to a cold meal. Quick and easy to make, it is a useful dish for a last-minute gathering.

Serves 4–6
½ red cabbage, thinly sliced
1 red (bell) pepper, chopped or very thinly sliced
½ red onion, chopped
60ml/4 tbsp red, white wine vinegar or cider vinegar
60ml/4 tbsp sugar, or to taste
120ml/4fl oz/½ cup Greek (US strained plain) yogurt or natural (plain) yogurt
120ml/4fl oz/½ cup mayonnaise, preferably home-made
1.5ml/¼ tsp curry powder
2–3 handfuls of raisins
salt and ground black pepper

1 Put the cabbage, red pepper and red onions in a bowl and toss to combine thoroughly.

2 Heat the vinegar and sugar in a small pan until the sugar has dissolved, then pour over the vegetables. Leave to cool slightly.

3 Mix together the yogurt and mayonnaise, then stir into the cabbage mixture. Season to taste with curry powder, salt and ground black pepper, then mix in the raisins.

4 Chill the salad for at least 2 hours before serving. Just before serving, drain off any excess liquid and briefly stir the slaw again.

Cook's Tip
If you have time, it is worth making your own mayonnaise.

Variation
• To make a tangy pareve slaw, suitable for serving with a meat meal, omit the natural (plain) yogurt and mayonnaise and add a little more vinegar.

Fennel coleslaw: Energy 145kcal/604kJ; Protein 1.9g; Carbohydrate 15.6g, of which sugars 15.3g; Fat 8.7g, of which saturates 1.2g; Cholesterol 0mg; Calcium 70mg; Fibre 3.8g; Sodium 46mg
Curried red cabbage slaw: Energy 286kcal/1194kJ; Protein 3.5g; Carbohydrate 31.6g, of which sugars 31g; Fat 17g, of which saturates 2.6g; Cholesterol 17mg; Calcium 108mg; Fibre 3.1g; Sodium 134mg

Orange & Chicory Salad with Walnuts

Chicory and oranges are both winter ingredients, so this salad is perfect as a light accompaniment to hearty winter meat dishes. The fresh flavours also go well with seafood dishes.

Serves 6
2 chicory (Belgian endive) heads
2 oranges
30ml/2 tbsp extra-virgin olive oil
25g/1oz/2 tbsp walnut halves, roughly chopped
salt and ground black pepper

1 Trim off the bottom of each chicory head and separate the leaves. Arrange on a serving platter.

2 Place one of the oranges on a chopping board and slice off the top and bottom to expose the flesh. Place the orange upright and, using a small sharp knife, slice down between the skin and the flesh. Do this all the way around until the orange is completely free of peel and pith. Repeat with the remaining orange, reserving any juice.

3 Holding one orange over a bowl to catch the juices, cut between the membrane to release the segments. Repeat with the second orange. Arrange the orange segments on the platter with the chicory.

4 Whisk the oil with any juice from the oranges, and season with salt and pepper to taste. Sprinkle the walnuts over the salad, drizzle over the dressing and serve immediately.

Cook's Tip
Blood oranges look especially attractive served in this dish.

Variation
Use young spinach leaves or rocket (arugula) instead of chicory.

Carrot & Orange Salad

This classic fruit and vegetable combination makes a wonderful, fresh-tasting salad. A great side dish for the winter months, it is particularly good with hot or cold poultry dishes.

Serves 4
450g/1lb carrots
2 large oranges
15ml/1 tbsp olive oil
30ml/2 tbsp lemon juice
pinch of sugar (optional)
30ml/2 tbsp chopped pistachio nuts or toasted pine nuts
salt and ground black pepper

1 Peel the carrots and grate (shred) them into a large serving bowl.

2 Cut a slice off the top and bottom of one orange. Place the orange upright on a board and cut off the skin, taking care to remove all the bitter white pith Repeat with the second orange, reserving any juice. Working over a bowl to catch the juices, cut between the membranes to release the segments.

3 Whisk together the olive oil, lemon juice and reserved orange juice in a bowl. Season with a little salt and pepper to taste, and add sugar, if you like.

4 Toss the orange segments together with the carrots and pour the dressing over. Scatter the salad with the pistachio nuts or pine nuts before serving.

Orange & chicory salad: Energy 81kcal/335kJ; Protein 1.2g; Carbohydrate 4.6g, of which sugars 3.9g; Fat 6.8g, of which saturates 0.8g; Cholesterol 0mg; Calcium 31mg; Fibre 1.2g; Sodium 3mg
Carrot & orange salad: Energy 137kcal/571kJ; Protein 2.9g; Carbohydrate 15.9g, of which sugars 15.1g; Fat 7.3g, of which saturates 1.1g; Cholesterol 0mg; Calcium 72mg; Fibre 4.4g; Sodium 72mg

Fennel, Orange & Rocket Salad

This light and refreshing salad is ideal to serve with spicy or rich foods. Zesty orange blends perfectly with the delicate flavour of fennel and the peppery rocket.

Serves 4
2 oranges, such as Jaffa, Shamouti
   or blood oranges
1 fennel bulb
115g/4oz rocket (arugula) leaves
50g/2oz/⅓ cup black olives

For the dressing
30ml/2 tbsp extra-virgin olive oil
15ml/1 tbsp balsamic vinegar
1 small garlic clove, crushed
salt and ground black pepper

1 Using a vegetable peeler, pare off strips of rind from the oranges, leaving the pith behind, then cut the pared rind into thin julienne strips. Blanch the strips in boiling water for a few minutes. Drain and set aside.

2 Cut a slice off the top and bottom of one orange. Place the orange upright on a board and cut off the skin, taking care to remove all the bitter white pith. Repeat with the second orange, reserving any juice. Slice the oranges into thin rounds.

3 Trim the fennel bulb, then cut in half lengthwise and slice across the bulb as thinly as possible, preferably in a food processor fitted with a slicing disc or using a mandolin.

4 Combine the slices of orange and fennel in a serving bowl and toss with the rocket leaves.

5 To make the dressing, mix together the oil, vinegar and garlic and season with salt and pepper to taste. Pour over the salad, toss together well and leave to stand for a few minutes. Sprinkle with the black olives and julienne strips of orange.

Variation
For a twist in flavour, substitute minneolas for the oranges.

Orange & Red Onion Salad with Cumin

Cumin and mint give this refreshing, quick-to-prepare salad a very Middle-Eastern flavour. Small, seedless oranges are most suitable, if available.

Serves 6
6 oranges
2 red onions
15ml/1 tbsp cumin seeds
5ml/1 tsp coarsely ground
   black pepper
15ml/1 tbsp chopped fresh mint
90ml/6 tbsp olive oil
salt
fresh mint sprigs and black
   olives, to serve

1 Slice the oranges thinly, catching any juices. Holding each orange slice in turn over a bowl, cut round with scissors to remove the peel and pith. Reserve the juice. Slice the onions thinly and separate into rings.

2 Arrange the orange and onion slices in layers in a shallow dish, sprinkling each layer with cumin seeds, black pepper, chopped mint, olive oil and salt to taste. Pour over the reserved orange juice.

3 Leave the salad to marinate in a cool place for about 2 hours. Scatter over the mint sprigs and black olives, and serve.

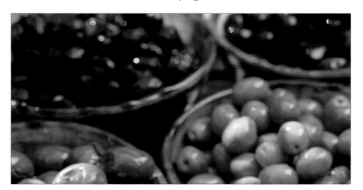

Asparagus & Orange Salad

This is a slightly unusual combination of ingredients with a simple dressing based on good-quality olive oil.

Serves 4

225g/8oz asparagus, trimmed
  and cut into 5cm/2in lengths
2 large oranges
2 well-flavoured tomatoes, cut
  into eighths
50g/2oz cos lettuce leaves
30ml/2 tbsp extra-virgin olive oil
2.5ml/½ tsp sherry vinegar
salt and ground black pepper

1 Cook the asparagus in boiling, salted water for 3–4 minutes, until just tender. The cooking time may vary according to the size of the asparagus stems. Drain and refresh under cold water, then leave on one side to cool.

2 Grate (shred) the rind from half one orange and reserve.

3 Cut a slice off the top and bottom of one orange to reveal the flesh. Place the orange upright on a board and, using a small sharp knife, cut off the skin, taking care to remove all the bitter white pith. Repeat with the second orange, reserving any juice.

4 Holding one orange over a bowl to catch the juices, cut between the membrane to release the segments. Repeat with the second orange. Reserve the juices.

5 Put the asparagus, orange segments, tomatoes and lettuce in a salad bowl.

6 Mix together the oil and vinegar, and add 15ml/1 tbsp of the reserved orange juice and 5ml/1 tsp of the grated rind. Season with salt and pepper to taste. Just before serving, pour the dressing over the salad and mix gently to coat the ingredients.

Cook's Tip
Do not overcook the asparagus; it should still be quite firm.

Black & Orange Salad

This dramatically colourful salad is ideal for serving with plainly grilled or barbecued meat and fish.

Serves 4

3 oranges
115g/4oz/1 cup pitted black
  olives
15ml/1 tbsp chopped fresh
  coriander (cilantro)
15ml/1 tbsp chopped
  fresh parsley

For the dressing
30ml/2 tbsp olive oil
15ml/1 tbsp lemon juice
2.5ml/½ tsp paprika
2.5ml/½ tsp ground cumin

1 Cut a slice off the top and bottom of one orange to reveal the flesh. Place the orange upright on a board and, using a small sharp knife, cut off the skin, taking care to remove all the bitter white pith. Repeat with the remaining oranges, then cut between the membranes to release the segments.

2 Place the orange segments in a salad bowl and add the black olives, coriander and parsley.

3 To make the dressing, blend together the olive oil, lemon juice, paprika and cumin.

4 Pour the dressing over the salad and toss gently. Chill for about 30 minutes and serve.

Variation
The strong flavours and vivid colours of this salad work brilliantly with couscous. Adapt the recipe by chopping the orange segments and olives quite finely (using a mandolin makes this a quick and easy job). Mix the finely chopped olives and oranges with the herbs and dressing into a bowl of cooked couscous while it is still warm. Either chill the salad or serve it immediately. It's delicious cold or warm – and perfect for a picnic with cold chicken or smoked ham.

Asparagus & orange salad: Energy 92kcal/384kJ; Protein 2.6g; Carbohydrate 7.2g, of which sugars 7.1g; Fat 6.1g, of which saturates 0.9g; Cholesterol 0mg; Calcium 46mg; Fibre 2.4g; Sodium 8mg
Black & orange salad: Energy 129kcal/537kJ; Protein 1.8g; Carbohydrate 11.1g, of which sugars 10.6g; Fat 9g, of which saturates 1.3g; Cholesterol 0mg; Calcium 79mg; Fibre 3g; Sodium 654mg

Orange & Water Chestnut Salad

Crisp water chestnuts combine with oranges to make a colourful and clean-tasting salad.

Serves 4
2 oranges
1 red onion, thinly sliced into rings
1 400g/14oz can drained water
    chestnuts, peeled and cut into
    strips
2 radicchio heads, cored, or
    1 red-leaf lettuce,
    leaves separated
45ml/3 tbsp chopped
    fresh parsley
45ml/3 tbsp chopped fresh basil
15ml/1 tbsp white wine vinegar
50ml/2fl oz/¼ cup walnut oil
salt and ground black pepper
1 fresh basil sprig, to garnish

1 Cut a slice off the top and bottom of one orange to reveal the flesh. Place the orange upright on a board and, using a small sharp knife, cut off the skin, taking care to remove all the bitter white pith. Repeat with the remaining orange.

2 Holding one peeled orange over a bowl, cut between the membranes to release the segments. Repeat with the remaining orange. Discard the membranes.

3 Put the onion in a colander and sprinkle with 5ml/1 tsp salt. Allow to drain for 15 minutes.

4 Put the oranges in a large bowl, add the water chestnuts and toss to mix.

5 Rinse the onion to remove excess salt and pat dry on kitchen paper. Toss with the water chestnuts and oranges.

6 Spread out the radicchio or red-leaf lettuce leaves in a large, shallow bowl or on a serving platter. Arrange the water chestnut, orange and onion mixture on top. Sprinkle with the chopped parsley and basil.

7 Put the vinegar, oil and salt and pepper to taste in a screw-top jar and shake well to combine. Pour the dressing over the salad and serve immediately, garnished with a sprig of basil.

Moroccan Date, Orange & Carrot Salad

Take exotic fresh dates and marry them with everyday ingredients, such as carrots and oranges, to create this deliciously different salad. It is excellent served with chargrilled lamb steaks or skewered lamb.

Serves 4
3 carrots
3 oranges
2 Little Gem (Bibb) lettuce,
    leaves separated
115g/4oz fresh dates, stoned
    (pitted) and cut into eighths
25g/1oz/¼ cup toasted whole
    almonds, chopped
salt and ground black pepper

1 Grate (shred) the carrots. Using a sharp knife, cut the peel and pith away from two of the oranges. Cut between the membranes to release the segments.

2 Line a serving dish or four individual plates with lettuce. Place the grated carrots on top and arrange the orange segments next to the carrot. Season with salt and ground black pepper. Pile the dates on top of the carrots, then sprinkle with the chopped, toasted almonds.

3 Squeeze the juice from the remaining orange and sprinkle over the salad. Chill the salad for an hour before serving.

Orange & water chestnut salad: Energy 110kcal/458kJ; Protein 1.5g; Carbohydrate 6.9g, of which sugars 6.6g; Fat 8.8g, of which saturates 0.8g; Cholesterol 0mg; Calcium 59mg; Fibre 2g; Sodium 20mg
Moroccan date, orange & carrot salad: Energy 147kcal/620kJ; Protein 3.8g; Carbohydrate 25g, of which sugars 24.3g; Fat 4.3g, of which saturates 0.5g; Cholesterol 0mg; Calcium 103mg; Fibre 5.3g; Sodium 34mg

Potato & Olive Salad

This delicious version of potato salad is simple and zesty – perfect as a quick and easy side salad.

Serves 4

8 large new potatoes
45–60ml/3–4 tbsp
  garlic-flavoured oil and
  vinegar dressing
60–90ml/4–6 tbsp chopped fresh
  herbs, such as coriander
  (cilantro) and chives
10–15 dry-fleshed black
  Mediterranean olives
pinch of ground cumin, to garnish

I Cut the new potatoes into chunks. Put them in a pan, pour in water to cover and add a pinch of salt. Bring to the boil, then reduce the heat and cook gently for about 10 minutes, or until the potatoes are just tender. Drain well and leave in a colander to dry thoroughly and cool slightly.

2 When the potatoes are cool enough to handle, chop them and put in a serving bowl.

3 Drizzle the garlic-flavoured dressing over the potatoes. Toss well together, then sprinkle with the chopped fresh herbs and black olives.

4 Chill in the refrigerator for at least 1 hour before serving. Serve garnished with a little ground cumin.

Cook's Tip
Similar in appearance to flat leaf parsley, fresh coriander (cilantro) has a distinctive pungent, almost spicy flavour that makes a delicious addition to salads. It is widely used in India, the Middle and Far East and in many eastern Mediterranean countries.

Potato, Caraway Seed & Parsley Salad

Leaving the potatoes to cool in garlic-infused oil with the caraway seeds helps them to absorb plenty of flavour.

Serves 4–6

675g/1½lb new potatoes,
  scrubbed
45ml/3 tbsp garlic-infused olive oil
15ml/1 tbsp caraway seeds,
  lightly crushed
45ml/3 tbsp chopped fresh
  parsley
salt and ground black pepper

I Cook the potatoes in salted, boiling water for about 10 minutes, or until just tender. Drain thoroughly and transfer to a large bowl.

2 Stir the oil, caraway seeds and some salt and pepper into the hot potatoes, then set aside to cool. When the potatoes are almost cold, stir in the parsley and serve.

Deli Potato Salad with Egg, Mayonnaise & Olives

Potato salad is synonymous with deli food and there are many varieties, some with soured cream, some with vinaigrette and others with vegetables. This tasty version includes a piquant mustard mayonnaise, chopped eggs and green olives.

Serves 6–8

1kg/2¼lb waxy salad potatoes,
  scrubbed
1 red, brown or white onion, finely
  chopped
2–3 celery sticks, finely chopped
60–90ml/4–6 tbsp chopped
  fresh parsley
15–20 pimiento-stuffed
  olives, halved
3 hard-boiled (hard-cooked)
  eggs, chopped
60ml/4 tbsp extra virgin olive oil
60ml/4 tbsp white wine vinegar
15–30ml/1–2 tbsp mild or
  wholegrain mustard
celery seeds, to taste (optional)
175–250ml/6–8fl oz/¾–1 cup
  mayonnaise
salt and ground black pepper
paprika, to garnish

I Put the potatoes in a pan, pour in water to cover and add a pinch of salt. Bring to the boil, then reduce the heat and cook gently for about 10 minutes, or until the potatoes are just tender. Drain well and return to the pan. Leave for 2–3 minutes to cool and dry a little.

2 When the potatoes are cool enough to handle but still very warm, cut them with a sharp knife into chunks or slices and place in a salad bowl.

3 Sprinkle the potatoes with salt and ground black pepper, then add the onion, celery, parsley, olives and the chopped eggs.

4 Place the olive oil in a small bowl, then whisk in the vinegar, mustard and celery seeds, if using. Pour the dressing over the salad and toss to combine.

5 Stir in enough mayonnaise to bind the salad together. Chill before serving, sprinkled with a little paprika.

Potato & Olive Salad: Energy 132kcal/548kJ; Protein 1.8g; Carbohydrate 12.4g, of which sugars 1.2g; Fat 8.6g, of which saturates 1.3g; Cholesterol 0mg; Calcium 42mg; Fibre 2.1g; Sodium 575mg
Potato, Caraway Seed & Parsley Salad: Energy 131kcal/549kJ; Protein 2.1g; Carbohydrate 18.3g, of which sugars 1.6g; Fat 5.9g, of which saturates 0.9g; Cholesterol 0mg; Calcium 22mg; Fibre 1.5g; Sodium 15mg
Deli potato salad: Energy 323kcal/1343kJ; Protein 5.2g; Carbohydrate 21.5g, of which sugars 2.7g; Fat 24.7g, of which saturates 4g; Cholesterol 88mg; Calcium 49mg; Fibre 2g; Sodium 149mg

Potato Salad with Capers & Black Olives

A dish from southern Italy, the combination of olives, capers and anchovies is quite perfect.

Serves 4–6
900g/2lb large white potatoes
50ml/2fl oz/¼ cup white
   wine vinegar
75ml/5 tbsp olive oil
30ml/2 tbsp chopped flat
   leaf parsley

30ml/2 tbsp capers, finely
   chopped
50g/2oz/½ cup pitted black
   olives, chopped in half
3 garlic cloves, finely chopped
50g/2oz marinated anchovies
   (unsalted)
salt and ground black pepper

1 Boil the potatoes in their skins in a large pan for 20 minutes or until just tender. Remove from the pan using a slotted spoon and place them in a separate bowl.

2 When the potatoes are cool enough to handle, carefully peel off the skins.

3 Cut the peeled potatoes into even chunks and place in a large, flat earthenware dish.

4 Mix together the vinegar and oil, season to taste and add the parsley, capers, olives and garlic. Toss carefully to combine and then pour over the potato chunks.

5 Lay the anchovies on top of the salad. Cover with a cloth and leave the salad to settle for 30 minutes or so before serving to allow the flavours to penetrate.

Variation
If you want to serve this dish to vegetarians, simply omit the anchovies, it tastes delicious even without them.

Potatoes with Egg & Lemon Dressing

This old favourite takes on a new lease of life when mixed with hard-boiled eggs and lemon juice. With its tangy flavour, it is the ideal salad to accompany a summer barbecue.

Serves 4
900g/2lb new potatoes
1 small onion, finely chopped

2 hard-boiled (hard-cooked) eggs,
   shelled
300ml/½ pint/1¼ cups
   mayonnaise
1 garlic clove, crushed
finely grated (shredded) rind and
   juice of 1 lemon
60ml/4 tbsp chopped fresh
   parsley, plus extra
   for garnishing
salt and ground black pepper

1 Scrub or scrape the potatoes. Put them in a pan, cover with cold water and add a pinch of salt. Bring to the boil, then simmer for 15 minutes, or until tender. Drain and allow to cool. Cut the potatoes into large dice, season well with salt and pepper and combine with the chopped onion.

2 Halve the eggs and set aside the yolk. Roughly chop the whites and place in a mixing bowl. Stir in the mayonnaise. Mix the garlic, lemon rind and lemon juice in a small bowl and stir into the mayonnaise mixture, combining thoroughly.

3 Stir the mayonnaise mixture into the potatoes, coating them well, then fold in the chopped parsley. Press the egg yolk through a sieve (strainer) and sprinkle on top. Serve cold or chilled, garnished with parsley.

Variation
For a change, replace the potato with cooked beetroot (beet). The mayonnaise will turn bright pink, which may surprise your guests, but the flavour is excellent. Alternatively, use a mixture of potatoes and beetroot.

Potato & Radish Salad

Radishes add a splash of crunch and peppery flavour to this honey-scented salad. So many potato salads are dressed in a thick sauce. This one, however, is quite light and colourful with a tasty yet delicate dressing.

Serves 4–6
450g/1lb new or salad potatoes
45ml/3 tbsp olive oil
15ml/1 tbsp walnut or hazelnut oil (optional)
30ml/2 tbsp wine vinegar
10ml/2 tsp coarse-grain mustard
5ml/1 tsp honey
about 6–8 radishes, thinly sliced
30ml/2 tbsp snipped chives
salt and ground black pepper

1 Cook the potatoes in their skins in a large pan of boiling salted water until just tender. Drain well and leave to cool slightly. When cool enough to handle, cut the potatoes in half, but leave any small ones whole. Place in a large bowl.

2 To make the dressing, place the oils, vinegar, mustard and honey in a bowl and season to taste with salt and pepper. Whisk together until thoroughly combined.

3 Toss the dressing into the potatoes in the bowl while they are still cooling and leave to stand for 1–2 hours to allow the flavours to penetrate.

4 Finally, mix in the sliced radishes and snipped chives and chill in the refrigerator until ready to serve.

5 Just before serving, toss the salad mixture together again, as some of the dressing may have settled on the bottom, and adjust the seasoning.

Variation
Sliced celery stick, diced red onion and/or chopped walnuts would make good alternatives to the radishes if you are unable to get hold of any.

Tangy Potato Salad

If you like a good kick of mustard and the distinctive flavour of tarragon, you'll love this combination.

Serves 8
1.3kg/3lb small new or salad potatoes
30ml/2 tbsp white wine vinegar
15ml/1 tbsp Dijon mustard
45ml/3 tbsp vegetable or olive oil
75g/3oz/6 tbsp chopped red onion
120ml/4fl oz/½ cup mayonnaise
30ml/2 tbsp chopped fresh tarragon, or 7.5ml/1½ tsp dried tarragon
1 celery stick, thinly sliced
salt and ground black pepper
celery leaves and tarragon leaves, to garnish

1 Cook the potatoes in their skins in boiling salted water for about 15–20 minutes until tender. Drain well.

2 Mix together the vinegar and Dijon mustard, then slowly whisk in the oil.

3 When the potatoes are cool enough to handle, slice them into a large bowl. Add the onion to the potatoes, then pour the dressing over them. Season with salt and pepper to taste, then toss gently to combine. Leave to stand for at least 30 minutes.

4 Mix together the mayonnaise and tarragon. Gently stir into the potatoes, together with the celery. Serve garnished with celery leaves and tarragon.

Cook's Tip
The delicious, distinctive tarragon flavour in this dish makes it the perfect partner to roast or grilled (broiled) chicken.

Variation
When available, use small red or even blue potatoes to give an interesting colour to the salad.

Hot Hot Cajun Potato Salad

Tabasco sauce gives this salad a punchy flavour.

Serves 6–8
8 waxy potatoes
1 green (bell) pepper, seeded and diced
1 large gherkin, chopped
4 spring onions (scallions), shredded
3 hard-boiled (hard-cooked) eggs, shelled and chopped
250ml/8fl oz/1 cup mayonnaise
15ml/1 tbsp Dijon mustard
salt and ground black pepper
Tabasco sauce, to taste
1–2 pinches cayenne pepper
sliced gherkin, to garnish
mayonnaise, to serve

1 Cook the potatoes in their skins in a large pan of salted boiling water until tender. Drain well and leave to cool.

2 When the potatoes are cool enough to handle, peel them and cut into coarse chunks. Transfer the potatoes to a large bowl and add the green pepper, gherkin, spring onions and hard-boiled eggs. Toss gently to mix.

3 In a separate bowl, mix the mayonnaise with the mustard and season with salt, black pepper and Tabasco sauce to taste.

4 Toss the dressing into the potato mixture and sprinkle with a pinch or two of cayenne. Serve the salad with mayonnaise and a garnish of sliced gherkin.

Spicy Potato Salad

This tasty salad is quick to prepare, and makes a satisfying accompaniment to plainly cooked meat or fish.

Serves 6
900g/2lb potatoes
2 red (bell) peppers, seeded and diced
2 celery sticks, finely chopped
1 shallot, finely chopped
2 or 3 spring onions (scallions), finely chopped
1 green chilli, seeded and finely chopped
1 garlic clove, crushed
10ml/2 tsp finely snipped fresh chives
10ml/2 tsp finely chopped fresh basil
15ml/1 tbsp finely chopped fresh parsley
15ml/1 tbsp single (light) cream
30ml/2 tbsp salad cream
15ml/1 tbsp mayonnaise
5ml/1 tsp prepared mild mustard
7.5ml/1½ tsp sugar
salt
snipped fresh chives, to garnish

1 Peel the potatoes. Boil in salted water for 10–12 minutes, until tender. Drain and cool, then cut into cubes and place in a large mixing bowl.

2 Add chopped red peppers, celery, shallot, spring onions and green chilli to the potatoes, together with the crushed garlic and chopped herbs, and stir gently to combine.

3 To make the dressing, blend the cream, salad cream, mayonnaise, mustard and sugar in a small bowl, stirring until the mixture is well combined.

4 Pour the dressing over the salad and toss gently to coat evenly. Serve garnished with the snipped chives.

Variations
If you prefer, leave out the salad cream and increase the amount of mayonnaise by 30ml/2 tbsp. To turn the salad into a light lunch dish, add some diced ham and a handful of cooked green beans that have been refreshed under cold running water.

Hot hot Cajun potato salad: Energy 289kcal/1197kJ; Protein 4g; Carbohydrate 10.3g, of which sugars 2.7g; Fat 26.1g, of which saturates 4.2g; Cholesterol 95mg; Calcium 21mg; Fibre 0.9g; Sodium 229mg
Spicy potato salad: Energy 178kcal/749kJ; Protein 3.9g; Carbohydrate 31.4g, of which sugars 8.7g; Fat 4.9g, of which saturates 1g; Cholesterol 5mg; Calcium 48mg; Fibre 3.3g; Sodium 118mg

Bulgur Wheat Salad

Bursting with summery flavours, this salad has a delicious texture and makes a change from a rice or pasta salad. Bulgur wheat is easy to prepare, too.

Serves 4

225g/8oz/1⅓ cups bulgur wheat
350ml/12fl oz/1½ cups
    vegetable stock
1 cinnamon stick
generous pinch of ground cumin
pinch of cayenne pepper
pinch of ground cloves
5ml/1 tsp salt
10 mangetouts (snow peas),
    topped and tailed
1 red and 1 yellow (bell) pepper,
    roasted, skinned, seeded
    and diced
2 plum tomatoes, peeled, seeded
    and diced
2 shallots, finely sliced
5 black olives, pitted and cut into
    quarters
30ml/2 tbsp each chopped fresh
    basil, mint and parsley
30ml/2 tbsp roughly chopped
    walnuts
30ml/2 tbsp balsamic vinegar
120ml/4fl oz/½ cup extra-virgin
    olive oil
ground black pepper
onion rings, to garnish

1 Place the bulgur wheat in a large bowl. Pour the stock into a pan and bring to the boil with the spices and salt.

2 Cook the stock for 1 minute, then pour, with the cinnamon stick, over the wheat. Leave to stand for 30 minutes.

3 In another bowl, mix together the mangetouts, peppers, tomatoes, shallots, olives, herbs and walnuts. Add the vinegar, olive oil and a little black pepper and stir thoroughly to mix.

4 Strain the bulgur wheat of any liquid and discard the cinnamon stick. Place in a serving bowl, stir in the fresh vegetable mixture and serve, garnished with onion rings.

Cook's Tip
Fresh herbs are essential for this salad. Dried herbs will not make a suitable substitute.

Cracked Wheat Salad with Oranges & Almonds

The citrus flavours of lemon and orange really come through in this tasty salad, which can be made several hours before serving.

Serves 4

150g/5oz/scant 1 cup
    bulgur wheat
600ml/1 pint/2½ cups water
1 small green (bell) pepper,
    seeded and diced
¼ cucumber, diced
15g/½oz/½ cup chopped
    fresh mint
60ml/4 tbsp flaked almonds,
    toasted
grated (shredded) rind and juice
    of 1 lemon
2 seedless oranges
salt and ground black pepper
fresh mint sprigs, to garnish

1 Place the bulgur wheat in a bowl, pour over the water and leave to soak for 20 minutes.

2 Line a colander with a clean dish towel. Turn the soaked bulgur wheat into the centre, let it drain, then gather up the sides of the dish towel and squeeze out any remaining liquid. Transfer the bulgur wheat to a large bowl.

3 Add the green pepper, diced cucumber, mint, toasted almonds and grated (shredded) lemon rind. Pour in the lemon juice and toss thoroughly to mix.

4 Cut the skin and pith from the oranges, then, working over a bowl to catch the juice, cut between the membranes to release the segments. Add the segments and the juice to the bulgur mixture, then season to taste with salt and pepper and toss lightly. Garnish with the mint sprigs and serve.

Cook's Tip
Bulgur wheat is also known as cracked wheat because the grains are cracked after hulling and steaming and before drying.

Bulgur wheat salad: Energy 429kcal/1782kJ; Protein 7.7g; Carbohydrate 52.1g, of which sugars 8.5g; Fat 21.7g, of which saturates 3g; Cholesterol 0mg; Calcium 70mg; Fibre 3g; Sodium 507mg
Cracked wheat salad: Energy 254kcal/1060kJ; Protein 7.8g; Carbohydrate 39g, of which sugars 9.8g; Fat 7.9g, of which saturates 0.6g; Cholesterol 0mg; Calcium 96mg; Fibre 3g; Sodium 10mg

Tabbouleh

This is a wonderfully refreshing, tangy salad of soaked bulgur wheat and masses of fresh mint, parsley and spring onions.

Serves 4–6

250g/9oz/1½ cups bulgur wheat
600ml/1 pint/2½ cups water
1 large bunch spring onions
  (scallions), thinly sliced
1 cucumber, finely chopped
  or diced
3 tomatoes, chopped
1.5–2.5ml/¼–½ tsp
  ground cumin
1 large bunch fresh parsley,
  chopped
1 large bunch fresh mint, chopped
juice of 2 lemons, or to taste
60ml/4 tbsp extra-virgin olive oil
salt
cos or romaine lettuce,
  to serve
olives and lemon wedges,
  to garnish

1 Place the bulgur wheat in a bowl, pour over the water and leave to soak for 20 minutes.

2 Line a colander with a clean dish towel. Turn the soaked bulgur wheat into the centre, let it drain, then gather up the sides of the dish towel and squeeze out any remaining liquid. Transfer the bulgur wheat to a large bowl.

3 Add the spring onions to the bulgur wheat, then mix and squeeze together with your hands to combine.

4 Add the cucumber, tomatoes, cumin, parsley and mint and mix well, then pour in the lemon juice and oil. Add salt to taste and toss to combine.

5 Heap the tabbouleh onto a bed of lettuce. Garnish with olives and lemon wedges.

Variations
- *Use couscous soaked in boiling water in place of the bulgur wheat.*
- *Use chopped fresh coriander (cilantro) instead of parsley.*
- *Try serving the salad with natural (plain) yogurt.*

Couscous Salad

Couscous has become an extremely popular salad ingredient, and there are many variations on the classic theme. This salad comes from Morocco.

Serves 4

275g/10oz/1⅔ cups couscous
550ml/18fl oz/2½ cups boiling
  vegetable stock
16–20 pitted black olives, halved
2 small courgettes (zucchini), cut
  into matchstick strips
25g/1oz/¼ cup flaked
  almonds, toasted
60ml/4 tbsp olive oil
15ml/1 tbsp lemon juice
15ml/1 tbsp chopped fresh
  coriander (cilantro)
15ml/1 tbsp chopped fresh
  parsley
good pinch of ground cumin
good pinch of cayenne pepper
salt
sprigs of coriander (cilantro),
  to garnish

1 Place the couscous in a bowl and pour over the boiling stock. Stir with a fork, then set aside for 10 minutes for the stock to be absorbed. Fluff up with a fork.

2 Add the olives, courgettes and almonds to the couscous and mix in gently.

3 Whisk the olive oil, lemon juice, coriander, parsley, cumin, cayenne and a pinch of salt in a bowl. Pour the dressing over the salad and toss to mix. Transfer to a serving dish and garnish with coriander sprigs.

Cook's Tip
This salad benefits from being made several hours ahead.

Variations
- *You can substitute ½ cucumber for the courgettes (zucchini) and pistachios for the almonds.*
- *For extra heat, add a pinch of chilli powder to the dressing.*

Tabbouleh: Energy 232kcal/965kJ; Protein 5.2g; Carbohydrate 34.6g, of which sugars 2.7g; Fat 8.4g, of which saturates 1.1g; Cholesterol 0mg; Calcium 51mg; Fibre 1.4g; Sodium 12mg
Couscous salad: Energy 324kcal/1344kJ; Protein 7.1g; Carbohydrate 37.4g, of which sugars 1.8g; Fat 17g, of which saturates 2.1g; Cholesterol 0mg; Calcium 80mg; Fibre 2.1g; Sodium 287mg

Fragrant Roasted Tomato Salsa

Roasting the tomatoes gives a greater depth to the flavour of this salsa, which also benefits from the warm, rounded flavour of roasted chillies. This salad is a classic accompaniment to tortillas and other Mexican dishes.

Serves 6
500g/1¼lb tomatoes, preferably beefsteak tomatoes
2 fresh Serrano chillies or other fresh red chillies
1 onion
juice of 1 lime
1 large bunch fresh coriander (cilantro)
salt

1 Preheat the oven to 200°C/400°F/Gas 6. Cut the tomatoes into quarters and place them in a roasting pan. Add the chillies and roast for 45 minutes to 1 hour, until the tomatoes and chillies are charred and softened.

2 Place the roasted chillies in a strong plastic bag. Tie the top to keep the steam in and set aside for 20 minutes. Leave the tomatoes to cool slightly, then use a small, sharp knife to remove the skins and dice the flesh.

3 Chop the onion finely, then place it in a bowl and add the lime juice and the diced tomatoes. Mix well.

4 Remove the chillies from the bag and peel off the skins. Cut off the stalks, then slit the chillies and scrape out the seeds with a sharp knife. Chop the chillies roughly and add them to the onion mixture. Mix well to combine.

5 Chop the coriander and add most of it to the salsa. Add salt to season, cover and chill for at least 1 hour before serving, sprinkled with the remaining chopped coriander.

> **Cook's Tip**
> This salsa will keep for a week in the refrigerator. It is a useful condiment for adding punchy flavour to a meal.

Classic Tomato Salsa

A classic Mexican salsa, full of fiery flavour. Use three chillies for a milder taste, up to six if you like it hot.

Serves 6
3–6 fresh serrano chillies
1 large white onion, finely chopped
grated (shredded) rind and juice of 2 limes, plus pared lime rind, to garnish
8 ripe, firm tomatoes
large bunch of fresh coriander (cilantro), chopped finely
1.5ml/¼ tsp caster (superfine) sugar
salt

1 To peel the chillies, spear them on a long-handled metal skewer and roast them over the flame of a gas burner until the skins blister and darken. Do not let the flesh burn. Alternatively, dry fry them in a griddle pan until the skins are scorched.

2 Place the roasted chillies in a strong plastic bag and tie the top of the bag. Set aside for about 20 minutes. Meanwhile, put the onion in a bowl with the lime rind and juice. The lime juice will soften the onion.

3 Remove the chillies from the bag and peel off the skins. Cut off the stalks, then slit the chillies and scrape out the seeds. Chop the flesh roughly and set aside.

4 Make a cut in the top of the tomatoes, then plunge into boiling water for 30 seconds. Refresh in cold water. Remove the skins completely. Dice the tomato flesh and put in a bowl.

5 Add the softened onion and lime juice mixture to the tomatoes, together with the coriander, chillies and the sugar. Mix gently until the sugar has dissolved. Cover and chill for 2–3 hours to allow the flavours to blend. Garnish with lime to serve.

> **Variation**
> Use spring onions (scallions) instead of white onion. For a smoky flavour use chipotle chillies instead of serrano chillies.

Classic tomato salsa: Energy 45kcal/190kJ; Protein 2.2g; Carbohydrate 8.2g, of which sugars 7g; Fat 0.7g, of which saturates 0.1g; Cholesterol 0mg; Calcium 43mg; Fibre 2.3g; Sodium 16mg
Fragrant roasted tomato salsa: Energy 22kcal/95kJ; Protein 1.2g; Carbohydrate 3.7g, of which sugars 3.4g; Fat 0.4g, of which saturates 0.1g; Cholesterol 0mg; Calcium 28mg; Fibre 1.4g; Sodium 11mg

Smoky Tomato Salsa

The smoky flavour in this recipe comes from the smoked bacon and the barbecue marinade. Served with sour cream, this salsa makes a great baked potato filler.

45ml/3 tbsp chopped fresh
  coriander (cilantro) or
  parsley leaves
1 garlic clove, finely chopped
15ml/1 tbsp smoky (barbecue)
  marinade
juice of 1 lime
salt and ground black pepper

Serves 4
450g/1lb tomatoes
4 rindless smoked streaky (fatty)
  bacon rashers (strips)
15ml/1 tbsp vegetable oil

1 Make a cut in the top of the tomatoes, then plunge into boiling water for 30 seconds. Refresh in cold water, then remove the skins. Halve the tomatoes, scoop out and discard the seeds, then finely dice the flesh.

2 Cut the smoked bacon into small pieces. Heat the oil in a frying pan and cook the bacon for 5 minutes, stirring occasionally, until crisp and browned. Remove from the heat and drain on kitchen paper. Leave to cool for a few minutes, then place in a mixing bowl.

3 Add the finely diced tomatoes and the chopped fresh coriander or parsley to the bowl. Stir in the finely chopped garlic, then add the liquid smoke and freshly squeezed lime juice. Season the salsa with salt and pepper to taste and mix well, using a wooden spoon or plastic spatula.

4 Spoon the smoky salsa into a serving bowl, cover with clear film (plastic wrap) and chill until ready to serve.

Variation
Give this smoky salsa an extra kick by adding a dash of Tabasco sauce or a pinch of dried chilli flakes.

Fresh Tomato & Tarragon Salsa

Plum tomatoes, garlic, olive oil and balsamic vinegar make for a very Mediterranean salsa – try serving this with grilled lamb cutlets or toss it with freshly cooked pasta.

Serves 4
8 plum tomatoes, or 500g/1¼lb
  sweet cherry tomatoes

60ml/4 tbsp olive oil or
  sunflower oil
15ml/1 tbsp balsamic vinegar
30ml/2 tbsp chopped fresh
  tarragon, plus extra shredded
  leaves, to garnish
1 small garlic clove, finely
  chopped or crushed
salt and ground black pepper

1 Make a cut in the top of the tomatoes, then plunge into boiling water for 30 seconds. Remove with a slotted spoon and refresh in cold water.

2 Slip off the tomato skins. Halve the tomatoes, scoop out and discard the seeds, then finely dice the flesh.

3 Whisk together the oil and balsamic vinegar with plenty of salt and pepper. Add the chopped fresh tarragon to the dressing and whisk to mix.

4 Mix the tomatoes and garlic in a bowl and pour the tarragon dressing over. Stand for 1 hour to allow the flavours to blend, before serving at room temperature. Garnish with coarsely chopped tarragon.

Cook's Tip
Be sure to serve this salsa at room temperature as the tomatoes taste less sweet, and rather acidic, when chilled.

Variation
Use a finely chopped red onion instead of the garlic. Stand the onion in some lime juice to soften before adding to the salsa.

Smoky tomato salsa: Energy 99kcal/412kJ; Protein 5g; Carbohydrate 3.6g, of which sugars 3.6g; Fat 7.3g, of which saturates 2g; Cholesterol 13mg; Calcium 17mg; Fibre 1.3g; Sodium 396mg
Fresh tomato & tarragon salsa: Energy 124kcal/512kJ; Protein 1.2g; Carbohydrate 4.2g, of which sugars 4.1g; Fat 11.5g, of which saturates 1.7g; Cholesterol 0mg; Calcium 29mg; Fibre 1.8g; Sodium 15mg

Orange, Tomato & Chive Salsa

Fresh chives and sweet oranges provide a very cheerful combination of flavours. This fruity salsa is very good served alongside other salads.

Serves 4

2 large, sweet oranges
1 beefsteak tomato, or
   2 plum tomatoes
bunch of fresh chives
1 garlic clove
30ml/2 tbsp extra-virgin olive oil
   or grapeseed oil
sea salt

1 Slice the base off 1 orange so that it will stand firmly on a chopping board. Using a large sharp knife, remove the peel by slicing from the top to the bottom of the orange. Repeat with the second orange.

2 Working over a bowl to catch the juice, cut the segments away from the membranes in each orange: slice towards the middle of the fruit, and slightly to one side of a segment, and then gently twist the knife to release the orange segment. Squeeze any juice from the remaining membrane.

3 Roughly chop the orange segments and add them to the bowl with the collected orange juice. Halve the tomato and use a teaspoon to scoop the seeds into the bowl. With a sharp knife, finely dice the tomato flesh and add to the oranges and juice in the bowl.

4 Hold the bunch of chives neatly together and use a pair of kitchen scissors to snip them into the bowl.

5 Thinly slice the garlic and stir it into the orange mixture. Pour the olive oil over the salad, season with sea salt and stir well to mix. Serve the salsa within 2 hours.

Variation
Add a sprinkling of chopped pistachios or toasted pine nuts.

Fiery Salsa

This is a scorchingly hot salsa for only the very brave! Spread it sparingly on to cooked meats and burgers or add a tiny amount to a curry or pot of chilli.

Serves 4–6

6 Scotch bonnet chillies
2 ripe tomatoes
4 standard green jalapeño chillies
30ml/2 tbsp chopped fresh
   parsley
30ml/2 tbsp olive oil
15ml/1 tbsp balsamic vinegar or
   sherry vinegar
salt

1 Skin the Scotch bonnet chillies, either by holding them in a gas flame for 3 minutes until the skin blackens and blisters, or by plunging them into boiling water. Then, using rubber gloves, rub off the skin from the chilli.

2 Hold each tomato in a gas flame for 3 minutes until the skin starts to come away, or plunge them into a bowl of boiling water. Remove the skins, halve the tomatoes, and remove the seeds. Chop the flesh very finely.

3 Try not to touch the Scotch bonnet chillies with your bare hands: use a fork to hold them and slice them open with a knife. Scrape out and discard the seeds. Finely chop the flesh.

4 Halve the jalapeño chillies, remove their seeds and finely slice them widthways into tiny strips. Mix both types of chillies, the tomatoes and the chopped parsley in a bowl.

5 In a small bowl, whisk the olive oil with the vinegar and a little salt. Pour this over the salsa and cover the dish. Chill before serving. The salsa will store for up to 3 days in the refrigerator.

Cook's Tip
If you have to touch the chillies with your hands, wear protective gloves. Do not touch your eyes when handling chillies.

Orange, tomato & chive salsa: Energy 91kcal/380kJ; Protein 1.3g; Carbohydrate 9.3g, of which sugars 9.3g; Fat 5.7g, of which saturates 0.8g; Cholesterol 0mg; Calcium 49mg; Fibre 2g; Sodium 7mg
Fiery salsa: Energy 42kcal/173kJ; Protein 0.7g; Carbohydrate 1.1g, of which sugars 1g; Fat 3.9g, of which saturates 0.6g; Cholesterol 0mg; Calcium 21mg; Fibre 0.7g; Sodium 6mg

Bloody Mary Salsa

Serve this perfect party salsa with sticks of crunchy celery or fingers of cucumber or, on a really special occasion, with freshly shucked oysters.

Serves 2
4 ripe tomatoes
1 celery stick
1 garlic clove

2 spring onions (scallions)
45ml/3 tbsp tomato juice
Worcestershire sauce, to taste
Tabasco sauce, to taste
10ml/2 tsp horseradish sauce
15ml/1 tbsp vodka
1 lemon
salt and ground black pepper

1 Halve the tomatoes, celery and garlic. Trim the spring onions.

2 Put the tomatoes, celery, garlic and spring onions in a blender or food processor. Process until finely chopped, then transfer the vegetable mixture to a serving bowl.

3 Stir in the tomato juice, a little at a time, then add a few drops of Worcestershire sauce and Tabasco sauce to taste. Mix well and set aside for 10–15 minutes.

4 Stir in the horseradish sauce and vodka. Squeeze the lemon and stir the juice into the salsa. Add salt and pepper to taste. Serve immediately, or cover and chill for 1–2 hours.

Cook's Tip
This is based on the famous Bloody Mary cocktail. To make the drink, mix 1 measure of vodka to 2 of tomato juice, with a dash of Tabasco and Worcestershire sauce, lemon juice and ice.

Variation
Blend 1–2 chopped, seeded, fresh red chillies with the tomatoes, instead of stirring in the Tabasco sauce.

Grilled Corn-on-the-Cob Salsa

This is an unusual salsa, made with deliciously sweet vegetables. Use cherry tomatoes for an extra special flavour, and combine with the ripest and freshest corn on the cob.

Serves 4
2 corn on the cob
30ml/2 tbsp melted butter
4 tomatoes
8 spring onions (scallions)
1 garlic clove, crushed
30ml/2 tbsp fresh lemon juice
30ml/2 tbsp olive oil
Tabasco sauce, to taste
salt and ground black pepper

1 Remove the husks and silky threads covering the corn on the cob. Brush the cobs with the melted butter and gently cook on the barbecue or grill (broil) them for 20–30 minutes, turning occasionally, until tender and tinged brown.

2 To remove the kernels, stand each cob upright on a chopping board and use a large, heavy knife to slice down the length of the cob and scrape off the kernels.

3 Make a cut in the top of the tomatoes, then plunge into boiling water for 30 seconds. Refresh in cold water, then slip off the skins and dice the tomato flesh.

4 Place 6 spring onions on a chopping board and chop finely. Mix with the garlic, corn and tomato in a small bowl.

5 Stir the lemon juice and olive oil together, adding Tabasco sauce, salt and pepper to taste. Pour this mixture over the salsa and stir well. Cover the salsa and leave at room temperature for 1–2 hours before serving, to allow the flavours to blend. Garnish with the remaining spring onions.

Cook's Tip
Make this colourful salsa in summer when fresh, ripe cobs of corn are readily available in the shops.

Bloody mary salsa: Energy 58kcal/243kJ; Protein 1.6g; Carbohydrate 6.9g, of which sugars 6.7g; Fat 1g, of which saturates 0.3g; Cholesterol 1mg; Calcium 23mg; Fibre 2.2g; Sodium 88mg
Grilled corn on the cob salsa: Energy 249kcal/1044kJ; Protein 4.1g; Carbohydrate 30.4g, of which sugars 13.3g; Fat 13.3g, of which saturates 5g; Cholesterol 16mg; Calcium 20mg; Fibre 2.7g; Sodium 326mg

Pinto Bean Salsa

The beans give this authentic Mexican salsa a pretty, speckled look. The smoky flavour of the chipotle chillies and the herby taste of the pasilla chilli contrast well with the tart tomatillos. Unusually, these are not cooked.

Serves 4

130g/4½ oz/generous ½ cup
    pinto beans, soaked overnight
    in water to cover
2 chipotle chillies
1 pasilla chilli
2 garlic cloves, peeled
½ onion
200g/7oz fresh tomatillos
salt

1 Drain the beans and put them in a large pan. Pour in water to cover and place the lid on the pan. Bring to the boil, lower the heat slightly and simmer the beans for 45–50 minutes or until tender. They should still have a little bite and should not have begun to disintegrate.

2 Drain, rinse under cold water, then drain again and turn into a bowl. Leave the beans until cold.

3 Soak the chipotle and pasilla chillies in hot water for about 10 minutes until softened. Drain, reserving the soaking water. Remove the stalks, then slit each chilli and scrape out the seeds with a small sharp knife. Chop the flesh finely and mix it to a smooth paste with a little of the soaking water.

4 Roast the garlic in a dry frying pan over a medium heat for a few minutes until the cloves starts to turn golden. Crush them, then add to the beans.

5 Chop the onion and tomatillos and stir into the beans. Add the chilli paste and mix well. Add salt to taste, cover and chill.

Cook's Tip
Canned tomatillos can be used, but to keep a clean, fresh flavour add a little lime juice.

Black Bean Salsa

This salsa has a very striking appearance with its black colouring. Leave the salad for a day or two after making to allow the flavours to develop fully.

Serves 4

130g/4½ oz/generous ½ cup
    black beans, soaked overnight
    in water to cover
1 pasado chilli
2 fresh red fresno chillies
1 red onion, finely chopped
grated (shredded) rind and juice
    of 1 lime
30ml/2 tbsp Mexican beer
15ml/1 tbsp olive oil
1 small bunch fresh coriander
    (cilantro), chopped
salt

1 Drain the beans and put them in a large pan. Pour in water to cover and place the lid on the pan. Bring to the boil, lower the heat slightly and simmer the beans for about 40 minutes or until tender. They should still have a little bite and should not have begun to disintegrate.

2 Drain, rinse under cold water, then drain again and leave the beans until cold.

3 Soak the pasado chilli in hot water for about 10 minutes until softened. Drain, remove the stalk, then slit the chilli and scrape out the seeds with a small sharp knife. Chop the flesh finely.

4 Spear the fresno chillies on a long-handled metal skewer and roast them over the flame of a gas burner until the skins blister and darken. Do not let the flesh burn. Alternatively, dry-fry them in a griddle pan until the skins are scorched. Then place the roasted chillies in a strong plastic bag and tie the top to keep the steam in. Set aside for 20 minutes.

5 Remove the chillies from the bag and peel off the skins. Slit them, remove the seeds and chop them finely.

6 Transfer the beans to a bowl and add the onion and both types of chilli. Stir in the lime rind and juice, beer, oil and coriander. Season with salt and mix well. Chill before serving.

Pinto bean salsa: Energy 105kcal/448kJ; Protein 8.5g; Carbohydrate 17.3g, of which sugars 3.4g; Fat 0.8g, of which saturates 0.1g; Cholesterol 0mg; Calcium 47mg; Fibre 5.8g; Sodium 13mg
Black bean salsa: Energy 126kcal/533kJ; Protein 8.5g; Carbohydrate 15.8g, of which sugars 1.9g; Fat 3.5g, of which saturates 0.5g; Cholesterol 0mg; Calcium 48mg; Fibre 5.3g; Sodium 10mg

Mexican Nopales Salsa

Nopales are the fleshy leaves of an edible cactus. Fresh nopales are hard to find outside Mexico, so look out for the canned version.

Serves 4
2 fresh red chillies
250g/9oz nopales (cactus paddles)
3 spring onions (scallions)
3 garlic cloves, peeled
1/2 red onion, chopped finely
100g/3 1/2 oz fresh tomatillos, chopped finely
2.5ml/1/2 tsp salt
150ml/1/4 pint/2/3 cup cider vinegar

1 Spear the chillies on a long-handled metal skewer and roast them over the flame of a gas burner (or under the grill) until the skins blister and darken. Do not let the flesh burn. Place the roasted chillies in a strong plastic bag and tie the top.

2 After 20 minutes, remove the chillies from the bag and peel off the skins. Cut off the stalks, then slit the chillies and scrape out the seeds. Chop the chillies roughly and set them aside.

3 Carefully remove the thorns from the nopales. Wearing gloves or holding each cactus paddle in turn with kitchen tongs, cut off the bumps that contain the thorns with a sharp knife.

4 Cut off and discard the thick base from each cactus paddle. Rinse the paddles well and cut them into strips then cut the strips into small pieces.

5 Bring a large pan of lightly salted water to the boil. Add the cactus strips, spring onions and garlic. Boil for 10–15 minutes, until the cactus is just tender. Drain the mixture, rinse under cold running water to remove any remaining stickiness, then drain again. Discard the spring onions and garlic.

6 Place the red onion and tomatillos in a bowl and add the cactus and chillies. Spoon into a large preserving jar, add the salt, pour in the vinegar and seal. Chill for at least 1 day, turning the jar occasionally to ensure that the nopales are marinated. The salsa will keep in the refrigerator for up to 10 days.

Sweet Potato Salsa

Eye-catchingly colourful and delightfully sweet, this delicious salsa makes the perfect accompaniment to hot, spicy Mexican dishes.

Serves 4
675g/1 1/2lb sweet potatoes
juice of 1 small orange
5ml/1 tsp crushed dried jalapeño chillies
4 small spring onions (scallions)
juice of 1 small lime (optional)
salt

1 Peel the sweet potatoes and dice the flesh finely. Bring a pan of water to the boil. Add the sweet potato and cook for 8–10 minutes, until just soft.

2 Drain off the cooking water from the sweet potato, cover the pan and put it back on the hob, having first turned off the heat. Leave the sweet potato for about 5 minutes to dry out, then transfer to a bowl and set aside.

3 Mix the orange juice and crushed dried chillies in a bowl. Chop the spring onions finely and add them to the orange juice and chilli mixture.

4 When the sweet potato is cool, add the orange juice mixture and toss carefully until all the pieces are coated.

5 Cover the bowl and chill for at least 1 hour, then taste and season with salt. Stir in the lime juice if you prefer a fresher taste to the salsa.

Cook's Tips
• This fresh and tasty salsa is also very good served with a simple grilled salmon fillet or other fish dishes, and makes a delicious accompaniment to veal escalopes or grilled chicken.
• The salsa will keep for 2–3 days in a covered bowl in the refrigerator. Leaving the salsa to stand in this way will also help the flavours to develop.

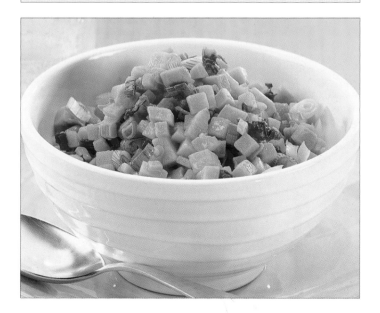

Mexican nopales salsa: Energy 16kcal/67kJ; Protein 0.8g; Carbohydrate 2.8g, of which sugars 2.4g; Fat 0.3g, of which saturates 0g; Cholesterol 0mg; Calcium 34mg; Fibre 1.3g; Sodium 41mg
Sweet potato salsa: Energy 153kcal/653kJ; Protein 2.4g; Carbohydrate 36.7g, of which sugars 9.9g; Fat 0.7g, of which saturates 0.2g; Cholesterol 0mg; Calcium 47mg; Fibre 4.2g; Sodium 69mg

Jicama Salsa

The jicama from Mexico, makes an unusual salsa with a delicious texture. Look out for this root vegetable in ethnic food stores.

Serves 4

1 small red onion
juice of 2 limes
3 small oranges
1 jicama, about 450g/1lb
1/2 cucumber
1 fresh red fresno chilli

1 Cut the onion in half, then slice each half finely. Place in a bowl, add the lime juice and leave to soak while you prepare the remaining ingredients.

2 Slice the top and bottom off each orange. Stand an orange on a board, then carefully slice off all the peel and pith. Hold the orange over a bowl and cut carefully between the membranes so that the segments fall into the bowl. Having cut out all the segments, squeeze the pulp over the bowl to extract the remaining juice.

3 Peel the jicama and rinse it in cold water. Cut it into quarters, then slice finely. Add to the bowl of orange juice.

4 Cut the unpeeled cucumber in half lengthwise, then use a teaspoon to scoop out the seeds. Slice the cucumber and add to the bowl. Remove the stalk from the chilli, slit it open and scrape out the seeds with a small sharp knife. Chop the flesh finely and add to the bowl.

5 Add the sliced onion to the bowl, with any remaining lime juice, and mix well. Cover and leave to stand at room temperature for at least 1 hour before serving. If not serving immediately, chill in the refrigerator for up to 3 days.

Cook's Tip
The jicama is a round, brown root vegetable with a texture somewhere between that of water chestnut and crisp apple. It can be eaten raw or cooked, and is always peeled.

Chayote Salsa

You can't get more Mexican than this salsa. The main ingredient, chayote – or vegetable pear as it is sometimes called – tastes rather like cucumber and makes a refreshing salsa. The contrast between the crisp chayote, cool melon and hot habañero sauce is stunning.

Serves 6

1 chayote, about 200g/7oz
1/2 small Galia melon
10ml/2 tsp habañero sauce or similar hot chilli sauce
juice of 1 lime
2.5ml/1/2 tsp salt
2.5ml/1/2 tsp sugar

1 Peel the chayote, then cut slices of flesh away from the stone. Cut the slices into thin strips. Cut the melon in half, scoop the seeds out, and cut each half into two pieces. Remove the skin and cut the flesh into small cubes. Place in a bowl with the chayote strips.

2 Mix the chilli sauce, lime juice, salt and sugar in a bowl. Stir until all the sugar has dissolved. Pour over the melon and chayote mixture and mix thoroughly. Chill for at least 1 hour before serving, or keep for up to 3 days in the refrigerator.

Cook's Tip
The chayote is a gourd-like fruit, shaped like a large pear. Several varieties grow in Mexico, the most common being white-fleshed and smooth-skinned, with a taste reminiscent of cucumber. Chayotes should be peeled before being eaten raw or cooked. The seed, which looks rather like a large, flat almond, is edible. In some countries, chayotes are called christophenes or choko. They are also used in Chinese cooking, so will be found in Oriental stores.

Variation
For extra colour, add finely diced red (bell) pepper or tomato.

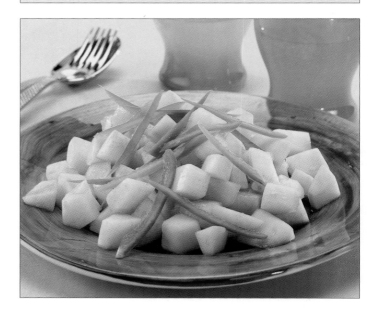

Jicama salsa: Energy 53kcal/224kJ; Protein 2g; Carbohydrate 11.1g, of which sugars 10.7g; Fat 0.4g, of which saturates 0g; Cholesterol 0mg; Calcium 102mg; Fibre 3.3g; Sodium 74mg
Chayote salsa: Energy 24kcal/102kJ; Protein 0.6g; Carbohydrate 5.4g, of which sugars 5.4g; Fat 0.2g, of which saturates 0g; Cholesterol 0mg; Calcium 25mg; Fibre 0.7g; Sodium 210mg

Onion Relish

This fiery side dish from Mexico is particularly good served with chicken, turkey or fish dishes.

Makes 1 small jar
2 fresh red fresno chillies
5ml/1 tsp allspice berries
2.5ml/½ tsp black peppercorns
5ml/1 tsp dried oregano
2 white onions
2 garlic cloves, peeled
100ml/3½fl oz/⅓ cup white wine vinegar
200ml/7fl oz/scant 1 cup cider vinegar
salt

1 Spear the fresno chillies on a long-handled metal skewer and roast them over the flame of a gas burner until the skins blister. Do not let the flesh burn. Alternatively, dry-fry them in a griddle pan until the skins are scorched. Place the roasted chillies in a strong plastic bag and tie the top. Set aside for 20 minutes.

2 Meanwhile, place the allspice, black peppercorns and oregano in a mortar or food processor. Grind slowly by hand with a pestle or process until coarsely ground.

3 Cut the onions in half and slice them thinly. Put them in a bowl. Dry roast the garlic in a heavy-based frying pan until golden, then crush and add to the onions in the bowl.

4 Remove the chillies from the bag and peel off the skins. Slit the chillies, scrape out the seeds, then chop them.

5 Add the ground spices to the onion mixture, followed by the chillies. Stir in both vinegars. Add salt to taste and mix thoroughly. Cover the bowl and chill in the refrigerator for at least 1 day before serving.

Cook's Tip
White onions have a pungent flavour and are good in this salsa. Spanish onions can also be used. Shallots also make an excellent pickle.

Chilli Strips with Lime

This fresh, tangy relish is ideal for serving with stews, rice dishes or bean dishes. The oregano adds a sweet note and the absence of sugar or oil makes this a very healthy choice.

Makes about 60ml/4 tbsp
10 fresh green chillies
½ white onion
4 limes
2.5ml/½ tsp dried oregano
salt

1 Roast the chillies in a griddle pan over a medium heat until the skins are charred and blistered. The flesh should not be allowed to blacken as this might make the salsa bitter. Place the roasted chillies in a strong plastic bag and tie the top to keep the steam in. Set aside for 20 minutes.

2 Meanwhile, slice the onion very thinly and put it in a large bowl. Squeeze the limes over a sieve (strainer) and add the juice to the bowl, with any pulp that gathers in the sieve. The lime juice will soften the onion. Stir in the oregano.

3 Remove the chillies from the bag and peel off the skins. Slit them, scrape out the seeds with a small sharp knife, then cut the chillies into long strips, which are called "rajas".

4 Add the chilli strips to the onion mixture and season with salt. Cover the bowl and chill for at least 1 day before serving, to allow the flavours to develop.

Cook's Tips
• This method of roasting chillies in a griddle pan is ideal if you need more than one or two chillies, or if you do not have a gas burner. If you prefer to roast the chillies over a burner, spear the chillies, four or five at a time, on a long-handled metal skewer and hold them over the flame until the skins begin to blister. Take care not to let them burn.
• This salsa will keep for up to 2 weeks in a covered bowl in the refrigerator. Use to add fiery flavour to a meal.

Onion relish: Energy 173kcal/721kJ; Protein 6.3g; Carbohydrate 35.1g, of which sugars 22.4g; Fat 2.1g, of which saturates 0.2g; Cholesterol 0mg; Calcium 118mg; Fibre 5.6g; Sodium 15mg
Chilli strips with lime: Energy 49kcal/204kJ; Protein 3.9g; Carbohydrate 7g, of which sugars 5.7g; Fat 0.7g, of which saturates 0g; Cholesterol 0mg; Calcium 52mg; Fibre 0.9g; Sodium 10mg

Quick-pickled Red Onions with Dill, Coriander & Juniper

Mild red onions are best for this quick pickle, which is based on a traditional Mexican method of pickling onions that was popularized by American cook Deborah Maddison. The pickle will keep in a covered jar in the refrigerator for up to one week, and is just the thing for adding a burst of flavour to a bland dish.

Serves 6

500g/1¼lb red onions, thinly sliced
250ml/8fl oz/1 cup rice wine vinegar or tarragon vinegar
5ml/1 tsp salt
15ml/1 tbsp caster (superfine) sugar
6 juniper berries, lightly crushed
30ml/2 tbsp chopped fresh dill
15ml/1 tbsp coriander seeds, bruised

1 Place the onions in a large bowl and pour over sufficient boiling water to cover. Immediately turn the onions into a colander, then set aside and allow to drain completely. Return the onions to the dried bowl.

2 In another bowl, mix together the vinegar, salt, sugar, juniper berries and chopped dill.

3 Heat the coriander seeds in a dry frying pan until they give off their aroma. Add the the toasted seeds to the vinegar mixture and stir. Pour the spiced vinegar over the onions, toss to mix, then leave to stand at room temperature for 1 hour. Drain before serving.

Variation
To make quick Mexican red onions, blanch 1 large sliced red onion, then toss with 5ml/1 tsp sugar and 105ml/7 tbsp lime juice or rice wine vinegar and a little finely chopped red or green chilli. Leave for 2–3 hours before draining, then season and serve. These onions are very good drained, then tossed with thinly sliced salted cucumber.

Tsatziki

Cool, creamy and refreshing, tzatziki is wonderfully easy to make and even easier to eat. Serve this classic Greek dip with toasted pitta bread as part of a salad spread, or with chargrilled vegetables.

Serves 4

1 mini cucumber, topped and tailed
4 spring onions (scallions)
1 garlic clove
200ml/7fl oz/scant 1 cup Greek (US strained plain) yogurt
45ml/3 tbsp chopped fresh mint
salt and ground black pepper
fresh mint sprig, to garnish
toasted pitta bread, to serve

1 Cut the cucumber into 5mm/¼in dice. Chop the spring onions and garlic very finely.

2 Beat the yogurt in a bowl until smooth, if necessary, then gently stir in the cucumber, spring onions, garlic and mint.

3 Add salt and plenty of ground black pepper to taste, then transfer the mixture to a serving bowl. Cover and chill in the refrigerator until ready to serve. Garnish with a mint sprig and serve with pitta bread.

Cook's Tip
Choose Greek-style (US strained plain) yogurt for this dip – it has a higher fat content than most yogurts, which gives the dish a deliciously rich, creamy texture.

Variation
A similar, but smoother, dip can be made in the food processor. Peel one mini cucumber and process with two garlic cloves and 75g/3oz/3 cups mixed fresh herbs to a purée. Stir the purée into 200ml/7fl oz/scant 1 cup soured cream and season to taste with salt and pepper.

Quick-pickled red onions: Energy 50kcal/209kJ; Protein 1.6g; Carbohydrate 10.3g, of which sugars 7.5g; Fat 0.6g, of which saturates 0.1g; Cholesterol 0mg; Calcium 43mg; Fibre 1.6g; Sodium 6mg
Tsatziki: Energy 67kcal/279kJ; Protein 4g; Carbohydrate 2.3g, of which sugars 1.6g; Fat 5.3g, of which saturates 2.6g; Cholesterol 0mg; Calcium 107mg; Fibre 0.3g; Sodium 39mg

Aromatic Guacamole

Guacamole is often served as a first course with corn chips for dipping. This chunky version is a great accompaniment for grilled fish, poultry or meat, especially steak.

Serves 4

2 large ripe avocados
1 small red onion, very finely chopped
1 red or green chilli, seeded and very finely chopped
½–1 garlic clove, crushed with a little salt (see Cook's Tip)
finely grated (shredded) rind of ½ lime and juice of 1–1½ limes
pinch of sugar
225g/8oz tomatoes, seeded and chopped
30ml/2 tbsp roughly chopped fresh coriander (cilantro)
2.5–5ml/½–1 tsp ground toasted cumin seeds
15ml/1 tbsp olive oil
15–30ml/1–2 tbsp sour cream (optional)
salt and ground black pepper
lime wedges dipped in sea salt, and fresh coriander (cilantro) sprigs, to garnish

1 Cut 1 avocado in half and remove the stone (pit). Scrape the flesh from both halves into a bowl and mash roughly with a fork.

2 Stir in the onion, chilli, garlic, lime rind, sugar, tomatoes and coriander. Add the ground cumin and season with salt and pepper to taste, then stir in the olive oil.

3 Halve and stone (pit) the remaining avocado. Dice the flesh and stir it into the guacamole.

4 Squeeze in fresh lime juice to taste, mix well, then cover and leave to stand for 15 minutes so that the flavour develops. Stir in the soured cream, if using. Serve with lime wedges dipped in sea salt, and fresh coriander sprigs.

Cook's Tip
To crush garlic, place a peeled clove on a chopping board and chop it roughly. Sprinkle over a little sea salt and, using the flat side of a large knife blade, gradually work the salt into the garlic.

Onion, Mango & Peanut Chaat

Chaats are spiced relishes of vegetables and nuts served with Indian meals. Amchoor (mango powder) adds a deliciously fruity sourness to this mixture of onions and mango.

Serves 4

90g/3½oz/scant 1 cup unsalted peanuts
15ml/1 tbsp peanut oil
1 onion, chopped
10cm/4in piece cucumber, seeded and cut into 5mm/¼in dice
1 mango, peeled, stoned (pitted) and diced
1 green chilli, seeded and chopped
30ml/2 tbsp chopped fresh coriander (cilantro)
15ml/1 tbsp chopped fresh mint
15ml/1 tbsp lime juice
pinch of light muscovado (brown) sugar

For the chaat masala
10ml/2 tsp ground toasted cumin seeds
2.5ml/½ tsp cayenne pepper
5ml/1 tsp mango powder (amchoor)
2.5ml/½ tsp garam masala
pinch of ground asafoetida
salt and ground black pepper

1 To make the chaat masala, grind all the spices together, then season with 2.5ml/½ tsp each of salt and pepper.

2 Fry the peanuts in the oil until lightly browned, then drain on kitchen paper until cool.

3 Put the onion in a mixing bowl with the cucumber, mango, chilli, fresh coriander and mint. Sprinkle in 5ml/1 tsp of the chaat masala. Stir in the peanuts and then add lime juice and/or sugar to taste. Set the mixture aside for 20–30 minutes for the flavours to develop.

4 Turn the mixture into a serving bowl, sprinkle another 5ml/ 1 tsp of the chaat masala over and serve.

Cook's Tip
Any remaining chaat masala can be put in a sealed jar and kept for 4–6 weeks.

Aromatic guacamole: Energy 182kcal/752kJ; Protein 2.4g; Carbohydrate 4.7g, of which sugars 3.3g; Fat 17.1g, of which saturates 3.5g; Cholesterol 0mg; Calcium 41mg; Fibre 4g; Sodium 14mg
Onion, mango & peanut chaat: Energy 189kcal/788kJ; Protein 6.9g; Carbohydrate 9.8g, of which sugars 6.6g; Fat 14g, of which saturates 2.4g; Cholesterol 0mg; Calcium 41mg; Fibre 2.4g; Sodium 4mg

Coconut Chutney with Onion & Chilli

Serve this exotic chutney as an accompaniment for Indian-style dishes or with a raita and other chutneys and poppadums as an interesting start to a meal.

Serves 4–6
200g/7oz fresh coconut, grated (shredded)
3–4 green chillies, seeded and chopped
20g/³⁄₄oz fresh coriander (cilantro), chopped
30ml/2 tbsp chopped fresh mint
30–45ml/2–3 tbsp lime juice
about 2.5ml/¹⁄₂ tsp salt
about 2.5ml/¹⁄₂ tsp caster (superfine) sugar
15–30ml/1–2 tbsp coconut milk (optional)
30ml/2 tbsp groundnut oil
5ml/1 tsp kalonji
1 small onion, very finely chopped
fresh coriander (cilantro) sprigs, to garnish

1 Place the coconut, chillies, coriander and mint in a food processor. Add 30ml/2 tbsp of the lime juice, then process until thoroughly chopped.

2 Scrape the mixture into a bowl and add more lime juice to taste. Add salt and sugar to taste. If the mixture is dry, stir in 15–30ml/1–2 tbsp coconut milk.

3 Heat the groundnut oil in a small pan and fry the kalonji until they begin to pop, then reduce the heat and add the onion. Fry, stirring frequently, for 4–5 minutes, until the onion softens but does not brown.

4 Stir the onion mixture into the coconut mixture and leave to cool. Garnish with coriander before serving.

> **Cook's Tips**
> • Kalonji are small black seeds which have a slightly bitter, yet pleasant, taste. They are fried to release their flavour.
> • Add more chillies if you prefer a chutney with a hotter flavour.

Green Vegetable Salad with Coconut Mint Dip

This is traditionally served with Malaysian meat dishes.

Serves 4–6
115g/4oz mangetouts (snow peas), halved
115g/4oz green beans, halved
¹⁄₂ cucumber, peeled, halved and sliced
115g/4oz Chinese leaves (Chinese cabbage), roughly shredded
115g/4oz beansprouts
salt

For the dressing
1 garlic clove, crushed
1 small fresh green chilli, seeded and finely chopped
10ml/2 tsp sugar
45ml/3 tbsp creamed coconut
75ml/5 tbsp boiling water
10ml/2 tsp fish sauce
45ml/3 tbsp vegetable oil
juice of 1 lime
30ml/2 tbsp chopped fresh mint

1 Bring a pan of lightly salted water to the boil. Blanch the mangetouts, green beans, beansprouts and cucumber for 4 minutes. Drain, refresh under cold water and drain again.

2 To make the dressing, pound the garlic, chilli and sugar together in a mortar with a pestle. Add the creamed coconut, water, fish sauce, vegetable oil, lime juice and mint. Stir well.

3 Arrange the blanched vegetables, Chinese leaves and beansprouts on a bed of lettuce in a basket. Pour the dressing into a shallow bowl and serve immediately.

> **Cook's Tip**
> Creamed coconut is sold in blocks from most supermarkets.

> **Variation**
> Vary the vegetables as you like – carrot sticks and red (bell) pepper strips would make a colourful addition.

Coconut chutney: Energy 145kcal/596kJ; Protein 1.6g; Carbohydrate 2.8g, of which sugars 2.5g; Fat 14.2g, of which saturates 9.3g; Cholesterol 0mg; Calcium 40mg; Fibre 3.3g; Sodium 11mg
Green vegetable salad: Energy 128kcal/530kJ; Protein 2.4g; Carbohydrate 5.2g, of which sugars 4.5g; Fat 11g, of which saturates 5.2g; Cholesterol 0mg; Calcium 31mg; Fibre 1.4g; Sodium 124mg

Plantain & Green Banana Salad

Beansprout & Mooli Salad

The plantains and bananas are cooked in their skins to keep their soft texture. They then absorb all the flavour of the dressing.

Serves 4
2 firm yellow plantains
3 green bananas

1 garlic clove, crushed
1 red onion
15–30ml/1–2 tbsp chopped fresh coriander (cilantro)
45ml/3 tbsp sunflower oil
25ml/1½ tbsp malt vinegar
salt and ground black pepper

1 Slit the plantains and bananas lengthwise along their natural ridges, then cut in half and place in a large pan.

2 Cover the plantains and bananas with water, add a little salt and bring to the boil. Boil gently for 20 minutes, until tender, then remove from the water. When they are cool enough to handle, peel and cut into medium-size slices.

3 Put the plantain and banana slices into a bowl and add the garlic, turning them with a wooden spoon to distribute the garlic evenly.

4 Halve the onion and slice thinly. Add to the bowl with the coriander, oil, vinegar and seasoning. Toss together to mix, then transfer to a serving bowl.

Ribbon-thin slices of fresh, crisp vegetables mixed with beansprouts make the perfect foil for an unusual Oriental dressing.

Serves 4
225g/8oz/1 cup beansprouts
1 cucumber
2 carrots
1 small Mooli (daikon) radish
1 small red onion, thinly sliced
2.5cm/1in fresh root ginger, peeled and cut into thin matchsticks

1 small red chilli, seeded and thinly sliced
handful of fresh coriander (cilantro) or mint leaves

For the Oriental dressing
15ml/1 tbsp rice wine vinegar
15ml/1 tbsp light soy sauce
15ml/1 tbsp Thai fish sauce
1 garlic clove, finely chopped
15ml/1 tbsp sesame oil
45ml/3 tbsp groundnut oil
30ml/2 tbsp sesame seeds, lightly toasted

1 To make the dressing, place all the dressing ingredients in a screw-top jar and shake well.

2 Wash the beansprouts and drain thoroughly in a colander.

3 Peel the cucumber, cut in half lengthwise and scoop out the seeds. Peel the cucumber flesh into long ribbon strips using a potato peeler.

4 Peel the carrots and radish into long strips in the same way as the cucumber.

5 Put the beansprouts in a shallow serving dish and add the carrots, radish and cucumber strips. Add the red onion, ginger, chilli and coriander or mint leaves and toss to mix. Pour the dressing over the salad just before serving.

Cook's Tip
The dressing can be made in advance. It will keep well for a couple of days if stored in the refrigerator or a cool place.

Plantain & green banana salad: Energy 242kcal/1019kJ; Protein 2.2g; Carbohydrate 40.9g, of which sugars 21g; Fat 8.9g, of which saturates 1.2g; Cholesterol 0mg; Calcium 35mg; Fibre 2.5g; Sodium 8mg
Beansprout & daikon salad: Energy 176kcal/728kJ; Protein 3.8g; Carbohydrate 6.7g, of which sugars 5.2g; Fat 15.1g, of which saturates 1.6g; Cholesterol 0mg; Calcium 82mg; Fibre 2.6g; Sodium 371mg

Lotus Stem Salad with Shallots & Shredded Fresh Basil

In this exotic Vietnamese-style salad, lotus stems absorb the flavours of the dressing while retaining a crunchy texture.

Serves 4

½ cucumber
225g/8oz jar preserved lotus stems, drained and cut into 5cm/2in strips
2 shallots, finely sliced
25g/1oz/½ cup fresh basil leaves, shredded
fresh coriander (cilantro) leaves, to garnish

For the dressing
juice of 1 lime
15–30ml/1–2 tbsp nuoc mam
1 red Thai chilli, seeded and finely chopped
1 garlic clove, crushed
15ml/1 tbsp sugar

1 To make the dressing, mix together the dressing ingredients in a bowl and set aside.

2 Peel the cucumber and cut it into thin 5cm/2in strips. Soak the strips in cold salted water for 20 minutes.

3 Put the lotus stems into a bowl of water. Using a pair of chopsticks, stir the water constantly so that the loose fibres of the stems wrap around the sticks. Drain the stems and put them in a bowl.

4 Drain the cucumber strips and add them to the bowl, then add the shallots, shredded basil leaves and the prepared dressing. Leave the salad to marinate for 20 minutes before serving. Garnish with fresh coriander leaves.

Cook's Tip
You may be lucky enough to find fresh lotus stems in an Asian market, but the ones preserved in brine are perfectly adequate for this recipe. Fresh lotus roots can also be used: peel and soak in water with a little lemon juice before adding to the salad.

Sweet-and-sour Cucumber with Chillies, Coriander & Mint

Cucumbers are sliced and dressed Thai-style with lime and herbs to make a delightful accompaniment to meat, poultry and seafood dishes. This salad is also a great addition to a summer barbecue or salad table.

Serves 4–6

2 cucumbers
30ml/2 tbsp sugar
100ml/3½fl oz/scant ½ cup rice wine vinegar
juice of half a lime
1–2 green Thai chillies, seeded and finely sliced
2 shallots, halved and finely sliced
1 small bunch each fresh coriander (cilantro) and mint, stalks removed, leaves roughly chopped
salt

1 Use a vegetable peeler to remove strips of the cucumber peel. Halve the cucumber lengthwise and cut into slices. Place the slices on a plate and sprinkle with a little salt. Leave to stand for 15 minutes, then rinse and drain.

2 In a bowl, mix the sugar with the vinegar until it has dissolved, then stir in the lime juice and a little salt to taste.

3 Add the chillies, shallots, herbs and cucumber to the dressing and leave to stand for 15–20 minutes before serving.

Lotus stem salad: Energy 43Kcal/181kJ; Protein 1g Carbohydrate 9g, of which sugars 6g; Fat 0g, of which saturates 0g; Cholesterol 0mg; Calcium 0mg; Fibre 0.5mg; Sodium 0.3g
Sweet-and-sour cucumber: Energy 59Kcal/248kJ; Protein 2g; Carbohydrate 12g, of which sugars 11g Fat 0g, of which saturates 0g; Cholesterol 0mg; Cacium 63mg; Fibre 0.8g; Sodium 0.2g

Sweet & Sour Salad

Acar Bening makes a perfect accompaniment to a variety of spicy dishes and curries, with its clean taste and bright, jewel-like colours. The pomegranate seeds, although not traditional, make a beautiful garnish. This is an essential dish for a buffet party.

Serves 8

1 small cucumber
1 onion, thinly sliced
1 small, ripe pineapple or 425g/15oz can pineapple rings
1 green (bell) pepper, seeded and thinly sliced
3 firm tomatoes, chopped
30ml/2 tbsp golden sugar
45–60ml/3–4 tbsp white wine vinegar
120ml/4fl oz/½ cup water
salt
seeds of 1–2 pomegranates, to garnish

1 Halve the cucumber lengthwise, remove the seeds, slice and spread on a plate with the onion. Sprinkle with salt. After 10 minutes, rinse with cold running water and pat dry.

2 If using a fresh pineapple, peel and core it, removing all the eyes, then cut it into bitesize pieces. If using canned pineapple, drain the rings and cut them into small wedges. Place the pineapple in a bowl with the cucumber, onion, green pepper and tomatoes.

3 Heat the sugar, vinegar and measured water in a pan, stirring until the sugar has dissolved. Remove the pan from the heat and leave to cool. When cold, add a little salt to taste and pour over the fruit and vegetables. Cover and chill until required. Serve in small bowls, garnished with pomegranate seeds.

> **Variation**
> *To make an Indonesian-style cucumber salad, salt a salad cucumber as described in the recipe. Make half the dressing and pour it over the cucumber. Add a few chopped spring onions (scallions). Cover and chill. Serve with toasted sesame seeds.*

Green Mango Salad

This exotic salad is delicious served with stir-fried prawns or seared beef. Green mangoes have dark green skins and light green flesh.

Serves 4

450g/1lb green mangoes
rind and juice of 2 limes
30ml/2 tbsp sugar
30ml/2 tbsp nuoc mam
2 green Thai chillies, seeded and finely sliced
1 small bunch fresh coriander (cilantro), stalks removed, finely chopped
salt

1 Peel, halve and stone (pit) the mango, then slice into thin strips.

2 In a bowl, mix together the lime juice and rind, sugar and nuoc mam. Add the mango strips with the chillies and coriander. Add salt to taste and leave to stand for 20 minutes to allow the flavours to mingle before serving.

Vietnamese Table Salad

Simple and attractive, this arranged salad makes a delightful accompaniment to lightly spiced finger food.

Serves 4–6

1 crunchy lettuce, leaves separated
½ cucumber, peeled and thinly sliced
1–2 carrots, finely sliced
200g/7oz/scant 1 cup beansprouts
1–2 unripe star fruit, finely sliced
1–2 green bananas, finely sliced
1 firm papaya, halved, seeded, peeled and finely sliced
1 bunch each fresh mint and basil, stalks removed
juice of 1 lime

1 Arrange the all the salad ingredients attractively on a plate, with the lettuce leaves on one side to use as wrappers.

2 Squeeze the lime juice over the fruits, particularly the bananas to help them retain their colour, and place the salad in the middle of the table.

Sweet & sour salad: Energy 38kcal/161kJ; Protein 0.9g; Carbohydrate 8.4g, of which sugars 8.1g; Fat 0.3g, of which saturates 0.1g; Cholesterol 0mg; Calcium 18mg; Fibre 1.5g; Sodium 6mg
Green mango salad: Energy 92kcal/391kJ; Protein 1g; Carbohydrate 22g, of which sugars 15g; Fat 0g, of which saturates 0g; Cholesterol 0mg; Calcium 32mg; Fibre 33g; Sodium 0.5mg
Vietnamese table salad: Energy 108kcal/455kJ; Protein 4g; Carbohydrate 21g, of which sugars 12g; Fat 1g, of which saturates 0g; Cholesterol 0mg; Calcium 110mg; Fibre 42g; Sodium 0.02mg

Sautéed Herb Salad with Chilli & Preserved Lemon

Firm-leafed fresh herbs, such as flat leaf parsley and mint tossed in a little olive oil and seasoned with salt, are fabulous to serve as a salad in a mezze spread or go wonderfully with spicy kebabs or tagines. Lightly sautéed with garlic and served warm with yogurt, this dish is delightful even on its own.

Serves 4
1 large bunch flat leaf parsley
1 large bunch fresh mint
1 large bunch fresh coriander (cilantro)
1 bunch rocket (arugula)
1 large bunch spinach leaves (about 115g/4oz)
60–75ml/4–5 tbsp olive oil
2 garlic cloves, finely chopped
1 green or red chilli, seeded and finely chopped
1/2 preserved lemon, finely chopped
salt and ground black pepper
45–60ml/3–4 tbsp Greek (US strained plain) yogurt, to serve

1 Roughly chop the herbs, rocket and spinach. Set aside.

2 Heat the olive oil in a wide, heavy pan. Stir in the garlic and chilli and fry until they begin to colour.

3 Toss in the herbs, rocket and spinach and cook gently, until they begin to soften and wilt.

4 Add the preserved lemon and season with salt and black pepper to taste.

5 Transfer the salad to a serving dish and serve warm with a dollop of yogurt.

> **Cook's Tip**
> *This is also good topped with garlic-flavoured yogurt. Simply stir a crushed garlic clove into the yogurt and season to taste.*

Simple Cooked Salad

This version of a popular Mediterranean recipe is a versatile side dish.

Serves 4
2 well-flavoured tomatoes, quartered
2 onions, chopped
1/2 cucumber, halved lengthwise, seeded and sliced
1 green (bell) pepper, halved, seeded and chopped
60ml/4 tbsp water

For the dressing
30ml/2 tbsp lemon juice
45ml/3 tbsp olive oil
2 garlic cloves, crushed
30ml/2 tbsp chopped fresh coriander (cilantro)
salt and ground black pepper

1 Put the prepared tomatoes, onions, cucumber and green pepper into a large pan. Add the water and simmer for 5 minutes. Leave to cool.

2 To make the dressing, whisk together the lemon juice, olive oil and garlic in a bowl.

3 Strain the vegetables, then transfer to a serving bowl. Pour the dressing over the salad, season with salt and pepper to taste and stir in the chopped coriander. Garnish with coriander sprigs and serve immediately.

Sautéed herb salad: Energy 157kcal/647kJ; Protein 2.9g; Carbohydrate 1.6g, of which sugars 1.5g; Fat 15.6g, of which saturates 2.6g; Cholesterol 0mg; Calcium 135mg; Fibre 2.1g; Sodium 70mg
Simple cooked salad: Energy 131kcal/540kJ; Protein 2.2g; Carbohydrate 11g, of which sugars 9.1g; Fat 8.9g, of which saturates 1.3g; Cholesterol 0mg; Calcium 55mg; Fibre 3g; Sodium 14mg

Leek & Egg Salad

Smooth-textured leeks are especially delicious warm when partnered with an earthy-rich sauce of parsley, olive oil and walnuts. Serve as a side salad with plainly-grilled or poached fish and new potatoes.

Serves 4

675g/1½lb young leeks
1 egg
fresh parsley sprigs, to garnish

For the dressing

25g/1oz fresh parsley
30ml/2 tbsp olive oil
juice of ½ lemon
50g/2oz/½ cup shelled, broken
    walnuts, toasted
5ml/1 tsp caster (superfine) sugar
salt and ground black pepper

1 Bring a pan of salted water to the boil. Cut the leeks into 10cm/4in lengths and rinse well to flush out any grit or soil. Cook the leeks for 8 minutes. Drain and part-cool under running water.

2 Lower the egg into boiling water and cook for 12 minutes. Cool under cold running water, shell and set aside.

3 To make the dressing, finely chop the parsley in a food processor. Add the olive oil, lemon juice and toasted walnuts. Blend for 1–2 minutes, until smooth.

4 Adjust the consistency with about 90 ml/6 tbsp water. Add the sugar and season to taste with salt and pepper.

5 Place the leeks on an serving plate, then spoon on the sauce. Finely grate (shred) the hard-boiled egg and scatter over the sauce. Garnish with the fresh parsley sprigs and serve while the leeks are still warm.

Cook's Tip
Toast walnuts in a dry non-stick pan (skillet).

Braised Artichokes with Fresh Peas

This artichoke dish has a unique delicacy. Shelling fresh peas is a little time-consuming but their matchless flavour makes the task very worthwhile. Sit on a step outside in the sunshine, and what at first seems a chore will be positively therapeutic.

Serves 4

4 globe artichokes
juice of 1½ lemons
150ml/ ¼ pint/⅔ cup
    extra-virgin olive oil
1 onion, thinly sliced
4–5 spring onions (scallions),
    roughly chopped
2 carrots, sliced in rounds
1.2kg/2½lb fresh peas in pods,
    shelled (this will give you about
    500–675g/1¼–1½lb peas)
450ml/¾ pint/scant 2 cups
    hot water
60ml/4 tbsp finely chopped
    fresh dill
salt and ground black pepper

1 To prepare the artichokes, trim the stalks of the artichokes close to the base, cut the very tips off the leaves and then divide them into quarters. Remove the inedible hairy choke (the central part), carefully scraping the hairs away from the heart at the base of the artichoke. Drop them into a bowl of water acidulated with about one-third of the lemon juice.

2 Heat the olive oil in a wide, shallow pan and add the onion and spring onions, and then a minute later, add the carrots. Sauté the mixture, stirring constantly, for a few seconds, then add the peas and stir for 1–2 minutes to coat them in the oil.

3 Pour in the remaining lemon juice. Let it bubble and evaporate for a few seconds, then add the hot water and bring to the boil. Drain the artichokes and add them to the pan, with salt and pepper to taste. Cover and cook gently for about 40–45 minutes, stirring occasionally.

4 Add the dill and cook for a further 5 minutes, or until the vegetables are tender. Serve hot or at room temperature.

Leek & egg salad: Energy 197kcal/817kJ; Protein 6.3g; Carbohydrate 6.5g, of which sugars 5.2g; Fat 16.4g, of which saturates 2.1g; Cholesterol 48mg; Calcium 73mg; Fibre 4.5g; Sodium 24mg
Braised artichokes with fresh peas: Energy 363kcal/1499kJ; Protein 10.3g; Carbohydrate 20.1g, of which sugars 8.3g; Fat 27.5g, of which saturates 4g; Cholesterol 0mg; Calcium 121mg; Fibre 9.2g; Sodium 91mg

Spinach & Roast Garlic Salad

Don't worry about the amount of garlic in this salad. During roasting, the garlic becomes sweet and subtle and loses its strong, pungent taste.

Serves 4
12 garlic cloves, unpeeled
60ml/4 tbsp extra-virgin olive oil
450g/1lb baby spinach leaves
50g/2oz/½ cup pine nuts,
    lightly toasted
juice of ½ lemon
salt and ground black pepper

1 Preheat the oven to 190°C/375°F/Gas 5. Place the garlic in a small roasting pan, toss in 30ml/2 tbsp of the olive oil and roast for about 15 minutes, until the garlic cloves are slightly charred around the edges.

2 While still warm, transfer the garlic to a salad bowl. Add the spinach, pine nuts, lemon juice, remaining olive oil and a little salt. Toss well and add black pepper to taste. Serve immediately, inviting guests to squeeze the softened garlic purée out of the skin to eat.

Cook's Tip
The spinach leaves need to be young and tender. Packs of baby spinach are sold in the salad sections of supermarkets.

Winter Vegetable Salad

This simple side salad is made with leeks, cauliflower and celery, flavoured with wine, herbs and juniper.

Serves 4
450g/1lb leeks
175ml/6fl oz/¾ cup white wine
5ml/1 tsp olive oil
30ml/2 tbsp lemon juice
2 bay leaves
1 fresh thyme sprig
4 juniper berries
1 small cauliflower, broken
    into florets
4 celery sticks, sliced on
    the diagonal
30ml/2 tbsp chopped
    fresh parsley
salt and ground black pepper

1 Trim the thick green leaves from the leeks and trim off the roots. Rinse well and cut into 2.5cm/1in lengths.

2 Put the wine, olive oil, lemon juice, bay leaves, thyme and juniper berries into a large, heavy-based pan and bring to the boil. Cover and leave to simmer for 20 minutes.

3 Add the leeks, cauliflower and celery. Simmer very gently for 5–6 minutes, or until just tender.

4 Remove the vegetables with a slotted spoon and transfer them to a serving dish. Briskly boil the cooking liquid until reduced by half. Pass through a sieve (strainer).

5 Stir the parsley into the liquid and season with salt and pepper to taste. Pour over the vegetables and leave to cool slightly. Serve at room temperature.

Cook's Tip
Do not overcook the cauliflower; it should have a bit of bite.

Variation
Vary the vegetables for this salad according to the season.

Radicchio, Artichoke & Walnut Salad

The distinctive, earthy taste of Jerusalem artichokes makes a lovely contrast to the sharp freshness of radicchio and lemon. Serve warm or cold as an accompaniment to grilled steak or meats.

Serves 4

1 large radicchio or 150g/5oz
    radicchio leaves
40g/1½oz/⅓ cup walnut pieces
45ml/3 tbsp walnut oil
thinly pared rind and juice
    of 1 lemon
500g/1¼lb Jerusalem artichokes
coarse sea salt and ground
    black pepper
fresh flat leaf parsley, to garnish

1 If using a whole radicchio, cut it into 8–10 wedges. Put the wedges or leaves in a flameproof dish. Scatter over the walnuts, then spoon over the walnut oil and season with salt and pepper. Grill (broil) for 2–3 minutes.

2 Fill a pan with cold water and add half the lemon juice. Using a small, sharp knife, peel the artichokes and cut up any large ones so that the pieces are all roughly the same size. Add them to the pan of acidulated water as you work.

3 Add a pinch of salt to the pan of artichokes, then bring to the boil and cook for 5–7 minutes until tender. Drain. Preheat the grill (broiler) to high.

4 Toss the artichokes into the salad with the remaining lemon juice and the pared rind. Season with coarse salt and pepper. Grill until beginning to brown. Serve garnished with torn parsley.

Cook's Tip
Jerusalem artichokes discolour very quickly once they have been peeled. Dropping them into water acidulated with a little lemon juice helps to prevent this.

Radicchio & Chicory Gratin

Creamy béchamel sauce, with its delicate flavour, is the perfect foil for these bitter-tasting salad leaves. Serve with grilled meat for a satisfying meal.

Serves 4
2 heads radicchio, quartered
    lengthwise
2 heads chicory (Belgian endive),
    quartered lengthwise

25g/1oz/½ cup drained
    sun-dried tomatoes in oil,
    coarsely chopped
25g/1oz/2 tbsp butter
15g/½oz/2 tbsp plain
    (all-purpose) flour
250ml/8fl oz/1 cup milk
pinch of freshly grated nutmeg
50g/2oz/½ cup grated
    Emmenthal cheese
salt and ground black pepper
chopped fresh parsley, to garnish

1 Preheat the oven to 180°C/350°F/Gas 4. Grease a 1.2 litre/ 2 pint/5 cup ovenproof dish and arrange the quartered radicchio and chicory in it.

2 Sprinkle over the sun-dried tomatoes and brush the vegetables with oil from the jar. Sprinkle with salt and pepper and cover the dish with foil. Bake for 15 minutes, then remove the foil and bake for a further 10 minutes.

3 To make the sauce, melt the butter in a small pan, stir in the flour and cook for 1 minute, stirring. Remove from the heat and gradually add the milk, whisking all the time. Return to the heat and bring to the boil, then simmer for about 3 minutes, stirring, to thicken. Season to taste and add the nutmeg.

4 Pour the sauce over the vegetables and sprinkle with the cheese. Bake for 20 minutes until golden. Garnish with parsley.

Cook's Tip
In Italy, radicchio and chicory are often cooked on a grill. To do this, prepare the vegetables as above and brush with olive oil. Place cut-side down on the grill for 7–10 minutes, until browned. Turn and cook the other side.

Radicchio, artichoke & walnut salad: Energy 179kcal/739kJ; Protein 2.7g; Carbohydrate 7.3g, of which sugars 7.1g; Fat 15.7g, of which saturates 1.4g; Cholesterol 0mg; Calcium 87mg; Fibre 3.1g; Sodium 21mg
Radicchio and chicory gratin: Energy 175kcal/728kJ; Protein 6.9g; Carbohydrate 9g, of which sugars 5.1g; Fat 12.9g, of which saturates 6.5g; Cholesterol 26mg; Calcium 219mg; Fibre 1.5g; Sodium 193mg

Grilled Fennel Salad

This is so typically Italian that if you close your eyes you could be on a Tuscan hillside, enjoying an elegant lunch. Fennel has many fans, but is often used only in its raw state or lightly braised, making this griddle recipe a delightful discovery.

Serves 6

3 sweet baby orange
(bell) peppers

5 fennel bulbs with green tops,
about 900g/2lb total weight
30ml/2 tbsp olive oil
15ml/1 tbsp cider or white wine
vinegar
45ml/3 tbsp extra-virgin olive oil
24 small niçoise olives
2 long sprigs of fresh savory,
leaves removed
salt and ground black pepper

1 Heat a griddle until a few drops of water sprinkled onto the surface evaporate instantly. Roast the baby peppers, turning them every few minutes until charred all over. Remove the pan from the heat, place the peppers in a bowl and cover with clear film (plastic wrap).

2 Remove the green fronds from the fennel and reserve. Slice the fennel lengthwise into five roughly equal pieces. If the root looks a little tough, cut it out. Place the fennel pieces in a flat dish, coat with the olive oil and season with salt and pepper. Rub off the charred skin from the grilled peppers, remove the seeds and cut the flesh into small dice.

3 Re-heat the griddle and test the temperature again, then lower the heat slightly and grill the fennel slices in batches for about 8–10 minutes, turning frequently, until they are branded with golden grill marks. Monitor the heat so they cook through without over charring. As each batch cooks, transfer it to a flat serving dish.

4 Whisk the vinegar and extra-virgin olive oil together, then pour over the fennel. Gently fold in the diced baby orange peppers and the niçoise olives. Tear the savory leaves and fennel fronds and scatter over the salad. Serve warm.

Globe Artichokes with Beans & Aïoli

Make the most of fresh artichokes when in season by serving them with a squeeze of lemon and this delicious Spanish garlic and mayonnaise dressing.

Serves 3
225g/8oz green beans
3 small globe artichokes

15ml/1 tbsp olive oil
pared rind of 1 lemon
coarse salt, for sprinkling
lemon wedges, to garnish

For the aïoli
6 large garlic cloves, thinly sliced
10ml/2 tsp white wine vinegar
250ml/8fl oz/1 cup olive oil
salt and ground black pepper

1 To make the aïoli, put the garlic and vinegar in a food processor or blender. With the motor running, slowly pour in the olive oil through the lid or feeder tube until the mixture is quite thick and smooth. Season with salt and pepper to taste.

2 To make the salad, cook the green beans in lightly salted boiling water for 1–2 minutes until slightly softened. Drain well.

3 Trim the artichoke stalks close to the base. Cook the artichokes in a large pan of salted water for about 30 minutes, or until you can easily pull away a leaf from the base. Drain. Cut the artichokes in half lengthwise and carefully scrape out the hairy choke using a teaspoon.

4 Arrange the artichokes and beans on serving plates and drizzle with the olive oil. Sprinkle the lemon rind over them and season to taste with coarse salt and a little pepper. Spoon the aïoli into the artichoke hearts and serve the salad warm, garnished with lemon wedges.

5 To eat the artichokes, squeeze a little lemon juice over them, then pull the leaves from the base one at a time and use to scoop a little of the aïoli sauce. Gently scrape away the white, fleshy end of each leaf with your teeth and discard the rest of the leaf. Eat the base of the artichoke with a knife and fork.

Grilled fennel salad: Energy 139kcal/574kJ; Protein 2.4g; Carbohydrate 8.7g, of which sugars 8.3g; Fat 10.8g, of which saturates 1.6g; Cholesterol 0mg; Calcium 49mg; Fibre 5.3g; Sodium 208mg
Globe artichokes with beans & aïoli: Energy 540kcal/2221kJ; Protein 2.1g; Carbohydrate 3.6g, of which sugars 2.9g; Fat 57.6g, of which saturates 8.2g; Cholesterol 0mg; Calcium 82mg; Fibre 3.1g; Sodium 80mg

Beetroot & Potato Salad

A brightly coloured salad with a lovely texture. The sweetness of the beetroot contrasts perfectly with the tangy dressing. Ideal with a selection of cold meats.

Serves 4

4 medium beetroot (beet)
4 potatoes, peeled and diced
1 red onion, finely chopped
150ml/¼ pint/⅔ cup natural (plain) yogurt
10ml/2 tsp cider vinegar
2 small sweet and sour cucumbers, finely chopped
10ml/2 tsp creamed horseradish
salt and ground black pepper
parsley sprigs, to garnish

1 Trim the leafy stalks of the beetroot down to about 2.5cm/1in of the root. Wash the beetroot but do not peel. Boil the unpeeled beetroot in a large pan of water for 40 minutes or until tender.

2 Meanwhile, boil the diced potatoes in a separate pan for 20 minutes until just tender.

3 When the beetroot are cooked, rinse and remove the skins. Chop into rough pieces and place in a bowl. Drain the potatoes and add to the bowl, together with the onions.

4 Mix the yogurt, vinegar, cucumbers and horseradish. Reserve a little for a garnish and pour the remainder over the salad. Toss and serve with parsley sprigs and remaining dressing.

Cook's Tip
If you are short of time, buy vacuum-packed ready-cooked and peeled beetroot, available in most supermarkets.

Variation
Add toasted chopped hazelnuts to the yogurt dressing.

Asparagus with Egg & Lemon Sauce

Eggs and lemons are often found in dishes from Greece, Turkey and the Middle East. This sauce has a tangy, fresh taste and brings out the best in asparagus.

Serves 4

675g/1½lb asparagus, woody ends removed, and tied into a bundle
15ml/1 tbsp cornflour (cornstarch)
10ml/2 tsp sugar
2 egg yolks
juice of 1½ lemons
salt

1 Cook the bundle of asparagus in boiling salted water for 7–10 minutes until just tender.

2 Drain well, reserving 200ml/7fl oz/scant 1 cup of the cooking liquid. Arrange the asparagus spears in a serving dish.

3 Blend the cornflour with the cooled, reserved cooking liquid in a small pan. Bring to the boil, stirring constantly, and cook over a gentle heat until the sauce thickens slightly. Stir in the sugar, then remove from the heat and allow to cool slightly.

4 Beat the egg yolks thoroughly with the lemon juice and gradually stir into the cooled sauce. Cook over a very low heat, stirring all the time, until the sauce is fairly thick. Be careful not to overheat the sauce or it may curdle. As soon as the sauce has thickened, remove the pan from the heat and continue stirring for 1 minute. Taste and add salt or sugar as necessary. Allow the sauce to cool slightly.

5 Stir the cooled sauce, then pour a little over the asparagus. Serve warm with the rest of the sauce.

Variation
This dish is also delicious served cold: chill for at least 2 hours.

Beetroot & potato salad: Energy 141kcal/597kJ; Protein 5.8g; Carbohydrate 28.8g, of which sugars 12.9g; Fat 1.2g, of which saturates 0.3g; Cholesterol 1mg; Calcium 107mg; Fibre 3.4g; Sodium 144mg
Asparagus with egg & lemon sauce: Energy 96kcal/399kJ; Protein 6.4g; Carbohydrate 9.5g, of which sugars 5.8g; Fat 3.8g, of which saturates 1g; Cholesterol 101mg; Calcium 59mg; Fibre 2.9g; Sodium 8mg

French Bean Salad

Green beans are delicious served with a simple vinaigrette dressing, but this slightly more elaborate dish turns them into something quite special.

Serves 4

450g/1lb green beans
15ml/1 tbsp olive oil
25g/1oz butter
½ garlic clove, crushed
50g/2oz/1 cup fresh white
  breadcrumbs

15ml/1 tbsp chopped
  fresh parsley
1 hard-boiled (hard-cooked) egg,
  finely chopped

For the dressing

30ml/2 tbsp olive oil
30ml/2 tbsp sunflower oil
10ml/2 tsp white wine vinegar
½ garlic clove, crushed
1.5ml/¼ tsp Dijon mustard
pinch of sugar
pinch of salt

1 Cook the green beans in boiling salted water for 5–6 minutes, until tender. Drain, refresh under cold running water and place in a serving bowl.

2 To make the dressing, mix all the ingredients thoroughly together. Pour over the beans and toss.

3 Heat the oil and butter in a non-stick pan and fry the garlic for 1 minute. Stir in the breadcrumbs and fry over a medium heat for about 3–4 minutes, until golden brown, stirring frequently.

4 Remove the pan from the heat and stir in the parsley and then the egg. Sprinkle the breadcrumb mixture over the green beans. Serve warm or at room temperature.

Variation

For a mixed bean salad, cook the green beans and dressing as above, then put the beans in a salad bowl with two finely chopped celery sticks, a few finely chopped spring onions (scallions), chopped parsley and a drained and rinsed can of red kidney beans or mixed beans. Toss in the dressing.

Green Beans with Almond Butter

A perfect accompaniment for baked or grilled oily fish.

Serves 4

350g/12oz green beans, trimmed
50g/2oz/¼ cup butter

50g/2oz/⅓ cup whole blanched
  almonds
grated (shredded) rind and juice
  of 1 unwaxed lemon
salt and ground black pepper

1 Cook the beans in a pan of salted boiling water for about 3 minutes, or until just tender. Drain well. Meanwhile, melt the butter in a large non-stick pan until foamy.

2 Add the almonds to the pan and cook, stirring occasionally, for 2–3 minutes, or until golden. Remove from the heat and toss with the beans, lemon rind and juice, and season.

Spicy Sweetcorn Salad

This brilliant, sweet-tasting salad is served warm with a spicy dressing.

Serves 4

30ml/2 tbsp vegetable oil
450g/1lb canned sweetcorn
1 gree (bell) pepper seeded
  and diced
1 small red chilli, seeded
  and diced
4 spring onions (scallions), sliced

45ml/3 tbsp chopped parsley
225g/8oz cherry tomatoes, halved
salt and ground black pepper

For the dressing

2.5ml/½ tsp sugar
30ml/2 tbsp white wine vinegar
2.5ml/½ tsp Dijon mustard
15ml/1 tbsp chopped fresh basil
15ml/1 tbsp mayonnaise
1.5ml/¼ tsp chilli sauce

1 Cook the drained sweetcorn, pepper, chilli and spring onions in the oil for 5 minutes, stirring, until softened. Transfer to a salad bowl. Stif in the parsley and the cherry tomatoes.

2 To make the dressing, whisk all the ingredients together. Pour over the sweetcorn mixture. Season with salt and pepper. Toss well to combine, then serve while the salad is still warm.

French bean salad: Energy 260kcal/1076kJ; Protein 5.2g; Carbohydrate 13.3g, of which sugars 3g; Fat 21.1g, of which saturates 5.6g; Cholesterol 61mg; Calcium 65mg; Fibre 2.8g; Sodium 151mg
Green beans with almond butter: Energy 191kcal/786kJ; Protein 4.4g; Carbohydrate 3.7g, of which sugars 2.6g; Fat 17.7g, of which saturates 7.2g; Cholesterol 27mg; Calcium 64mg; Fibre 2.9g; Sodium 78mg
Spicy sweetcorn salad: Energy 205kcal/863kJ; Protein 4.3g; Carbohydrate 32.5g, of which sugars 15.3g; Fat 7.3g, of which saturates 1.1g; Cholesterol 3mg; Calcium 39mg; Fibre 3.4g; Sodium 298mg

Brown Bean Salad

Brown beans, sometimes called *ful medames*, are available from health-food shops and Middle-Eastern grocery stores. Dried broad beans or black or red kidney beans make a good substitute.

Serves 6
350g/12oz/1½ cups dried
  brown beans
3 fresh thyme sprigs
2 bay leaves
1 onion, halved
4 garlic cloves, crushed
7.5ml/1½ tsp crushed
  cumin seeds
3 spring onions (scallions),
  finely chopped
90ml/6 tbsp chopped
  fresh parsley
20ml/4 tsp lemon juice
90ml/6 tbsp olive oil
3 hard-boiled (hard-cooked) eggs,
  roughly chopped
1 pickled cucumber,
  roughly chopped
salt and ground black pepper

1 Put the beans in a bowl with plenty of cold water and leave to soak overnight. Drain, transfer to a pan and cover with fresh water. Bring to the boil and boil rapidly for 10 minutes.

2 Reduce the heat and add the thyme, bay leaves and onion. Simmer very gently for about 1 hour, until tender. Drain and discard the herbs and onion.

3 Place the beans in a large bowl. Mix together the garlic, cumin seeds, spring onions, parsley, lemon juice and oil in a small bowl, and add a little salt and pepper. Pour over the beans and toss the ingredients lightly together.

4 Gently stir in the chopped hard-boiled eggs and pickled cucumber. Transfer the bean salad to a serving dish and serve immediately.

> **Variation**
> To ring the changes, try using crumbled feta cheese or goat's cheese instead of the hard-boiled (hard-cooked) egg.

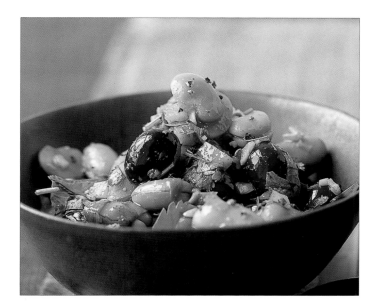

Broad Bean Salad

The Moroccan technique of marrying broad beans with preserved lemons creates a flavourful side salad.

Serves 4
2kg/4½lb broad (fava) beans
  in the pod
60–75ml/4–5 tbsp olive oil
juice of ½ lemon
2 garlic cloves, chopped
5ml/1 tsp ground cumin
10ml/2 tsp paprika
small bunch of fresh coriander
  (cilantro)
1 preserved lemon, chopped
handful of black olives, to garnish
salt and ground black pepper

1 Bring a large pan of salted water to the boil. Meanwhile, pod the broad beans. Put the shelled beans in the pan and boil for about 2 minutes.

2 Drain and refresh the beans under cold running water. Drain well. Slip off and discard the thick outer skin to reveal the smooth, bright green beans underneath.

3 Put the beans in a heavy pan and add the olive oil, lemon juice, garlic, cumin and paprika. Cook the beans gently over a low heat for about 10 minutes, then season to taste with salt and pepper and leave to cool in the pan until warm.

4 Transfer the warm beans to a serving bowl, scraping all the juices from the pan. Finely chop the fresh coriander and add to the beans with the preserved lemon. Toss together, then garnish with the black olives and serve immediately.

> **Cook's Tip**
> To make preserved lemons, scrub and quarter lemons almost through to the base, then rub the cut sides with salt. Pack tightly into a large sterilized jar. Half fill the jar with more salt, adding some bay leaves, peppercorns and cinnamon, if you like. Cover completely with lemon juice. Cover with a lid and store for 2 weeks, shaking the jar daily. Add a little olive oil to seal and use within 1–6 months, washing off the salt before use.

Broad bean salad: Energy 272kcal/1143kJ; Protein 16.6g; Carbohydrate 24.6g, of which sugars 2.9g; Fat 12.7g, of which saturates 1.8g; Cholesterol 0mg; Calcium 142mg; Fibre 13.6g; Sodium 21mg
Brown bean salad: Energy 300kcal/1258kJ; Protein 16.6g; Carbohydrate 27.1g of which sugars 2.5g; Fat 14.8g, of which saturates 2.5g; Cholesterol 95mg; Calcium 99mg; Fibre 9.9g; Sodium 50mg

Stewed Aubergine

Stewing aubergines with tomatoes, red wine and garlic really brings out the best in this delectable Mediterranean vegetable.

Serves 4
1 large aubergine (eggplant)
60–90ml/4–6 tbsp olive oil
2 shallots, thinly sliced
4 tomatoes, quartered
2 garlic cloves, thinly sliced
60ml/4 tbsp red wine
30ml/2 tbsp chopped fresh
    parsley, plus extra to garnish
30–45ml/2–3 tbsp virgin olive oil
    (if serving cold)
salt and ground black pepper

1 Slice the aubergine into 1cm/½in rounds. Layer the aubergine slices in a colander, sprinkling each layer with a little salt. Leave to drain over a sink or plate for about 20 minutes.

2 Rinse the aubergine slices well, then press between several layers of kitchen paper to remove any excess liquid.

3 Heat 30ml/2 tbsp of the oil in a large frying pan (skillet) until smoking. Add one layer of aubergine slices and fry, turning once, until golden brown. Transfer to a plate covered with kitchen paper. Heat more oil and fry the second batch in the same way.

4 Heat 15ml/1 tbsp of oil in a pan and cook the shallots for 5 minutes until golden. Cut the aubergine into strips and add to the shallots with the tomatoes, garlic and wine. Cover and simmer for 30 minutes.

5 Stir in the parsley, and check the seasonings. Sprinkle with a little more parsley and serve hot. To serve cold, dribble a little virgin olive oil over the dish before it goes on the table.

Cook's Tip
Heat the oil before adding the aubergine (eggplant) slices and do not be tempted to add more oil once the aubergines are cooking as they will absorb cold oil, resulting in a greasy dish.

Roast Mediterranean Vegetables with Pecorino

Aubergines, courgettes, peppers and tomatoes make a marvellous medley when roasted and served drizzled with fragrant olive oil. Shavings of sheep's milk Pecorino add the perfect finishing touch.

Serves 4-6
1 aubergine (eggplant), sliced
2 courgettes (zucchini), sliced
2 red or yellow (bell) peppers,
    seeded and quartered
1 large onion, thickly sliced
2 large carrots, cut into sticks
4 firm plum tomatoes, halved
extra-virgin olive oil, for brushing
    and sprinkling
45ml/3 tbsp chopped
    fresh parsley
45ml/3 tbsp pine nuts,
    lightly toasted
125g/4oz piece of
    Pecorino cheese
salt and ground black pepper

1 Layer the aubergine slices in a colander, sprinkling each layer with a little salt. Leave to drain over a sink or plate for about 20 minutes, then rinse thoroughly under cold running water, drain well and pat dry with kitchen paper. Preheat the oven to 220°C/425°F/Gas 7.

2 Spread out the aubergine slices, courgettes, peppers, onion, carrots and tomatoes in one or two large roasting pans. Brush the vegetables lightly with olive oil and roast them in the oven for about 20 minutes or until they are lightly browned and the skins on the peppers have begun to blister.

3 Transfer the vegetables to a large serving platter. If you like, peel the peppers. Trickle over any vegetable juices from the pan and season to taste with salt and pepper. As the vegetables cool, sprinkle them with more oil (preferably extra-virgin olive oil). When they are at room temperature, mix in the parsley and pine nuts.

4 Using a vegetable peeler, shave the Pecorino and scatter the shavings over the vegetables.

Stewed aubergine: Energy 135kcal/560kJ; Protein 1.4g; Carbohydrate 5.2g, of which sugars 4.7g; Fat 11.6g, of which saturates 1.7g; Cholesterol 0mg; Calcium 17mg; Fibre 2.5g; Sodium 10mg
Roast Mediterranean vegetables: Energy 202kcal/839kJ; Protein 12g; Carbohydrate 10g, of which sugars 9.3g; Fat 12.9g, of which saturates 4.8g; Cholesterol 21mg; Calcium 300mg; Fibre 4g; Sodium 244mg

Lentil Salad with Red Onion & Garlic

This delicious, garlicky lentil salad is perfect served with meaty kebabs. It can be served warm or cooled. As a finishing touch, serve it with a generous spoonful of thick, creamy yogurt.

Serves 4

45ml/3 tbsp olive oil
2 red onions, chopped
2 tomatoes, peeled, seeded and chopped
10ml/2 tsp ground turmeric
10ml/2 tsp ground cumin
175g/6oz/¾ cup brown or green lentils, picked over and rinsed
900ml/1½ pints/3¾ cups vegetable stock or water
4 garlic cloves, crushed
1 small bunch fresh coriander (cilantro), finely chopped
salt and ground black pepper
1 lemon, cut into wedges, to serve

1 Heat 30ml/2 tbsp of the oil in a large pan or flameproof casserole and fry the onions until soft.

2 Add the tomatoes, turmeric and cumin, then stir in the lentils. Pour in the stock or water and bring to the boil, then reduce the heat and simmer until the lentils are tender and almost all the liquid has been absorbed.

3 In a separate pan, fry the garlic in the remaining oil until brown and frizzled.

4 Toss the garlic into the lentils with the fresh coriander and season to taste. Serve warm or at room temperature, with wedges of lemon for squeezing over.

Cook's Tip
If you prefer, you can replace the lentils with mung beans – they work just as well. When including this type of dish in a mezze spread, it is worth balancing it with a dip such as zahdouk and a fruity salad for the different textures.

Grilled Mixed Onion Salad

This salad is brilliant served with grilled meat and fish.

Serves 4

6 red spring onions (scallions), trimmed
6 green salad onions, trimmed and split lengthwise
250g/9oz small or baby (pearl) onions, peeled and left whole
2 pink onions, sliced horizontally into 5mm/4in rounds
2 red onions, sliced
into wedges
2 small yellow onions, sliced into wedges
4 banana shallots, halved lengthwise
200g/7oz shallots
45ml/3 tbsp olive oil, plus extra for drizzling
juice of 1 lemon
45ml/3 tbsp chopped fresh flat leaf parsley
30ml/2 tbsp balsamic vinegar
salt and ground black pepper

1 Preheat the grill. Spread the onions and shallots in a large flat dish. Whisk the oil and lemon juice together and pour over. Turn the onions and shallots in the dressing to coat them evenly. Season to taste.

2 Put the onions and shallots on a griddle or perforated metal vegetable basket placed on the grill rack. Cook for 5–7 minutes, turning occasionally. Alternatively, cook the onions under a conventional grill (broiler).

3 Just before serving, add the parsley and gently toss to mix, then drizzle over the balsamic vinegar and extra olive oil.

Lentil salad: Energy 266kcal/1116kJ; Protein 12.5g; Carbohydrate 35.1g, of which sugars 9.2g; Fat 9.4g, of which saturates 1.4g; Cholesterol 0mg; Calcium 73mg; Fibre 4.8g; Sodium 29mg
Barbecued mixed onion salad: Energy 183kcal/762kJ; Protein 4.5g; Carbohydrate 22.6g, of which sugars 16.7g; Fat 9.1g, of which saturates 1.2g; Cholesterol 0mg; Calcium 100mg; Fibre 5g; Sodium 17mg

Roasted Beetroot with Horseradish Dressing

Fresh beetroot is enjoying a well-deserved renaissance. Roasting gives it a delicious sweet flavour, which contrasts wonderfully with this sharp, tangy dressing.

Serves 4
450g/1lb baby beetroot (beet),
   preferably with leaves
15ml/1 tbsp olive oil

For the dressing
30ml/2 tbsp lemon juice
30ml/2 tbsp mirin or saké
120ml/8 tbsp olive oil
30ml/2 tbsp creamed horseradish
salt and ground black pepper

1 Cook the unpeeled beetroot in boiling salted water for 30 minutes. Drain, add the olive oil and toss gently. Preheat the oven to 200°C/400°F/Gas 6.

2 Place the beetroot on a baking sheet and roast for about 40 minutes or until tender when pierced with a knife.

3 Meanwhile, make the dressing. Whisk together the lemon juice, mirin or saké, olive oil and horseradish until smooth and creamy. Season with salt and pepper to taste.

4 Peel the beetroot, cut it in half, place in a bowl and add the dressing. Toss gently and serve immediately.

Cook's Tips
• *This salad is probably at its best served warm, but you can make it in advance, if you wish, and serve it at room temperature. Add the dressing just before serving.*
• *Beetroot has a reputation for containing cancer-fighting compounds and is thought to enhance the immune system. It is a powerful blood-purifier and is rich in iron, vitamins C and A, and folates, which are essential for healthy cells.*

Moroccan Carrot Salad

A cumin and coriander vinaigrette lifts this carrot salad out of the ordinary. Fresh tasting and lightly spiced, it makes a lovely accompaniment for all sorts of dishes.

Serves 4–6
3–4 carrots
pinch of sugar
3–4 garlic cloves, chopped
1.5ml/¼ tsp ground cumin,
   or to taste

juice of ½ lemon
30–45ml/2–3 tbsp extra-virgin
   olive oil
15–30ml/1–2 tbsp red wine
   vinegar or fruit vinegar, such
   as raspberry
30ml/2 tbsp chopped fresh
   coriander (cilantro) leaves or
   a mixture of coriander
   and parsley
salt and ground black pepper
fresh coriander (cilantro) sprigs,
   to garnish (optional)

1 Thinly slice the carrots. Cook the carrots by either steaming or boiling in lightly salted water until they are just tender but not soft. Drain well, leave for a few moments to dry, then put them in a serving bowl.

2 Add the sugar, chopped garlic, ground cumin, lemon juice, olive oil and red wine vinegar to the carrots and toss them together. Add the chopped herbs and season with salt and pepper to taste. Serve warm, garnished with coriander sprigs, if using.

Roasted beetroot with horseradish: Energy 254kcal/1052kJ; Protein 2.1g; Carbohydrate 10g, of which sugars 9.1g; Fat 22.2g, of which saturates 3.2g; Cholesterol 1mg; Calcium 26mg; Fibre 2.3g; Sodium 143mg
Moroccan carrot salad: Energy 53kcal/220kJ; Protein 0.6g; Carbohydrate 4.2g, of which sugars 3.9g; Fat 3.9g, of which saturates 0.6g; Cholesterol 0mg; Calcium 29mg; Fibre 1.6g; Sodium 15mg

Carrot Salad

Packed with exotic spices, this colourful Middle-Eastern salad is sure to go down well. It is delicious served with a topping of tangy, garlicky yogurt.

Serves 4
450g/1lb carrots, cut into sticks
30–45ml/2–3 tbsp olive oil
juice of 1 lemon
2–3 garlic cloves, crushed
10ml/2 tsp sugar
5–10ml/1–2 tsp cumin
 seeds, roasted
5ml/1 tsp ground cinnamon
5ml/1 tsp paprika
1 small bunch fresh coriander
 (cilantro), finely chopped
1 small bunch fresh mint, finely
 chopped
salt and ground black pepper

1 Steam the carrots over boiling water for about 15 minutes, or until tender.

2 While they are still warm, toss the carrots in a serving bowl with the olive oil, lemon juice, garlic and sugar.

3 Season to taste, then add the cumin seeds, cinnamon and paprika. Finally, toss in the fresh coriander and mint, and serve warm or at room temperature.

Cook's Tip
To roast the cumin seeds, stir them in a heavy pan over a low heat until they change colour slightly and emit a warm, nutty aroma. Be careful not to burn them.

Variation
For a spiced carrot dip, put 3 grated carrots, 1 chopped onion and the grated rind and juice of 2 oranges in a pan with 15ml/1 tbsp hot curry paste. Bring to the boil, then simmer for 10 minutes until tender. Process until smooth, allow to cool. Stir in 150ml/¼ pint/⅔ cup natural (plain) yogurt. Add a handful basil, then season with lemon juice and salt and pepper. Serve.

Young Vegetables with Tarragon

The vegetables for this bright, fresh dish are just lightly cooked to bring out their different flavours. The tarragon adds a wonderful depth to the salad. Try serving as a light side dish with fish and seafood dishes.

Serves 4
5 spring onions (scallions)
50g/2oz/¼ cup butter
1 garlic clove, crushed
115g/4oz asparagus tips
115g/4oz mangetouts
 (snow peas), trimmed
115g/4oz broad (fava) beans
2 Little Gem (Bibb) lettuces
5ml/1 tsp finely chopped
 fresh tarragon
salt and ground black pepper

1 Cut the spring onions into quarters lengthwise and fry gently over a medium-low heat in half the butter with the garlic.

2 Add the asparagus tips, mangetouts and broad beans. Mix well to coat all the pieces with oil.

3 Add enough water to just cover the base of the pan, then season with salt and pepper to taste. Bring to the boil, then allow to simmer gently for a few minutes.

4 Cut the lettuce into quarters and add to the pan. Cook for 3 minutes, then remove from the heat, swirl in the remaining butter and the tarragon, season and serve.

Carrot salad: Energy 114kcal/473kJ; Protein 1.6g; Carbohydrate 13.2g, of which sugars 11.2g; Fat 6.5g, of which saturates 1g; Cholesterol 0mg; Calcium 61mg; Fibre 3.3g; Sodium 34mg
Young vegetables with tarragon: Energy 149Kcal/619kJ; Protein 4.7g; Carbohydrate 6.1g, of which sugars 3g; Fat 12g, of which saturates 7.3g; Cholesterol 29mg; calcium 55mg; Fibre 3.5g; Sodium 89mg

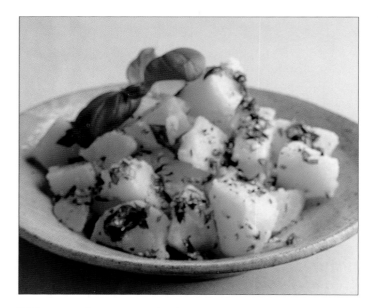

Feta & Mint Potato Salad

The oddly named pink fir apple potatoes are perfect for this salad, and taste great with feta cheese, yogurt and fresh mint. This dish goes very well with salmon and roasted chicken.

Serves 4

500g/1¼ lb pink fir
  apple potatoes
90g/3½ oz feta cheese, crumbled

For the dressing

225g/8oz/1 cup natural
  (plain) yogurt
15g/½oz/½ cup fresh
  mint leaves
30ml/2 tbsp mayonnaise
salt and ground black pepper

1 Steam the potatoes over a pan of boiling water for about 20 minutes, until tender.

2 Meanwhile, make the dressing. Mix the yogurt and mint in a food processor and pulse until the mint leaves are finely chopped. Scrape the mixture into a small bowl, stir in the mayonnaise and season to taste with salt and pepper.

3 Drain the potatoes well and transfer them to a large bowl. Spoon the dressing over the potatoes and scatter the feta cheese on top. Serve immediately.

Cook's Tip
Pink fir apple potatoes have a smooth waxy texture and retain their shape when cooked. Charlotte, Belle de Fontenay and other special salad potatoes could be used instead.

Variations
• *Crumbled Kefalotiri or young Manchego could be used instead of the feta.*
• *For a richer dressing, use Greek (US strained plain) yogurt.*

Warm Potato Salad with Herb Dressing

Toss the potatoes in the dressing as soon as possible, so the flavours are fully absorbed. Use the best olive oil for an authentic Mediterranean taste.

Serves 6

1kg/2¼lb waxy or salad potatoes
90ml/6 tbsp extra-virgin olive oil
juice of 1 lemon
1 garlic clove, very finely chopped
30ml/2 tbsp chopped fresh herbs
  such as parsley, basil or thyme
salt and ground black pepper
basil leaves, to garnish

1 Cook the potatoes in their skins in boiling salted water, or steam them until tender.

2 Meanwhile, make the dressing. Mix together the olive oil, lemon juice, garlic and herbs and season thoroughly.

3 Drain the potatoes and leave to cool slightly. When they are cool enough to handle, peel them. Cut the potatoes into chunks and place in a large bowl.

4 Pour the dressing over the potatoes while they are still warm and mix well. Serve immediately, garnished with basil leaves and ground black pepper.

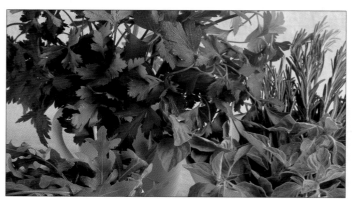

Feta & mint potato salad: Energy 229kcal/959kJ; Protein 8.7g; Carbohydrate 25g, of which sugars 6.3g; Fat 11.2g, of which saturates 4.4g; Cholesterol 22mg; Calcium 204mg; Fibre 1.3g; Sodium 419mg
Warm potato salad with herb dressing: Energy 218kcal/913kJ; Protein 3g; Carbohydrate 27g, of which sugars 2.3g; Fat 11.6g, of which saturates 1.7g; Cholesterol 0mg; Calcium 23mg; Fibre 2g; Sodium 21mg

New Potato & Quail's Egg Salad

Freshly cooked eggs and tender potatoes mix perfectly with the flavour of celery salt and the peppery-tasting rocket leaves.

Serves 6
900g/2lb new potatoes
50g/2oz/4 tbsp butter
15ml/1 tbsp snipped chives
a pinch of celery salt
a pinch of paprika
12 quail's eggs
a few rocket (arugula) leaves
salt and ground black pepper
snipped chives, to garnish

1 Boil the potatoes in a large pan of salted water for about 20 minutes or until tender.

2 Meanwhile, beat the butter and chives together with the celery salt and the paprika.

3 While the potatoes are cooking, boil the eggs for 3 minutes, then drain and plunge into a bowl of cold water. Peel the eggs under running water.

4 Arrange the rocket leaves on individual plates or a serving platter and top with the eggs.

5 Drain the potatoes and add the seasoned butter. Toss well to melt the butter and carefully spoon the potatoes onto the plates of rocket and egg. Garnish the salad with a few more snipped chives and serve immediately.

Cook's Tips
• You can buy bags of rocket, on its own, or mixed with other leaves, in many supermarkets. It is also easy to grow from seed and makes a worthwhile addition to a herb patch.
• Tiny quail's eggs are available from larger supermarkets and butchers. They make an attractive addition to any salad. If unavailable, use hen's eggs, quartered.

Warm Hazelnut & Pistachio Salad

Two kinds of crunchy nuts turn ordinary potato salad into a really special accompaniment. This would be lovely with cold sliced roast beef, tongue or ham, but you can also serve it on its own as a healthy snack.

Serves 4
900g/2lb small new or
*   salad potatoes*
30ml/2 tbsp hazelnut or
*   walnut oil*
60ml/4 tbsp sunflower oil
juice of 1 lemon
25g/1oz/¼ cup hazelnuts
15 pistachio nuts
salt and ground black pepper
flat leaf parsley sprig, to garnish

1 Cook the potatoes in their skins in boiling salted water for about 10–15 minutes until tender. Drain the potatoes well and leave to cool slightly.

2 Meanwhile, mix together the hazelnut or walnut oil with the sunflower oil and lemon juice. Season well with salt and ground black pepper.

3 Using a sharp knife, roughly chop the hazelnuts and pistachios.

4 Put the cooled potatoes in a large bowl and pour the dressing over. Toss to combine. Sprinkle the salad with the chopped nuts and serve immediately, garnished with parsley.

New potato & quail's egg salad: Energy 204kcal/855kJ; Protein 5.7g; Carbohydrate 24.2g, of which sugars 2g; Fat 10.1g, of which saturates 5.3g; Cholesterol 113mg; Calcium 25mg; Fibre 1.5g; Sodium 102mg
Warm hazelnut & pistachio salad: Energy 369kcal/1541kJ; Protein 5.4g; Carbohydrate 36.9g, of which sugars 3.4g; Fat 23.2g, of which saturates 2.6g; Cholesterol 0mg; Calcium 27mg; Fibre 2.9g; Sodium 45mg

Curried Potato Salad with Mango Dressing

This sweet and spicy salad is a wonderful accompaniment to roasted meats.

Serves 4–6
900g/2lb new potatoes
15ml/1 tbsp olive oil
1 onion, sliced into rings
1 garlic clove, crushed
5ml/1 tsp ground cumin
5ml/1 tsp ground coriander
1 mango, peeled, stoned (pitted) and diced
30ml/2 tbsp demerara (raw) sugar
30ml/2 tbsp lime juice
15ml/1 tbsp sesame seeds
salt and ground black pepper
deep fried coriander (cilantro) leaves, to garnish

1 Cut the potatoes in half, then cook them in their skins in boiling salted water until tender. Drain well.

2 Heat the oil in a frying pan (skillet) and fry the onion and garlic over a low heat for 10 minutes until they start to brown.

3 Stir in the ground cumin and coriander and fry for a few seconds. Stir in the mango and sugar and fry for 5 minutes, until soft. Remove the pan from the heat and squeeze in the lime juice. Season with salt and pepper.

4 Place the potatoes in a large bowl and spoon the mango dressing over. Sprinkle with sesame seeds and serve while the dressing is still warm. Garnish with the coriander leaves.

Cook's Tip
To prepare the mango, cut through the mango lengthwise on either side of the stone (pit) to slice off two sections. Leaving the skin on each section, cross hatch the flesh, then bend it back so that the cubes stand proud of the skin. Slice them off with a small knife. Peel the remaining central section of the mango, then cut off the remaining flesh in chunks and dice.

Warm Potato Salad with Bacon Dressing

This tasty summer salad becomes a favourite with all who try it. Use real new-season potatoes rather than all-year "baby" potatoes, if possible, and also dry-cured bacon. Using superior ingredients makes this a special dish and it's ideal for outdoor eating or a party.

Serves 4–6
900g/2lb small new potatoes
1 fresh mint sprig
15–30ml/1–2 tbsp olive oil
1 onion, chopped
175g/6oz streaky (fatty) or back (lean) bacon, diced
2 garlic cloves, crushed
30ml/2 tbsp chopped parsley
1 small bunch chives, chopped
15ml/1 tbsp wine vinegar, or cider vinegar
15ml/1 tbsp wholegrain mustard
salt and ground black pepper

1 Scrape or rub off the skins from the new potatoes, and cook in salted water with the mint for about 10 minutes, or until just tender. Drain, cool a little, then turn into a salad bowl.

2 Heat the oil in a frying pan, then add the onion and cook gently until just softening. Add the diced bacon to the pan and cook for 3–5 minutes, until beginning to crisp up.

3 Add the crushed garlic and cook for another minute or so, and then add the chopped herbs, the vinegar and mustard. Season with salt and pepper to taste, remembering that the bacon may be quite salty.

4 Pour the dressing over the potatoes. Toss gently to mix, and serve warm.

Variation
Finely chopped spring onions (scallions) can replace the chopped chives and/or chopped parsley, if you like.

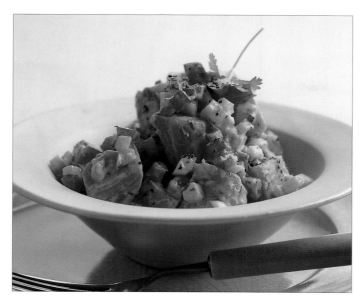

Baked Sweet Potato Salad

This salad has a truly tropical taste and is ideal served with Asian or Caribbean dishes.

Serves 4–6
1kg/2¼lb sweet potatoes
1 red (bell) pepper, seeded and
   finely diced
3 celery sticks, finely diced
¼ red onion, finely chopped
1 fresh red chilli, finely chopped
salt and ground black pepper
coriander (cilantro) leaves,
   to garnish

For the dressing
45ml/3 tbsp chopped fresh
   coriander (cilantro)
juice of 1 lime
150ml/¼ pint/⅔ cup natural
   (plain) yogurt

1 Preheat the oven to 200°C/400°F/Gas 6. Wash the potatoes, and pierce them all over with a fork. Place in the oven and bake for about 40 minutes, or until tender.

2 Meanwhile, make the dressing. Whisk together the coriander, lime juice and yogurt in a small bowl and season to taste with salt and pepper. Chill in the refrigerator while you prepare the remaining salad ingredients.

3 In a large bowl, mix the diced red pepper, celery, chopped onion and chilli together.

4 Remove the potatoes from the oven. As soon as they are cool enough to handle, peel them and cut them into cubes. Add them to the bowl. Drizzle the dressing over and toss carefully. Taste and adjust the seasoning, if necessary. Serve, garnished with coriander leaves.

Cook's Tip
It is generally thought that the seeds are the hottest part of a chilli. In fact, they contain no capsaicin – the hot element – but it is intensely concentrated in the flesh surrounding them. Removing the seeds usually removes this extra-hot flesh.

Sweet Potato & Carrot Salad

This warm salad has a sweet-and-sour taste, and lots of contrasting texture.

Serves 4
1 medium sweet potato
2 carrots, cut into thick
   diagonal slices
3 tomatoes
75g/3oz/½ cup canned
   chickpeas, drained
8–10 iceberg lettuce leaves

For the dressing
15ml/1 tbsp clear honey
90ml/6 tbsp natural (plain) yogurt
2.5ml/½ tsp salt
5ml/1 tsp ground black pepper

For the garnish
15ml/1 tbsp walnuts
15ml/1 tbsp sultanas
   (golden raisins)
1 small onion, cut into rings

1 Peel the sweet potato and cut roughly into cubes. Boil it until it is soft but not mushy, then cover the pan and set aside.

2 Boil the carrots for just a few minutes, making sure that they remain crunchy. Drain both the carrots and sweet potato and place in a mixing bowl.

3 Slice the tops off the tomatoes, then scoop out the seeds with a spoon and discard. Roughly chop the tomato flesh. Add the chickpeas and tomatoes to the sweet potato and carrots and mix gently.

4 Slice the lettuce into strips across the leaves. Line a salad bowl with the lettuce. Place the sweet potato mixture on top.

5 To make the dressing, whisk together the honey, yogurt, salt and black pepper in a small bowl. Garnish the salad with the walnuts, sultanas and onion rings, then pour the dressing over the top just before serving.

Cook's Tip
This salad also makes an excellent lunch or supper dish when served with a sweet mango chutney and warm naan bread.

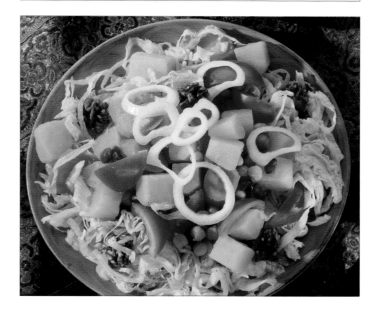

Baked sweet potato salad: Energy 176kcal/750kJ; Protein 4g; Carbohydrate 40.4g, of which sugars 14.1g; Fat 1g, of which saturates 0.3g; Cholesterol 0mg; Calcium 116mg; Fibre 5.2g; Sodium 103mg
Sweet potato & carrot salad: Energy 153kcal/648kJ; Protein 4.7g; Carbohydrate 26.7g, of which sugars 15.4g; Fat 3.9g, of which saturates 0.6g; Cholesterol 0mg; Calcium 88mg; Fibre 3.9g; Sodium 95mg

Warm Halloumi & Fennel Salad

The firm texture of halloumi cheese makes it perfect for the barbecue, as it keeps its shape very well. Combined with the delicate flavour of fennel, it makes a lovely chargrilled salad.

Serves 4
200g/7oz halloumi cheese, thickly sliced
2 fennel bulbs, trimmed and thinly sliced
30ml/2 tbsp roughly chopped fresh oregano
45ml/3 tbsp lemon-infused olive oil
salt and ground black pepper

1 Put the halloumi, fennel and oregano in a bowl and drizzle over the lemon-infused oil. Season with salt and black pepper to taste. (Halloumi is a fairly salty cheese, so be very careful when adding extra salt.)

2 Cover the bowl with clear film (plastic wrap) and chill for about 2 hours to allow the flavours to develop.

3 Place the halloumi and fennel on a griddle pan or over the barbecue, reserving the marinade, and cook for about 3 minutes on each side, until charred.

4 Divide the halloumi and fennel among four serving plates and drizzle over the reserved marinade. Serve immediately.

Halloumi & Grape Salad

Sweet, juicy grapes really complement the distinctive salty flavour of halloumi cheese in this delectable warm salad from Cyprus.

Serves 4
150g/5oz mixed green salad leaves
75g/3oz seedless green grapes
75g/3oz seedless black grapes
250g/9oz halloumi cheese
45ml/3 tbsp olive oil
fresh young thyme leaves or dill, to garnish

For the dressing
60ml/4 tbsp olive oil
15ml/1 tbsp lemon juice
2.5ml/½ tsp caster (superfine) sugar
15ml/1 tbsp chopped fresh thyme or dill
salt and ground black pepper

1 To make the dressing, mix together the olive oil, lemon juice and sugar. Season with salt and pepper to taste. Stir in the thyme or dill and set aside.

2 Toss together the salad leaves and the green and black grapes, then transfer to a large serving plate.

3 Thinly slice the cheese. Heat the oil in a large frying pan. Add the cheese and fry briefly until turning golden on the underside. Turn the cheese with a fish slice or metal spatula and cook the other side until golden.

4 Arrange the cheese on top of the salad. Pour over the dressing, garnish with thyme or dill and serve immediately.

Cook's Tips
• Most supermarkets sell ready-mixed bags of prepared salad leaves, which are ideal for use in this recipe. Experiment with various combinations to find the lettuce flavours that you like best. A mix of rocket (arugula), spinach and watercress is good. or try a mix with fresh herbs included.
• Halloumi cheese is now widely available from most large supermarkets and Greek delicatessens.

Warm halloumi & fennel salad: Energy 215kcal/889kJ; Protein 10.2g; Carbohydrate 1.8g, of which sugars 1.7g; Fat 18.6g, of which saturates 8.1g; Cholesterol 29mg; Calcium 205mg; Fibre 2.4g; Sodium 209mg
Halloumi & grape salad: Energy 365kcal/1513kJ; Protein 12.2g; Carbohydrate 7.2g, of which sugars 7.2g; Fat 32.2g, of which saturates 11.4g; Cholesterol 36mg; Calcium 250mg; Fibre 0.8g; Sodium 250mg

Cabbage Salad

This is a simple and delicious way of serving a somewhat mundane vegetable. Classic Thai flavours permeate this colourful warm salad.

Serves 4–6
30ml/2 tbsp vegetable oil
2 large fresh red chillies, seeded and cut into thin strips

6 garlic cloves, thinly sliced
6 shallots, thinly sliced
1 small cabbage, shredded
30ml/2 tbsp coarsely chopped roasted peanuts, to garnish

For the dressing
30ml/2 tbsp Thai fish sauce
grated (shredded) rind of 1 lime
30ml/2 tbsp fresh lime juice
120ml/4fl oz/½ cup coconut milk

1 To make the dressing, mix the fish sauce, lime rind and juice and coconut milk in a bowl. Whisk until thoroughly combined and set aside.

2 Heat the oil in a wok. Stir-fry the chillies, garlic and shallots over a medium heat for 3–4 minutes, until the shallots are brown and crisp. Remove with a slotted spoon and set aside.

3 Bring a large pan of lightly salted water to the boil. Add the cabbage and blanch for 2–3 minutes. Turn into a colander, drain well and transfer to a bowl.

4 Whisk the dressing again, add it to the warm cabbage and toss to mix. Transfer the salad to a serving dish. Sprinkle with the fried shallot mixture and the peanuts. Serve immediately.

Cook's Tip
Buy coconut milk in cans from supermarkets and ethnic stores.

Variation
Other vegetables, such as cauliflower, broccoli and Chinese leaves (Chinese cabbage), can be cooked in this way.

Stir-fried Pineapple with Ginger & Chilli

Throughout South-east Asia, fruit is often treated like a vegetable and tossed in a salad, or stir-fried, to accompany spicy dishes.

Serves 4
30ml/2 tbsp groundnut (peanut) oil
2 garlic cloves, finely shredded
40g/1½oz fresh root ginger, peeled and finely shredded

2 red Thai chillies, seeded and finely shredded
1 pineapple, trimmed, peeled, cored and cut into bitesize chunks
15ml/1 tbsp Thai fish sauce
30ml/2 tbsp soy sauce
15ml–30ml/1–2 tbsp sugar
30ml/2 tbsp roasted unsalted peanuts, finely chopped
1 lime, cut into quarters, to serve

1 Heat a large wok or heavy pan and add the oil. Stir in the garlic, ginger and chilli. Stir-fry until they begin to colour.

2 Add the pineapple and stir-fry until the edges turn golden.

3 Stir in the fish sauce, soy sauce and sugar to taste and continue to stir-fry until the pineapple begins to caramelize.

4 Transfer the salad to a serving dish, sprinkle with the roasted peanuts and serve with lime wedges.

Cabbage salad: Energy 798kcal/3334kJ; Protein 38.5g; Carbohydrate 131.8g, of which sugars 127.7g; Fat 14.3g, of which saturates 1.4g; Cholesterol 0mg; Calcium 1259mg; Fibre 53.7g; Sodium 461mg
Stir-fried pineapple: Energy 203kcal/844kJ; Protein 2.7g; Carbohydrate 16g, of which sugars 15.4g; Fat 14.7g, of which saturates 1.9g; Cholesterol 0mg; Calcium 31mg; Fibre 1.8g; Sodium 810mg

Thai Asparagus

This is an excitingly different way of cooking asparagus. The crunchy texture is retained and the flavour is complemented by the addition of galangal and chilli.

Serves 4

350g/12oz asparagus stalks
30ml/2 tbsp vegetable oil
1 garlic clove, crushed
15ml/1 tbsp sesame
    seeds, toasted
2.5cm/1in piece fresh galangal,
    finely shredded
1 fresh red chilli, seeded and
    finely chopped
15ml/1 tbsp Thai fish sauce
15ml/1 tbsp light soy sauce
45ml/3 tbsp water
5ml/1 tsp palm sugar (jaggery) or
    light muscovado (brown) sugar

1 Snap the asparagus stalks. They will break naturally at the junction between the woody base and the more tender portion of the stalk. Discard the woody parts of the stems.

2 Heat the vegetable oil in a wok and stir-fry the garlic, sesame seeds and galangal for 3–4 seconds, until the garlic is just beginning to turn golden.

3 Add the asparagus stalks and chilli, toss to mix, then add the fish sauce, soy sauce, water and sugar. Using two spoons, toss over the heat for a further 2 minutes, or until the asparagus just begins to soften and the liquid is reduced by half.

4 Carefully transfer to a warmed platter and serve immediately.

> **Cook's Tip**
> Galangal root belongs to the ginger family but has a more aromatic flavour. The pinkish skin has distinctive rings on it.

> **Variation**
> Try this with broccoli or pak choi (bok choy). The sauce also works very well with green beans.

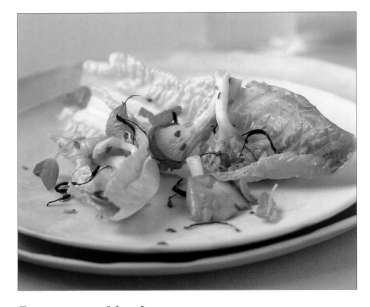

Fragrant Mushrooms in Lettuce Leaves

This quick and easy vegetable dish is served on lettuce leaf "saucers" so can be eaten with the fingers.

Serves 2

30ml/2 tbsp vegetable oil
2 garlic cloves, finely chopped
2 baby cos or romaine lettuces,
    or 2 Little Gem (Bibb) lettuces
1 lemon grass stalk,
    finely chopped
2 kaffir lime leaves, rolled in
    cylinders and thinly sliced
200g/7oz/3 cups oyster or
    chestnut mushrooms, sliced
1 small fresh red chilli, seeded
    and finely chopped
juice of ½ lemon
30ml/2 tbsp light soy sauce
5ml/1 tsp palm sugar (jaggery) or
    light muscovado (brown) sugar
1 small bunch fresh mint, leaves
    removed from the stalks

1 Heat the oil in a wok or frying pan. Add the garlic and cook over a medium heat, stirring occasionally, until golden. Do not let it burn or it will taste bitter.

2 Meanwhile, divide up the lettuces into separate, individual leaves and set aside.

3 Increase the heat under the wok or pan and add the lemon grass, lime leaves and mushrooms. Stir-fry for about 2 minutes.

4 Add the chilli, lemon juice, soy sauce and sugar to the wok or pan. Toss the mixture over the heat to combine the ingredients together, then stir-fry for a further 2 minutes.

5 Arrange the lettuce leaves on a large plate. Spoon a small amount of the mushroom mixture onto each leaf, top with a mint leaf and serve immediately.

> **Cook's Tip**
> If you can't find kaffir leaves, use freshly grated (shredded) lime rind instead.

Pak Choi with Lime Dressing

If you like your food hot and spicy, then this is the dish for you! The fiery flavours pack a punch.

Serves 4

30ml/2 tbsp oil
3 fresh red chillies, cut into thin strips
4 garlic cloves, thinly sliced
6 spring onions (scallions), sliced diagonally
2 pak choi (bok choy), shredded
15ml/1 tbsp crushed peanuts

For the dressing

30ml/2 tbsp fresh lime juice
15–30ml/1–2 tbsp Thai fish sauce
250ml/8fl oz/1 cup coconut milk

1 To make the dressing, put the lime juice and fish sauce in a bowl and mix well, then gradually whisk in the coconut milk until thoroughly combined.

2 Heat the oil in a wok and stir-fry the chillies for 2–3 minutes, until crisp. Transfer to a plate using a slotted spoon. Add the garlic to the wok and stir-fry for 30–60 seconds, until golden brown. Transfer to the plate.

3 Stir-fry the white parts of the spring onions for about 2–3 minutes, then add the green parts and stir-fry for 1 minute more. Transfer to the plate.

4 Bring a large pan of lightly salted water to the boil and add the pak choi. Stir twice, then drain immediately.

5 Place the pak choi in a large bowl, add the dressing and toss to mix. Spoon into a large serving bowl and sprinkle with the crushed peanuts and the stir-fried chilli mixture. Serve warm.

Cook's Tip

• Thai fish sauce is traditionally used for this dressing, but if you are cooking for vegetarians, mushroom sauce is a suitable vegetarian alternative.
• If pak choi is unavailable, use Chinese cabbage instead.

Thai Rice Salad

This is a lovely, soft, fluffy rice dish, perfumed with limes and fresh lemon grass.

Serves 4

2 limes
1 lemon grass stalk
225g/8oz/generous 1 cup brown long grain rice
15ml/1 tbsp olive oil
1 onion, chopped
2.5cm/1in piece fresh root ginger, peeled and finely chopped
7.5ml/1½ tsp coriander seeds
7.5ml/1½ tsp cumin seeds
750ml/1¼ pints/3 cups vegetable stock
60ml/4 tbsp chopped fresh coriander (cilantro)
spring onion (scallion) finely sliced, and toasted coconut strips, to garnish
lime wedges, to serve

1 Pare the limes using a canelle knife (zester) or a fine grater, taking care to avoid cutting the bitter pith. Set aside. Finely chop the lower portion of the lemon grass stalk and set aside.

2 Rinse the rice in plenty of cold water until the water runs clear. Turn into a sieve (strainer) and drain thoroughly.

3 Heat the olive oil in a pan. Add the onion, ginger, spices, lemon grass and lime rind and cook gently over a low heat, stirring occasionally, for about 3 minutes until the onion is soft.

4 Add the drained rice and cook. stirring constantly, for 1 minute, then pour in the stock and bring to the boil.

5 Reduce the heat to very low and cover the pan with a tight-fitting lid. Cook gently for 30 minutes, then check the rice. If it is still crunchy, re-cover and leave for 3–5 minutes more. Remove the pan from the heat when done.

6 Stir in the fresh coriander, fluff up the grains, cover the pan again and leave for about 10 minutes.

7 Transfer to a serving dish or individual bowls, garnish with spring onion and toasted coconut, and serve with lime wedges.

Pak choi with lime dressing: Energy 104kcal/434kJ; Protein 3.3g; Carbohydrate 5.2g, of which sugars 4.8g; Fat 8g, of which saturates 1.2g; Cholesterol 0mg; Calcium 116mg; Fibre 1.5g; Sodium 408mg
Thai rice salad: Energy 125kcal/523kJ; Protein 2.6g; Carbohydrate 20.9g, of which sugars 1.4g; Fat 4.1g, of which saturates 0.6g; Cholesterol 0mg; Calcium 38mg; Fibre 1.3g; Sodium 7mg

Parsley & Rocket Salad with Black Olive & Garlic Dressing

A light dish, but full of flavour, this salad is perfect for a lunchtime snack. Use the best Parmesan cheese – parmigiano reggiano – for a great taste experience.

Serves 6
1 garlic clove, halved
115g/4oz good white bread, cut into 1cm/½in thick slices
45ml/3 tbsp olive oil, plus extra for shallow frying
75g/3oz rocket (arugula) leaves
75g/3oz baby spinach

25g/1oz flat leaf parsley, stalks removed
45ml/3 tbsp salted capers, rinsed and dried
40g/1½oz Parmesan cheese, pared into shavings

For the dressing
25ml/5 tsp black olive paste
1 garlic clove, finely chopped
5ml/1 tsp Dijon mustard
75ml/5 tbsp olive oil
10ml/2 tsp balsamic vinegar
ground black pepper

1 To make the dressing, whisk the black olive paste, garlic and mustard together in a bowl. Gradually whisk in the olive oil, then the vinegar. Adjust the seasoning with black pepper – the dressing should be sufficiently salty.

2 Heat the oven to 190°C/375°F/Gas 5. Rub the halved garlic clove over the bread and cut or tear the slices into bitesize croûtons. Toss them in the oil and place on a small baking tray. Bake for 10–15 minutes, stirring once, until golden brown. Cool on kitchen paper.

3 Mix the rocket, spinach and parsley in a large salad bowl.

4 Heat a shallow layer of olive oil in a frying pan. Add the capers and fry briefly until crisp. Scoop out straight away and drain on kitchen paper.

5 Toss the dressing and croûtons into the salad and divide it among 6 bowls or plates. Scatter the Parmesan shavings and the fried capers over the top and serve immediately.

Avocado, Red Onion & Spinach Salad with Polenta Croûtons

The simple lemon dressing gives a sharp tang to this sophisticated salad, while the croûtons, with their crunchy golden exterior and soft centre, add a contrast.

Serves 4
1 large red onion, cut into wedges
300g/11oz ready-made polenta, cut into 1cm/½in cubes

olive oil, for brushing
225g/8oz baby spinach leaves
1 avocado
5ml/1 tsp lemon juice

For the dressing
60ml/4 tbsp extra-virgin olive oil
juice of ½ lemon
salt and ground black pepper

1 Preheat the oven to 200°C/400°F/Gas 6. Place the onion wedges and polenta cubes on a lightly oiled baking sheet and bake for 25 minutes, or until the onion is tender and the polenta is crisp and golden, turning everything frequently to prevent sticking. Leave to cool slightly.

2 Meanwhile, make the dressing. Place the olive oil and lemon juice in a screw-top jar. Add salt and pepper to taste, close the jar tightly and shake vigorously to combine.

3 Place the spinach in a serving bowl. Peel, stone (pit) and slice the avocado, then toss the slices in the lemon juice to prevent them from discolouring. Add to the spinach with the onions.

4 Pour the dressing over the salad and toss gently. Sprinkle the polenta croûtons on top or hand them round separately.

Cook's Tip
Polenta is a type of cornmeal, popular in Italian cooking. To make polenta cubes, simply cook the polenta grains in salted water, according to the packet instructions, until thick. Spread the polenta on a board, leave to cool, then cut into cubes.

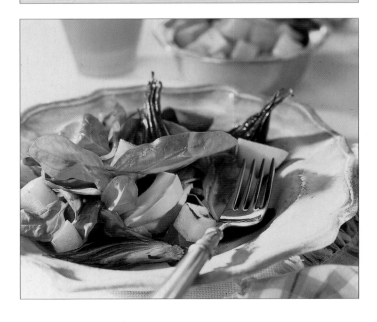

Parsley & rocket salad: Energy 262kcal/1084kJ; Protein 9.8g; Carbohydrate 12.7g, of which sugars 3.5g; Fat 19.3g, of which saturates 3.7g; Cholesterol 7mg; Calcium 437mg; Fibre 4.5g; Sodium 565mg
Avocado, red onion & spinach: Energy 442kcal/1838kJ; Protein 9.3g; Carbohydrate 57.4g, of which sugars 1.8g; Fat 18.8g, of which saturates 2.7g; Cholesterol 0mg; Calcium 105mg; Fibre 3.9g; Sodium 81mg

Moroccan Vegetable Salad

This fresh and invigorating salad makes a satisfying vegetarian salad. Arrange it carefully for the best effect.

Serves 4
1 large cucumber, thinly sliced
2 cold, boiled potatoes, sliced
1 each red, yellow and green
   (bell) peppers, seeded and
   thinly sliced
300g/11oz/2⅔ cups pitted olives
½–1 hot fresh chilli, chopped or
   2–3 shakes of cayenne pepper
3–5 garlic cloves, chopped
3 spring onions (scallions), sliced
   or 1 red onion, finely chopped
60–90ml/4–6 tbsp extra-virgin
   olive oil
15–30ml/1–2 tbsp white
   wine vinegar
juice of ½ lemon, or to taste
15–30ml/1–2 tbsp chopped fresh
   mint leaves
15–30ml/1–2 tbsp chopped fresh
   coriander (cilantro) leaves
salt (optional)

1 Arrange the cucumber, potato and pepper slices and the pitted olives on a serving plate or in a dish.

2 Sprinkle the chopped fresh chilli or cayenne pepper over the salad and season with salt, if you like. (Olives tend to be very salty so you may not wish to add any extra salt.)

3 Sprinkle the garlic, onions, olive oil, vinegar and lemon juice over the salad. Chill before serving, sprinkled with the chopped mint leaves and coriander leaves.

Cook's Tip
For a satisfying, well-balanced vegetarian meal, serve this salad with a spicy lentil soup and chunks of wholemeal (whole-wheat) bread, or Italian focaccia, flavoured with onions, olives or sun-dried tomato.

Variation
Serve the salad garnished with sliced or diced cooked beetroot (beet) for extra colour and a delicious flavour.

Israeli Chopped Vegetable Salad

This summery salad makes a lovely light meal when served with chunks of warm olive bread.

Serves 4–6
1 each red, green and yellow (bell)
   peppers, halved and seeded
1 carrot
1 cucumber
6 tomatoes
3 garlic cloves, finely chopped
3 spring onions (scallions),
   thinly sliced
30ml/2 tbsp chopped fresh
   coriander (cilantro) leaves
30ml/2 tbsp each chopped fresh
   dill, parsley and mint leaves
½–1 hot fresh chilli,
   chopped (optional)
45–60ml/3–4 tbsp extra-virgin
   olive oil
juice of 1–1½ lemons
salt and ground black pepper

1 Using a sharp knife, finely dice the red, green and yellow peppers, carrot, cucumber and tomatoes and place them in a large mixing bowl.

2 Add the garlic, spring onions, coriander, dill, parsley, mint and chilli, if using, to the chopped vegetables in the mixing bowl and toss together to combine.

3 Pour the olive oil and lemon juice over the vegetables, season with salt and pepper to taste and toss together. Chill for at least 1 hour before serving.

Cook's Tip
A very popular dish in Israel, this colourful salad is best made in summer when there is an abundance of fresh herbs.

Variation
This salad lends itself to endless variety: add olives, diced beetroot (beet) or potatoes, omit the chilli, vary the herbs, use lime or lemon in place of the vinegar or add a good pinch of ground cumin. It is always wonderful.

Israeli chopped vegetable salad: Energy 91kcal/378kJ; Protein 1.6g; Carbohydrate 7.8g, of which sugars 7.4g; Fat 6.1g, of which saturates 0.9g; Cholesterol 0mg; Calcium 35mg; Fibre 2.6g; Sodium 16mg
Moroccan vegetable salad: Energy 269kcal/1115kJ; Protein 4g; Carbohydrate 18.7g, of which sugars 10.8g; Fat 20.3g, of which saturates 3.1g; Cholesterol 0mg; Calcium 99mg; Fibre 6.1g; Sodium 1705mg

Piquant Roasted Pepper Salad

This is the Moroccan cousin of gazpacho – roasting the peppers adds a sweet richness to the salad, which contrasts superbly with the tangy flavour of preserved lemons.

Serves 4
3 green (bell) peppers, quartered
4 large tomatoes
2 garlic cloves, finely chopped

30ml/2 tbsp olive oil
30ml/2 tbsp lemon juice
good pinch of paprika
pinch of ground cumin
¼ preserved lemon
salt and ground black pepper
fresh coriander (cilantro) and flat leaf parsley, to garnish

1 Grill (broil) the peppers skin-side up until the skins are blistered and charred. Place in a plastic bag and tie the ends. Leave for about 10 minutes, or until the peppers are cool enough to handle, then peel off the skins.

2 Cut the peppers into small pieces, discarding the seeds and core, and place in a serving dish.

3 Plunge the tomatoes into a pan of boiling water for about 30 seconds, then refresh in cold water. Peel off the skins and remove the seeds and cores. Chop coarsely and add to the peppers. Sprinkle the garlic on top and chill for 1 hour.

4 Blend together the olive oil, lemon juice, paprika and cumin and pour over the salad. Season with salt and pepper.

5 Rinse the preserved lemon in cold water and remove the flesh and pith. Cut the peel into slivers and sprinkle over the salad. Garnish with coriander and flat leaf parsley.

Cook's Tip
It is always better to use fresh, rather than bottled lemon juice; as a guide, 30ml/2 tbsp is the average yield from half a lemon.

Tomato, Bean & Fried Basil Salad

Various canned beans or chickpeas can be used instead of mixed beans in this simple dish, as they all taste good and make a wholesome vegetarian salad.

Serves 4
15g/½oz/½ cup fresh basil
75ml/5 tbsp extra-virgin olive oil
300g/11oz cherry tomatoes
400g/14oz can mixed beans, drained and rinsed
salt and ground black pepper

1 Reserve one-third of the basil leaves for garnish, then tear the remainder into pieces. Pour the olive oil into a small pan. Add the torn basil and heat gently for 1 minute, until the basil sizzles and begins to colour.

2 Halve the cherry tomatoes and put in a bowl with the beans. Pour in the basil oil and add a little salt and plenty of freshly ground black pepper. Toss the ingredients together gently.

3 Cover the salad and leave to marinate at room temperature for at least 30 minutes. Serve sprinkled with the remaining basil.

Cook's Tip
Infusing basil in hot oil brings out its wonderful, aromatic flavour, which works so well in almost any tomato dish.

Piquant roasted pepper salad: Energy 113kcal/469kJ; Protein 2.2g; Carbohydrate 12.3g, of which sugars 11.9g; Fat 6.4g, of which saturates 1g; Cholesterol 0mg; Calcium 19mg; Fibre 3.3g; Sodium 15mg

Tomato, bean & fried basil salad: Energy 404kcal/1701kJ; Protein 22.8g; Carbohydrate 46.5g, of which sugars 4.9g; Fat 15.4g, of which saturates 2.3g; Cholesterol 0mg; Calcium 113mg; Fibre 16.6g; Sodium 26mg

Sun-ripened Tomato & Feta Salad with Lamb's Lettuce

This tasty salad is a version of a traditional Greek salad, with the addition of plenty of lamb's lettuce.

Serves 4
225g/8oz tomatoes
1 red onion, thinly sliced
1 green (bell) pepper, seeded and
  sliced into thin ribbons
1 piece of cucumber, about
15cm/6in in length, peeled and
  sliced in rounds
150g/5oz feta cheese, cubed
a large handful of lamb's lettuce
  (corn salad)
8–10 black olives
90–105ml/6–7 tbsp extra-virgin
  olive oil
15ml/1 tbsp lemon juice
1.5ml/¼ tsp dried oregano
salt and ground black pepper

1 Cut the tomatoes into quarters and place them in a salad bowl. Add the onion, green pepper, cucumber, feta, lamb's lettuce and black olives.

2 Sprinkle the extra-virgin olive oil, lemon juice and oregano on top. Add salt and ground black pepper to taste, then toss to coat everything in the olive oil and lemon, and to amalgamate the flavours.

3 If possible, allow the salad to stand for 10–15 minutes at room temperature before serving.

Chinese Sautéed Green Bean Salad

The smoky flavour of the dried shrimps adds an extra dimension to these greeen beans, and because the dish is so low in saturated fat, you can eat it to your heart's content.

Serves 4
25g/1oz dried shrimps
450g/1lb green beans
15ml/1 tbsp vegetable oil
3 garlic cloves, finely chopped
5 spring onions (scallions), cut
  into 2.5cm/1in lengths
15ml/1 tbsp light soy sauce
salt

1 Put the dried shrimps in a bowl and pour over the warm water to cover. Stir, cover the bowl with clear film (plastic wrap) and leave to soak for 1 hour.

2 Using a sharp knife, trim the green beans neatly, then bunch them together on a board and slice them in half.

3 Bring a large pan of lightly salted water to the boil and cook the beans for 3–4 minutes until crisp-tender. Drain, refresh under cold water and drain again. Pat the beans dry with kitchen paper.

4 Drain the dried shrimps, reserving the soaking water for adding to fish soup, if you like.

5 Heat the oil in a non-stick frying pan (skillet) or wok until very hot. Stir-fry the garlic and spring onions for 30 seconds, then add the shrimps. Mix lightly.

6 Add the green beans and soy sauce. Toss the mixture over the heat until the beans are hot. Serve immediately on a warmed dish.

Cook's Tip
Don't be tempted to use too many dried shrimps, as they have a high salt content and strong flavour.

Sun-ripened tomato & feta salad: Energy 283Kcal/1168kJ; Protein 7.2g; Carbohydrate 6.8g, of which sugars 6.3g; Fat 25.4g, of which saturates 7.7g; Cholesterol 26mg; Calcium 158mg; Fibre 1.9g; Sodium 717mg
Chinese sautéed green bean salad: Energy 64Kcal/264kJ; Proteint 4.5g; Carbohydrate 4g, of which sugars 2.9g; Fat 3.5g, fo which saturates 0.5g; Cholesterol 19mg; Calcium 90mg; Fibre 2.7g; Sodium 163mg.

Roasted Peppers with Tomatoes

This Mediterranean-style dish is a real treat, whether you are a vegetarian or not. If you have time, make and dress this salad an hour or two before serving, as this will allow the juices to mingle and create the best mouthwatering salad.

Serves 4
1 red (bell) pepper
1 yellow (bell) pepper
4 ripe plum tomatoes, sliced

2 canned artichokes, drained
  and quartered
4 sun-dried tomatoes in oil,
  drained and thinly sliced
15ml/1 tbsp capers, drained
1 garlic clove, sliced

For the dressing
15ml/1 tbsp balsamic vinegar
5ml/1 tsp lemon juice
75ml/5 tbsp extra-virgin olive oil
chopped fresh mixed herbs
salt and ground black pepper

1 Cut the peppers in half, and remove the seeds and stalks. Cut into quarters and place on a grill (broiler) pan covered with foil. Cook, skin-side up, under a grill (broiler) set on high, until the skin chars. Transfer to a bowl and cover with crumpled kitchen paper. Leave the peppers to cool.

2 Rub the skin off the peppers, remove the seeds and cores, then cut into strips.

3 Arrange the pepper strips, fresh plum tomatoes and canned artichokes on a serving dish. Sprinkle over the sun-dried tomatoes, capers and garlic.

4 To make the dressing, put the balsamic vinegar and lemon juice in a bowl and whisk in the olive oil, then the chopped herbs. Season with salt and pepper. Pour the dressing over the salad 1–2 hours before the salad is served, if possible.

Variation
The flavour of the salad can be varied by using different herbs in the dressing. For a nutty flavour add a handful of pine nuts.

Fattoush

This simple salad has been served for centuries in the Middle East. A wonderful concoction of peppers, tomatoes, cucumber and fresh herbs, it makes a clean-tasting light meal.

Serves 4
1 yellow or red (bell) pepper,
  seeded and sliced
1 large cucumber,
  roughly chopped
4–5 tomatoes, chopped

1 bunch spring onions
  (scallions), sliced
30ml/2 tbsp finely chopped
  fresh parsley
30ml/2 tbsp finely chopped
  fresh mint
30ml/2 tbsp finely chopped
  fresh coriander (cilantro)
2 garlic cloves, crushed
juice of 1½ lemons
45ml/3 tbsp olive oil
salt and ground black pepper
2 pitta breads, to serve

1 Place the yellow or red pepper, cucumber and tomatoes in a large salad bowl. Add the spring onions, with the finely chopped parsley, mint and coriander.

2 To make the dressing, mix the garlic with the lemon juice in a bowl. Gradually whisk in the olive oil, then season to taste with salt and black pepper. Pour the dressing over the salad and toss lightly to mix.

3 Toast the pitta bread, in a toaster or under a hot grill (broiler) until crisp. Serve with the salad.

Cook's Tip
People either love or hate fresh coriander (cilantro). If you hate it, omit it and double the quantity of parsley.

Variations
If you prefer, make this salad in the traditional way. After toasting the pitta breads until crisp, crush them in your hand and sprinkle over the salad before serving.

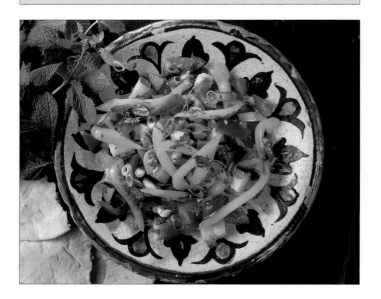

Roasted peppers with tomatoes: Energy 216kcal/890kJ; Protein 1.5g; Carbohydrate 8.1g, of which sugars 7.9g; Fat 19.9g, of which saturates 2.9g; Cholesterol 0mg; Calcium 22mg; Fibre 2.4g; Sodium 24mg
Fattoush: Energy 120kcal/499kJ; Protein 2.4g; Carbohydrate 7.7g, of which sugars 7.5g; Fat 9.1g, of which saturates 1.4g; Cholesterol 0mg; Calcium 54mg; Fibre 3g; Sodium 18mg

Date, Orange & Carrot Salad

A simple oil-free dressing is perfect on this juicy salad.

Serves 4
1 Little Gem (Bibb) lettuce
2 carrots, finely grated (shredded)
2 oranges, segmented

115g/4oz/²⁄₃ cup fresh dates, stoned (pitted) and sliced
30ml/2 tbsp toasted almonds
30ml/2 tbsp lemon juice
5ml/1 tsp caster (superfine) sugar
1.5ml/¼ tsp salt
15ml/1 tbsp orange flower water

1 Spread out the lettuce leaves on a platter. Place the carrot in the centre. Surround it with the oranges, dates and almonds.

2 Mix together the lemon juice, sugar, salt and orange flower water. Sprinkle over the salad and serve chilled.

Roasted Pepper & Tomato Salad

This is one of those lovely recipes that brings together perfectly the colours, flavours and textures of southern Italian food. It is best to serve this dish at room temperature.

Serves 4
3 red (bell) peppers
6 large plum tomatoes
2.5ml/½ tsp dried red chilli flakes

1 red onion, finely sliced
3 garlic cloves, finely chopped
grated (shredded) rind and juice of 1 lemon
45ml/3 tbsp chopped fresh flat leaf parsley
30ml/2 tbsp extra-virgin olive oil
salt
black and green olives and extra chopped flat leaf parsley, to garnish

1 Preheat the oven to 220°C/425°F/ Gas 7. Place the peppers on a baking sheet and roast for 10 minutes until the skins are slightly blackened. Add the tomatoes to the baking sheet and bake for a further 5 minutes.

2 Place the charred peppers in a plastic bag. Close the top, trapping in the steam. Set the pepper aside, with the tomatoes, until they are cool.

3 Skin and seed the peppers. Chop the peppers and tomatoes roughly and place them both in a mixing bowl.

4 Add the chilli flakes, onion, garlic, lemon rind and juice. Sprinkle over the parsley. Mix the ingredients together, then transfer to a serving dish.

5 Season with salt, drizzle over the olive oil and sprinkle the olives and extra parsley over the top.

> **Cook's Tip**
> These peppers will keep for several weeks if the peeled pepper pieces are placed in a jar of olive oil, with a tight-fitting lid. Store in the refrigerator.

Panzanella

Open-textured, Italian-style bread is essential for this colourful Tuscan salad.

Serves 6
10 thick slices day-old Italian style bread, about 275g/10oz
1 cucumber, peeled and cut into chunks
5 tomatoes, seeded and diced

1 large red onion, chopped
175g/6oz/1½ cups pitted black or green olives
20 fresh basil leaves, torn

For the dressing
60ml/4 tbsp extra-virgin olive oil
15ml/1 tbsp red or white wine vinegar
salt and ground black pepper

1 Soak the bread in water to cover for about 2 minutes, then lift it out and squeeze gently, first with your hands and then in a dish towel to remove any excess water.

2 Whisk the oil, vinegar and seasoning together. Mix the cucumber, tomatoes, onion and olives in a bowl.

3 Break the bread into chunks and add to the bowl with the basil. Pour the dressing over the salad, and toss before serving.

Roasted pepper & tomato salad: Energy 126kcal/527kJ; Protein 2.9g; Carbohydrate 14.6g, of which sugars 13.8g; Fat 6.6g, of which saturates 1.1g; Cholesterol 0mg; Calcium 49mg; Fibre 4.4g; Sodium 22mg
Date, orange & carrot salad: Energy 138kcal/582kJ; Protein 3.6g; Carbohydrate 21.8g, of which sugars 21.4g; Fat 4.7g, of which saturates 0.4g; Cholesterol 0mg; Calcium 90mg; Fibre 3.9g; Sodium 18mg
Panzanella: Energy 239kcal/1003kJ; Protein 5.5g; Carbohydrate 29.6g, of which sugars 7.1g; Fat 11.8g, of which saturates 1.6g; Cholesterol 0mg; Calcium 93mg; Fibre 3.3g; Sodium 905mg

Avocado, Tomato & Orange Salad

This salad has a feel of the Mediterranean – avocados are grown in many parts of the region and add a delicious flavour and texture to this dish. Take care to find avocados that are fully ripe, but not over-ripe.

Serves 4
2 oranges
4 well-flavoured tomatoes
2 small avocados
60ml/4 tbsp extra-virgin olive oil
30ml/2 tbsp lemon juice
15ml/1 tbsp chopped fresh
   parsley
1 small onion, sliced into rings
salt and ground black pepper
25g/1oz/¼ cup flaked (sliced)
   almonds and olives, to garnish

1 Peel the oranges and slice into thick rounds. Plunge the tomatoes into boiling water for 30 seconds, then refresh in cold water. Peel off the skins, cut the tomatoes into quarters, remove the seeds and chop roughly.

2 Cut the avocados in half, remove the stones (pits) and carefully peel away the skin. Cut into chunks.

3 Whisk together the olive oil, lemon juice and parsley. Season with salt and pepper to taste. Toss the avocados and tomatoes in half the dressing.

4 Arrange the sliced oranges on a plate and scatter over the onion rings. Drizzle the remaining dressing over the oranges, then carefully spoon the avocados, tomatoes, almonds and olives on top of the salad.

Cook's Tip
Use avocados that are just ripe for this salad. They should yield to gentle pressure. Avoid any avocados with bruised areas, or that feel very soft. Unripe avocados will ripen in 4–7 days if stored at room temperature; they will ripen even sooner if you have bananas in the same bowl.

Nopalitos Salad

This unusual salad captures the authentic taste of Mexico. Nopalitos – strips of pickled cactus paddles – are sold in cans or jars, and are very useful for making quick and easy salads like this one.

Serves 4
300g/11oz/scant 2 cups drained
   canned nopalitos
1 red (bell) pepper
30ml/2 tbsp olive oil
2 garlic cloves, sliced
½ red onion, thinly sliced
120ml/4fl oz/½ cup cider vinegar
small bunch of fresh coriander
   (cilantro), chopped
salt

1 Preheat the grill (broiler). Put the nopalitos in a bowl. Pour over water to cover and set aside for 30 minutes. Drain the nopalitos, replace with fresh water and leave to soak for a further 30 minutes.

2 Place the red pepper halves cut-side down in a grill pan. Grill (broil) the peppers until the skins blister and char, then put the pepper halves in a strong plastic bag, tie the top securely to keep the steam in, and set aside for 20 minutes.

3 Heat the oil in a small frying pan (skillet) and fry the garlic over a low heat until the slices start to turn golden. Using a slotted spoon, transfer them to a salad bowl. Pour the garlic-flavoured oil into a bowl and set it aside to cool.

4 Add the red onion slices to the salad bowl, then pour over the vinegar. Remove the red pepper from the bag, peel off the skins, then cut the flesh into thin strips. Add the peppers and onions to the salad bowl.

5 Drain the nopalitos thoroughly and add them to the salad, with the cooled garlic-flavoured oil and a little salt, to taste. Toss lightly, then chill until needed.

6 Sprinkle the chopped fresh coriander over the salad just before serving.

Italian Salad

A combination of antipasto ingredients and potatoes makes this a very substantial vegetarian dish.

Serves 6

1 aubergine (eggplant), sliced
75ml/5 tbsp olive oil
2 garlic cloves, cut into slivers
4 sun-dried tomatoes in oil, halved
2 red (bell) peppers, halved, seeded and cut into large chunks
2 large baking potatoes, cut into wedges
10ml/2 tsp mixed dried Italian herbs
30–45ml/2–3 tbsp balsamic vinegar
salt and ground black pepper

1 Preheat the oven to 200°C/400°F/Gas 6. Place the aubergines in a medium roasting pan with the olive oil, garlic and sun-dried tomatoes. Lay the pepper chunks over the aubergines.

2 Arrange the potato wedges on top of the other ingredients in the roasting pan. Scatter the mixed herbs over and season with salt and black pepper. Cover the pan with foil and bake in the oven for 45 minutes.

3 Remove from the oven and turn the vegetables over. Then return to the oven and cook uncovered for 30 minutes. Transfer the vegetables to a serving dish with a slotted spoon. Add the vinegar and seasoning to the pan, whisk and pour over the

Smoky Aubergine & Pepper Salad

Cooking the aubergines whole, over an open flame, gives them a distinctive smoky flavour and aroma, as well as tender, creamy flesh. The subtle flavour of the roasted aubergine contrasts wonderfully with the sweet flavour of the peppers.

Serves 4–6

2 aubergines (eggplants)
2 red (bell) peppers
3–5 garlic cloves, chopped, or more to taste
2.5ml/½ tsp ground cumin
juice of ½–1 lemon, to taste
2.5ml/½ tsp sherry or wine vinegar
45–60ml/3–4 tbsp extra-virgin olive oil
1–2 shakes of cayenne pepper, Tabasco or other hot pepper sauce
coarse sea salt
chopped fresh coriander (cilantro), to garnish

To serve

pitta bread wedges or thinly sliced French bread or ciabatta bread
sesame seed crackers
cucumber slices

1 Place the aubergines and peppers directly over a medium-low gas flame or on the coals of a barbecue. Turn the vegetables frequently until the skins are blistered and charred.

2 Put the aubergines and peppers in a plastic bag or in a bowl and seal tightly. Leave to cool for about 30 minutes.

3 Peel the vegetables, reserving the juices, and roughly chop the flesh. Put the flesh in a bowl with the reserved juices.

4 Add the garlic, cumin, lemon juice, vinegar, olive oil, hot pepper seasoning and salt. Mix well to combine. Turn the mixture into a serving bowl and garnish with coriander. Serve with bread, sesame seed crackers and cucumber slices.

Cook's Tip
Shape and size are not important when choosing aubergines; the essentials are tight, glossy skins and a fairly firm texture.

Italian salad: Energy 154kcal/644kJ; Protein 2.2g; Carbohydrate 15.6g, of which sugars 3.1g; Fat 9.7g, of which saturates 1.5g; Cholesterol 0mg; Calcium 12mg; Fibre 2.2g; Sodium 17mg
Smoky aubergine & pepper salad: Energy 81kcal/335kJ; Protein 1.3g; Carbohydrate 5.6g, of which sugars 5.2g; Fat 6.1g, of which saturates 0.9g; Cholesterol 0mg; Calcium 13mg; Fibre 2.6g; Sodium 4mg

Ensaladilla

A Spanish version of what is commonly known as Russian salad, this dish is a meal in itself.

Serves 4

8 new potatoes, scrubbed and quartered
I large carrot, diced
115g/4oz fine green beans, cut into 2cm/³⁄₄in lengths
75g/3oz/³⁄₄ cup peas
¹⁄₂ Spanish onion, chopped
4 cornichons or small gherkins, sliced
I small red (bell) pepper, seeded and diced

50g/2oz/¹⁄₂ cup pitted black olives
15ml/1 tbsp drained pickled capers
15ml/1 tbsp freshly squeezed lemon juice
30ml/2 tbsp chopped fresh fennel or parsley
salt and ground black pepper

For the aïoli

2 garlic cloves, finely chopped
2.5ml/¹⁄₂ tsp salt
150ml/¹⁄₄ pint/²⁄₃ cup mayonnaise

1 To make the aïoli, crush the garlic with the salt in a mortar with a pestle, then whisk or stir into the mayonnaise.

2 Cook the potatoes and diced carrot in a pan of boiling lightly salted water for 5–8 minutes until almost tender. Add the beans and peas to the pan and cook for 2 minutes, or until all the vegetables are tender. Drain well.

3 Transfer the vegetables to a large bowl. Add the onion, cornichons or gherkins, red pepper, olives and capers. Stir in the aïoli and season to taste with pepper and lemon juice.

4 Toss the vegetables and aïoli together, adjust the seasoning and chill well. Serve garnished with fennel or parsley.

Variation
This salad is delicious using any combination of chopped, cooked vegetables. Use whatever is available.

Lentil & Cabbage Salad

A warm, crunchy salad that makes a satisfying meal if served with crusty French bread or wholemeal rolls.

Serves 4–6

225g/8oz/1 cup Puy lentils
1.5 litres/2¹⁄₄ pints/6¹⁄₄ cups cold water
3 garlic cloves
I bay leaf

I small onion, peeled and studded with 2 cloves
15ml/1 tbsp olive oil
I red onion, finely sliced
15ml/1 tbsp fresh thyme leaves
350g/12oz cabbage, finely shredded
finely grated (shredded) rind and juice of I lemon
15ml/1 tbsp raspberry vinegar
salt and ground black pepper

1 Rinse the lentils in cold water and place in a large pan with the cold water, one of the garlic cloves, the bay leaf and clove-studded onion. Bring to the boil and cook for 10 minutes.

2 Reduce the heat, cover and simmer gently for 15–20 minutes. Drain and discard the onion, garlic and bay leaf.

3 Crush the remaining garlic cloves. Heat the oil in a large pan. Add the red onion, crushed garlic and thyme and cook for 5 minutes, until softened.

4 Add the cabbage and cook for 3–5 minutes, until just cooked but still crunchy. Stir in the cooked lentils, lemon rind and juice and the raspberry vinegar. Season with salt and black pepper to taste and serve warm.

Cook's Tip
The small, green Puy lentils, from France, have a fine flavour and are well worth using in this recipe.

Variation
Use spinach instead of cabbage; just cook briefly until wilted.

Ensaladilla: Energy 397kcal/1645kJ; Protein 4.9g; Carbohydrate 25.3g, of which sugars 7.8g; Fat 31.4g, of which saturates 4.9g; Cholesterol 28mg; Calcium 47mg; Fibre 4.4g; Sodium 609mg
Lentil & cabbage salad: Energy 155kcal/656kJ; Protein 9.9g; Carbohydrate 24.8g, of which sugars 4.3g; Fat 2.5g, of which saturates 0.3g; Cholesterol 0mg; Calcium 50mg; Fibre 3.2g; Sodium 18mg

Caribbean Potato Salad

Colourful vegetables in a creamy smooth dressing make this piquant salad ideal to serve on its own or with a vegetable flan.

Serves 6

900g/2lb small waxy or salad potatoes
2 red (bell) peppers, seeded and diced
2 celery sticks, finely chopped
1 shallot, finely chopped
2 or 3 spring onions (scallions), finely chopped
1 mild fresh green chilli, seeded and finely chopped
1 garlic clove, crushed
10ml/2 tsp finely snipped chives
10ml/2 tsp finely chopped basil
15ml/1 tbsp finely chopped parsley
15ml/1 tbsp single (light) cream
30ml/2 tbsp salad cream
15ml/1 tbsp mayonnaise
5ml/1 tsp Dijon mustard
7.5ml/1/2 tbsp sugar
snipped chives and chopped red chilli, to garnish

1 Cook the potatoes in a large pan of boiling water until tender but still firm. Drain and set aside. When cool enough to handle, cut the potatoes into 2.5cm/1in cubes and place in a large salad bowl.

2 Add the peppers, celery, shallot and spring onions to the potatoes in the salad bowl, together with the chilli, garlic and all the chopped herbs.

3 Mix together the cream, salad cream, mayonnaise, mustard and sugar in a small bowl. Stir well until the mixture is thoroughly combined and forms a smooth dressing.

4 Pour the dressing over the potato mixture and stir gently to coat. Serve garnished with snipped chives and chopped red chilli.

Variation
To turn this salad into a more substantial meal-in-one, add quartered hard-boiled (hard-cooked) eggs and cooked green beans, serve on a bed of lettuce and top with sliced olives.

Pumpkin Salad

Red wine vinegar brings out the sweetness of the pumpkin. No salad leaves are used, just plenty of fresh parsley. A great dish for a cold buffet.

Serves 4

1 large red onion, peeled and very thinly sliced
200ml/7fl oz/scant 1 cup olive oil
60ml/4 tbsp red wine vinegar
675g/1 1/2lb pumpkin, peeled and cut into 4cm/1 1/2 in pieces
40g/1 1/2oz/3/4 cup fresh flat leaf parsley leaves, chopped
salt and ground black pepper
fresh flat leaf parsley sprigs, to garnish (optional)

1 Mix the onion, olive oil and vinegar in a large bowl. Season with salt and pepper, then stir well to combine.

2 Put the pumpkin pieces in a large pan of cold salted water. Bring to the boil, then lower the heat and simmer gently for 15–20 minutes. Drain.

3 Immediately add the drained pumpkin to the bowl containing the dressing and toss lightly with your hands. Leave to cool. Stir in the chopped parsley, cover with clear film (plastic wrap) and chill until needed.

4 Allow the salad to come back to room temperature before serving. Garnish with fresh parsley sprigs, if you like.

Caribbean potato salad: Energy 176kcal/742kJ; Protein 3.8g; Carbohydrate 31.3g, of which sugars 8.7g; Fat 4.8g, of which saturates 1g; Cholesterol 5mg; Calcium 42mg; Fibre 3.2g; Sodium 92mg
Pumpkin salad: Energy 404kcal/1663kJ; Protein 1.7g; Carbohydrate 5.2g, of which sugars 4g; Fat 42g, of which saturates 6.1g; Cholesterol 0mg; Calcium 73mg; Fibre 2.4g; Sodium 4mg

Sweet & Sour Artichoke Salad

This Italian salad combines spring vegetables with a deliciously piquant sauce called *agrodolce*.

Serves 4
juice of 1 lemon
6 small globe artichokes
30ml/2 tbsp olive oil
2 medium onions,
    roughly chopped
175g/6oz/1 cup broad (fava)
    beans (shelled weight)

300ml/½ pint/1¼ cups water
175g/6oz/1½ cups fresh or
    frozen peas (shelled weight)
salt and ground black pepper
fresh mint leaves, to garnish

For the sauce
120ml/4fl oz/½ cup white
    wine vinegar
15ml/1 tbsp caster (superfine)
    sugar
a handful of fresh mint leaves,
    roughly torn

1 Fill a bowl with cold water and add the lemon juice. Pull off the outer leaves from the artichokes and discard them. Cut the artichokes into quarters and place them in the bowl of acidulated water to prevent them from discolouring.

2 Heat the oil in a large, heavy-based pan. Add the onions and fry over a low heat, stirring occasionally, until they are golden.

3 Stir in the beans, then drain the artichokes and add them to the pan. Pour in the measured water. Bring the water to the boil, lower the heat, cover and cook for 10–15 minutes.

4 Add the peas, season to taste with salt and pepper and cook for 5 minutes more, stirring from time to time, until the vegetables are tender. Drain thoroughly. Place in a bowl, leave to cool, then cover and chill.

5 To make the sauce, mix all the ingredients in a small pan. Heat gently for 2–3 minutes, until the sugar has dissolved. Simmer for about another 5 minutes, stirring occasionally. Remove from the heat and leave to cool.

6 To serve, drizzle the sauce over the vegetables and garnish with the fresh mint leaves.

Artichokes with Garlic, Lemon & Olive Oil

With a lovely combination of simple ingredients, this salad really brings out the flavour of the artichokes.

Serves 4
4 globe artichokes
juice of 1–2 lemons, plus extra to
    acidulate water
60ml/4 tbsp extra-virgin olive oil

1 onion, chopped
5–8 garlic cloves, roughly chopped
    or thinly sliced
30ml/2 tbsp chopped
    fresh parsley
120ml/4fl oz/½ cup dry
    white wine
120ml/4fl oz/½ cup vegetable
    stock or water
salt and ground black pepper

1 To prepare the artichokes, trim the stalks of the artichokes close to the base, cut the very tips off the leaves and then divide them into quarters. Remove the inedible hairy choke (the central part), carefully scraping the hairs away from the heart at the base of the artichoke. Put in a bowl of water that has had lemon juice added to it.

2 Heat the oil in a pan, add the onion and garlic and fry for 5 minutes until softened. Stir in the parsley and cook for a few seconds. Add the wine, stock and drained artichokes. Season with half the lemon juice, salt and pepper.

3 Bring the mixture to the boil, then lower the heat, cover and simmer for 10–15 minutes until the artichokes are tender. Lift out with a slotted spoon and transfer to a serving dish.

4 Bring the cooking liquid to the boil and boil until reduced to about half. Pour over the artichokes and drizzle over the remaining lemon juice. Adjust the seasoning. Cool before serving.

Cook's Tip
Placing trimmed artichokes in a bowl of water acidulated with lemon juice prevents them discolouring.

Pear & Pecan Nut Salad

Chicory, Carrot & Rocket Salad

Toasted pecan nuts have a special affinity with crisp white pears. Their robust flavours combine well with a rich cheese and chive dressing to make this a salad to remember.

Serves 4
75g/3oz/½ cup shelled pecan
  nuts, roughly chopped
3 crisp pears

1 escarole or round
  (butterhead) lettuce
1 radicchio
175g/6oz young spinach,
  stems removed
30ml/2 tbsp blue cheese and
  chive dressing
salt and ground black pepper
crusty bread, to serve

1 Toast the shelled pecan nuts under a medium grill (broiler) to bring out their flavour.

2 Cut the pears into even slices, leaving the skins intact but discarding the cores.

3 Separate the leaves on the lettuce and radicchio, then place in a large bowl with the spinach. Add the pear slices and toasted pecans.

4 Pour over the blue cheese dressing and toss well. Distribute among four large serving plates and season with salt and pepper. Serve the salad with warm crusty bread.

Cook's Tips
• To make blue cheese and chive dip, add 50ml/2fl oz/
¼ cup soured cream and 50g/2oz crumbled blue cheese to
75ml/3fl oz/⅓ cup mayonnaise. Stir in a few drops of white
wine vinegar, 15ml/1 tbsp snipped fresh chives and ground
black pepper to taste. Beat well to combine.
• The pecan nuts will burn quickly under the grill, so keep a
constant watch over them and remove them as soon as they
change colour.

A bright and colourful salad, which is ideal for a party. Use watercress if you are unable to obtain any rocket.

Serves 4–6
3 carrots
about 50g/2oz fresh rocket
  (arugula) or watercress,
1 large head chicory
  (Belgian endive)
Parmesan cheese, to garnish

For the dressing
45ml/3 tbsp sunflower oil
15ml/1 tbsp hazelnut or walnut
  oil (optional)
30ml/2 tbsp cider or wine vinegar
10ml/2 tsp clear honey
5ml/1 tsp grated (shredded)
  lemon rind
15ml/1 tbsp poppy seeds
salt and ground black pepper

1 Coarsely grate (shred) the carrots and put in a large bowl. Roughly chop the rocket or watercress and add to the bowl of carrots. Mix together and season well with salt and pepper.

2 Put the dressing ingredients in a screw-top jar, close the lid tightly and shake the jar vigorously to mix well.

3 Pour the dressing onto the carrots and green leaves. Toss the salad thoroughly.

4 Line a shallow salad bowl with the chicory leaves and spoon the salad into the centre. Chill for 1 hour, then garnish with Parmesan shavings.

Pear & pecan nut salad: Energy 233kcal/965kJ; Protein 4.2g; Carbohydrate 15.3g, of which sugars 14.9g; Fat 17.6g, of which saturates 1.2g; Cholesterol 3mg; Calcium 129mg; Fibre 5.1g; Sodium 151mg
Chicory, carrot & rocket salad: Energy 90kcal/374kJ; Protein 1.2g; Carbohydrate 5.2g, of which sugars 5g; Fat 7.3g, of which saturates 1g; Cholesterol 0mg; Calcium 51mg; Fibre 1.6g; Sodium 16mg

Courgettes, Carrots & Pecan Salad

In this vegetarian lunch dish, hunks of warm fried courgettes are served with a crisp tangy salad in pockets of pitta bread.

Serves 2

2 carrots
25g/1oz/¼ cup pecan nuts
4 spring onions (scallions), sliced
50ml/2fl oz/¼ cup Greek
    (US strained plain) yogurt
35ml/7 tsp olive oil
5ml/1 tsp lemon juice
15ml/1 tbsp chopped fresh mint
2 courgettes (zucchini)
25g/1oz/¼ cup plain
    (all-purpose) flour
2 pitta breads
salt and ground black pepper
shredded lettuce, to serve

1 Coarsely grate (shred) the carrots into a bowl. Stir in the pecans and spring onions and toss well.

2 To make the dressing, whisk the yogurt with 7.5ml/1½ tsp of the olive oil, the lemon juice and the mint. Stir the dressing into the carrot mixture and mix well. Cover and chill until required.

3 Cut the courgettes diagonally into slices. Season the flour with salt and pepper. Spread it out on a plate and turn the courgette slices in it until they are well coated.

4 Heat the remaining oil in a large frying pan (skillet). Add the coated courgette slices and cook for 3–4 minutes, turning once, until browned. Drain the courgettes on kitchen paper.

5 Make a slit in each pitta bread to form a pocket. Fill the pittas with the carrot mixture and the courgette slices. Serve on a bed of shredded lettuce.

> **Cook's Tip**
> Warm the pitta breads in the oven or under a medium grill (broiler). Do not fill the pitta breads too soon or the carrot mixture will make the bread soggy.

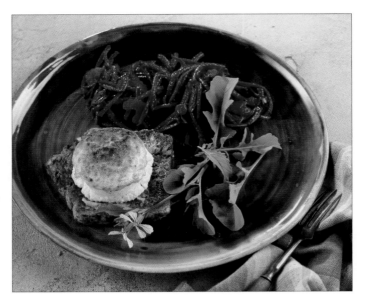

Toasted Crottins with Beetroot Salad

Small goat's cheese rounds are grilled to a delicious, nutty creaminess in a matter of minutes for serving on thinly sliced walnut bread toast. A salad of grated raw beetroot, celery and spring onions makes a colourful accompaniment.

Serves 4

2 raw beetroots (beet), about
    200g/7oz total weight
1 celery stick
2 spring onions (scallions)
60ml/4 tbsp French dressing
generous pinch of ground cumin
4 small slices of walnut bread
4 crottins (small goat's
    milk cheeses), about
    60g/2¼oz each
a little butter, for spreading
salt and ground black pepper
rocket (arugula) or watercress
    leaves, to serve

1 Peel the beetroots and grate (shred) coarsely. Ideally, the beetroot should be served raw, but, if you prefer, blanch it in boiling water for 3 minutes, then drain, refresh under cold running water and drain again. Put the beetroot in a bowl.

2 Slice the celery and spring onions finely and toss with the beetroot, dressing and cumin. Add salt and pepper to taste. Leave to marinate for 1 hour or so, if possible, then mound onto four salad plates.

3 Preheat the grill (broiler). Toast the walnut bread lightly on each side. Keep warm.

4 Place a sheet of foil on the rack, add the crottins and grill (broil) for 3–5 minutes until they turn golden brown on top and just start to melt.

5 Meanwhile, butter the toast lightly. Place on the plates, then, using a palette knife, transfer the crottins to the toast and serve immediately, accompanied by the beetroot salad and rocket or watercress leaves.

White Beans with Green Peppers in Spicy Dressing

Tender white beans are delicious in this spicy sauce with the bite of fresh, crunchy green pepper.

Serves 4

750g/1²⁄₃lb tomatoes, diced
1 onion, finely chopped
¹⁄₂–1 mild fresh chilli, finely chopped
1 green (bell) pepper, seeded and chopped
pinch of sugar
4 garlic cloves, chopped
400g/14oz can cannellini beans, drained
45–60ml/3–4 tbsp olive oil
grated (shredded) rind and juice of 1 lemon
15ml/1 tbsp cider vinegar or wine vinegar
salt and ground black pepper
chopped fresh parsley, to garnish

1 Put the tomatoes, onion, chilli, green pepper, sugar, garlic, cannellini beans, salt and plenty of ground black pepper in a large bowl and toss together until well combined.

2 Add the olive oil, grated (shredded) lemon rind, lemon juice and vinegar to the salad and toss lightly to combine. Chill before serving, garnished with chopped parsley.

> **Variation**
> Substitute flageolets for the cannellini beans, or try using haricots (navy beans). They will all taste and look attractive.

White Bean Salad with Roasted Red Pepper Dressing

The speckled herb and red pepper dressing adds a wonderful colour contrast to this salad, which is best served warm. Canned beans are used for convenience – substitute cooked, dried beans, if you prefer.

Serves 4

1 large red (bell) pepper
60ml/4 tbsp olive oil
1 large garlic clove, crushed
25g/1oz/1 cup fresh oregano leaves or flat leaf parsley
15ml/1 tbsp balsamic vinegar
400g/14oz/3 cups canned flageolet beans, drained and rinsed
200g/7oz/1 1/2 cups can cannellini beans, drained and rinsed
salt and ground black pepper

1 Preheat the oven to 200°C/400°F/Gas 6. Place the red pepper on a baking sheet, brush with oil and roast for 30 minutes or until the skin blisters and the flesh is soft.

2 Remove the pepper from the oven and place in a plastic bag. Seal and leave to cool. (This makes the skin easier to remove.)

3 When the pepper is cool enough to handle, remove it from the bag and peel off the skin. Rinse under cold running water. Slice the pepper in half, remove the seeds and dice. Set aside.

4 Heat the remaining oil in a pan and cook the garlic for 1 minute until soft. Remove from the heat, then add the oregano, the red pepper and any juices, and the balsamic vinegar. Put the beans in a large bowl and pour over the dressing. Season to taste, then stir gently. Serve warm.

> **Cook's Tip**
> Low in fat, cannellini beans should be a regular part of a healthy balanced diet. They are also a good source of minerals.

White beans with green peppers: Energy 226kcal/947kJ; Protein 8.8g; Carbohydrate 27.6g, of which sugars 12.9g; Fat 9.6g, of which saturates 1.5g; Cholesterol 0mg; Calcium 92mg; Fibre 9g; Sodium 409mg
White bean salad: Energy 165kcal/686kJ; Protein 4.1g; Carbohydrate 11.9g, of which sugars 4.6g; Fat 11.6g, of which saturates 1.7g; Cholesterol 0mg; Calcium 52mg; Fibre 4.1g; Sodium 199mg

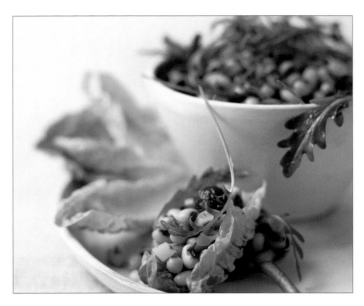

Warm Black-eyed Bean Salad with Rocket

This is an easy dish, as black-eyed beans do not need to be soaked overnight. By adding spring onions and lots of aromatic dill, they are transformed into a refreshing and healthy meal.

Serves 4

275g/10oz/1½ cups black-eyed
   beans (peas)
5 spring onions (scallions), sliced
   into rounds
a large handful of fresh rocket
   (arugula) leaves, chopped
   if large
45–60ml/3–4 tbsp chopped
   fresh dill
150ml/¼ pint/⅔ cup extra-virgin
   olive oil
juice of 1 lemon, or to taste
10–12 black olives
salt and ground black pepper
small cos or romaine lettuce
   leaves, to serve

1 Thoroughly rinse the beans and drain them well. Turn them into a pan and pour in cold water to just about cover them. Slowly bring to the boil over a low heat. As soon as the water is boiling, remove the pan from the heat and drain the water off immediately.

2 Put the beans back in the pan with fresh cold water to cover and add a pinch of salt – this will make their skins harder and stop them from disintegrating when they are cooked.

3 Bring the beans to the boil over a medium heat, then lower the heat and cook them until they are soft but not mushy. They will take 20–30 minutes only, so keep an eye on them.

4 Drain the beans, reserving 75–90ml/5–6 tbsp of the cooking liquid. Transfer the beans to a large salad bowl. Immediately add the spring onions, rocket, dill, oil, lemon juice, olives and the reserved liquid. Season with salt and pepper, then mix well.

5 Serve immediately, piled onto the lettuce leaves, or leave to cool slightly and serve later.

Bean Feast with Tomato & Avocado Salsa

This is a very quick and easy recipe using canned beans, although it could be made with dried beans, if you like.

Serves 4

15ml/1 tbsp olive oil
1 small onion, finely chopped
3 garlic cloves, finely chopped
1 fresh red Ancho chilli, seeded
   and finely chopped
1 red (bell) pepper, seeded and
   coarsely chopped
2 plum tomatoes, chopped
2 bay leaves
10ml/2 tsp chopped
   fresh oregano
10ml/2 tsp ground cumin
5ml/1 tsp ground coriander
2.5ml/½ tsp ground cloves
15ml/1 tbsp soft dark
   brown sugar
400g/14oz can red kidney beans,
   rinsed and drained
400g/14oz can flageolet or
   cannellini beans, rinsed, drained
400g/14oz can borlotti beans,
   rinsed and drained
300ml/½ pint/1¼ cups
   vegetable stock
salt and ground black pepper
fresh coriander (cilantro),
   to garnish

For the salsa

1 ripe, but firm, avocado
45ml/3 tbsp fresh lime juice
1 small red onion, chopped
1 small fresh hot green chilli,
   seeded and chopped
5 ripe plum tomatoes, skinned
   and chopped
45ml/3 tbsp chopped fresh
   coriander (cilantro)

1 Heat the oil and fry the onion for 3 minutes, until softened. Add the garlic, chilli, pepper, tomatoes, herbs and spices.

2 Stir well and cook for a further 3 minutes, then add the sugar, beans and stock and cook for 8 minutes. Season with salt and plenty of ground black pepper.

3 To make the salsa, peel and stone (pit) the avocado. Cut the flesh into 1cm/½in dice. Place in a bowl with the lime juice and stir to mix. Add the red onion, chilli, tomatoes and coriander. Season with black pepper and mix. Spoon the beans into a warmed serving dish and serve with the tomato and avocado salsa, garnished with sprigs of fresh coriander.

Black-eyed bean salad: Energy 238kcal/1007kJ; Protein 16.1g; Carbohydrate 31g, of which sugars 2.4g; Fat 6.4g, of which saturates 0.9g; Cholesterol 0mg; Calcium 114mg; Fibre 12.3g; Sodium 580mg
Bean feast: Energy 463kcal/1955kJ; Protein 24.1g; Carbohydrate 72.3g, of which sugars 28.3g; Fat 10.5g, of which saturates 2g; Cholesterol 0mg; Calcium 268mg; Fibre 23.8g; Sodium 1196mg

Goat's Cheese Salad with Hazelnut Dressing

A herb-flavoured salad tossed with crunchy, toasted hazelnuts and topped with fresh-tasting goat's cheese makes a delightful lunch dish. Serve the salad with crusty French-style bread or Melba toast.

Serves 4

175g/6oz mixed salad leaves, such as lamb's lettuce, rocket (arugula), radicchio, frisée or cress

a few fresh large-leaf herbs, such as chervil and flat leaf parsley
15ml/1 tbsp toasted hazelnuts, roughly chopped
15–20 goat's cheese balls or cubes

For the dressing
30ml/2 tbsp hazelnut oil, olive oil or sunflower oil
5–10ml/1–2 tsp sherry vinegar or good wine vinegar, to taste
salt and ground black pepper

1 Tear up any large salad leaves. Put all the leaves into a large salad bowl with the fresh herbs and most of the toasted, chopped nuts (reserve a few for the garnish).

2 To make the dressing, whisk the hazelnut, olive or sunflower oil and vinegar together, and then season with salt and pepper.

3 Just before serving, toss the salad in the dressing and divide it among four serving plates. Arrange the drained goat's cheese on the leaves and sprinkle over the remaining chopped nuts.

Cook's Tip
A grilled (broiled) slice from a goat's cheese log can replace the cheese balls or cubes, just to ring the changes.

Variation
Toasted flaked (sliced) almonds could replace the hazelnuts, teamed with extra-virgin olive oil.

Goat's Cheese & Fig Salad

Fresh figs and walnuts, goat's cheese and couscous make a tasty salad, full of texture. The dressing has no vinegar, depending instead on the acidity of the goat's cheese.

Serves 4

175g/6oz/1 cup couscous
30ml/2 tbsp toasted buckwheat
1 egg, hard-boiled/(hard-cooked)
30ml/2 tbsp chopped parsley

60ml/4 tbsp olive oil
45ml/3 tbsp walnut oil
115g/4oz rocket (arugula) leaves
½ frisée lettuce
175g/6oz crumbly white goat's cheese
50g/2oz/½ cup broken walnuts, toasted
4 ripe figs, trimmed and almost cut into four (leave the pieces joined at the base)

1 Place the couscous and toasted buckwheat in a bowl, cover with boiling water and leave to soak for 15 minutes. Place in a strainer to drain off any remaining water, then spread out on a metal tray and allow to cool.

2 Shell the hard-boiled egg and grate (shred) finely. Toss the grated (shredded) egg, parsley, couscous and buckwheat together in a bowl.

3 Combine the olive and walnut oils and use half to moisten the couscous mixture.

4 Toss the salad leaves in the remaining oil and distribute between four large serving plates. Pile the couscous mixture into the centre of each plate and crumble the goat's cheese over the top. Scatter with toasted walnuts, place a fig in the centre of each plate and serve immediately.

Cook's Tip
Goat's cheeses vary in strength from the youngest, which are soft and mild, to strongly-flavoured, mature cheeses, which have a firm and crumbly texture. The crumbly varieties are best suited to salads.

Goat's cheese & fig salad: Energy 581kcal/2410kJ; Protein 17g; Carbohydrate 35.9g, of which sugars 13.3g; Fat 41.9g, of which saturates 11.4g; Cholesterol 88mg; Calcium 189mg; Fibre 3.5g; Sodium 301mg
Goat's cheese salad: Energy 225kcal/9310kJ; Protein 11g; Carbohydrate 1.4g, of which sugars 1.3g; Fat 19.5g, of which saturates 8.7g; Cholesterol 41mg; Calcium 138mg; Fibre 1.2g; Sodium 325mg

Grilled Halloumi & Bean Salad with Skewered Potatoes

Halloumi, the hard, white salty goat's milk cheese that squeaks when you bite it, grills really well and is the perfect complement to fresh-tasting vegetables.

Serves 4

20 baby new potatoes, total weight about 300g/11oz
200g/7oz extra-fine green beans, trimmed
675g/1½lb broad (fava) beans, shelled weight 225g/8oz
200g/7oz halloumi cheese, cut into 5mm/¼in slices
1 garlic clove, crushed to a paste with a large pinch of salt
90ml/6 tbsp olive oil
5ml/1 tsp cider vinegar or white wine vinegar
15g/½oz/½ cup fresh basil leaves, shredded
45ml/3 tbsp chopped fresh savory
2 spring onions (scallions), finely sliced
salt and ground black pepper

1 Thread five potatoes onto each skewer, and cook in a large pan of salted boiling water for about 7 minutes or until almost tender. Add the green beans and cook for 3 minutes more. Add the broad beans and cook for just 2 minutes. Drain all the vegetables in a large colander.

2 Refresh the cooked broad beans under cold water. Pop each broad bean out its skin to reveal the bright green inner bean. Place in a bowl, cover and set aside.

3 Preheat a grill (broiler) or griddle. Place the halloumi slices and the potato skewers in a wide dish. Whisk the garlic and oil together with a generous grinding of black pepper. Add to the dish and toss the halloumi and potato skewers in the mixture.

4 Cook the cheese and potato skewers under the grill or on the griddle for about 2 minutes on each side.

5 Add the vinegar to the oil and garlic remaining in the dish and whisk to mix. Toss in the beans, herbs and spring onions, with the cooked halloumi. Serve with the potato skewers.

Salad of Roasted Shallots & Butternut Squash with Feta Cheese

This is especially good served with a grain or starchy salad, based on rice or couscous, for example. Serve with plenty of good bread to mop up the juices.

Serves 4–6

75ml/5 tbsp olive oil
15ml/1 tbsp balsamic vinegar, plus a little extra to taste
15ml/1 tbsp sweet soy sauce
350g/12oz shallots, peeled but left whole
3 fresh red chillies
1 butternut squash, peeled, seeded and cut into chunks
5ml/1 tsp finely chopped fresh thyme
15g/½oz flat leaf parsley
1 small garlic clove, finely chopped
75g/3oz walnuts, chopped
150g/5oz feta cheese
salt and ground black pepper

1 Preheat the oven to 200°C/400°F/Gas 6. Beat the oil, vinegar and soy sauce together in a large bowl, then season with salt and pepper.

2 Toss the shallots and two of the chillies in the oil mixture and turn into a large roasting pan or ovenproof dish. Roast for 15 minutes, stirring once or twice.

3 Add the butternut squash and roast for a further 30–35 minutes, stirring once, until the squash is tender and browned. Remove from the oven, stir in the chopped thyme and set the vegetables aside to cool.

4 Chop the parsley and garlic together and mix with the walnuts. Seed and finely chop the remaining chilli.

5 Stir the parsley, garlic and walnut mixture into the vegetables. Add chopped chilli to taste and adjust the seasoning, adding a little extra balsamic vinegar to taste.

6 Crumble the feta and add to the salad. Transfer to a serving dish and serve immediately.

Halloumi & bean salad: Energy 393kcal/1635kJ; Protein 16.5g; Carbohydrate 20.8g, of which sugars 3.4g; Fat 27.7g, of which saturates 9.4g; Cholesterol 29mg; Calcium 263mg; Fibre 6.3g; Sodium 215mg
Roasted shallots & butternut squash: Energy 275kcal/1136kJ; Protein 7.7g; Carbohydrate 9.3g, of which sugars 7g; Fat 23.2g, of which saturates 5.6g; Cholesterol 18mg; Calcium 165mg; Fibre 2.9g; Sodium 541mg

Potato & Feta Salad

This flavourful potato salad is easy to assemble, making it a perfect lunch or dinner dish for a busy day.

Serves 4

115g/4oz feta cheese
500g/1¼lb small new potatoes
5 spring onions (scallions), green
  and white parts
  finely chopped
15ml/1 tbsp rinsed bottled capers
8–10 black olives
45ml/3 tbsp finely chopped fresh
  flat leaf parsley
30ml/2 tbsp finely chopped mint
salt and ground black pepper

For the dressing

90–120ml/6–8 tbsp extra-virgin
  olive oil
juice of 1 lemon, or to taste
45ml/3 tbsp Greek (US strained
  plain) yogurt
45ml/3 tbsp finely chopped
  fresh dill, plus a few sprigs,
  to garnish
5ml/1 tsp French mustard

1 Chop the feta cheese into small, even cubes and crumble slightly into a bowl. Set aside.

2 Bring a pan of lightly salted water to the boil and cook the potatoes in their skins for 25–30 minutes, or until tender. Take care not to let them become soggy and disintegrate. Drain them thoroughly and let them cool a little.

3 When the potatoes are cool enough to handle, peel them with your fingers and place them in a large bowl. If they are very small, keep them whole; otherwise cut them into large cubes. Add the chopped spring onions, capers, olives, feta cheese and fresh herbs, and toss gently to mix.

4 To make the dressing, place the extra-virgin olive oil in a bowl with the lemon juice. Whisk thoroughly for a few minutes until the dressing emulsifies and thickens; you may need to add a little more olive oil if it does not thicken.

5 Whisk in the yogurt, dill and mustard, with salt and pepper to taste. Dress the salad while the potatoes are still warm, tossing lightly to coat them.

Aubergine & Butternut Salad with Crumbled Feta

This delightful salad not only tastes good, but looks very appetizing. Watch out for slivered pistachios in Middle-Eastern shops: their colour combines brilliantly with the orange butternut.

Serves 4

2 aubergines (eggplants)
1 butternut squash, about
  1kg/2¼lb, peeled
120ml/4fl oz/½ cup extra-virgin
  olive oil
5ml/1 tsp paprika
150g/5oz feta cheese
50g/2oz/⅓ cup pistachio nuts,
  roughly chopped
salt and ground black pepper

1 Slice the aubergines widthways into 5mm/¼in rounds. Spread them out on a tray and sprinkle with a little salt. Leave for 30 minutes. Slice the squash in the same way, scooping out any seeds with a spoon. Place the butternut squash slices in a bowl, season lightly and toss with 30ml/2 tbsp of the oil.

2 Heat the griddle until a few drops of water sprinkled onto the surface evaporate instantly. Lower the heat a little and cook the butternut squash slices in batches. Sear for about 1½ minutes on each side, then put them on a tray. Continue until all the slices have been cooked, then dust with paprika.

3 Pat the aubergine slices dry. Toss with the remaining oil and season lightly. Cook in the same way as the squash. Mix the cooked aubergine and squash together in a bowl. Crumble the feta over the warm salad, scatter the chopped pistachio nuts over the top and dust with the remaining paprika.

Cook's tip

The vegetables are also delicious cooked directly on a charcoal barbecue. When the coals are medium-hot, sear the vegetables for about 2 minutes on each side.

Potato & feta salad: Energy 138Kcal/566kJ; Protein 1.3g; carbohydrate 1.2g, of which sugars 1.1g; Fat 14.2g, of which saturates 2g; Cholesterol 0mg; Cacium 75mg;Fibre 1.4g; Sodium 40mg
Aubergine & butternut salad: Energy 385kcal/1593kJ; Protein 10.7g; Carbohydrate 9.2g, of which sugars 7g; Fat 34.2g, of which saturates 9.1g; Cholesterol 26mg; Calcium 231mg; Fibre 4.8g; Sodium 608mg

Roquefort & Walnut Salad

This delicious, fresh-tasting salad makes a wonderful light lunch dish. The combination of luxurious fresh figs with the tangy blue cheese and crunchy nuts is quite exquisite.

Serves 4

45ml/3 tbsp walnut oil
juice of I lemon
mixed salad leaves
4 fresh figs
115g/4oz Roquefort cheese, cut
into small chunks
75g/3oz/¾ cup walnut halves
salt and ground black pepper

I Whisk together the walnut oil and lemon juice in a bowl until emulsified, then season with salt and pepper.

2 Wash and dry the salad leaves then tear them gently into bitesize pieces. Place in a mixing bowl and toss with the dressing. Transfer to a large serving dish or divide among four individual plates, ensuring a good balance of colour and texture on each plate.

3 Cut the figs into quarters and add to the salad leaves. Sprinkle the cheese over the salad, crumbling it slightly. Then sprinkle over the walnuts, breaking them up roughly in your fingers as you work. Serve immediately.

Cook's Tip
Look for dark green salad leaves, such as lamb's lettuce and rocket (arugula), and reds, such as lollo rosso, as well as some crunchy leaves, such as Little Gem (Bibb), to add interest.

Variations
The figs may be replaced with ripe nectarines or peaches if you prefer. Wash and cut in half, discard the stone (pit), then cut each half into three or four slices. If the skin is very tough, you may need to remove it completely.

Roquefort & Flageolet Bean Salad with Honey Dressing

Pungent and creamy, classic sheep's milk Roquefort goes particularly well with pale green flageolet beans and a light sweet-sour dressing.

Serves 4

150g/5oz/scant I cup dried
flageolet or cannellini beans,
soaked overnight in water
I bay leaf
I sprig of thyme
I small onion, sliced
30ml/2 tbsp chopped parsley

30ml/2 tbsp chopped walnuts
200g/7oz Roquefort cheese,
lightly crumbled
salt and ground black pepper
red and green salad leaves,
to serve

For the dressing
60ml/4 tbsp extra-virgin olive oil
30ml/2 tbsp rice wine vinegar
or half wine vinegar and
half water
5ml/I tsp French mustard
10ml/2 tsp clear honey

I Drain the beans and put them in a pan. Cover with cold water. Bring to the boil. Cook for 10 minutes, then reduce the heat. Add the bay leaf, thyme and onion and simmer for 20–25 minutes until the beans are tender.

2 Drain the beans, discarding the herbs but not the onion. Transfer to a bowl, season and leave until just warm.

3 To make the dressing, mix the oil, vinegar or vinegar and water, mustard and honey in a small bowl. Add salt to taste and a generous grinding of pepper. Pour over the beans. Add the parsley and walnuts.

4 Gently mix the crumbled Roquefort into the salad. Serve the salad at room temperature with red and green salad leaves.

Variations
Try using another flavourful blue cheese instead of Roquefort. The salad is also great with cooked lentils instead of the beans.

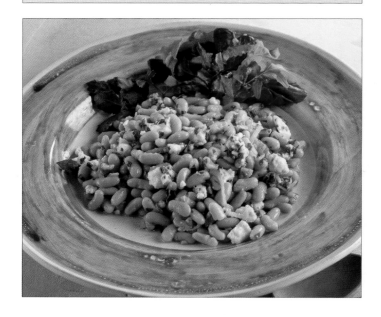

Roquefort & walnut salad: Energy 415Kcal/1726kL; Protein 10.6g; Carbohydrate 26.6g, of which sugars 26.4g; Fat 30.3g, of which saturates 7.3g; Cholesterol 22mg; Calcium 286mg; fibre 4.5g; sodium 383mg
Roquefort & flageolet bean salad: Energy 524kcal/2179kJ; Protein 25.3g; Carbohydrate 20.2g, of which sugars 4.2g; Fat 38.5g, of which saturates 16.4g; Cholesterol 56mg; Calcium 440mg; Fibre 7g; Sodium 927mg

Quail's Egg Salad with Bishop Kennedy Cheese

Bishop Kennedy is produced in Scotland and is a full-fat soft cheese, with its rind washed in malt whisky to produce a distinctive orangey red crust and a strong creamy taste. It is perfect combined with softly cooked quail's eggs in this unusual salad. If the cheese is unavailable, use another variety with lots of flavour.

Serves 4
8 quail's eggs
vinegar, for poaching
½ red onion, finely chopped
½ leek, cut into fine strips and blanched
75g/3oz Bishop Kennedy cheese, finely diced
½ red cabbage, shredded
mixed salad leaves, including Little Gem (Bibb) lettuce and lollo bionda
10ml/2 tsp pine nuts
French dressing, to serve

1 To poach the quail's eggs you need a shallow pan of simmering water with a dash of vinegar added, an eggcup, a slotted spoon, a pan of iced water. Using a thin knife, carefully break the shell of an egg and open it up into the eggcup.

2 Gently lower the cup into the simmering water, allowing some water to cover and firm up the egg, then let it slide into the water and cook for about 2 minutes. The white should change from opaque to just white. Lift the egg out with a slotted spoon and put it straight into iced water.

3 When all the eggs are cooked lift them out of the water and dry them on kitchen paper. This last bit can be done just before you assemble the salad since the quail's eggs will keep in cold water for up to 2 days.

4 Combine the salad ingredients, including the pine nuts (which can be lightly toasted if you like).

5 Toss with French dressing to coat. To serve, place the diced Bishop Kennedy and the quail's eggs on top of the salad.

Springtime Salad with Quail's Eggs

Enjoy some of the best early season garden vegetables in this crunchy green salad. Quail's eggs add a touch of sophistication and elegance.

Serves 4
175g/6oz broad (fava) beans
175g/6oz fresh peas
175g/6oz asparagus
175g/6oz very small new potatoes, scrubbed
45ml/3 tbsp good lemon mayonnaise
45ml/3 tbsp soured cream or crème fraîche
½ bunch fresh mint, chopped, plus whole leaves for garnishing
8 quail's eggs, soft-boiled and peeled
salt and ground black pepper

1 Cook the broad beans, peas, asparagus and new potatoes in separate pans of lightly salted boiling water until just tender. Drain, refresh under cold water, and drain again.

2 When the vegetables are completely cold, mix them lightly together in a large bowl.

3 Mix the mayonnaise with the soured cream or crème fraîche and chopped mint in a bowl. Stir in salt and pepper, if needed.

4 Pour the dressing over the salad and toss to coat.

5 Add the quail's eggs and whole mint leaves and toss very gently to mix. Serve immediately.

Cook's Tip
To make your own lemon mayonnaise, combine two egg yolks, 5ml/1 tsp Dijon mustard, and the grated (shredded) rind and juice of half a lemon in a blender or food processor. Add salt and pepper to taste. Process to combine. With the motor running, add about 250ml/8fl oz/1 cup mild olive oil (or a mixture of olive oil and sunflower oil) through the lid or feeder tube, until the mixture emulsifies. Trickle the oil in at first, then add it in a steady stream.

Quail's egg salad: Energy 231kcal/956kJ; Protein 11.7g; Carbohydrate 5.3g, of which sugars 4.8g; Fat 17.7g, of which saturates 5.6g; Cholesterol 132mg; Calcium 203mg; Fibre 2.3g; Sodium 183mg
Springtime salad: Energy 256kcal/1067kJ; Protein 12.5g; Carbohydrate 19.3g, of which sugars 3.6g; Fat 14.9g, of which saturates 3.7g; Cholesterol 110mg; Calcium 100mg; Fibre 6.1g; Sodium 101mg

Chilli Salad Omelette with Hummus

These delicate omelettes filled with healthy and nutritious salad make a refreshing lunch option. The omelettes are made in advance for quick, last-minute assembly.

Serves 4

4 eggs
15ml/1 tbsp cornflour (cornstarch)
15ml/1 tbsp water
115g/4oz/1 cup shredded salad vegetables
60ml/4 tbsp chilli salad dressing
60–75ml/4–5 tbsp hummus
4 cooked bacon rashers (strips), chopped
salt and ground black pepper

1 Beat together the eggs, cornflour and the water. Heat a lightly oiled frying pan (skillet) and pour a quarter of the mixture into the pan, tipping it to spread it out evenly. Cook the omelette gently. Remove from the pan, then make 3 more omelettes. Stack between sheets of baking parchment, then chill.

2 When ready to serve, toss the shredded salad vegetables together with about 45ml/3 tbsp of the dressing.

3 Spread half of each omelette with hummus, top with the salad vegetables and chopped bacon and fold in half. Drizzle the rest of the dressing over the filled omelettes before serving.

Fried Egg Salad

Chillies and eggs may seem unlikely partners, but they actually work well together. The peppery flavour of the watercress makes it the perfect foundation for this tasty salad.

Serves 2

15ml/1 tbsp groundnut (peanut) oil
1 garlic clove, thinly sliced
4 eggs
2 shallots, thinly sliced
2 small fresh red chillies, seeded and thinly sliced
½ small cucumber, finely diced
1cm/½in piece fresh root ginger, peeled and grated
juice of 2 limes
30ml/2 tbsp soy sauce
5ml/1 tsp caster (superfine) sugar
small bunch coriander (cilantro)
bunch watercress, coarsely chopped

1 Heat the oil in a frying pan (skillet). Add the garlic and cook over a low heat until it starts to turn golden. Crack in the eggs. Break the yolks with a wooden spatula, then fry until the eggs are almost firm. Remove from the pan and set aside.

2 Mix the shallots, chillies, cucumber and ginger in a bowl. In a separate bowl, whisk the lime juice with the soy sauce and caster sugar. Pour this dressing over the vegetables and toss lightly together.

3 Reserve a few coriander sprigs for the garnish. Chop the rest and add to the salad. Toss it again.

4 Reserve a few watercress sprigs and arrange the remainder on two plates. Cut the fried eggs into slices and divide them between the watercress mounds. Spoon the shallot mixture over them and serve, garnished with coriander and watercress.

Variation
For a milder version, omit the chilli and add chopped red pepper: roast the pepper first, for a sweeter flavour.

Chilli salad omelettes: Energy 173kcal/720kJ; Protein 11.8g; Carbohydrate 5.7g, of which sugars 0.8g; Fat 11.7g, of which saturates 3.1g; Cholesterol 204mg; Calcium 45mg; Fibre 0.6g; Sodium 558mg
Fried egg salad: Energy 235kcal/977kJ; Protein 14.8g; Carbohydrate 6.4g, of which sugars 5.6g; Fat 17.2g, of which saturates 3.9g; Cholesterol 381mg; Calcium 154mg; Fibre 1.2g; Sodium 1234mg

Warm Dressed Salad with Poached Eggs

Soft poached eggs, hot croûtons and cool, crisp salad leaves with a warm dressing make a lively and unusual combination.

Serves 2

½ small loaf Granary (whole-wheat) bread
45ml/3 tbsp walnut oil
2 eggs
115g/4oz mixed salad leaves
45ml/3 tbsp extra-virgin olive oil
2 garlic cloves, crushed
15ml/1 tbsp balsamic or sherry vinegar
50g/2oz piece of Parmesan cheese, shaved
ground black pepper (optional)

1 Carefully cut off the crust from the Granary loaf and discard it. Cut the bread into 2.5cm/1in cubes.

2 Heat the walnut oil in a large, heavy frying pan (skillet). Add the bread cubes and cook over a low heat for about 5 minutes, turning and tossing the cubes occasionally, until they are crisp and golden brown all over.

3 Bring a pan of water to the boil. Break each egg into a cup, one at a time, and carefully slide each one into the water. Gently poach the eggs over a low heat for about 4 minutes, until lightly cooked and the whites have just set.

4 Meanwhile, divide the salad leaves among two plates. Arrange the croûtons over the leaves.

5 Wipe the frying pan clean with kitchen paper. Heat the olive oil in the pan, add the garlic and vinegar and cook over a high heat for 1 minute. Pour the warm dressing over the salad on each plate.

6 Lift out each poached egg, in turn, with a slotted spoon and place one on top of each of the salads. Top with thin shavings of Parmesan and a little freshly ground black pepper, to taste. Serve immediately.

Artichoke & Egg Salad

Artichoke hearts are best when cut from fresh artichokes, but can also be bought frozen.

Serves 4

4 large artichokes or 4 frozen artichoke hearts, thawed
½ lemon
4 eggs, hard-boiled (hard-cooked) and shelled
fresh parsley sprigs, to garnish

For the mayonnaise

1 egg yolk
10ml/2 tsp Dijon mustard
15ml/1 tbsp white wine vinegar
250ml/8 fl oz/1 cup olive or vegetable oil
30ml/2 tbsp chopped fresh parsley
salt and ground black pepper

1 If using fresh artichokes, wash them. Squeeze the lemon and put the juice and the squeezed half in a bowl of cold water.

2 Prepare the artichokes one at a time. Cut off only the tip from the stem. Peel the stem with a small knife, pulling upwards towards the leaves. Pull off the small leaves around the stem and continue snapping off the upper part of the dark outer leaves until you reach the taller inner leaves. Cut the tops off the leaves with a sharp knife. Place the artichoke in the acidulated water. Repeat with the other artichokes.

3 Boil or steam the fresh artichokes until just tender (when a leaf comes away easily when pulled). Cook frozen artichoke hearts according to the packet instructions. Allow them to cool completely.

4 To make the mayonnaise, combine the egg yolk, mustard and vinegar in a mixing bowl. Add salt and pepper to taste. Add the oil in a thin stream, beating with a wire whisk. When thick and smooth, stir in the parsley. Cover and chill until needed.

5 If using fresh artichokes, pull off the leaves. Cut the stems off level with the base. Scrape off the hairy "choke" with a knife.

6 Cut the eggs and artichokes into wedges. Arrange on a serving plate, spoon the mayonnaise over the top, garnish with parsley sprigs and serve.

Warm dressed salad: Energy 908kcal/3803kJ; Protein 35.3g; Carbohydrate 94.8g, of which sugars 5.8g; Fat 45.8g, of which saturates 10.9g; Cholesterol 215mg; Calcium 747mg; Fibre 6.6g; Sodium 1433mg
Artichoke & egg salad: Energy 493kcal/2034kJ; Protein 7.9g; Carbohydrate 1.3g, of which sugars 1.2g; Fat 51g, of which saturates 7.1g; Cholesterol 241mg; Calcium 100mg; Fibre 1.7g; Sodium 137mg

Coronation Salad

The famous salad dressing used in this dish was created especially for the coronation dinner of Queen Elizabeth II. It is a wonderful accompaniment to hard-boiled eggs and vegetables.

Serves 6
450g/1lb new potatoes
45ml/3 tbsp French dressing
3 spring onions (scallions), chopped
6 eggs, hard-boiled (hard-cooked)
    and halved
frilly lettuce leaves
1/4 cucumber, cut into thin strips
6 large radishes, sliced
1 carton salad cress
salt and ground black pepper

For the coronation dressing
30ml/2 tbsp olive oil
1 small onion, chopped
15ml/1 tbsp mild curry powder or
    korma spice mix
10ml/2 tsp tomato purée (paste)
30ml/2 tbsp lemon juice
30ml/2 tbsp sherry
300ml/1/2 pint/1 1/4 cups
    mayonnaise
150ml/1/4 pint/2/3 cup natural
    (plain) yogurt

1 Boil the potatoes in salted water until tender. Drain, then transfer to a large bowl and toss in the French dressing while they are still warm.

2 Stir in the spring onions and the salt and pepper to taste, and allow to cool thoroughly.

3 Meanwhile, make the coronation dressing. Heat the oil in a small pan and fry the onion for 3 minutes, until soft. Stir in the curry powder or spice mix and fry for a further 1 minute. Remove from the heat and mix in the tomato purée, lemon juice, sherry, mayonnaise and yogurt.

4 Stir the dressing into the potatoes, add the eggs, then chill. Line a serving platter with lettuce leaves and pile the salad in the centre. Scatter over the cucumber, radishes and cress.

Cook's Tip
Make your own mayonnaise and French dressing, if time allows.

Marinated Courgette & Flageolet Bean Salad

Serve this healthy salad as a light meal or as an accompaniment to a main course. It has a wonderful bright green colour and is perfect for a summer lunch.

Serves 4
2 courgettes (zucchini), halved
    lengthwise and sliced
400g/14oz can flageolet or
    cannellini beans, drained
    and rinsed
45ml/3 tbsp garlic-infused olive oil
grated (shredded) rind and juice
    of 1 unwaxed lemon
salt and ground black pepper

1 Cook the courgettes in boiling salted water for 2–3 minutes, or until just tender. Drain and refresh under cold running water.

2 Transfer the drained courgettes to a bowl with the beans and stir in the oil, lemon rind and juice and some salt and pepper.

3 Chill for 30 minutes before serving.

Variation
To add extra flavour to the salad add 30ml/2 tbsp chopped basil and mint before chilling.

Coronation salad: Energy 587kcal/2429kJ; Protein 10.1g; Carbohydrate 17.1g, of which sugars 4.7g; Fat 51.6g, of which saturates 8.8g; Cholesterol 228mg; Calcium 97mg; Fibre 1.1g; Sodium 401mg
Courgette & flageolet bean salad: Energy 188kcal/785kJ; Protein 8.3g; Carbohydrate 19.2g, of which sugars 4.9g; Fat 9.2g, of which saturates 1.4g; Cholesterol 0mg; Calcium 90mg; Fibre 6.9g; Sodium 391mg

Green Bean & Sweet Red Pepper Salad

A galaxy of colour and texture, with a jolt of heat from the chilli, will make this a favourite salad.

Serves 4

350g/12oz cooked green
  beans, quartered
2 red (bell) peppers, seeded
  and chopped
2 spring onions (scallions), both
  white and green parts, chopped
1 or more drained pickled
  serrano chillies, well rinsed,
  seeded and chopped
1 iceberg lettuce, coarsely
  shredded, or mixed salad leaves
green olives, to garnish

For the dressing

45ml/3 tbsp red wine vinegar
135ml/9 tbsp olive oil
salt and ground black pepper

1 Combine the green beans, peppers, spring onions and chilli(es) in a salad bowl.

2 To make the dressing, pour the vinegar into a bowl. Add salt and pepper to taste, then gradually whisk in the olive oil until well combined.

3 Pour the dressing over the prepared vegetables and toss lightly together to mix and coat thoroughly.

4 Line a large serving platter with the shredded lettuce or mixed salad leaves and arrange the vegetable mixture attractively on top. Garnish with the olives and serve.

Cook's Tip
Use a seeded, finely chopped fresh red chilli, if you prefer.

Variation
For extra flavour, top with shavings of Parmesan cheese.

Green Green Salad

You could make this lovely dish any time of the year with frozen vegetables and still get a pretty salad.

Serves 4

175g/6oz shelled broad
  (fava) beans
115g/4oz green beans, quartered
115g/4oz mangetouts
  (snow peas)
8–10 small fresh mint leaves
3 spring onions (scallions),
  chopped

For the dressing

60ml/4 tbsp olive oil
15ml/1 tbsp cider vinegar
15ml/1 tbsp chopped fresh mint
1 garlic clove, crushed
salt and ground black pepper

1 Plunge the broad beans into a pan of boiling water and bring back to the boil. Remove from the heat immediately and plunge into cold water. Drain.

2 Repeat the blanching process in step 1 with the green beans.

3 In a large bowl, mix the blanched broad beans and green beans with the raw mangetouts, mint leaves and spring onions.

4 In another bowl, mix together the olive oil, vinegar, chopped mint, garlic and seasoning.

5 Pour the dressing over the salad and toss well. Chill until ready to serve.

Chargrilled Pepper Salad with Pesto

The ingredients of this colourful salad are simple and few, but the overall flavour is quite intense.

Serves 4

1 large red (bell) pepper, halved and seeded
1 large green (bell) pepper, halved and seeded
250g/9oz/2¼ cups dried fusilli tricolore or other pasta shapes
1 handful fresh basil leaves
1 handful fresh coriander (cilantro) leaves
1 garlic clove
salt and ground black pepper

For the dressing
30ml/2 tbsp pesto
juice of ½ lemon
60ml/4 tbsp extra-virgin olive oil

1 Place the red and green pepper halves, skin-side up, on a grill (broiler) rack and grill (broil) until the skins have blistered and are beginning to char. Transfer the peppers to a bowl, cover with crumpled kitchen paper and leave to cool slightly. When they are cool enough to handle, rub off the skins and discard.

2 Bring a large pan of salted water to the boil, add the pasta and cook according to the packet instructions, until *al dente*.

3 Meanwhile, whisk together the pesto, lemon juice and olive oil in a large bowl. Season to taste with salt and pepper.

4 Drain the cooked pasta well and add to the bowl of dressing. Toss thoroughly to mix and set aside to cool.

5 Chop the pepper flesh and add to the pasta. Put most of the basil and coriander and all the garlic on a board and chop them. Add the herb mixture to the pasta and toss, then season to taste, if necessary, and serve, garnished with the herb leaves.

Cook's Tip
Serve the salad at room temperature or lightly chilled, whichever you prefer.

Roasted Plum Tomato & Rocket Salad

This is a good side salad to accompany a cheese flan or a fresh herb pizza.

Serves 4

450g/1lb ripe baby Italian plum tomatoes, halved lengthwise
75ml/5 tbsp extra-virgin olive oil
2 garlic cloves, cut into thin slivers
225g/8oz/2 cups dried pasta shapes
30ml/2 tbsp balsamic vinegar
2 pieces sun-dried tomato in olive oil, drained and chopped
large pinch of sugar
1 handful rocket (arugula) leaves
salt and ground black pepper

1 Preheat the oven to 190°C/375°F/Gas 5. Arrange the halved tomatoes, cut side up, in a roasting pan. Drizzle 30ml/2 tbsp of the oil over them and sprinkle with the slivers of garlic and salt and pepper to taste. Roast for 20 minutes, turning once.

2 Meanwhile, bring a large pan of lightly salted water to the boil, add the pasta and cook according to the packet instructions, until it is *al dente*.

3 Put the remaining oil in a large bowl with the vinegar, sun-dried tomatoes and sugar with salt and pepper to taste.

4 Drain the pasta, add it to the bowl of dressing and toss to mix. Add the roasted tomatoes and mix gently.

5 Just before serving, add the rocket leaves, toss lightly and taste for seasoning. Serve at room temperature or chilled.

Variations
• If you are in a hurry and don't have time to roast the tomatoes, you can make the salad with halved raw tomatoes instead, but make sure that they are really ripe.
• If you like, add 150g/5oz mozzarella cheese, drained and diced, with the rocket.

Chargrilled pepper salad: Energy 379kcal/1593kJ; Protein 11.7g; Carbohydrate 52.3g, of which sugars 7.7g; Fat 15.1g, of which saturates 3.3g; Cholesterol 8mg; Calcium 138mg; Fibre 3.9g; Sodium 91mg
Plum tomato & rocket salad: Energy 339kcal/1427kJ; Protein 7.9g; Carbohydrate 45.5g, of which sugars 5.6g; Fat 15.3g, of which saturates 2.2g; Cholesterol 0mg; Calcium 47mg; Fibre 3.4g; Sodium 16mg

Country Pasta Salad with Fresh Cherry Tomatoes

Colourful, tasty and nutritious, this is the ideal pasta salad for a summer picnic, and makes the most of the deliciously sweet cherry tomatoes available in the markets.

Serves 6

300g/11oz/2¾ cups dried fusilli or other pasta shapes
150g/5oz green beans, cut into 5cm/2in lengths
1 potato, about 150g/5oz, diced into small pieces
200g/7oz cherry tomatoes, halved
2 spring onions (scallions), finely chopped or 90g/3½oz white of leek, finely chopped
90g/3½oz Parmesan cheese, diced or coarsely shaved
6–8 pitted black olives, cut into rings
15–30ml/1–2 tbsp capers, to taste

For the dressing

90ml/6 tbsp extra-virgin olive oil
15ml/1 tbsp balsamic vinegar
15ml/1 tbsp chopped fresh flat leaf parsley
salt and ground black pepper

1 Bring a large pan of salted water to the boil, add the pasta and cook according to the packet instructions, until *al dente*. Drain, cool and rinse under cold water, then shake the colander to remove as much water as possible. Leave to drain and dry.

2 Cook the beans and diced potato in a pan of salted boiling water for 5–6 minutes, or until tender. Drain and leave the vegetables to cool.

3 To make the dressing, put olive oil, balsamic vinegar and parsley in a large serving bowl with salt and pepper to taste and whisk well to mix.

4 Add the cherry tomatoes, spring onions or leek, Parmesan, olive rings and capers to the dressing, then the cold pasta, beans and potato. Toss well to mix. Cover and leave to stand for about 30 minutes. Taste the salad and adjust the seasoning before serving.

Summer Salad

Ripe red tomatoes, mozzarella and olives make a good base for a fresh and tangy salad that is perfect for a light summer lunch.

Serves 4

350g/12oz/3 cups dried penne or other pasta shapes
150g/5oz packet mozzarella di bufala, drained and diced
3 ripe tomatoes, diced
10 pitted black olives, sliced
10 pitted green olives, sliced
1 spring onion (scallion), thinly sliced on the diagonal
1 handful fresh basil leaves

For the dressing

90ml/6 tbsp extra-virgin olive oil
15ml/1 tbsp balsamic vinegar or lemon juice
salt and ground black pepper

1 Bring a large pan of salted water to the boil, add the pasta and cook according to the packet instructions, until *al dente*. Drain and rinse under cold running water, then drain thoroughly again. Leave the pasta to drain.

2 To make the dressing, whisk the olive oil and balsamic vinegar or lemon juice in a large bowl with a little salt and pepper.

3 Add the pasta, mozzarella, tomatoes, olives and spring onion to the dressing and toss together well. Adjust the seasoning and garnish with basil before serving.

Variation
Make the salad more substantial by adding other ingredients, such as sliced peppers, toasted pine nuts, canned artichoke hearts, baby corn cobs – whatever you have to hand.

Cook's Tip
Mozzarella made from buffalo milk has more flavour than the type made with cow's milk. It is now widely available.

Country pasta salad: Energy 388kcal/1625kJ; Protein 13.5g; Carbohydrate 43.4g, of which sugars 4g; Fat 19g, of which saturates 5.1g; Cholesterol 15mg; Calcium 221mg; Fibre 3.3g; Sodium 547mg
Summer salad: Energy 635kcal/2658kJ; Protein 18.7g; Carbohydrate 67.2g, of which sugars 5.3g; Fat 34.2g, of which saturates 9.1g; Cholesterol 22mg; Calcium 210mg; Fibre 5.5g; Sodium 1845mg

Avocado, Tomato & Mozzarella Pasta Salad

When avocados are in season, there is no better way to serve them than with juicy tomatoes in a simple pasta salad.

Serves 4
175g/6oz dried farfalle
   (pasta bows)
6 ripe red tomatoes
225g/8oz mozzarella cheese
1 large ripe avocado
30ml/2 tbsp pine nuts, toasted
1 fresh basil sprig, to garnish

For the dressing
90ml/6 tbsp olive oil
30ml/2 tbsp wine vinegar
5ml/1 tsp balsamic vinegar
   (optional)
5ml/1 tsp wholegrain mustard
pinch of sugar
salt and ground black pepper
chopped fresh basil, to garnish

1 Cook the pasta in plenty of boiling salted water according to the packet instructions. Drain well and cool.

2 Slice the tomatoes and mozzarella into thin rounds. Halve the avocado, remove the stone (pit), and peel off the skin. Slice the flesh lengthwise.

3 Whisk together all the dressing ingredients, except the chopped fresh basil, in a small bowl.

4 Just before you are ready to serve, arrange alternate slices of tomato, mozzarella and avocado in a spiral pattern, just slightly overlapping, around the edge of a large serving platter.

5 Toss the pasta with half the dressing and the chopped basil. Pile into the centre of the platter. Pour over the remaining dressing, scatter over the pine nuts and garnish with basil.

> **Cook's Tip**
> To ripen avocados, put them into a paper bag with an apple or potato and leave in a warm place for 2–3 days.

Roast Pepper & Mushroom Pasta Salad

A combination of grilled peppers and two different kinds of mushroom makes this salad colourful as well as nutritious. Serve with chunks of ciabatta or a flavoured focaccia for a scrumptious meal.

Serves 6
1 red (bell) pepper, halved
1 yellow (bell) pepper, halved
1 green (bell) pepper, halved
350g/12oz dried whole-wheat
   pasta shells or fusilli
30ml/2 tbsp olive oil
45ml/3 tbsp balsamic vinegar
75ml/5 tbsp tomato juice
30ml/2 tbsp chopped fresh basil
15ml/1 tbsp chopped fresh thyme
175g/6oz/2¼ cups shiitake
   mushrooms, diced
175g/6oz/2¼ cups oyster
   mushrooms, sliced
400g/14oz can black-eyed beans
   (peas), drained and rinsed
115g/4oz/¾ cup sultanas
   (golden raisins)
2 bunches spring onions
   (scallions), finely chopped
salt and ground black pepper

1 Preheat the grill (broiler) to hot. Put the peppers cut-side down on a grill pan rack and place under the grill for 10–15 minutes, until the skins are charred. Put in a bowl, cover crumpled kitchen paper and set aside to cool.

2 Meanwhile, bring a large pan of lightly salted water to the boil, add the pasta and cook according to the packet instructions, until *al dente*. Drain thoroughly.

3 Mix together the oil, vinegar, tomato juice, basil and thyme, add to the warm pasta and toss.

4 Remove and discard the skins from the peppers. Seed and slice and add to the pasta.

5 Add the mushrooms, beans, sultanas and spring onions to the pasta and season with salt and pepper to taste. Toss the ingredients to mix and serve immediately. Alternatively, cover and chill in the refrigerator before serving.

Avocado, tomato & mozzarella pasta salad: Energy 585kcal/2436kJ; Protein 18.3g; Carbohydrate 36.9g, of which sugars 5.4g; Fat 41.4g of which saturates 12.2g; Cholesterol 33mg; Calcium 228mg; Fibre 3.8g; Sodium 236mg
Roast pepper & mushroom pasta salad: Energy 390kcal/1650kJ; Protein 15.6g; Carbohydrate 71.8g, of which sugars 25.4g; Fat 6.5g, of which saturates 1g; Cholesterol 0mg; Calcium 126mg; Fibre 12.5g; Sodium 380mg

Whole-wheat Pasta Salad

Roquefort & Walnut Pasta Salad

This substantial vegetarian salad is easily assembled from any combination of seasonal vegetables. Use raw or lightly blanched vegetables, or a mixture of both to ring the changes.

Serves 8
450g/1lb dried whole-wheat
  pasta, such as fusilli or penne
45ml/3 tbsp olive oil
2 carrots
1 small head broccoli, halved
115g/4oz/1 cup shelled peas,
  fresh or frozen
1 red or yellow (bell) pepper,
  halved and seeded

2 celery stalks
4 spring onions (scallions)
1 large tomato
50g/2oz/1/2 cup pitted
  olives, halved
75g/3oz/2/3 cup diced Cheddar or
  mozzarella, or a combination

For the dressing
45ml/3 tbsp balsamic or
  wine vinegar
60ml/4 tbsp olive oil
15ml/1 tbsp Dijon mustard
15ml/1 tbsp sesame seeds
10ml/2 tsp finely chopped mixed
  fresh herbs, such as parsley,
  thyme and basil
salt and ground black pepper

1 Bring a large pan of salted water to the boil, add the pasta and cook according to the packet instructions, until al dente. Drain, and rinse under cold water to stop the cooking. Drain well and turn into a large bowl. Toss with the olive oil and allow to cool completely.

2 Lightly blanch the carrots, broccoli and peas in a large pan of boiling water. Refresh under cold water. Drain well.

3 Chop the carrots and broccoli into bitesize pieces and add to the pasta with the peas. Slice the pepper, celery, spring onions and tomato into small pieces. Add them to the salad with the olives.

4 To make the dressing, whisk the vinegar with the oil and mustard in a small bowl. Stir in the sesame seeds and herbs and season with salt and pepper. Whisk well to combine, then pour over the salad. Toss to mix, then stir in the cheese. Leave to stand for 15 minutes before serving.

This is a simple, earthy salad, relying totally on the quality of the ingredients.

Serves 4
225g/8oz/2 cups dried pasta
  shapes, such as penne
selection of salad leaves, such as
  rocket (arugula), frisée, lamb's

lettuce, spinach or radicchio
30ml/2 tbsp walnut oil
60ml/4 tbsp sunflower oil
30ml/2 tbsp red wine vinegar or
  sherry vinegar
225g/8oz Roquefort cheese,
  roughly crumbled
115g/4oz/1 cup walnut halves
salt and ground black pepper

1 Bring a large pan of salted water to the boil, add the pasta and cook according to the packet instructions, until al dente. Drain well and cool. Place the salad leaves in a bowl.

2 Whisk together the walnut oil, sunflower oil and vinegar. Season with salt and pepper to taste.

3 Pile the pasta in the centre of the salad leaves, scatter over the crumbled Roquefort and pour over the dressing. Sprinkle the walnuts over the top. Toss the salad just before serving.

Cook's Tip
Toast the walnuts under the grill to add extra flavour.

Whole-wheat pasta salad: Energy 374kcal/1569kJ; Protein 14g; Carbohydrate 43.7g, of which sugars 6.9g; Fat 16.9g, of which saturates 4.1g; Cholesterol 9mg; Calcium 145mg; Fibre 8.1g; Sodium 354mg
Roquefort & walnut pasta salad: Energy 731kcal/3042kJ; Protein 22.5g; Carbohydrate 42.6g, of which sugars 2.6g; Fat 53.5g, of which saturates 14.3g; Cholesterol 42mg; Calcium 316mg; Fibre 2.7g; Sodium 690mg

Pasta, Asparagus & Potato Salad

Made with whole-wheat pasta, this delicious salad is a real treat, especially when made with fresh asparagus just in season.

Serves 4
225g/8oz/2 cups dried whole-wheat pasta shapes
60ml/4 tbsp extra-virgin olive oil
350g/12oz baby new potatoes
225g/8oz asparagus
115g/4oz piece Parmesan cheese
salt and ground black pepper

1 Bring a large pan of salted water to the boil, add the pasta and cook according to the packet instructions, until *al dente*. Drain well and toss with the olive oil while the pasta is still warm. Season with salt and ground black pepper.

2 Cook the potatoes in boiling salted water for 15 minutes, or until tender. Drain and toss together with the pasta.

3 Trim any woody ends off the asparagus and halve the stalks if very long. Blanch in boiling salted water for 6 minutes, until bright green and still crunchy. Drain. Plunge into cold water to refresh. Drain and dry on kitchen paper.

4 Toss the asparagus with the potatoes and pasta, adjust the seasoning to taste and transfer to a shallow serving bowl. Using a vegetable peeler, shave the Parmesan over the salad.

Pasta Salad with Olives

This delicious salad combines all the flavours of the Mediterranean. It is an excellent way of serving pasta and is particularly nice on hot summer days.

Serves 6
450g/1lb/4 cups dried pasta shapes, such as shells, farfalle or penne
60ml/4 tbsp extra-virgin olive oil
10 sun-dried tomatoes, thinly sliced
30ml/2 tbsp capers, in brine or salted
75g/3oz/²⁄₃ cup black olives, pitted
2 garlic cloves, finely chopped
45ml/3 tbsp balsamic vinegar
45ml/3 tbsp chopped fresh parsley
salt and ground black pepper

1 Bring a large pan of salted water to the boil, add the pasta and cook according to the packet instructions, until *al dente*. Drain, and rinse under cold water. Drain well and turn into a large bowl. Toss with the olive oil and set aside.

2 Soak the tomatoes in a bowl of hot water for 10 minutes, then drain, reserving the soaking liquid. Rinse the capers well. If they have been preserved in salt, soak them in a little hot water for 10 minutes. Rinse again.

3 Combine the olives, tomatoes, capers, garlic and vinegar in a small bowl. Season with salt and pepper.

4 Stir the vegetable mixture into the pasta and toss well. Add 30–45ml/2–3 tbsp of the tomato water if the salad seems too dry. Toss with parsley and leave the salad to stand for 15 minutes before serving.

Variations
* *You could use green olives instead of the black variety to ring the changes.*
* *Pimiento stuffed olives would add extra colour.*
* *Add chopped fresh tomatoes to enhance the tomato flavour.*

Pasta, Olive & Avocado Salad

The ingredients of this salad are united by a wonderful sun-dried tomato and fresh basil dressing.

Serves 6
225g/8oz/2 cups dried fusilli pasta or other pasta shapes
115g/4oz can sweetcorn, drained, or frozen sweetcorn, thawed
1/2 red (bell) pepper, seeded and diced
8 black olives, pitted and sliced
3 spring onions (scallions), finely chopped
2 medium avocados
15ml/1 tbsp lemon juice

For the dressing
2 sun-dried tomato halves, loose-packed (not preserved in oil)
25ml/1 1/2 tbsp balsamic or white wine vinegar
25ml/1 1/2 tbsp red wine vinegar
1/2 garlic clove, crushed
2.5ml/1/2 tsp salt
75ml/5 tbsp olive oil
15ml/1 tbsp sliced fresh basil

1 To make the dressing, drop the sun-dried tomatoes into a pan containing 2.5cm/1in boiling water and simmer for about 3 minutes until tender. Drain and chop finely.

2 Combine the sun-dried tomatoes, both vinegars, garlic and salt in a food processor. With the machine running, add the olive oil in a stream. Stir in the basil.

3 Bring a large pan of salted water to the boil, add the pasta and cook according to the packet instructions, until *al dente*. Drain, and rinse under cold water. Drain well.

4 In a large bowl, combine the pasta, drained sweetcorn, diced red pepper, olives and spring onions. Add the dressing and toss well to coat thoroughly.

5 Just before serving, peel and stone (pit) the avocados and cut the flesh into cubes. Sprinkle with the lemon juice to stop the flesh from discolouring.

6 Mix the avocado gently into the pasta, then transfer the salad to a serving dish. Serve at room temperature.

Vegetable Pasta Salad

A colourful medley of crisp vegetables, tossed with freshly cooked pasta, is ideal for an easy lunch or supper.

Serves 4
225g/8oz/2 cups dried pasta shapes
25g/1oz/2 tbsp butter
45ml/3 tbsp extra-virgin olive oil
1 small leek, thinly sliced
2 carrots, diced
2.5ml/1/2 tsp sugar
1 courgette (zucchini), diced
75g/3oz green beans, cut into 2cm/3/4in lengths
75g/3oz fresh or frozen peas
1 handful fresh flat leaf parsley, finely chopped
2 ripe Italian plum tomatoes, chopped
salt and ground black pepper

1 Bring a large pan of salted water to the boil, add the pasta and cook according to the packet instructions, until al dente.

2 Meanwhile, heat the butter and oil in a pan. When the mixture sizzles, add the leek and carrots. Sprinkle the sugar over and cook, stirring frequently, for about 5 minutes.

3 Stir in the courgette, green beans, peas and plenty of salt and pepper. Cover and cook over a low to medium heat for 5–8 minutes until the vegetables are tender, stirring occasionally. Stir in the parsley and chopped plum tomatoes.

4 Drain the pasta, add the vegetables, then toss to combine.

Pasta, olive & avocado salad: Energy 329kcal/1374kJ; Protein 6.5g; Carbohydrate 31.1g, of which sugars 3.7g; Fat 20.6g, of which saturates 3.6g; Cholesterol 0mg; Calcium 26mg; Fibre 3.9g; Sodium 412m.
Vegetable pasta salad: Energy 201kcal/829kJ; Protein 5.5g; Carbohydrate 12g, of which sugars 7.2g; Fat 14.8g, of which saturates 4.7g; Cholesterol 13mg; Calcium 68mg; Fibre 5.5g; Sodium 57mg

Roasted Vegetable Pasta Salad

Nothing could be simpler – or more delicious – than tossing freshly cooked pasta with roasted vegetables. The flavour is superb.

Serves 6

1 red (bell) pepper, seeded and
   cut into 1cm/½in squares
1 yellow or orange (bell) pepper,
   seeded and cut into
   1cm/½in squares
1 small aubergine (eggplant),
   roughly diced
2 courgettes (zucchini), sliced

75ml/5 tbsp extra-virgin olive oil
15ml/1 tbsp chopped fresh flat
   leaf parsley
5ml/1 tsp dried oregano or
   marjoram
250g/9oz baby Italian plum
   tomatoes, hulled and
   halved lengthwise
2 garlic cloves, roughly chopped
350–400g/12–14oz/3–3½ cups
   dried pasta shells
salt and ground black pepper
4–6 fresh marjoram or oregano
   flowers, to garnish

1 Preheat the oven to 190°C/375°F/Gas 5. Rinse the prepared peppers, aubergine and courgettes under cold running water, then drain. Transfer the vegetables to a large roasting pan.

2 Pour 45ml/3 tbsp of the olive oil over the vegetables and sprinkle with the fresh and dried herbs. Add salt and pepper to taste and stir well. Roast for about 30 minutes, stirring two or three times.

3 Stir the halved tomatoes and chopped garlic into the vegetable mixture, then roast for 20 minutes more, stirring once or twice during the cooking time.

4 Meanwhile, bring a large pan of salted water to the boil, add the pasta and cook according to the instructions on the packet, or until *al dente*.

5 Drain the pasta and transfer it to a warmed bowl. Add the roasted vegetables and the remaining oil and toss well.

6 Serve the pasta and vegetables hot in warmed bowls, sprinkling each portion with a few herb flowers.

Bountiful Bean & Nut Salad

This is a good multi-purpose dish. It can be a cold main course, a buffet party dish, or a salad on the side.

Serves 6

75g/3oz/½ cup red kidney, pinto
   or borlotti beans
75g/3oz/½ cup white cannellini
   or butter beans
30ml/2 tbsp olive oil
175g/6oz cooked fresh
   green beans
3 spring onions (scallions), sliced
1 small yellow or red (bell)
   pepper, sliced

1 carrot, coarsely grated
30ml/2 tbsp dried topping
   onions or sun-dried
   tomatoes, chopped
50g/2oz/½ cup unsalted cashew
   nuts or almonds, chopped

For the dressing

45ml/3 tbsp sunflower oil
30ml/2 tbsp red wine vinegar
15ml/1 tbsp wholegrain mustard
5ml/1 tsp caster (superfine) sugar
5ml/1 tsp dried mixed herbs
salt and ground black pepper

1 Soak the beans, overnight if possible, then drain and rinse well. Place in a pan, cover with cold water and cook according to the instructions on the packet.

2 Drain the beans and transfer to a large serving bowl. Add the olive oil and season with salt and pepper. Toss well to coat, then leave to cool for 30 minutes.

3 Add the green beans, spring onions, peppers and carrot to the bowl and stir to combine.

4 To make the dressing, put all the ingredients in a jar, close the lid tightly and shake to mix. Toss the dressing into the salad and adjust the seasoning. Serve sprinkled with the topping onions and sun-dried tomatoes, if using, and the chopped nuts.

Cook's Tip
This salad keeps well for up to 3 days in the refrigerator, making it ideal for entertaining.

Roasted vegetable salad: Energy 319kcal/1343kJ; Protein 8.8g; Carbohydrate 49.6g, of which sugars 8g; Fat 10.8g, of which saturates 1.6g; Cholesterol 0mg; Calcium 34mg; Fibre 4g; Sodium 9mg
Bountiful bean & nut salad: Energy 230kcal/959kJ; Protein 8.6g; Carbohydrate 17.8g, of which sugars 5.7g; Fat 14.3g, of which saturates 2.2g; Cholesterol 0mg; Calcium 51mg; Fibre 5.8g; Sodium 73mg

Fruity Brown Rice Salad

An Oriental-style dressing gives this colourful rice salad extra piquancy.

Serves 4–6
115g/4oz/⅔ cup brown rice
1 small red (bell) pepper, seeded and diced
200g/7oz can sweetcorn kernels, drained
45ml/3 tbsp sultanas (golden raisins)
225g/8oz can pineapple pieces in fruit juice
15ml/1 tbsp light soy sauce
15ml/1 tbsp sunflower oil
15ml/1 tbsp hazelnut oil
1 garlic clove, crushed
5ml/1 tsp finely chopped fresh root ginger
salt and ground black pepper
4 spring onions (scallions), diagonally sliced, to garnish

1 Bring a large pan of salted water to the boil and cook the brown rice for about 30 minutes, or until it is just tender. Drain thoroughly, rinse under cold water and drain again. Cool.

2 Turn the rice into a bowl and add the red pepper, sweetcorn and sultanas. Drain the pineapple pieces, reserving the juice, then add them to the rice mixture and toss lightly.

3 Pour the reserved pineapple juice into a clean screw-top jar. Add the soy sauce, sunflower and hazelnut oils, garlic and chopped root ginger and season to taste with salt and pepper. Close the jar tightly and shake vigorously.

4 Pour the dressing over the salad and toss well. Scatter the spring onions over the top and serve.

> **Cook's Tips**
> • *Hazelnut oil gives a distinctive flavour to any salad dressing and is especially good for leafy salads that need a bit of a lift. It is like olive oil, in that it contains mainly monounsaturated fats.*
> • *Brown rice is often mistakenly called wholegrain. In fact, the outer husk is completely inedible and is removed from all rice, but the bran layer is left intact on brown rice.*

Wilted Spinach with Rice & Dill

This is a delicious vegetarian dish that can be made in very little time. In Greece it is particularly popular during periods of fasting, when meat is avoided for religious reasons.

Serves 6
675g/1½lb fresh spinach, trimmed of any hard stalks
105ml/7 tbsp extra-virgin olive oil
1 large onion, chopped
juice of ½ lemon
150ml/¼ pint/⅔ cup water
115g/4oz/generous ½ cup long grain rice
30ml/2 tbsp chopped fresh dill, plus extra sprigs to garnish
salt and ground black pepper

1 Thoroughly wash the spinach in cold water and drain. Repeat four or five times until the spinach is completely clean and free of grit, then drain thoroughly. Brush off the excess water with kitchen paper and coarsely shred the spinach.

2 Heat the olive oil in a large pan and sauté the onion until softened. Add the spinach and stir for a few minutes to coat it with the oil.

3 As soon as the spinach looks wilted, add the lemon juice and the measured water and bring to the boil. Add the rice and chopped dill, then cover and cook gently for about 10 minutes or until the rice is cooked to your taste. If it looks too dry, add a little extra hot water.

4 Spoon the rice into a serving dish and sprinkle the sprigs of dill over the top. Serve hot or at room temperature.

> **Cook's Tip**
> *This dish makes a nourishing vegetarian meal when accompanied by chickpea rissoles, served with a fresh tomato sauce. Alternatively, it is excellent as a light lunch dish, served with warm walnut bread.*

Fruity brown rice salad: Energy 189kcal/799kJ; Protein 3g; Carbohydrate 35.5g, of which sugars 14.4g; Fat 4.9g, of which saturates 0.6g; Cholesterol 0mg; Calcium 20mg; Fibre 2g; Sodium 94mg
Wilted spinach with rice & dill: Energy 325kcal/1343kJ; Protein 7.8g; Carbohydrate 29.9g, of which sugars 5.6g; Fat 19.2g, of which saturates 2.7g; Cholesterol 0mg; Calcium 327mg; Fibre 4.8g; Sodium 242mg

Simple Rice Salad

A quick and easy dish of fresh salad vegetables tossed into cooled rice.

Serves 6

275g/10oz/1½ cups long grain rice
1 bunch spring onions (scallions), finely sliced
1 green (bell) pepper, seeded and finely diced
1 yellow (bell) pepper, seeded and finely diced
½ fresh green chilli, chopped
225g/8oz tomatoes, peeled, seeded and chopped
30ml/2 tbsp chopped fresh flat leaf parsley

For the dressing

75ml/5 tbsp mixed olive oil and extra-virgin olive oil
15ml/1 tbsp lemon juice
5ml/1 tsp strong Dijon mustard
salt and ground black pepper

1 Cook the rice in a large pan of lightly salted boiling water for 10–12 minutes, until tender. Drain the rice well, rinse thoroughly under cold running water and drain again. Leave the rice to cool completely.

2 Place the rice in a large serving bowl. Add the spring onions, peppers, tomatoes and parsley or coriander.

3 To make the dressing, place all the ingredients in a screw-top jar, close the lid tightly and shake vigorously until well mixed. Stir the dressing into the rice and season with salt and pepper.

Tomato Rice & Beans with Avocado Salsa

Tasty rice and beans, served on tortillas, with a tangy avocado and onion salsa, is a supper dish with bags of Mexican flavour.

Serves 4

40g/1½oz/¼ cup dried kidney beans or 75g/3oz/1½ cup canned kidney beans, rinsed and drained
8 tomatoes, halved and seeded
2 garlic cloves, chopped
1 onion, sliced
45ml/3 tbsp olive oil
225g/8oz/generous 1 cup long grain brown rice, rinsed
600ml/1 pint/2½ cups vegetable stock
2 carrots, diced
75g/3oz/¾ cup green beans
salt and ground black pepper
4 wheat tortillas and soured cream, to serve

For the avocado salsa

1 avocado
juice of 1 lime
1 small red onion, diced
1 small fresh red chilli, seeded and chopped
15ml/1 tbsp chopped fresh coriander (cilantro)

1 If using dried kidney beans, place in a bowl, cover with cold water and leave to soak overnight, then drain and rinse well. Place in a pan with enough water to cover and bring to the boil. Boil rapidly for 10 minutes, then reduce the heat. Simmer for 40–50 minutes until tender; drain and set aside.

2 To make the avocado salsa, halve and stone (pit) the avocado. Peel and dice the flesh, then toss it in the lime juice. Add the onion, chilli and coriander. Mix well.

3 Preheat the grill (broiler) to high. Place the tomatoes, garlic and onion on a baking tray. Pour over 15ml/1 tbsp of the oil and toss to coat. Grill (broil) for 10 minutes or until the tomatoes and onions are softened, turning once. Set the vegetables aside and leave to cool.

4 Heat the remaining oil in a pan, add the rice and cook for 2 minutes, stirring, until light golden.

5 Purée the cooled tomatoes and onion in a food processor or blender, then add the mixture to the rice and cook for a further 2 minutes, stirring frequently.

6 Pour in the vegetable stock, then cover the pan and cook gently for 20 minutes, stirring occasionally.

7 Stir 30ml/2 tbsp of the kidney beans into the salsa. Add the rest to the rice mixture with the carrots and green beans, and cook for 10 minutes until the vegetables are tender. Season well. Remove the pan from the heat and leave to stand, covered, for 15 minutes.

8 Meanwhile, warm the wheat tortillas under the grill.

9 Place one tortilla on each serving plate. Spoon the hot rice and bean mixture on top. Serve immediately, with the avocado salsa and a bowl of soured cream.

Spanish Rice Salad

Ribbons of green and yellow pepper add colour and flavour to this simple salad.

Serves 6

275g/10oz/1½ cups long grain rice
1 bunch spring onions (scallions), thinly sliced
1 green (bell) pepper, seeded and sliced
1 yellow (bell) pepper, seeded and sliced
3 tomatoes, peeled, seeded and chopped
30ml/2 tbsp chopped fresh coriander (cilantro)

For the dressing

75ml/5 tbsp mixed sunflower and olive oil
15ml/1 tbsp rice vinegar
5ml/1 tsp Dijon mustard
salt and ground black pepper

1 Bring a large pan of lightly salted water to the boil and cook the rice for 10–12 minutes, until tender but still slightly firm at the centre of the grain. Do not overcook. Drain, rinse under cold water and drain again. Leave until cold.

2 Place the rice in a large serving bowl. Add the spring onions, peppers, tomatoes and coriander.

3 To make the dressing, mix the oils, vinegar and mustard in a screw-top jar with a tight-fitting lid and season to taste with salt and pepper. Shake vigorously. Stir 60–75ml/4–5 tbsp of the dressing into the rice and adjust the seasoning, if necessary.

4 Cover and chill for about 1 hour before serving. Offer the remaining dressing separately.

Variations
• Cooked garden peas, cooked diced carrot and drained, canned sweetcorn can be added to this versatile salad.
• This recipe works well with long grain rice, but if you can obtain Spanish rice, it will be more authentic. This has a rounder grain, a little like risotto rice.

Couscous with Eggs & Tomato

This tasty Middle-Eastern vegetarian dish is quick to make with the easy-to-use couscous available today.

Serves 4

675g/1½lb plum tomatoes, roughly chopped
4 garlic cloves, chopped
75ml/5 tbsp olive oil
½ fresh red chilli, seeded and chopped
10ml/2 tsp soft light brown sugar
4 eggs
1 large onion, chopped
2 celery sticks, finely sliced
50g/2oz/⅓ cup sultanas (golden raisins)
200g/7oz/generous 1 cup ready-to-use couscous
350ml/12fl oz/1½ cups hot vegetable stock
salt and ground black pepper

1 Preheat the oven to 200°C/400°F/Gas 6. Spread out the tomatoes and garlic in a roasting pan, drizzle with 30ml/2 tbsp of the oil, sprinkle with the chopped chilli and sugar, salt and pepper, and roast for 20 minutes.

2 Meanwhile, cook the eggs in boiling water for 4 minutes, then plunge them straight into cold water and leave until cold. Carefully peel off the shells.

3 Heat 15–30ml/1–2 tbsp of the remaining olive oil in a large pan and fry the onion and celery until softened. Add the sultanas, couscous and hot stock, and set aside until all the liquid has been absorbed. Stir gently, adding extra hot stock if necessary, and season to taste. Turn the mixture into a large heated serving dish, bury the eggs in the couscous and cover with foil. Keep warm in the oven.

4 Remove the tomato mixture from the oven and press it through a strainer placed over a bowl. Add 15ml/1 tbsp boiling water and the rest of the olive oil and stir to make a smooth, rich sauce.

5 Remove the couscous mixture from the oven and locate the eggs. Spoon a little tomato sauce over the top of each egg. Serve immediately, with the rest of the sauce handed separately.

Spanish rice salad: Energy 246kcal/1028kJ; Protein 4.7g; Carbohydrate 42.4g, of which sugars 5.6g; Fat 6.3g, of which saturates 0.8g; Cholesterol 0mg; Calcium 24mg; Fibre 1.7g; Sodium 33mg
Couscous with eggs & tomato: Energy 418kcal/1744kJ; Protein 12.1g; Carbohydrate 49.3g, of which sugars 21g; Fat 20.6g, of which saturates 3.7g; Cholesterol 190mg; Calcium 85mg; Fibre 3.4g; Sodium 99mg

Grilled Aubergine & Couscous Salad

Easy to make, yet packed with Mediterranean flavours, this delicious couscous salad is wonderful served with a crisp green salad.

Serves 2
1 large aubergine (eggplant)
30ml/2 tbsp olive oil
115g/4oz packet garlic
   and coriander (cilantro)
   flavoured couscous
30ml/2 tbsp chopped fresh mint
salt and ground black pepper
fresh mint leaves, to garnish

1 Preheat the grill (broiler) to high. Cut the aubergine into large chunky pieces and toss them with the olive oil. Season with salt and ground black pepper to taste and spread the aubergine pieces on a non-stick baking sheet. Grill (broil) for 5–6 minutes, turning occasionally, until golden brown.

2 Meanwhile, prepare the couscous in boiling water, according to the instructions on the packet.

3 Stir the grilled aubergine and chopped mint into the couscous, toss the salad thoroughly to spread the flavours, and serve immediately, garnished with mint leaves.

Cook's Tip
Packets of flavoured couscous are available in most supermarkets – you can use whichever you like, but garlic and coriander (cilantro) is particularly good for this recipe.

Variation
A similar dish, which is also popular around Greece, uses grilled (broiled) courgettes (zucchini) instead of, or as well as, the aubergine. Slice the courgettes into thin rounds or ovals, brush with olive oil, and place under a hot grill (broiler) for a few minutes on each side.

Bulgur Wheat & Cherry Tomato Salad

This appetizing salad is ideal served with fresh crusty bread and home-made chutney or pickle.

Serves 6
350g/12oz/2 cups bulgur wheat
225g/8oz frozen broad
   (fava) beans
115g/4oz/1 cup frozen petits
   pois (baby peas)
225g/8oz cherry tomatoes, halved
1 sweet onion, chopped
1 red (bell) pepper, seeded
   and diced
50g/2oz mangetouts
   (snow peas), chopped
50g/2oz watercress
45ml/3 tbsp chopped fresh
   herbs, such as parsley, basil
   and thyme

For the dressing
75ml/5 tbsp olive oil
15ml/1 tbsp white wine vinegar
5ml/1 tsp mustard powder
salt and ground black pepper

1 Put the bulgur wheat into a large bowl. Add enough cold water to come 2.5cm/1in above the level of the wheat. Leave to soak for approximately 30 minutes.

2 Turn the soaked bulgur wheat into a sieve (strainer) lined with a clean dish towel. Drain the wheat well and use the dish towel to squeeze out any excess water.

3 Cook the broad beans and petits pois in a pan of boiling water for about 3 minutes, until tender. Drain thoroughly and mix with the prepared bulgur wheat in a bowl.

4 Add the cherry tomatoes, onion, pepper, mangetouts and watercress to the bulgur wheat mixture and mix. Combine all the ingredients for the dressing, season and stir well.

5 Add the herbs to the salad, season and add enough dressing to taste. Toss the ingredients together.

6 Serve immediately or cover and chill in the refrigerator before serving.

Fennel & Egg Tabbouleh with Herbs

This Middle-Eastern classic is given a different twist with the addition of aniseed-flavoured fennel and tangy black olives.

Serves 4
250g/9oz/1 cup bulgur wheat
4 small eggs
1 fennel bulb
1 bunch of spring onions (scallions), chopped
25g/1oz/1/2 cup drained sun-dried tomatoes in oil, sliced
45ml/3 tbsp chopped fresh parsley
30ml/2 tbsp chopped fresh mint
75g/3oz/1/2 cup black olives
60ml/4 tbsp olive oil
30ml/2 tbsp garlic oil
30ml/2 tbsp lemon juice
50g/2oz/1/2 cup chopped hazelnuts, toasted
1 open-textured loaf or 4 pitta breads, warmed
salt and ground black pepper

1 Put the bulgur wheat into a large bowl. Add enough cold water to come 2.5cm/1in above the level of the wheat. Leave to soak for approximately 30 minutes.

2 Turn the soaked bulgur wheat into a sieve (strainer) lined with a clean dish towel. Drain the wheat well and use the dish towel to squeeze out any excess water. Leave to cool.

3 Cook the eggs in boiling water for 8 minutes. Cool under running water, peel and quarter.

4 Halve and finely slice the fennel. Boil in salted water for 6 minutes, then drain and cool under running water. Drain again thoroughly.

5 Combine the eggs, fennel, spring onions, sun-dried tomatoes, parsley, mint and olives with the bulgur wheat.

6 Put the olive oil, garlic oil and lemon juice in a small bowl and whisk together with a fork. Add to the bulgur wheat salad, toss well, then add the nuts. Season with salt and pepper to taste, then tear the bread into pieces and add to the salad. Serve the salad immediately.

Tabbouleh with Tomatoes & Apricots

A marvellous combination of vegetables and fruity flavours, this colourful dish is the epitomé of Middle-Eastern cooking.

Serves 4
250g/9oz/1 1/2 cups bulgur wheat
4 tomatoes
4 baby courgettes (zucchini), thinly sliced
4 spring onions (scallions), sliced
8 ready-to-eat dried apricots, chopped
40g/1 1/2oz/1/4 cup raisins or sultanas (golden raisins)
juice of 1 lemon
30ml/2 tbsp tomato juice
45ml/3 tbsp chopped fresh mint
1 garlic clove, crushed
salt and ground black pepper
sprig of fresh mint, to garnish

1 Put the bulgur wheat into a large bowl. Add enough cold water to come 2.5cm/1in above the level of the wheat. Leave to soak for 30 minutes, then turn into a sieve (strainer) lined with a clean dish towel. Drain well and squeeze out any water.

2 Meanwhile, cut a mark in the top of the tomatoes and plunge into boiling water for 30 seconds, then refresh in a bowl of cold water. Peel off the skins. Halve the tomatoes, remove the seeds and cores, and chop roughly.

3 In a bowl, mix the tomatoes, courgettes, spring onions and dried fruit with the bulgur wheat.

4 Put the lemon and tomato juice, mint, garlic clove and salt and pepper to taste in a small bowl and whisk together with a fork. Pour over the salad and mix well. Chill for at least 1 hour. Serve garnished with a sprig of mint.

Cook's Tip
Also known as cracked wheat, bulgur wheat has been partially cooked, so it requires only a short soaking before being used in a salad. It is very handy for a quick meal.

Lentil, Tomato & Cheese Salad

In this hearty salad, lentils are teamed up with crumbly cheese, red onion and fresh-tasting tomatoes to provide a wholesome vegetarian main course with lots of texture contrasts. Serve with a tossed green salad and poppy seed rolls for a complete meal.

Serves 6
200g/7oz/scant 1 cup lentils (preferably Puy lentils), soaked for about 3 hours in cold water to cover
1 red onion, chopped
1 bay leaf
60ml/4 tbsp extra-virgin olive oil
45ml/3 tbsp chopped fresh parsley
30ml/2 tbsp chopped fresh oregano or marjoram
250g/9oz cherry tomatoes, halved
250g/9oz feta, goat's milk cheese or Caerphilly cheese, crumbled
salt and ground black pepper
30–45ml/2–3 tbsp lightly toasted pine nuts
leaves of chicory (Belgian endive), frisée and fresh herbs, to garnish

1 Drain the lentils and place them in a large pan. Pour in plenty of cold water and add the onion and bay leaf. Bring to the boil, boil hard for 10 minutes, then lower the heat and simmer for 20 minutes or according to the instructions on the packet.

2 Drain the lentils, discard the bay leaf and transfer them to a bowl. Add salt and pepper to taste. Toss with the olive oil. Set aside to cool, then mix with the fresh parsley, oregano or marjoram and cherry tomatoes.

3 Add the cheese. Line a serving dish with chicory or frisée leaves and pile the salad in the centre. Scatter over the pine nuts and garnish with fresh herbs.

> **Cook's Tip**
> The small blue-green Puy lentils from France are perfect for salads; flat green Continental lentils or massor dhal lentils from India are also a good choice.

Fragrant Lentil & Spinach Salad

This earthy salad is great for a picnic or barbecue.

Serves 6
225g/8oz/1 cup Puy lentils
1 fresh bay leaf
1 celery stick
1 fresh thyme sprig
30ml/2 tbsp olive oil
1 onion, finely sliced
10ml/2 tsp crushed toasted cumin seeds
400g/14oz young spinach leaves
30–45ml/2–3 tbsp chopped fresh parsley, plus a few extra sprigs for garnishing
salt and ground black pepper

For the dressing
45ml/3 tbsp extra-virgin olive oil
5ml/1 tsp Dijon mustard
15–25ml/3–5 tsp red wine vinegar
1 small garlic clove, finely chopped
2.5ml/½ tsp grated (shredded) lemon rind

1 Rinse the lentils and place them in a large pan. Add water to cover. Tie the bay leaf, celery and thyme into a bundle and add to the pan, then bring to the boil. Lower the heat to a steady boil. Cook the lentils for 30–45 minutes, until just tender.

2 Meanwhile, make the dressing. Mix the oil and mustard with 15ml/1 tbsp of the vinegar. Add the garlic and lemon rind, and whisk to mix. Season well with salt and pepper.

3 Drain the lentils and discard the herbs. Transfer them to a serving bowl, add most of the dressing and toss well. Set aside and stir occasionally.

4 Heat the oil in a pan and cook the onion for 4–5 minutes, until it starts to soften. Add the cumin and cook for 1 minute.

5 Add the spinach and season to taste, then cover and cook for 2 minutes. Stir, then cook again briefly until wilted.

6 Stir the spinach into the lentils and leave the salad to cool to room temperature. Stir in the remaining dressing and chopped parsley. Adjust the seasoning, adding more vinegar if necessary. Spoon onto a serving platter, scatter some parsley sprigs over, and serve at room temperature with toasted French bread.

Lentil, tomato & cheese salad: Energy 341kcal/1423kJ; Protein 16.1g; Carbohydrate 22g, of which sugars 3.7g; Fat 21.6g, of which saturates 7.2g; Cholesterol 29mg; Calcium 188mg; Fibre 2.7g; Sodium 619mg
Fragrant lentil & spinach salad: Energy 224kcal/938kJ; Protein 11g; Carbohydrate 23.2g, of which sugars 2.5g; Fat 10.3g, of which saturates 1.5g; Cholesterol 0mg; Calcium 136mg; Fibre 3.4g; Sodium 132mg

Sweet & Hot Vegetable Noodles

This noodle dish has the colour of fire, but only the mildest suggestion of heat.

Serves 4

130g/4½oz dried rice noodles
30ml/2 tbsp groundnut
   (peanut) oil
2.5cm/1in piece fresh root ginger,
   sliced into thin batons
1 garlic clove, crushed
130g/4½oz drained canned
   bamboo shoots, cut into batons
2 carrots, sliced into batons
130g/4½oz/1½ cups
   beansprouts

1 small white cabbage, shredded
30ml/2 tbsp soy sauce
30ml/2 tbsp plum sauce
10ml/2 tsp sesame oil
15ml/1 tbsp palm sugar (jaggery)
   or light muscovado
   (brown) sugar
juice of ½ lime
90g/3½oz mooli (daikon), sliced
   into thin batons
small bunch fresh coriander
   (cilantro), chopped
60ml/4 tbsp sesame
   seeds, toasted

1 Cook the noodles in a large pan of boiling water, following the instructions on the packet.

2 Heat the oil in a wok or large pan and stir-fry the ginger and garlic for 2–3 minutes on a medium heat, until golden.

3 Drain the noodles and set them aside. Add the bamboo shoots to the wok, increase the heat to high and stir-fry for 5 minutes. Add the carrots, beansprouts and cabbage and stir-fry for a further 5 minutes, until they are beginning to char.

4 Stir in the sauces, sesame oil, sugar and lime juice. Add the mooli and coriander, toss to mix, then spoon into a warmed bowl, sprinkle with sesame seeds and serve immediately.

Cook's Tip
Use a large, sharp knife for shredding cabbage. Remove tough outer leaves, then cut into quarters. Cut off the hard core from each quarter, then place flat side down and slice into shreds.

Fried Tofu & Rice Noodle Salad

A light and refreshing salad, this is a meal in itself. Extremely easy to assemble, it is excellent as a last-minute supper dish.

Serves 4

200g/7oz cellophane noodles
8 spring onions (scallions), thinly
   sliced
300g/11oz marinated
   deep-fried tofu

about 2.5ml/½ tsp dried chilli
   flakes
grated (shredded) rind and juice
   of 1 lemon
5cm/2in piece fresh root ginger,
   sliced into fine batons (optional)
1 bunch fresh coriander (cilantro)
   or parsley, chopped
about 30ml/2 tbsp soy sauce
30ml/2 tbsp toasted sesame oil
65g/2½oz/½ cup sesame or
   sunflower seeds, toasted,
   or 75g/3oz/¾ cup peanuts

1 Cover the noodles with boiling water, leave for 5–10 minutes, or according to the packet instructions, then drain and rinse under cold running water. Place in a large bowl.

2 Add the spring onions, tofu and chilli flakes to the noodles, together with the lemon rind and juice, ginger, if using, coriander, soy sauce, sesame oil and seeds or nuts. Toss together, then add salt and pepper to taste and serve.

Cook's Tip
Made from bean curd, tofu is a good source of protein for vegetarians. It is bland in taste but absorbs marinades well.

Variations
• *Try making a thin egg omelette seasoned with soy sauce and a pinch of sugar then rolled up and finely sliced. Use with or instead of the marinated tofu.*
• *Peanuts could be toasted and chopped and used instead of the sesame or sunflower seeds.*
• *Green beans or mangetouts (snow peas) can be blanched and used with or instead of the coriander (cilantro).*

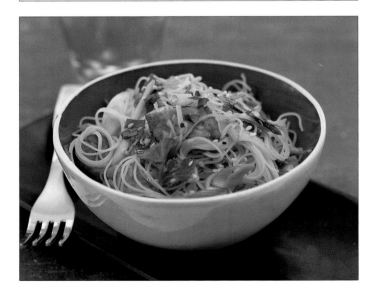

Sweet & hot vegetable noodles: Energy 368kcal/1530kJ; Protein 8.8g; Carbohydrate 45.8g, of which sugars 17.6g; Fat 16.5g, of which saturates 2.3g; Cholesterol 0mg; Calcium 200mg; Fibre 6.2g; Sodium 650mg
Fried tofu & rice noodle salad: Energy 699kcal/2898kJ; Protein 23.7g; Carbohydrate 43.6g, of which sugars 1.9g; Fat 47.1g, of which saturates 5.7g; Cholesterol 0mg; Calcium 1235mg; Fibre 1.6g; Sodium 554mg

VEGETARIAN SALADS

Noodles with Pineapple, Ginger & Chillies

Fragrant and fruity, this noodle dish makes an exotic change from pasta. The pineapple is glazed to give a delicious sweetness, while garlic and chilli add a savoury note.

Serves 4
275g/10oz dried udon noodles
½ pineapple, peeled, cored and
    sliced into 4cm/1½in rings
45ml/3 tbsp soft light
    brown sugar
60ml/4 tbsp fresh lime juice
60ml/4 tbsp coconut milk
30ml/2 tbsp grated (shredded)
    fresh root ginger
2 garlic cloves, finely chopped
1 ripe mango or 2 peaches,
    finely diced
freshly ground black pepper

For the garnish
2 spring onions (scallions),
    finely sliced
2 red chillies, seeded and
    finely shredded
fresh mint leaves

1 Cook the noodles in a large pan of boiling water until tender, according to the instructions on the packet. Drain, refresh under cold water and drain again.

2 Place the pineapple rings on a flameproof dish, sprinkle with 30ml/2 tbsp of the sugar and grill (broil) for about 5 minutes or until golden. Cool slightly and cut into small dice.

3 Mix the lime juice and coconut milk in a salad bowl. Add the remaining brown sugar, with the ginger and garlic, and whisk well. Add the noodles and pineapple. Add the mango or peaches and toss. Scatter over the spring onions, chillies and mint leaves before serving.

> **Cook's Tip**
> The Japanese udon noodles are made from wheat flour. They are white and are usually fairly thick with a slightly chewy texture. They are often used in soups and are eaten hot or cold.

Hot & Sour Noodle Salad

Noodles make the perfect basis for a salad, absorbing the dressing and providing a contrast in texture to the crisp vegetables.

Serves 2
200g/7oz dried thin rice noodles
1 small bunch fresh coriander
    (cilantro)
2 tomatoes, seeded and sliced
130g/4½oz baby corn
    cobs, sliced
4 spring onions (scallions),
    thinly sliced
1 red (bell) pepper, seeded and
    finely chopped
juice of 2 limes
2 small fresh green chillies,
    seeded and finely chopped
10ml/2 tsp sugar
115g/4oz/1 cup peanuts, toasted
    and chopped
30ml/2 tbsp soy sauce
salt

1 Bring a large pan of lightly salted water to the boil. Snap the noodles into short lengths, add to the pan and cook for 3–4 minutes. Drain, then rinse under cold water and drain again.

2 Set aside a few coriander leaves for the garnish. Chop the remaining leaves and place them in a large serving bowl.

3 Put the noodles into the bowl with the chopped coriander. Add the tomato slices, corn cobs, spring onions, red pepper, lime juice, chillies, sugar and toasted peanuts.

4 Season with the soy sauce, then taste and add a little salt if you think the mixture needs it.

5 Toss the salad lightly but thoroughly, then garnish with the reserved coriander leaves and serve immediately.

> **Variation**
> If you are not a fan of the strong taste of coriander (cilantro), try swapping in Thai basil for this recipe. It has a subtle, yet distinctive flavour that complements chilli and lime juice well. Thai basil is now available as a fresh herb in many Oriental markets and supermarkets.

Rice Noodles with Fresh Herbs

Rice noodles simply tossed with crunchy salad vegetables, fresh herbs and sharp flavourings make a delicious and satisfying vegetarian snack.

Serves 4
half a small cucumber
4–6 lettuce leaves

1 bunch mixed fresh basil, coriander (cilantro), mint and oregano
225g/8oz dried rice sticks (vermicelli)
115g/4oz/1/2 cup beansprouts
juice of half a lime
soy sauce, to drizzle (optional)

1 Peel the cucumber, cut it in half lengthwise, remove the seeds, and cut into matchsticks. Using a sharp knife, cut the lettuce into fine shreds. Remove the stalks from the herbs and shred the leaves.

2 Add the rice sticks to a pan of boiling water, loosening them gently, and cook for 3–4 minutes, or until white and just tender. Drain, rinse under cold water, and drain again.

3 In a bowl, toss the shredded lettuce, beansprouts and cucumber together, then toss in the shredded herbs. Add the noodles and lime juice and toss together.

4 Drizzle with a little soy sauce, if using, and serve immediately.

Thai Noodle Salad

The addition of coconut milk and sesame oil gives an unusual nutty flavour to the dressing for this colourful noodle salad.

Serves 4–6
350g/12oz somen noodles
1 large carrot, cut into thin strips
1 bunch asparagus, trimmed and cut into 4cm/1 1/2in lengths
1 red (bell) pepper, seeded and cut into fine strips
115g/4oz mangetouts (snow peas), topped, tailed and halved
115g/4oz baby corn cobs, halved lengthwise
115g/4oz beansprouts
115g/4oz can water chestnuts, drained and finely sliced

1 lime, cut into wedges, 50g/2oz/1/2 cup roasted peanuts, roughly chopped, and fresh coriander (cilantro) leaves, to garnish

For the dressing
45ml/3 tbsp roughly torn fresh basil
75ml/5 tbsp roughly chopped fresh mint
250ml/8fl oz/1 cup coconut milk
30ml/2 tbsp dark sesame oil
15ml/1 tbsp grated (shredded) fresh root ginger
2 garlic cloves, finely chopped
juice of 1 lime
2 spring onions (scallions), finely chopped
salt and cayenne pepper

1 To make the dressing, combine the herbs, coconut milk, sesame oil, ginger, garlic, lime juice and spring onions in a large bowl and mix well. Season to taste with salt and cayenne pepper.

2 Cook the noodles in a pan of boiling water, according to the instructions on the packet, until just tender. Drain, rinse under cold running water and drain again.

3 Cook all the vegetables, except the water chestnuts, in separate pans of boiling, lightly salted water until they are tender but still crisp. Drain, plunge them immediately into cold water and drain again.

4 Toss the noodles, vegetables, water chestnuts and dressing together. Arrange on individual serving plates and garnish the salads with the lime wedges, chopped peanuts and coriander.

Rice noodles with fresh herbs: Energy 217kcal/908kJ; Protein 6.4g; Carbohydrate 46.1g, of which sugars 1.5g; Fat 0.6g, of which saturates 0.1g; Cholesterol 0mg; Calcium 51mg; Fibre 1.3g; Sodium 11mg
Thai noodle salad: Energy 365kcal/1521kJ; Protein 6g; Carbohydrate 55.1g, of which sugars 6.7g; Fat 12.8g, of which saturates 2.3g; Cholesterol 0mg; Calcium 61mg; Fibre 2.5g; Sodium 280mg

Sesame Noodle Salad

Toasted sesame oil adds a nutty flavour to this salad, which is at its best when served warm.

Serves 2–4

250g/9oz medium egg noodles
200g/7oz/1¾ cups sugar snap
   peas or mangetouts (snow
   peas), sliced diagonally
2 carrots, cut into fine
   julienne strips
2 tomatoes, seeded and diced
15ml/1 tbsp sesame seeds
30ml/2 tbsp chopped fresh
   coriander (cilantro), plus

coriander sprigs, to garnish
3 spring onions (scallions),
   shredded

For the dressing

10ml/2 tsp light soy sauce
30ml/2 tbsp toasted sesame
   seed oil
15ml/1 tbsp sunflower oil
4cm/1½in piece of fresh root
   ginger, finely grated
1 garlic clove, crushed

1 Bring a large pan of water to the boil, add the noodles and remove the pan from the heat. Cover and leave to stand for about 4 minutes, until the noodles are just tender.

2 Meanwhile, bring a second, smaller pan of water to the boil. Add the sugar snap peas or mangetouts, bring back to the boil and cook for 2 minutes. Drain and refresh under cold water, then drain again.

3 To make the dressing, put the soy sauce, sesame seed and sunflower oils, ginger and garlic in a screw-top jar. Close tightly and shake vigorously to mix.

4 Drain the noodles thoroughly and turn them into a large bowl. Add the peas or mangetouts, carrots, tomatoes and coriander. Pour the dressing over the top, and toss thoroughly with your hands to combine.

5 Sprinkle the salad with the sesame seeds, garnish with the shredded spring onions and coriander sprigs and serve while the noodles are still warm.

Sesame Noodle Salad with Hot Peanuts

An Eastern-inspired salad with crunchy vegetables and a light soy dressing. The hot peanuts make a surprisingly successful union with the cold noodles.

Serves 4

350g/12oz egg noodles
2 carrots, cut into fine
   julienne strips
½ cucumber, peeled, seeded and
   cut into 1cm/½in cubes
115g/4oz celeriac, peeled and
   cut into fine julienne strips
6 spring onions (scallions),
   finely sliced

8 canned water chestnuts, drained
   and finely sliced
175g/6oz/1⅔ cups beansprouts
1 small fresh green chilli, seeded
   and finely chopped
30ml/2 tbsp sesame seeds and
   115g/4oz/1 cup peanuts,
   to serve

For the dressing

15ml/1 tbsp dark soy sauce
15ml/1 tbsp light soy sauce
15ml/1 tbsp clear honey
15ml/1 tbsp Chinese rice wine
   or dry sherry
15ml/1 tbsp sesame oil

1 Cook the egg noodles in boiling water, according to the instructions on the packet.

2 Drain the noodles, refresh in cold water, then drain again. Mix the noodles together with all of the prepared vegetables. Preheat the oven to 200°C/400°F/ Gas 6.

3 Combine the dressing ingredients in a small bowl, then toss into the noodle and vegetable mixture. Divide the salad between 4 plates.

4 Place the sesame seeds and peanuts on separate baking trays and place in the oven. Take the sesame seeds out after 5 minutes and continue to cook the peanuts for another 5 minutes until evenly browned.

5 Sprinkle the sesame seeds and peanuts evenly over each salad portion and serve at once.

Basmati and Blue Lentil Salad

Puy lentils from France (sometimes known as blue lentils) are small, deliciously nutty pulses. In this recipe, they blend beautifully with aromatic basmati rice.

Serves 6
115g/4oz/⅔cup Puys de dome lentils, soaked
225g/8oz/1¼ cups basmati rice, rinsed well
2 carrots, coarsely grated
⅓ cucumber, halved, seeded and coarsely grated
3 spring onions (scallions), sliced

45 ml/3 tbsp fresh parsley, chopped

For the dressing
30ml/2 tbsp sunflower oil
30ml/2 tbsp extra-virgin olive oil
30ml/2 tbsp wine vinegar
30ml/2 tbsp fresh lemon juice
good pinch of sugar
salt and ground black pepper

1 Soak the dried lentils in plenty of cold water for 30 minutes.

2 Make the dressing by shaking all the dressing ingredients together in a screw-topped jar. Adjust the seasoning and sugar to taste. Set aside.

3 Drain the lentils, then pour them into a large pan of unsalted water. Bring this to the boil and cook the lentils for 20–25 minutes or until soft. Drain thoroughly.

4 Boil the basmati rice for 10 minutes, or according to the instructions on the packet, then drain.

5 Using a large mixing bowl, toss together the rice and lentils in the dressing and season well. Leave, uncovered, to cool.

6 Once the rice mixture is cold, add the prepared carrots, cucumber, onions and parsley. Chill.

7 Spoon the cooled salad into an attractive bowl when ready to serve.

Thai Rice & Sprouting Beans

Thai rice has a delicate fragrance and texture that is delicious whether served hot or cold. This salad is a colourful collection of popular Thai flavours.

Serves 6
30ml/2 tbsp sesame oil
30ml/2 tbsp fresh lime juice
1 small fresh red chilli, seeded and chopped
1 garlic clove, crushed
10ml/2 tsp grated (shredded) fresh root ginger
30ml/2 tbsp light soy sauce
5ml/1 tsp clear honey

45ml/3 tbsp pineapple juice
15ml/1 tbsp wine vinegar
225g/8oz/1¼ cups Thai fragrant rice, lightly boiled
2 spring onions (scallions), sliced
2 rings canned pineapple in natural juice, chopped
150g/5oz/1¼ cups sprouted lentils or beansprouts
1 small red (bell) pepper, sliced
1 celery stick, sliced
50g/2oz/½ cup unsalted cashew nuts, roughly chopped
30ml/2 tbsp toasted sesame seeds
salt and ground black pepper

1 Whisk together the sesame oil, lime juice, chilli, garlic, ginger, soy sauce, honey, pineapple juice and vinegar in a large bowl. Stir in the lightly boiled rice.

2 Toss in all the remaining ingredients and mix well. This dish can be served warm or lightly chilled. If the rice grains stick together on cooling, simply stir them with a metal spoon.

Basmati & blue lentil salad: Energy 231kcal/961kJ; Protein 4.2g; Carbohydrate 34.3g, of which sugars 2.2g; Fat 8.4g, of which saturates 1.2g; Cholesterol 1mg; Calcium 39mg; Fibre 1.2g; Sodium 16mg
Thai rice & sprouting beans: Energy 281kcal/1171kJ; Protein 6.7g; Carbohydrate 38.2g, of which sugars 6.6g; Fat 11.3g, of which saturates 1.8g; Cholesterol 0mg; Calcium 60mg; Fibre 1.8g; Sodium 387mg

Fruit & Raw Vegetable Gado-Gado

A banana leaf, which can be bought from Asian stores, can be used instead of the mixed salad leaves to line the platter for a special occasion.

Serves 6

½ cucumber
2 pears (not too ripe) or
    175g/6oz wedge of yam bean
1–2 eating apples
juice of ½ lemon
mixed salad leaves
6 small tomatoes, cut in wedges
3 slices fresh pineapple, cored
    and cut in wedges
3 eggs, hard-boiled (hard-cooked)
    and shelled

175g/6oz egg noodles, cooked,
    cooled and chopped
deep-fried onions, to garnish

For the peanut sauce

2–4 fresh red chillies, seeded
    and ground, or 15ml/1 tbsp
    chilli sambal
300ml/½ pint/1¼ cups
    coconut milk
350g/12oz/1¼ cups crunchy
    peanut butter
15ml/1 tbsp dark soy sauce or
    dark brown sugar
5ml/1 tsp tamarind pulp, soaked
    in 45ml/3 tbsp warm water
coarsely crushed peanuts
salt

1 To make the peanut sauce, put the ground chillies or chilli sambal in a pan. Pour in the coconut milk, then stir in the peanut butter. Heat gently, stirring, until well blended.

2 Simmer gently until the sauce thickens, then stir in the soy sauce or sugar. Strain in the tamarind juice, add salt to taste and stir well. Spoon into a small serving bowl and sprinkle with a few coarsely crushed peanuts.

3 To make the salad, core the cucumber and peel the pears or yam bean. Cut them into matchsticks. Finely shred the apples and sprinkle them with the lemon juice.

4 Spread a bed of lettuce leaves on a flat platter, then pile the fruit and vegetables on top.

5 Add the sliced or quartered hard-boiled eggs, the chopped noodles and the deep-fried onions. Serve immediately, with the peanut sauce.

Gado-Gado Salad with Peanut Sambal

This classic Indonesian salad combines lightly steamed vegetables and hard-boiled eggs with a richly flavoured peanut dressing.

Serves 6

225g/8oz new potatoes, halved
2 carrots, cut into sticks
115g/4oz green beans
½ small cauliflower, broken into
    florets
¼ firm white cabbage, shredded
200g/7oz bean or lentil sprouts
4 eggs, hard-boiled (hard-cooked)
    and quartered
bunch of watercress (optional)

For the sauce

90ml/6 tbsp crunchy
    peanut butter
300ml/½ pint/1¼ cups
    cold water
1 garlic clove, crushed
30ml/2 tbsp dark soy sauce
15ml/1 tbsp dry sherry
10ml/2 tsp caster
    (superfine) sugar
15ml/1 tbsp fresh lemon juice

1 Place the halved potatoes in a metal colander or steamer and set over a pan of gently boiling water. Cover the pan or steamer with a lid and cook the potatoes for 10 minutes.

2 Add the rest of the vegetables to the steamer and steam for a further 10 minutes, until tender. Cool and arrange on a platter with the egg quarters and the watercress, if using.

3 Beat together all the ingredients for the sauce in a large mixing bowl until smooth. Drizzle a little sauce over the salad then pour the rest into a small bowl and serve separately.

Variation

There are a range of nut butters available in supermarkets and health-food stores. Try using hazelnut, almond or cashew nut butter in place of peanut butter to create a milder sauce.

Raw vegetable gado-gado: Energy 495kcal/2066kJ; Protein 18.7g; Carbohydrate 30.8g, of which sugars 23.3g; Fat 34g, of which saturates 8.5g; Cholesterol 97mg; Calcium 91mg; Fibre 6.9g; Sodium 489mg
Gado-gado salad: Energy 199kcal/831kJ; Protein 10.5g; Carbohydrate 14g, of which sugars 6.6g; Fat 11.3g, of which saturates 2.9g; Cholesterol 127mg; Calcium 58mg; Fibre 3.1g; Sodium 819mg

Raw Vegetable Yam

In Thai cooking, "yam" dishes are salads made with raw or lightly cooked vegetables, dressed with a special spicy sauce. They are a real treat.

Serves 4

50g/2oz watercress or baby spinach, chopped
¹/₂ cucumber, finely diced
2 celery sticks, finely diced
2 carrots, finely diced
1 red (bell) pepper, seeded and finely diced
2 tomatoes, seeded and finely diced
small bunch fresh mint, chopped
90g/3¹/₂oz cellophane noodles

For the yam

2 small fresh red chillies, seeded and finely chopped
60ml/4 tbsp light soy sauce
45ml/3 tbsp lemon juice
5ml/1 tsp palm sugar (jaggery) or light muscovado (brown) sugar
60ml/4 tbsp water
1 head pickled garlic, finely chopped, plus 15ml/1 tbsp vinegar from the jar
50g/2oz/scant ¹/₂ cup peanuts, roasted and chopped
90g/3¹/₂oz fried tofu, finely chopped
15ml/1 tbsp sesame seeds, toasted

1 Place the watercress or spinach, cucumber, celery, carrots, red pepper and tomatoes in a serving bowl. Add the chopped mint and toss together.

2 Soak the noodles in boiling water for 3 minutes, or according to the packet instructions, then drain well and snip with scissors into shorter lengths. Add them to the vegetables.

3 To make the yam, put the chopped chillies in a pan and add the soy sauce, lemon juice, sugar and water. Place over a medium heat and stir until the sugar has dissolved.

4 Add the garlic, with the pickling vinegar from the jar, then mix in the chopped nuts, tofu and toasted sesame seeds.

5 Pour the yam over the vegetables and noodles, toss together until well mixed, and serve immediately.

Cambodian Soya Beansprout Salad

Unlike mung beansprouts, soya beansprouts are slightly poisonous raw and need to be par-boiled before using. Tossed in a salad and served with noodles and rice they make a perfect light meal.

Serves 4

450g/1lb fresh soya beansprouts
2 spring onions (scallions), finely sliced

1 small bunch fresh coriander (cilantro), stalks removed

For the dressing

15ml/1 tbsp sesame oil
30ml/2tbsp light soy sauce
15ml/1 tbsp white rice vinegar
10ml/2 tsp palm sugar (jaggery)
1 fresh red chilli, seeded and finely sliced
15g/¹/₂ oz fresh young root ginger, finely shredded

1 To make the dressing, in a bowl, beat the oil, soy sauce and rice vinegar with the sugar, until it dissolves. Stir in the chilli and ginger and leave to stand for 30 minutes.

2 Bring a pan of salted water to the boil. Drop in the beansprouts and blanch for a minute only. Drain and refresh under cold water until cool. Drain again and put them into a clean dish towel. Shake out the excess water.

3 Put the beansprouts into a bowl with the spring onions. Pour over the dressing and toss well. Garnish with coriander leaves and serve immediately.

Raw vegetable yam: Energy 276kcal/1152kJ; Protein 12.1g; Carbohydrate 28.8g, of which sugars 9g; Fat 12.4g, of which saturates 1.5g; Cholesterol 0mg; Calcium 415mg; Fibre 3.1g; Sodium 1101mg
Cambodian soya beansprout salad: Energy 95kcal/396kJ; Protein 4.5g; Carbohydrate 8.4g, of which sugars 5.6g; Fat 5.6g, of which saturates 0.5g; Cholesterol 3mg; Calcium 54mg; Fibre 2.4g; Sodium 79mg

Green Papaya Salad

This salad appears in many guises in South-east Asia. As green (or unripe) papaya is not easy to get hold of, finely grated carrots, cucumber or green apple can be used instead. Alternatively, use very thinly sliced white cabbage.

Serves 4
1 green papaya
4 garlic cloves, roughly chopped
15ml/1 tbsp chopped shallots
3–4 fresh red chillies, seeded
  and sliced
2.5ml/½ tsp salt
2–3 snake beans or 6
  green beans, cut into
  2cm/¾in lengths
2 tomatoes, cut into thin wedges
45ml/3 tbsp light soy sauce
15ml/1 tbsp caster
  (superfine) sugar
juice of 1 lime
30ml/2 tbsp crushed roasted
  peanuts
sliced fresh red chillies, to garnish

1 Cut the papaya in half lengthwise. Scrape out the seeds with a spoon, then remove the peel using a swivel vegetable peeler or a small sharp knife. Shred the flesh finely using a food processor or grater (shredder).

2 Put the garlic, shallots, chillies and salt in a large mortar and grind to a paste with a pestle. Add the shredded papaya, a little at a time, pounding until it becomes slightly limp and soft.

3 Add the sliced beans and wedges of tomato to the mortar and crush them lightly with the pestle.

4 Season the mixture with soy sauce, sugar and lime juice. Transfer the salad to a serving dish, sprinkle with crushed peanuts and garnish with sliced red chillies.

> **Cook's Tip**
> Snake beans are extremely long, green, stringless beans. They are available from Oriental stores.

Bamboo Shoot Salad

This hot, sharp-flavoured salad originated in north-eastern Thailand. Use canned whole bamboo shoots, if you can find them – they have more flavour than sliced ones. Serve with noodles and stir-fried vegetables.

Serves 4
400g/14oz canned bamboo
  shoots, in large pieces
25g/1oz/about 3 tbsp
  glutinous rice
30ml/2 tbsp chopped shallots
15ml/1 tbsp chopped garlic
45ml/3 tbsp chopped spring
  onions (scallions)
30ml/2 tbsp light soy sauce
30ml/2 tbsp fresh lime juice
5ml/1 tsp sugar
2.5ml/½ tsp dried chilli flakes
20–25 small fresh mint leaves
15ml/1 tbsp toasted
  sesame seeds

1 Rinse the bamboo shoots under cold running water, then drain them and pat them thoroughly dry with kitchen paper and set them aside.

2 Dry-roast the rice in a frying pan until it is golden brown. Leave to cool slightly, then turn into a mortar and grind to fine crumbs with a pestle.

3 Transfer the rice to a bowl and add the shallots, garlic, spring onions, soy sauce, lime juice, sugar, chillies and half the mint leaves. Mix well.

4 Add the bamboo shoots to the bowl and toss to mix. Serve sprinkled with the toasted sesame seeds and the remaining fresh mint leaves.

> **Cook's Tip**
> Glutinous rice does not, in fact, contain any gluten – it's just sticky. It is very popular in South-east Asian cooking.

Green papaya salad: Energy 109kcal/461kJ; Protein 3.4g; Carbohydrate 16.5g, of which sugars 15.9g; Fat 3.8g, of which saturates 0.7g; Cholesterol 0mg; Calcium 40mg; Fibre 3.5g; Sodium 811mg
Bamboo shoot salad: Energy 72kcal/305kJ; Protein 3.9g; Carbohydrate 13g, of which sugars 6.2g; Fat 0.7g, of which saturates 0.1g; Cholesterol 0mg; Calcium 31mg; Fibre 1.9g; Sodium 185mg

Salad Rolls with Pumpkin, Tofu, Peanuts & Basil

This is a type of "do-it-yourself" dish. You place all the ingredients on the table with the rice wrappers for everyone to assemble their own rolls.

Serves 4–5
about 30ml/2 tbsp groundnut
  (peanut) or sesame oil
175g/6oz tofu, rinsed and
  patted dry
4 shallots, halved and sliced
2 garlic cloves, finely chopped
350g/12oz pumpkin flesh, cut
  into strips

1 carrot, cut into strips
15ml/1 tbsp soy sauce
120ml/4fl oz/½ cup water
3–4 green Thai chillies, seeded
  and finely sliced
1 small, crispy lettuce, torn
  into strips
1 bunch fresh basil,
  stalks removed
115g/4oz/⅔ cup roasted
  peanuts, chopped
100ml/3½ fl oz/scant ½ cup
  hoisin sauce
20 dried rice wrappers
salt

1 Heat a heavy pan and smear with a little oil. Place the block of tofu in the pan and sear on both sides. Transfer to a plate and cut into thin strips.

2 Heat 30ml/2 tbsp oil in the pan and stir in the shallots and garlic. Add the pumpkin and carrot, then pour in the soy sauce and the water. Add a little salt to taste and cook gently until the vegetables have softened but still have a bite to them.

3 Meanwhile, arrange the tofu, chillies, lettuce, basil, peanuts and hoisin sauce in separate dishes and put them on the table. Provide a small bowl of hot water for each person, and place the stack of rice wrappers beside each. Turn the cooked vegetable mixture into a dish and add to the bowls of ingredients on the table.

4 To eat, take a rice wrapper and dip it in hot water for a few seconds to soften. Lay the wrapper flat and layer a little of each ingredient in a neat stack on top. Roll up the wrapper to eat.

Japanese Salad

Delicate and refreshing, this combines a mild-flavoured, sweet-tasting seaweed with crisp radishes, cucumber and beansprouts.

Serves 4
15g/½oz/ ½ cup dried hijiki
250g/9oz/1¼ cups radishes,
  sliced into very thin rounds
1 small cucumber, cut into
  thin sticks
75g/3oz/¾ cup beansprouts

For the dressing
15ml/1 tbsp sunflower oil
15ml/1 tbsp toasted sesame oil
5ml/1 tsp light soy sauce
30ml/2 tbsp rice vinegar or
  15ml/1 tbsp wine vinegar
15ml/1 tbsp mirin or dry sherry

1 Place the hijiki in a bowl and add cold water to cover. Soak for 10–15 minutes, until it is rehydrated, then drain, rinse under cold running water and drain again. It should have almost trebled in volume.

2 Place the hijiki in a pan of water. Bring to the boil, then lower the heat and simmer for about 30 minutes, or until tender. Drain thoroughly.

3 Meanwhile, make the dressing. Place the sunflower and sesame oils, soy sauce, vinegar and mirin or sherry in a screw-top jar. Shake vigorously to combine.

4 Arrange the hijiki in a shallow bowl or platter with the radishes, cucumber and beansprouts. Pour the dressing over the salad and toss lightly.

Cook's Tip
Hijiki is a type of seaweed. A rich source of minerals, it comes from Japan, where it has a distinguished reputation for enhancing beauty and adding lustre to hair. Look for hijiki in Oriental food stores.

Salad rolls: Energy 312kcal/1300kJ; Protein 11.2g; Carbohydrate 28.9g, of which sugars 10.4g; Fat 16.9g, of which saturates 2.9g; Cholesterol 0mg; Calcium 231mg; Fibre 3.3g; Sodium 547mg
Japanese salad: Energy 68Kcal/280kJ; Protein 1.4g; Carbohydrate 2.8g, of which sugars 2.4g; fat 5.8g, of which saturates 0.8g; Cholesterol 0mg; Calcium 23mg; Fibre 1.1g; Sodium 276mg

Spanish Seafood Salad

This salad is a very pretty arrangement of fresh mussels, prawns and squid rings served on a colourful bed of salad vegetables. In Spain, canned albacore tuna is also often included in this type of simple salad.

Serves 6
115g/4oz prepared squid rings
12 fresh mussels, scrubbed and
   beards removed
1 large carrot
6 crisp lettuce leaves
10cm/4in piece cucumber,
   finely diced
115g/4oz cooked peeled
   prawns (shrimp)
15ml/1 tbsp drained
   pickled capers

For the dressing
30ml/2 tbsp freshly squeezed
   lemon juice
45ml/3 tbsp virgin olive oil
15ml/1 tbsp chopped
   fresh parsley
salt and ground black pepper

1 Put the squid rings into a metal sieve (strainer) or vegetable steamer. Place the sieve or steamer over a pan of simmering water, cover with a lid and steam the squid for 2–3 minutes until it just turns white. Cool under cold running water to prevent further cooking and drain thoroughly on kitchen paper.

2 Discard any open mussels that do not close when tapped. Cover the base of a large pan with water, add the mussels, then cover and steam for a few minutes until they open. Discard any that remain shut.

3 Using a swivel-style vegetable peeler, cut the carrot into wafer-thin ribbons. Tear the lettuce into pieces and arrange on a serving plate. Scatter the carrot ribbons on top, then sprinkle over the diced cucumber.

4 Arrange the mussels, prawns and squid rings over the salad and scatter the capers over the top.

5 To make the dressing, put all the ingredients in a small bowl and whisk well to combine. Drizzle over the salad. Serve at room temperature.

Seafood Salad with Fragrant Herbs

This is a spectacular salad. The luscious combination of prawns, scallops and squid, makes it the ideal choice for a special celebration.

Serves 4–6
250ml/8fl oz/1 cup fish stock
   or water
350g/12oz squid, cleaned and cut
   into rings
12 raw king prawns (jumbo
   shrimp), peeled, with tails intact
12 scallops
50g/2oz cellophane noodles,
   soaked in warm water for
   30 minutes
½ cucumber, cut into thin batons
1 lemon grass stalk,
   finely chopped
2 kaffir lime leaves,
   finely shredded
2 shallots, thinly sliced
30ml/2 tbsp chopped spring
   onions (scallions)
30ml/2 tbsp fresh coriander
   (cilantro) leaves
12–15 fresh mint leaves,
   coarsely torn
4 fresh red chillies, seeded and
   cut into slivers
juice of 1–2 limes
30ml/2 tbsp Thai fish sauce
fresh coriander sprigs, to garnish

1 Pour the fish stock or water into a medium pan, set over a high heat and bring to the boil. Cook each type of seafood separately in the stock for 3–4 minutes. Remove with a slotted spoon and set aside to cool.

2 Drain the noodles. Using scissors, cut them into short lengths, about 5cm/2in long. Place them in a serving bowl and add the cucumber, lemon grass, kaffir lime leaves, shallots, spring onions, coriander, mint and chillies.

3 Pour the lime juice and fish sauce over the noodle salad. Mix well, then add the seafood. Toss lightly. Garnish with the fresh coriander sprigs and serve immediately.

Cook's Tip
To peel the large prawns (shrimp), gently pull off the head, then peel off the body shell, pulling up from the legs. Using a sharp knife, gently prise out the black vein running down the back.

Insalata Di Mare

Served warm or chilled, this stunning seafood salad is guaranteed to impress. The classic dressing sets off the shellfish perfectly.

Serves 4–6

450g/1lb fresh mussels, scrubbed and beards removed
450g/1lb small clams, scrubbed
105ml/7 tbsp dry white wine
225g/8oz squid, cleaned
4 large scallops, with their corals
30ml/2 tbsp olive oil
2 garlic cloves, finely chopped
1 small dried red chilli, crumbled
225g/8oz whole cooked prawns (shrimp), in the shell
6–8 large chicory (Belgian endive) leaves
6–8 radicchio leaves
15ml/1 tbsp chopped flat leaf parsley, to garnish

For the dressing

5ml/1 tsp Dijon mustard
30ml/2 tbsp white wine or cider vinegar
5ml/1 tsp lemon juice
120ml/4fl oz/½ cup extra-virgin olive oil
salt and ground black pepper

1 Put the mussels and clams in a large pan with the white wine. Cover and cook over a high heat, shaking the pan occasionally, for about 4 minutes, until they have opened. Discard any that remain closed.

2 Use a slotted spoon to transfer the shellfish to a bowl, then strain and reserve the cooking liquid. Set aside.

3 Cut the squid into thin rings; chop the tentacles. Leave small squid whole. Halve the scallops horizontally.

4 Heat the oil in a frying pan, add the garlic, chilli, squid, scallops and corals, and sauté for about 2 minutes, until just cooked and tender. Using a slotted spoon, remove the squid and scallops from the pan, reserving the the oil in the pan.

5 When the shellfish are cool enough to handle, shell them, keeping a dozen of each in the shell. Peel all but 6–8 of the prawns. Pour the shellfish cooking liquid into a small pan, set over a high heat and reduce by half.

6 Mix all the shelled and unshelled mussels and clams with the squid and scallops, then add the prawns.

7 To make the dressing, whisk the mustard with the vinegar and lemon juice and season to taste. Add the olive oil, whisk vigorously, then whisk in the reserved cooking liquid and the oil from the frying pan. Pour the dressing over the seafood mixture and toss lightly to coat well.

8 Arrange the chicory and radicchio leaves around the edge of a large serving dish and pile the seafood salad into the centre. Sprinkle with the chopped parsley and serve immediately.

Cook's Tip
You can vary the seafood in this Italian salad according to what is available at the time, but try to include at least two kinds of shellfish and some squid for the best effect.

Prawn Salad

A pretty combination of pink prawns and green avocado, this salad makes a stylish light meal.

Serves 4

450g/1lb cooked peeled prawns (shrimp)
juice of 1 lime
3 tomatoes
1 ripe but firm avocado
30ml/2 tbsp hot chilli sauce
5ml/1 tsp sugar
150ml/¼ pint/⅔ cup soured cream
2 Little Gem (Bibb) lettuces, separated into leaves
salt and ground black pepper
fresh basil leaves and strips of green (bell) pepper, to garnish

1 Put the prawns in a large bowl, add the lime juice and salt and pepper. Toss lightly and leave to marinate.

2 Cut a cross in the base of each tomato. Place the tomatoes into just-boiled water for 30 seconds, then remove with a slotted spoon and plunge into cold water. Drain, then peel off the skins. Chop the flesh into 2cm cubes, discarding the seeds.

3 Halve, pit and skin the avocado and chop into 2cm chunks. Add the chopped avocado and tomato to the prawns.

4 Mix the hot chilli sauce, sugar and soured cream in a bowl. Fold into the prawn mixture. Line a bowl with lettuce leaves, then top with the prawns. Chill for at least 1 hour, then garnish with fresh basil and strips of green pepper.

Insalata di mare: Energy 284kcal/1186kJ; Protein 24.5g; Carbohydrate 3g, of which sugars 1g; Fat 18.2g, of which saturates 2.8g; Cholesterol 167mg; Calcium 113mg; Fibre 0.5g; Sodium 785mg
Prawn salad: Energy 221kcal/920kJ; Protein 21.8g; Carbohydrate 3.8g, of which sugars 3.5g; Fat 13.2g, of which saturates 5.9g; Cholesterol 242mg; Calcium 141mg; Fibre 1.3g; Sodium 232mg

Prawn & Mint Salad

Fresh, uncooked prawns make all the difference to this salad as cooking them in butter adds to the piquant flavour. Garnish with shavings of fresh coconut for a tropical topping.

Serves 4

12 large raw prawns (shrimp)
15ml/1 tbsp unsalted butter
15ml/1 tbsp Thai fish sauce
juice of 1 lime
45ml/3 tbsp thin coconut milk
5ml/1 tsp caster (superfine) sugar
1 garlic clove, crushed
2.5cm/1in fresh root ginger, peeled and grated (shredded)
2 red chillies, seeded and finely chopped
30ml/2 tbsp fresh mint leaves
225g/8oz light green lettuce leaves
ground black pepper

1 Carefully peel the uncooked prawns, removing and discarding the heads and outer shells, but leaving the tails intact.

2 Using a sharp knife, carefully remove the dark-coloured vein that runs along the back of each prawn.

3 Melt the butter in a large frying pan. When it begins to foam, add the prawns and toss over a high heat until they turn pink. Remove from the heat; it is important not to cook them for too long so that their tenderness is retained.

4 In a small bowl mix the fish sauce, lime juice, coconut milk, sugar, garlic, ginger and chillies together. Season to taste with freshly ground black pepper.

5 Toss the warm prawns into the sauce with the mint leaves. Arrange the lettuce leaves on a serving plate and place the prawn and mint mixture in the centre.

Cook's Tip

If you can't find any fresh, uncooked prawns you could use frozen ones. Completely thaw the prawns, then toss very quickly in the hot butter to make the most of their flavour.

San Francisco Salad

This is a truly glamorous Californian creation.

Serves 4

900g/2lb langoustines or Dublin Bay prawns (jumbo shrimp)
50g/2oz bulb fennel, sliced
2 ripe tomatoes, quartered, and 4 small tomatoes
30ml/2 tbsp olive oil, plus extra for moistening the leaves
60ml/4 tbsp brandy
150ml/¼ pint/⅔ cup dry white wine
200ml/7fl oz can lobster or crab bisque
30ml/2 tbsp chopped fresh tarragon
45ml/3 tbsp double (heavy) cream
225g/8oz green beans, cooked and refreshed
2 oranges, divided into segments
175g/6oz lamb's lettuce (corn salad)
115g/4oz rocket (arugula) leaves
½ frisée lettuce
salt and cayenne pepper

1 Put the langoustines in a large pan of salted boiling water and simmer for 10 minutes. Refresh under cold running water.

2 Preheat the oven to 220°C/425°F/Gas 7. Twist the tails from the langoustines, reserving four whole ones for garnishing. Peel the shells from the tail meat. Put the tail peelings, carapace and claws in a heavy roasting pan with the fennel and medium tomatoes. Toss with the olive oil and roast for 20 minutes.

3 Remove the roasting pan from the oven and place it over a medium heat on top of the stove. Add the brandy and ignite, then add the wine and simmer briefly.

4 Transfer the contents of the roasting pan to a food processor and reduce to a coarse purée: this will take only 10–15 seconds. Rub the purée through a fine nylon sieve (strainer) into a bowl. Add the lobster or crab bisque, tarragon and cream. Season to taste with salt and a little cayenne pepper.

5 Moisten the salad leaves with olive oil and divide between four plates. Fold the langoustine tails into the dressing and place on the leaves. Add the beans, orange segments and small tomatoes. Garnish with a whole langoustine and serve warm.

Prawn & mint salad: Energy 83kcal/347kJ; Protein 9.8g; Carbohydrate 2.5g, of which sugars 1.7g; Fat 3.8g, of which saturates 2.1g; Cholesterol 106mg; Calcium 86mg; Fibre 0.5g; Sodium 144mg
San Francisco salad: Energy 345kcal/1438kJ; Protein 23.6g; Carbohydrate 16.3g, of which sugars 14.4g; Fat 14.6g, of which saturates 5.2g; Cholesterol 85mg; Calcium 257mg; Fibre 5.1g; Sodium 1591mg

Ghanaian Prawn Salad

The addition of plantain, which is first cooked in its skin, brings an unusual flavour to this salad.

Serves 4

115g/4oz cooked peeled
  prawns (shrimp)
1 garlic clove, crushed
7.5ml/1½ tsp vegetable oil
2 eggs
1 yellow plantain, halved

4 lettuce leaves
2 tomatoes
1 red (bell) pepper, seeded
1 avocado
juice of 1 lemon
1 carrot
200g/7oz can tuna or
  sardines, drained
1 green chilli, finely chopped
30ml/2 tbsp chopped spring
  onion (scallion)
salt and ground black pepper

1 Put the prawns and garlic in a small bowl. Sprinkle a little salt and pepper over and toss.

2 Heat the oil in a small pan, add the prawns and cook over a low heat for a few minutes, stirring constantly. Transfer the prawns to a plate to cool.

3 Hard-boil (hard-cook) the eggs in boiling water, place in cold water to cool, then shell and cut into slices.

4 Boil the unpeeled plantain in a pan of water for 15 minutes, cool, then peel and cut the flesh into thick slices.

5 Shred the lettuce and arrange on a large serving plate. Slice the tomatoes and red pepper. Halve the avocado, then remove the stone (pit) and skin. Slice the avocado neatly, sprinkling it with a little lemon juice.

6 Cut the carrot into matchstick-size pieces and arrange on top of the lettuce with the tomatoes, red pepper and avocado.

7 Add the plantain slices, hard-boiled eggs, prawns and tuna or sardines. Sprinkle with the remaining lemon juice, then scatter the chilli and spring onion on top. Season with salt and pepper to taste and serve immediately.

Prawn & Artichoke Salad

The mild flavours of prawns and artichoke hearts are complemented here by a zingy herb dressing.

Serves 4

1 garlic clove
10ml/2 tsp Dijon mustard
60ml/4 tbsp red wine vinegar
150ml/¼ pint/⅔ cup olive oil

45ml/3 tbsp shredded fresh basil
  leaves or 30ml/2 tbsp finely
  chopped fresh parsley
1 red onion, very finely sliced
350g/12oz cooked peeled
  prawns (shrimp)
400g/14oz can artichoke hearts
½ iceberg lettuce
salt and ground black pepper

1 Chop the garlic, then crush it to a pulp with 5ml/1 tsp salt, using the flat edge of a heavy knife blade. Mix the garlic and mustard to a paste in a small bowl.

2 Beat in the vinegar and finally the olive oil, beating hard to make a thick, creamy dressing.

3 Season the dressing with black pepper and, if necessary, additional salt.

4 Stir the basil or parsley into the dressing, followed by the sliced onion. Leave the mixture to stand for 30 minutes at room temperature, then stir in the prawns and chill for 1 hour, or until ready to serve.

5 Drain the artichoke hearts and halve each one. Shred the lettuce finely.

6 Arrange a bed of lettuce on a serving platter or four individual salad plates and spread the artichoke hearts on top. Immediately before serving, pour the prawns and their marinade over the top of the salad.

Variation
Vary the salad leaves as you wish, choosing the best in season.

Seafood Salad with Fruity Dressing

White fish is briefly seared, then served with prawns and salad tossed in an oil-free apricot and apple dressing. The fruity flavours delicately enhance the fish in this Japanese recipe.

Serves 4
1 baby (pearl) onion,
  sliced lengthwise
dash of lemon juice
400g/14oz seabass, filleted
30ml/2 tbsp sake

4 large king prawns (jumbo
  shrimp), peeled, with tails intact
about 400g/14oz mixed
  salad leaves

For the fruity dressing
2 ripe apricots, peeled and
  stoned (pitted)
1/4 apple, peeled and cored
60ml/4 tbsp dashi stock or the
  same amount of water and
  5ml/1 tsp dashi-no-moto
10ml/2 tsp shoyu
salt and ground white pepper

1 Soak the onion slices in ice-cold water for 30 minutes, then drain thoroughly.

2 Bring a pan half-full of water to the boil. Add a dash of lemon juice and plunge the fish fillet into it. Remove after 30 seconds, and cool immediately under cold running water for 30 seconds to stop the cooking. Cut crossways into 8mm/⅓in thick slices.

3 Pour the sake into a small pan, bring to the boil, then add the prawns. Cook for 1 minute, or until the colour of the prawns has completely changed to pink.

4 Cool immediately under cold running water for 30 seconds to again stop the cooking. Cut the prawns crossways into 1cm/½in thick slices.

5 Slice one apricot very thinly, then set aside. Process the remaining apricot and dressing ingredients in a food processor. Add salt, if required, and pepper. Chill.

6 Place some of the leaves on four plates. Mix the fish, prawn, apricot and onion slices in a bowl. Add the remaining leaves, then pour on the dressing and toss well. Heap up on the plates.

Prawn, Melon & Chorizo Salad

This is a rich and colourful salad. It tastes best when made with fresh prawns.

Serves 4
450g/1lb/4 cups cooked white
  long grain rice
1 avocado
15ml/1 tbsp lemon juice
½ small Galia melon, cut into
  wedges
15g/½oz/1 tbsp butter

½ garlic clove
115g/4oz raw prawns (shrimp),
  peeled and deveined
25g/1oz chorizo sausage,
  finely sliced
flat leaf parsley, to garnish

For the dressing
75ml/5 tbsp natural (plain) yogurt
45ml/3 tbsp mayonnaise
15ml/1 tbsp olive oil
3 fresh tarragon sprigs
freshly ground black pepper

1 Put the cooked rice in a large salad bowl.

2 Peel the avocado and cut it into chunks. Place in a mixing bowl and toss lightly with the lemon juice. Slice the melon off the rind, cut the flesh into chunks, and add to the avocado.

3 Melt the butter in a small pan and gently fry the garlic for 30 seconds. Add the prawns and cook for about 3 minutes until evenly pink. Add the chorizo and stir-fry for 1 minute more.

4 Tip the mixture into the bowl with the avocado and melon chunks. Mix lightly, then leave to cool.

5 Make the dressing by mixing together all the ingredients in a food processor or blender. Stir half of the mixture into the rice and the remainder into the prawn and avocado mixture. Pile the salad on top of the rice. Chill for about 30 minutes before serving, garnished with flat leaf parsley sprigs.

Cook's Tip
Select a ripe and flavourful, but not overly soft avocado, so that the chunks retain their shape and don't colour the dressing.

Prawn, melon & chorizo salad: Energy 414kcal/1734kJ; Protein 10.8g; Carbohydrate 44.6g, of which sugars 8.8g; Fat 22.6g, of which saturates 5.8g; Cholesterol 75mg; Calcium 102mg; Fibre 1.5g; Sodium 236mg
Seafood salad: Energy 164kcal/691kJ; Protein 25g; Carbohydrate 5g, of which sugars 4.6g; Fat 3.2g, of which saturates 0.5g; Cholesterol 129mg; Calcium 185mg; Fibre 1.5g; Sodium 299mg

Aubergine Salad with Shrimp & Egg

An appetizing and unusual salad that you will find yourself making over and over again. Roasting the aubergines really brings out their flavour.

Serves 4–6

2 aubergines (eggplants)
15ml/1 tbsp vegetable oil
30ml/2 tbsp dried shrimp, soaked in warm water for 10 minutes
15ml/1 tbsp coarsely chopped garlic
1 hard-boiled (hard-cooked) egg, chopped
4 shallots, thinly sliced into rings
fresh coriander (cilantro) leaves and 2 fresh red chillies, seeded and sliced, to garnish

For the dressing

30ml/2 tbsp fresh lime juice
5ml/1 tsp palm sugar (jaggery) or light muscovado (brown) sugar
30ml/2 tbsp Thai fish sauce

1 Preheat the oven to 180°C/350°F/Gas 4. Prick the aubergines several times with a skewer, then place them directly on the shelf of the oven for about 1 hour, turning at least twice. Remove the aubergines. Set aside until cool enough to handle.

2 Meanwhile, make the dressing. Put the lime juice, sugar and fish sauce in a small bowl. Whisk well with a fork or balloon whisk. Cover with clear film (plastic wrap) and set aside.

3 Remove the skin from the cooled aubergines and cut the flesh into medium slices.

4 Heat the oil in a small frying pan (skillet). Drain the dried shrimp thoroughly and add them to the pan with the garlic. Cook over a medium heat for about 3 minutes, until golden. Remove from the pan and set aside.

5 Arrange the aubergine slices on a serving dish. Top with the chopped hard-boiled egg, shallot rings and dried shrimp mixture. Drizzle over the dressing and garnish with the coriander and red chillies. Serve immediately.

Pink & Green Salad

Spiked with a little fresh chilli, this pretty salad makes a delicious light lunch served with hot ciabatta rolls and a glass of sparkling dry Italian white wine. It's also a good choice for a buffet party.

Serves 4

225g/8oz/2 cups dried farfalle
1 small fresh red chilli, seeded and very finely chopped
juice of 1/2 lemon
60ml/4 tbsp chopped fresh basil
30ml/2 tbsp chopped fresh coriander (cilantro)
60ml/4 tbsp extra virgin olive oil
15ml/1 tbsp mayonnaise
250g/9oz/1 1/2 cups peeled cooked prawns (shrimp)
1 avocado
salt and ground black pepper

1 Cook the pasta in a large pan of lightly salted boiling water according to the packet instructions.

2 Meanwhile, put the lemon juice and chilli in a bowl with half the basil and coriander and salt and pepper to taste. Whisk well to mix, then whisk in the oil and mayonnaise until thick. Add the prawns and gently stir to coat in the dressing.

3 Drain the pasta and rinse under cold running water until cold. Leave to drain and dry, shaking the colander occasionally.

4 Halve, stone (pit) and peel the avocado, then cut the flesh into neat dice. Add to the prawns and dressing with the pasta. Toss well to mix and adjust the seasoning.

5 Serve at once, sprinkled with basil and coriander.

Cook's Tip

This pasta salad can be made several hours ahead of time, without the avocado. Cover the bowl with clear film (plastic wrap) and chill in the refrigerator. Prepare the avocado and add it to the salad just before serving or it will discolour.

Aubergine salad: Energy 58kcal/242kJ; Protein 4.6g; Carbohydrate 3.1g, of which sugars 2.8g; Fat 3.2g, of which saturates 0.6g; Cholesterol 57mg; Calcium 74mg; Fibre 1.5g; Sodium 230mg
Pink & green salad: Energy 420kcal/1761kJ; Protein 19g; Carbohydrate 42.8g, of which sugars 2.6g; Fat 20.3g, of which saturates 3.2g; Cholesterol 125mg; Calcium 112mg; Fibre 3.6g; Sodium 146mg

Potato & Mussel Salad with Shallot & Chive Dressing

A tangy dressing is a perfect partner to sweet mussels.

Serves 4
675g/1½lb salad potatoes
1kg/2¼lb fresh mussels, scrubbed
    and beards removed
200ml/7fl oz/ scant 1 cup
    dry white wine
15g/½oz flat leaf parsley, chopped
salt and ground black pepper
snipped fresh chives, to garnish
watercress sprigs, to serve

For the dressing
105ml/7 tbsp mild olive oil
15–30ml/1–2 tbsp white
    wine vinegar
5ml/1 tsp Dijon mustard
1 large shallot, finely chopped
15ml/1 tbsp snipped fresh chives
45ml/3 tbsp double (heavy)
    cream
pinch of caster (superfine) sugar

1 Cook the potatoes in boiling, salted water for 15–20 minutes, or until tender. Drain, cool, then peel. Slice the potatoes into a bowl and toss with 30ml/2 tbsp of the oil for the dressing.

2 Discard any open mussels that do not close when sharply tapped. Bring the white wine to the boil in a large, heavy pan. Add the mussels, cover and boil vigorously, shaking the pan occasionally, for 3–4 minutes, until the mussels have opened. Discard any mussels that have not opened. Drain and shell the mussels, reserving the cooking liquid.

3 Boil the reserved cooking liquid until reduced to about 45ml/3 tbsp. Pass through a fine sieve (strainer) over the potatoes. Toss.

4 To make the dressing, whisk together the remaining oil with 15ml/1 tbsp vinegar, the mustard, shallot and chives. Whisk in the cream to form a thick dressing. Adjust the seasoning, adding more vinegar and/or a pinch of sugar to taste.

5 Toss the mussels with the potatoes, mix in the dressing and parsley, sprinkle with snipped chives and serve with watercress.

Salade Mouclade

A delightful French-style salad of mussels dressed in a light curry cream sauce, served on a bed of lentils.

Serves 4
45ml/3 tbsp olive oil
1 onion, finely chopped
350g/12oz/1½ cups Puy or
    green lentils, soaked for 2 hours
900ml/1½ pints/3¾ cups
    vegetable stock
2kg/4½lb fresh mussels in their
shells, cleaned, and
    beards removed
75ml/5 tbsp white wine
2.5ml/½ tsp curry paste
pinch of saffron
30ml/2 tbsp double
    (heavy) cream
2 large carrots, cut into batons
4 celery sticks, cut into batons
900g/2lb young spinach, stems
    removed
15ml/1 tbsp garlic oil
salt and cayenne pepper

1 Heat the oil in a heavy pan and soften the onion for 6–8 minutes. Add the drained lentils and stock, bring to the boil and simmer for 45 minutes. Remove from the heat and cool.

2 Discard any open mussels that do not close if given a sharp tap. Place the mussels in a large pan, add the wine, cover and steam over a high heat for 12 minutes. Strain, reserving the cooking liquid. Discard any mussels that have not opened during the cooking. Shell all but four of the mussels.

3 Pass the mussel liquid through a fine sieve (strainer) or muslin into a wide, shallow pan. Add the curry paste and saffron, then reduce over a high heat until almost dry. Remove from the heat, stir in the cream, season and combine with the mussels.

4 Cook the carrot and celery batons in salted boiling water for 3 minutes. Drain, cool and moisten with olive oil. Wash the spinach, put the wet leaves into a large pan, cover and steam for 30 seconds. Immerse in cold water then press the leaves dry in a colander. Moisten with garlic oil and season.

5 Spoon the lentils into the centre of four plates. Place heaps of spinach around the edge, with carrot and celery on top. Spoon over the mussels and garnish with the whole mussels.

Potato & mussel salad: Energy 455kcal/1899kJ; Protein 16.7g; Carbohydrate 29.2g, of which sugars 3.8g; Fat 27.5g, of which saturates 6.9g; Cholesterol 45mg; Calcium 197mg; Fibre 2.5g; Sodium 185mg
Salade Mouclade: Energy 628kcal/2646kJ; Protein 50.8g; Carbohydrate 63.7g, of which sugars 11.2g; Fat 19.1g, of which saturates 4.6g; Cholesterol 90mg; Calcium 560mg; Fibre 11.5g; Sodium 902mg

Seafood Salad

This is a very special salad which can be served as a first course or main meal. The choice of pasta shape is up to you, but one of the unusual "designer" shapes would suit it well.

Serves 4–6
450g/1lb fresh mussels
250ml/8fl oz/1 cup dry white wine
2 garlic cloves, roughly chopped
1 handful of fresh flat leaf parsley
175g/6oz/1 cup prepared squid rings
175g/6oz/1½ cups small dried pasta shapes
175g/6oz/1 cup peeled cooked prawns (shrimp)

For the dressing
90ml/6 tbsp extra-virgin olive oil
juice of 1 lemon
5–10ml/1–2 tsp capers, to taste, roughly chopped
1 garlic clove, crushed
1 small handful fresh flat leaf parsley, finely chopped
salt and ground black pepper

1 Scrub the mussels under cold running water to remove the beards. Discard any that are open or that do not close when sharply tapped against the work surface.

2 Pour half the wine into a large pan, add the garlic, parsley and mussels. Cover the pan tightly and bring to the boil over a high heat. Cook for about 5 minutes, shaking the pan frequently, until the mussels are open.

3 Turn the mussels and their liquid into a sieve (strainer) set over a bowl. Leave the mussels until cool enough to handle. Reserve a few mussels for garnishing, then remove the rest from their shells, tipping the liquid from the mussels into the bowl of cooking liquid. Discard any closed mussels.

4 Return the mussel cooking liquid to the pan and add the remaining wine and the squid rings. Bring to the boil, cover and simmer gently, stirring occasionally, for 30 minutes or until the squid is tender. Leave the squid to cool in the cooking liquid.

5 Meanwhile, cook the pasta according to packet instructions and whisk all the dressing ingredients in a large bowl, adding a little salt and pepper to taste.

6 Drain the cooked pasta well, add it to the bowl of dressing and toss well to mix. Leave to cool.

7 Turn the cooled squid into a sieve (strainer) and drain well, then rinse lightly under the cold tap. Add the squid, mussels and prawns to the dressed pasta and toss well to mix. Cover the bowl tightly with clear film (plastic wrap) and chill in the refrigerator for about 4 hours. Toss well and adjust the seasoning to taste before serving.

> **Cook's Tip**
> For a quick and easy short cut, buy ready-prepared seafood salad from an Italian delicatessen and toss it with the cooked pasta and dressing.

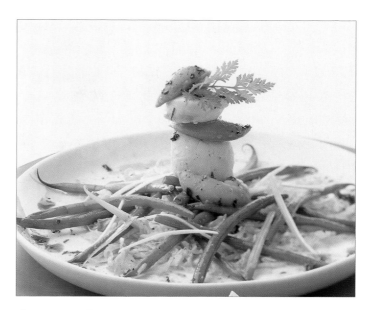

Queen Scallop & Green Bean Salad

This is a sensational dish to serve at a dinner party.

Serves 4
115g/4oz fine green beans, trimmed
2 good handfuls of frisée or batavia lettuce leaves, finely shredded
15g/½ oz/1 tbsp butter
15ml/1 tbsp hazelnut oil
20 shelled queen scallops, with corals if possible
2 spring onions (scallions), very thinly sliced lengthwise
salt and ground black pepper
4 fresh chervil sprigs, to garnish

For the dressing
10ml/2 tsp sherry vinegar
30ml/2 tbsp hazelnut oil
15ml/1 tbsp finely chopped fresh mint leaves

1 Cook the beans in a pan of lightly salted boiling water for about 5 minutes, until crisp-tender. Drain, refresh under cold water, drain again and set aside.

2 Put the salad leaves in a bowl. Mix the dressing, seasoning with salt and pepper, and toss into the salad. Arrange on four plates.

3 Heat the butter and hazelnut oil in a frying pan (skillet) until sizzling, then add the scallops and their corals and sauté for about 1 minute, tossing the scallops until they have just turned opaque. Stir in the beans and spring onions. Spoon the vegetables over the salad and pile the scallops and corals into a tower. Garnish with chervil and serve immediately.

Seafood salad: Energy 294kcal/1235kJ; Protein 17.3g; Carbohydrate 22.4g, of which sugars 1.4g; Fat 12.8g, of which saturates 1.9g; Cholesterol 132mg; Calcium 99mg; Fibre 1.3g; Sodium 140mg
Queen scallop salad: Energy 213kcal/887kJ; Protein 19g; Carbohydrate 5.4g, of which sugars 2.3g; Fat 12.9g, of which saturates 3.4g; Cholesterol 43mg; Calcium 59mg; Fibre 1.8g; Sodium 160mg

Genoese Squid Salad

Crab Salad with Rocket

This Italian-style salad is good for summer days, when green beans and new potatoes are at their best.

Serves 4–6
450g/1lb prepared squid, cut into rings
4 garlic cloves, roughly chopped
300ml/½ pint/1¼ cups Italian red wine
450g/1lb waxy new potatoes, scrubbed
225g/8oz green beans, trimmed and cut into short lengths
2–3 sun-dried tomatoes in oil, drained and thinly sliced lengthwise
60ml/4 tbsp extra virgin olive oil
15ml/1 tbsp red wine vinegar
salt and ground black pepper

1 Preheat the oven to 180°C/350°F/Gas 4. Put the squid rings in an earthenware dish with half the garlic, the wine and pepper to taste. Cover and cook for 45 minutes, or until the squid is tender.

2 Meanwhlile, put the potatoes in a pan, cover with cold water and add a good pinch of salt. Bring to the boil, cover and simmer for about 15 minutes, until tender. Using a slotted spoon, lift out the potatoes and set aside. Add the beans to the boiling water and cook for 3 minutes. Drain.

3 When the potatoes are cool enough to handle, slice them thickly on the diagonal and place them in a bowl with the warm beans and sun-dried tomatoes. Whisk the oil, vinegar and the remaining garlic in a bowl and add salt and pepper to taste. Pour over the potato mixture.

4 Drain the squid and discard the liquid. Add the squid to the potato mixture and mix very gently. Arrange on individual plates and season liberally with pepper before serving.

Cook's Tip
The French potato called Charlotte is perfect for this salad because it retains its shape when boiled.

If the dressed crabs are really small, pile the salad back into the shells for an alternative presentation.

Serves 4
white and brown meat from 4 small fresh dressed crabs, about 450g/1lb
1 small red (bell) pepper, seeded and finely chopped
1 small red onion, finely chopped
30ml/2 tbsp drained capers
30ml/2 tbsp chopped fresh coriander (cilantro)
grated (shredded) rind and juice of 2 lemons
a few drops of Tabasco sauce
salt and ground black pepper
lemon rind strips, to garnish

For the salad
40g/1½ oz rocket (arugula) leaves
30ml/2 tbsp sunflower oil 15ml/1 tbsp fresh lime juice

1 Put the white and brown crab meat, red pepper, onion, capers and chopped coriander in a bowl. Add the lemon rind and juice and toss gently to mix together. Season with a few drops of Tabasco sauce, according to taste, then add a little salt and ground black pepper.

2 Wash the rocket leaves and thoroughly pat dry on kitchen towels. Divide the rocket between four individual plates. Whisk together the oil and lime juice in a small bowl. Dress the rocket leaves, then carefully pile the crab salad on top and serve garnished with lemon rind strips.

Genoese squid salad: Energy 239kcal/999kJ; Protein 13.6g; Carbohydrate 14.3g, of which sugars 1.9g; Fat 10.9g, of which saturates 1.7g; Cholesterol 169mg; Calcium 31mg; Fibre 1.6g; Sodium 94mg
Crab salad: Energy 164kcal/686kJ; Protein 21.4g; Carbohydrate 4.3g, of which sugars 3.8g; Fat 6.9g, of which saturates 0.8g; Cholesterol 81mg; Calcium 167mg; Fibre 1.5g; Sodium 625mg

Avocado, Crab & Coriander Salad

The sweet richness of crab combines especially well with creamy avocado, tangy coriander and fresh-tasting tomato. Serve with warm French bread for a special lunch or supper dish.

Serves 4
675g/1½lb small new potatoes
1 fresh mint sprig
900g/2lb boiled crabs or 275g/10oz frozen crab meat
1 endive (US chicory) or round (butterhead) lettuce, leaves separated
175g/6oz lamb's lettuce (corn salad) or young spinach leaves
1 large ripe avocado
175g/6oz cherry tomatoes
freshly grated (shredded) nutmeg
salt and ground black pepper

For the dressing
75ml/5 tbsp olive oil
15ml/1 tbsp lime juice
45ml/3 tbsp chopped fresh coriander (cilantro)
2.5ml/½ tsp caster (superfine) sugar

1 Scrape or peel the potatoes. Cover with water, add a good pinch of salt and a sprig of mint. Bring to the boil and simmer for about 15 minutes, until tender. Drain the potatoes, cover and keep warm until needed.

2 Remove the legs and claws from each crab. Crack these open with the back of a chopping knife and remove the white meat.

3 Turn each crab on its back and push the rear leg section away with the thumb and forefinger of each hand. Remove the flesh from inside the shell.

4 Discard the "dead men's fingers", the soft gills which the crab uses to filter impurities in its diet. Apart from these and the shell, everything else is edible, both white and dark meat.

5 Split the central body section open with a knife and remove the white and dark flesh with a pick or skewer.

6 Combine all the dressing ingredients in a screw-top jar and shake. Put the salad leaves in a large bowl, pour the dressing over and toss well.

7 Cut the avocado in half, remove the stone (pit), then peel and slice into even pieces.

8 Divide the leaves among four serving plates. Top with the avocado, crab, tomatoes and warm new potatoes. Season with salt, pepper and freshly grated nutmeg and serve.

Cook's Tip
Young crabs offer the sweetest meat, but are more fiddly to prepare than older, larger ones. The hen crab carries more flesh than the cock which is considered to have a better overall flavour. The cock crab is identified by his narrow apron flap at the rear. The hen has a broad flap, under which she carries her eggs. Frozen crab meat is a good alternative to fresh and retains much of its original sweetness.

Turnips with prawns and mangetouts

This dish transforms turnips into something sophisticated and surprising.

Serves 4
8 small turnips, peeled
600ml/1 pint/2½ cups water and 7.5ml/1½ tsp intsant dashi powder
10ml/2 tsp shoyu (use the japanese pale awakuchi soy sauce if available)
60ml/4 tbsp mirin
30ml/2 tbsp sake
16 medium raw tiger prawns (jumbo shrimp), head and shells removed but with tails left intact
dash of rice vinegar
90g/3½oz mangetouts (snow peas)
30ml/2 tbsp sunflower oil
5ml/1 tsp cornflour (cornstarch)
salt

1 Par-boil the turnips for 3 minutes. Drain, then place them side by side in a deep pan. Add the prepared dashi stock and cover with a saucer to submerge the turnips. Bring to the boil, then add the shoyu, 5ml/1 tsp salt, the mirin and sake. Reduce the heat to very low, cover and simmer for 30 minutes.

2 Devein the prawns. Blanch them in boiling water with the vinegar until the colour just changes. Drain.

3 Cook the mangetouts in lightly salted water for 3 minutes. Drain well, then set aside.

4 Remove the saucer and add the cooked prawns to the turnip stock for about 4 minutes to warm through. Take out the turnips, drain and place in individual bowls. Reserve the prawns

5 Mix the cornflour with 15ml/1 tbsp water and add to the pan that held the turnips. Increase the heat a little and shake the pan gently until the liquid thickens slightly.

6 Place the mangetouts on the turnips with prawns on top, and pout about 30ml/2 tbsp of hot liquid from the pan into each bowl. Serve immediately.

Millionaire's Lobster Salad

When you're in a decadent mood, this salad will satisfy your every whim.

Serves 4
1 medium lobster, cooked
675g/1½lb new potatoes, scrubbed
½ frisée lettuce
175g/6oz lamb's lettuce (corn salad) leaves
60ml/4 tbsp extra-virgin olive oil
200g/7oz can young artichokes in brine, quartered
4 oranges, peeled and divided into segments
2 ripe tomatoes, peeled, seeded and diced
1 small bunch fresh tarragon, chervil or flat leaf parsley
salt

For the dressing
30ml/2 tbsp frozen concentrated orange juice, thawed
75g/3oz/6 tbsp unsalted butter, diced
salt and cayenne pepper

1 Twist off the legs and claws of the lobster, and separate the tail from the body. Break the claws with a hammer and remove the meat. Cut the tail piece open from the underside, slice the meat and set aside.

2 Bring the potatoes to the boil in salted water and simmer for about 15 minutes, until tender. Drain, cover and keep warm.

3 To make the dressing, measure the orange juice into a heatproof bowl and set it over a pan containing 2.5cm/1in simmering water. Heat the juice for 1 minute, turn off the heat, then whisk in the butter a little at a time until the dressing reaches a coating consistency.

4 Season to taste with salt and a pinch of cayenne pepper, cover and keep warm.

5 Dress the salad leaves with olive oil, then divide between four large serving plates. Moisten the potatoes, artichokes and orange segments with olive oil and distribute among the leaves. Lay the sliced lobster over the salad, spoon on the warm dressing, add the diced tomato and decorate with the fresh herbs. Serve at room temperature.

Warm Fish Salad with Mango Dressing

An exotic dressing combines the flavour of rich mango with hot chilli, ginger and lime – the perfect foil to the fish. For al fresco eating, cook the fish on the barbecue.

Serves 4
1 baguette
4 redfish, black bream or porgy, each about 275g/10oz
15ml/1 tbsp vegetable oil
1 mango
1cm/½in fresh root ginger
1 red chilli, seeded and finely chopped
30ml/2 tbsp lime juice
30ml/2 tbsp chopped fresh coriander (cilantro)
175g/6oz young spinach
150g/5oz pak choi (bak choy)
175g/6oz cherry tomatoes, halved

1 Preheat the oven to 180°C/350°F/Gas 4. Cut the baguette into 20cm/8in lengths. Slice lengthwise, then cut into thick fingers. Place the bread on a baking sheet and leave to dry in the oven for 15 minutes.

2 Preheat the grill (broiler) or light the barbecue and allow the embers to settle. Slash the fish deeply on both sides and moisten with oil. Grill (broil) or barbecue the fish for 6 minutes, turning once.

3 Peel the mango and cut in half; discard the stone. Thinly slice one half and set aside. Place the other half in a food processor.

4 Peel the ginger, grate (shred) finely, then add to the mango in the food processor with the chilli, lime juice and coriander. Process until smooth. Adjust the dressing to a pouring consistency with 30–45ml/2–3 tbsp water.

5 Divide the spinach and pak choi leaves between four serving plates. Place the fish on top of the leaves. Spoon the mango dressing over the fish and finish with the reserved slices of mango and the tomato halves. Serve with fingers of the crispy baguette.

Millionaire's lobster salad: Energy 662kcal/2775kJ; Protein 51.5g; Carbohydrate 47.7g, of which sugars 22.7g; Fat 30.7g, of which saturates 12g; Cholesterol 260mg; Calcium 325mg; Fibre 6.9g; Sodium 900mg
Warm fish salad: Energy 457kcal/1937kJ; Protein 33.7g; Carbohydrate 64.1g, of which sugars 10.6g; Fat 9.1g, of which saturates 0.8g; Cholesterol 48mg; Calcium 317mg; Fibre 5.5g; Sodium 872mg

Skate with Bitter Salad Leaves

Skate has a delicious sweet flavour, enhanced here by orange. It contrasts well with any bitter leaves – buy a bag of mixed salad leaves for contrasting textures and flavours.

Serves 4
800g/1¾lb skate wings
15ml/1 tbsp white wine vinegar
4 black peppercorns
1 fresh thyme sprig
1 orange

175g/6oz bitter salad leaves, such
    as frisée, rocket (arugula),
    radicchio, escarole, lamb's
    lettuce (corn salad)
    and watercress
2 tomatoes, peeled, seeded
    and diced
crusty bread, to serve

For the dressing
15ml/1 tbsp white wine vinegar
45ml/3 tbsp extra-virgin olive oil
1 bunch spring onions (scallions),
    whites finely chopped
salt, paprika and black pepper

1 Put the skate wings into a large shallow pan, cover with cold water and add the vinegar, peppercorns and thyme. Bring to the boil, then poach gently for 8–10 minutes, until the flesh comes away easily from the bones.

2 Pare of a few strips of rind from the orange, then cut the rind into fine shreds and reserve. Remove the remaining peel from the orange, taking care to remove all the pith. Slice the orange flesh into thin rounds.

3 To make the dressing, whisk together the vinegar, oil and spring onions and season with salt, paprika and pepper. Put the salad leaves in a large bowl, pour over the dressing and toss.

4 Flake the fish, discarding the bones, and add to the salad. Add the reserved orange rind, the orange slices and tomatoes, toss gently and serve with crusty bread.

> **Cook's Tip**
> Skate is a flat fish and the "wings" contain many bones, but once cooked, the flesh falls off easily and it tastes succulent.

Red Mullet with Raspberry Dressing

The partnership of red mullet and raspberry vinegar is delicious in this light salad. Keep to the "red" theme by including salad leaves such as red oakleaf lettuce and baby red-stemmed chard. If red mullet is not available, use small red snapper fillets.

Serves 4
8 red mullet fillets, scaled
15ml/1 tbsp olive oil
15ml/1 tbsp raspberry vinegar
175g/6oz mixed dark green and
    red salad leaves, such as lamb's
    lettuce (corn salad), oakleaf
    lettuce and rocket (arugula)
salt and ground black pepper

For the raspberry dressing
115g/4oz/1 cup raspberries,
    puréed and sieved (strained)
30ml/2 tbsp raspberry vinegar
60ml/4 tbsp extra-virgin olive oil
1.5–2.5ml/¼–½ tsp caster
    (superfine) sugar

1 Lay the red mullet fillets in a shallow dish. Whisk together the olive oil and raspberry vinegar, add a pinch of salt and drizzle the mixture over the fish. Cover and leave to marinate in a cool place for 1 hour.

2 Meanwhile, make the raspberry dressing. Whisk together the puréed raspberries, vinegar, olive oil and sugar in a bowl, then season to taste with salt and pepper.

3 Wash and dry the salad leaves, put them in a bowl, pour over most of the dressing and toss lightly.

4 Heat a ridged griddle pan or frying pan (skillet) until very hot, add the red mullet fillets and fry for 2–3 minutes on each side, until just cooked. Cut the fillets diagonally in half to make rough diamond shapes.

5 Arrange a tall heap of salad in the middle of each serving plate. Prop up four red mullet fillet halves on each salad mound and spoon the reserved dressing around the edge.

Red mullet with raspberry dressing: Energy 333kcal/1391kJ; Protein 38.2g; Carbohydrate 2.1g, of which sugars 2.1g; Fat 19.2g, of which saturates 1.7g; Cholesterol 0mg; Calcium 152mg; Fibre 1.1g; Sodium 184mg
Skate with bitter salad leaves: Energy 230kcal/965kJ; Protein 31.6g; Carbohydrate 4.8g, of which sugars 4.8g; Fat 9.5g, of which saturates 1.3g; Cholesterol 0mg; Calcium 118mg; Fibre 1.5g; Sodium 247mg

Hake & Potato Salad

Hake is excellent served cold, and delicious with a piquant dressing.

Serves 4
450g/1lb hake fillets
150ml/¼ pint/⅔ cup fish stock
1 onion, thinly sliced
1 bay leaf
450g/1lb cooked baby potatoes
1 red (bell) pepper, seeded
 and diced
115g/4oz/1 cup petits pois (baby
 peas), cooked
2 spring onions (scallions), sliced
½ cucumber, unpeeled and diced
4 large red lettuce leaves
salt and ground black pepper

For the dressing
150ml/¼ pint/⅔ cup Greek
 (US strained plain) yogurt
30ml/2 tbsp olive oil
juice of ½ lemon
15–30ml/1–2 tbsp capers

For the garnish
2 hard-boiled (hard-cooked) eggs,
 finely chopped
15ml/1 tbsp finely chopped fresh
 flat leaf parsley
15ml/1 tbsp finely chopped chives

1 Put the hake in a shallow pan with the fish stock, onion slices and bay leaf. Bring to the boil over a medium heat. Lower the heat and poach the fish gently for about 10 minutes, until it flakes easily when tested with the tip of a sharp knife. Leave it to cool, then remove and discard the skin and any remaining bones, and separate the flesh into large flakes.

2 Halve the potatoes unless they are tiny and place in a bowl with the red pepper, petits pois, spring onions and cucumber. Stir in the flaked hake and season to taste with salt and pepper.

3 Stir all the dressing ingredients together in a bowl. Season with salt and pepper and toss gently into the salad. Place a lettuce leaf on each plate and spoon the salad over it. Mix the hard-boiled eggs with the parsley and chives. Sprinkle the mixture over each salad.

> **Variation**
> This is equally good made with halibut, monkfish or cod.

Whitefish Salad

Smoked whitefish is wonderful made into a salad with mayonnaise and soured cream and served with pumpernickel or rye bread. If you can't find smoked whitefish, use any other smoked firm white fish such as halibut.

Serves 4–6
1 smoked whitefish, skinned
 and boned
2 celery sticks, chopped
½ red, white or yellow onion
 or 3–5 spring onions
 (scallions), chopped
45ml/3 tbsp mayonnaise
45ml/3 tbsp soured cream
 or Greek (US strained
 plain) yogurt
juice of ½–1 lemon
1 round (butterhead) lettuce,
 leaves separated
ground black pepper
5–10ml/1–2 tsp chopped fresh
 parsley, to garnish

1 Break the smoked fish into bitesize pieces. In a bowl, combine the chopped celery, onion or spring onion, mayonnaise, and soured cream or yogurt, and add lemon juice to taste.

2 Fold the fish into the mixture and season with pepper. Arrange the lettuce leaves on serving plates, then spoon the whitefish salad on top. Serve chilled, sprinkled with parsley.

Provencal Aïoli with Salt Cod

Salt cod is superb with garlic-flavoured mayonnaise.

Serves 6
1kg/2¼lb salt cod, soaked
 overnight in water to cover
1 fresh bouquet garni
18 small new potatoes, scrubbed
1 large fresh mint sprig, torn
225g/8oz green beans, trimmed
225g/8oz broccoli florets
6 hard-boiled (hard-cooked) eggs
12 baby carrots
1 large red (bell) pepper, seeded
 and cut into strips
2 fennel bulbs, cut into strips
18 red or yellow cherry tomatoes
6 large whole cooked prawns
 (shrimp), to garnish

For the aïoli
600ml/1 pint/2½ cups
 home-made mayonnaise
2 fat garlic cloves, (or more if you
 are feeling brave), crushed
cayenne pepper

1 Drain the cod and put into a shallow pan with enough water to barely cover. Add the bouquet garni. Bring to the boil, then cover and poach very gently for about 10 minutes, until the fish flakes easily. Drain and set aside.

2 Cook the potatoes in lightly salted water with mint. Drain and set aside. Boil the beans and broccoli in separate pans for 3–5 minutes, so that they are still very crisp. Refresh under cold water, drain again, then set aside.

3 Remove the skin from the cod and break the flesh into large flakes. Shell and halve the eggs lengthwise. Arrange the cod, eggs, vegetables and garnish on a platter.

4 To make the aïoli, stir the cayenne and crushed garlic into the mayonnaise and serve with the salad.

Hake & potato salad: Energy 373kcal/1561kJ; Protein 31.2g; Carbohydrate 29.1g, of which sugaars 8.8g; fat 15.8g, of which saturates 4.2g; Cholesterol 121mg; Calcium 129mg; Fibre 4.3g; Sodium 192mg
Whitefish Salad: Energy 112kcal/469kJ; Protein 10.1g; Carbohydrate 1g, of which sugars 1g; Fat 7.6g, of which saturates 1.9g; Cholesterol 28mg; Calcium 29mg; Fibre 0.3g; Sodium 421mg
Aïoli with Salt Cod: Energy 1099kcal/4567kJ; Protein 66.5g; Carbohydrate 21.4g, of which sugars 10.2g; Fat 83.9g, of which saturates 13.6g; Cholesterol 364mg; Calcium 140mg; Fibre 5.6g; Sodium 1217mg

Warm Monkfish Salad

Monkfish has a matchless flavour and benefits from being cooked simply. Teaming it with wilted baby spinach and toasted pine nuts is inspirational.

Serves 4

2 monkfish fillets, about
　350g/12oz each
25g/1oz/¼ cup pine nuts

15ml/1 tbsp olive oil
15g/½oz/1 tbsp butter
225g/8oz baby spinach leaves,
　washed and stalks removed
salt and ground black pepper

For the dressing

5ml/1 tsp Dijon mustard
5ml/1 tsp sherry vinegar
60ml/4 tbsp olive oil
1 garlic clove, crushed

1 Holding the knife at a slight angle, cut each monkfish fillet into 12 diagonal slices. Season lightly and set aside.

2 Heat an empty frying pan (skillet), put in the pine nuts and shake them about for a while, until golden brown. Do not burn. Transfer to a plate; set aside.

3 To make the dressing, whisk all the ingredients together until smooth and creamy. Pour the dressing into a small pan, season to taste with salt and black pepper and heat gently.

4 Heat the oil and butter in a ridged griddle pan or frying pan until sizzling. Add the monkfish slices and cook for only 20–30 seconds on each side.

5 Put the spinach leaves in a large bowl and pour over the warm dressing. Sprinkle on the toasted pine nuts, reserving a few, and toss together well. Divide the dressed spinach leaves between four serving plates and arrange the monkfish slices on top. Sprinkle the reserved pine nuts on top and serve.

> **Variation**
> The spinach can be substituted with mixed salad leaves and a few capers added to the dressing to give a more tangy taste.

Warm Swordfish & Rocket Salad

Swordfish is robust enough to take the sharp flavours of rocket and Pecorino cheese. If you can't find Pecorino cheese, then use a good Parmesan instead.

Serves 4

4 swordfish steaks, about
　175g/6oz each
75ml/5 tbsp extra-virgin olive oil,
　plus extra for serving

juice of 1 lemon
30ml/2 tbsp finely chopped
　fresh parsley
115g/4oz rocket (arugula) leaves,
　stalks trimmed
115g/4oz Pecorino cheese
salt and ground black pepper

1 Lay the swordfish steaks in a shallow, non-metallic dish. Mix 60ml/4 tbsp of the olive oil with the lemon juice. Pour over the fish. Season, sprinkle on the parsley and turn the fish to coat, cover and leave to marinate for 10 minutes.

2 Heat a ridged griddle pan or the grill (broiler) until very hot. Take the fish out of the marinade and pat it dry with kitchen paper. Cook for 2–3 minutes on each side, until the swordfish is just cooked through, but still juicy.

3 Meanwhile, put the rocket leaves in a bowl and season with a little salt and plenty of pepper. Add the remaining 15ml/1 tbsp olive oil and toss well. Shave the Pecorino over the top.

4 Place the swordfish steaks on four individual plates and arrange a little mound of salad on each steak. Serve with extra olive oil for drizzling over the swordfish.

> **Cook's Tip**
> Swordfish has a firm texture which makes it ideal for grilling or barbecuing, but it needs to be marinated to keep it moist during cooking. If you have difficulty finding swordfish, tuna steaks can be used instead with great success.

Warm monkfish salad: Energy 331kcal/1379kJ; Protein 29.9g; Carbohydrate 1.2g, of which sugars 1.1g; fat 23g, of which saturates 4.9g; Cholesterol 34mg; Calcium 110mg; Fibre 1.3g; Sodium 137mg
Swordfish & rocket salad: Energy 378kcal/1579kJ; protein 43.7g; carbohydrate 0.5g, of which sugars 0.5g; Fat 22.3g, of which saturates 8.3g; cholesterol 101mg; Calcium 407mg; Fibre 0.7g; Sodium 587mg

Smoked Eel & Chicory Salad

Smoked eel has become increasingly popular recently and is seen on some of the most sophisticated tables. It tastes marvellous in a salad with a refreshing citrus dressing.

Serves 4

450g/1lb smoked eel fillets, skinned and cut diagonally into 8 pieces
2 large heads of chicory (Belgian endive), separated
4 radicchio leaves
flat leaf parsley leaves, to garnish

For the citrus dressing

1 lemon
1 orange
5ml/1 tsp sugar
5ml/1 tsp Dijon mustard
90ml/6 tbsp sunflower oil
15ml/1 tbsp chopped fresh parsley
salt and ground black pepper

1 To make the dressing, using a canelle knife (zester), carefully remove the rind in strips from the lemon and the orange. Squeeze the juice of both fruits. Set the lemon juice aside and pour the orange juice into a small pan. Stir in the rinds and sugar. Bring to the boil and reduce by half. Leave to cool.

2 Whisk the Dijon mustard, reserved lemon juice and the sunflower oil together in a bowl. Add the orange juice mixture, then stir in the chopped fresh parsley. Season to taste with salt and ground black pepper and whisk again.

3 Arrange the chicory leaves in a circle on individual plates. Take the radicchio leaves and arrange them on the plates, between the chicory leaves.

4 Drizzle a little of the dressing over the leaves and place four pieces of eel in a star shape in the middle. Garnish with parsley leaves and serve. Offer the remaining dressing separately.

> **Variation**
> This salad can also be made with other hot-smoked fish such as trout or mackerel.

Avocado & Smoked Fish Salad

Avocado and smoked fish make a good combination. Flavoured with herbs and spices, they create a delectable all-in-one salad.

Serves 4

2 avocados
1/2 cucumber
15ml/1 tbsp lemon juice
2 firm tomatoes
1 green chilli
salt and ground black pepper

For the fish salad

15g/1/2oz/1 tbsp butter or margarine
1/2 onion, finely sliced
5ml/1 tsp mustard seeds
225g/8oz smoked mackerel, flaked
30ml/2 tbsp fresh chopped coriander (cilantro) leaves
2 firm tomatoes, peeled and chopped
15ml/1 tbsp lemon juice

1 To make the fish salad, melt the butter or margarine in a frying pan (skillet), add the onion and mustard seeds and fry for about 5 minutes, until the onion is soft.

2 Add the mackerel, coriander, tomatoes and lemon juice and cook over a low heat for 2–3 minutes. Remove from the heat and leave to cool.

3 To make the avocado salad, slice the avocados and cucumber thinly. Place together in a bowl and sprinkle with the lemon juice. Slice the tomatoes and remove the seeds. Finely chop the chilli.

4 Place the fish mixture in the centre of a serving plate.

5 Arrange the avocado, cucumber and tomato salad decoratively around the fish salad. Sprinkle the top with the finely chopped chilli and a little salt and pepper and serve.

> **Variation**
> Smoked haddock or cod can also be used in this salad, or a mixture of mackerel and haddock.

Smoked eel & chicory salad: Energy 368kcal/1526kJ; Protein 19.9g; Carbohydrate 6.1g, of which sugars 5g; Fat 29.9g, of which saturates 5.4g; Cholesterol 169mg; Calcium 69mg; Fibre 1.6g; Sodium 142mg
Avocado & smoked fish salad: Energy 351kcal/1454kJ; Protein 13g; Carbohydrate 6g, of which sugars 4.9g; Fat 30.6g, of which saturates 7.7g; Cholesterol 67mg; Calcium 58mg; Fibre 3.7g; Sodium 462mg

Smoked Trout & Noodle Salad

It is important to use ripe juicy tomatoes for this salad.

Serves 4
225g/8oz somen noodles
2 smoked trout, skinned
   and boned
30ml/2 tbsp snipped chives
2 hard-boiled eggs (hard-cooked),
   chopped
lime halves, to serve

For the dressing
6 ripe plum tomatoes
2 shallots, finely chopped
30ml/2 tbsp tiny capers, rinsed
30ml/ 2 tbsp chopped
   fresh tarragon
finely grated (shredded) rind and
   juice of 1/2 orange
60ml/ 4 tbsp extra-virgin olive oil
salt and ground black pepper

1 To make the dressing, cut the tomatoes into chunks. Place in a bowl with the shallots, capers, tarragon, orange rind and juice and olive oil. Season with salt and pepper and mix well. Leave at room temperature for 1–2 hours.

2 Cook the noodles until just tender. Drain, rinse and drain again. Toss the noodles into the dressing, season with salt and pepper to taste, and divide between the serving plates.

3 Flake the trout over the noodles, then sprinkle the chives and chopped egg over the top. Add the lime halves and serve.

Smoked Trout & Horseradish Salad

In the summer, when lettuce leaves are sweet and crisp, partner them with fillets of smoked trout, warm new potatoes and a creamy horseradish dressing.

Serves 4
675g/1 1/2lb new potatoes
4 smoked trout fillets

115g/4oz mixed lettuce leaves
4 slices dark rye bread,
   cut into fingers
salt and ground black pepper

For the dressing
60ml/4 tbsp creamed horseradish
60ml/4 tbsp groundnut
   (peanut) oil
15ml/1 tbsp white wine vinegar
10ml/2 tsp caraway seeds

1 Put the potatoes in a pan of salted water and bring to the boil. Simmer for about 15 minutes until tender. Remove the skin from the trout fillets and lift the flesh from the bone.

2 To make the dressing, place all the ingredients in a jar and shake vigorously. Season the lettuce with salt and pepper and moisten them with the dressing. Divide between four plates.

3 Flake the trout fillets and cut the potatoes in half. Scatter them together with the rye bread fingers over the salad leaves and toss to mix. Season the salad to taste and serve.

> **Cook's Tip**
> In some cases it is better to season the leaves rather than the dressing when making a salad.

Smoked Trout Pasta Salad

Choose hollow pasta shapes, such as shells or penne, which trap the creamy filling, creating tasty mouthfuls of trout, fennel and spring onion. The addition of dill is not only attractive, but also gives the salad a subtle aniseed flavour.

Serves 8
15g/1/2oz/1 tbsp butter
1 fennel bulb, finely chopped
6 spring onions (scallions), 2 finely
   chopped and 4 thinly sliced
225g/8oz smoked trout fillets,
   skinned and flaked
45ml/3 tbsp chopped fresh dill
120ml/4fl oz/1/2 cup mayonnaise
10ml/2 tsp lemon juice
30ml/2 tbsp whipping cream
450g/1lb small pasta shapes,
   such as shells
salt and ground black pepper
fresh dill sprigs, to garnish

1 Melt the butter in a small non-stick pan. Add the fennel and finely chopped spring onions and fry over a medium heat for 3–5 minutes. Transfer to a large bowl and leave to cool slightly.

2 Add the sliced spring onions, trout, dill, mayonnaise, lemon juice and cream to the bowl with the fennel. Season lightly with salt and pepper and mix gently until well blended.

3 Bring a large pan of lightly salted water to the boil. Add the pasta. Cook according to the instructions on the packet until *al dente*. Drain thoroughly and leave to cool.

4 Add the pasta to the vegetable and trout mixture and toss to coat evenly. Adjust the seasoning. Serve the salad lightly chilled or at room temperature, garnished with the sprigs of dill.

> **Variations**
> This pasta salad works well with any type of fresh, cooked fish fillets, including salmon. Alternatively, try using a 200g/7oz can of tuna in brine in place of the trout.

Smoked trout & noodle salad: Energy 474kcal/1979kJ; Protein 26g; Carbohydrate 51.5g, of which sugars 5.3g; Fat 17.6g, of which saturates 3.1g; Cholesterol 121mg; Calcium 49mg; Fibre 1.5g; Sodium 1464mg
Smoked trout & horseradish: Energy 428kcal/1797kJ; Protein 25.3g; Carbohydrate 41.8g, of which sugars 5.4g; Fat 18.9g, of which saturates 2.6g; Cholesterol 28mg; Calcium 84mg; Fibre 3.7g; Sodium 1712mg
Smoked trout pasta salad: Energy 369kcal/1550kJ; Protein 14.5g; Carbohydrate 42.7g, of which sugars 2.8g; Fat 16.8g of which saturates 4g; Cholesterol 29mg; Calcium 32mg; Fibre 2.4g; Sodium 614mg

Spiced Trout Salad

In this make-ahead salad, the trout is marinated in a mixture of coriander, ginger and chilli and served with cold baby roast potatoes.

Serves 4

2.5cm/1in piece fresh root ginger, peeled and finely grated (shredded)
1 garlic clove, crushed
5ml/1 tsp hot chilli powder
15ml/1 tbsp coriander seeds, lightly crushed
grated rind and juice of 2 lemons
60ml/4 tbsp olive oil
450g/1lb trout fillet, skinned
900g/2lb new potatoes
5–10ml/1–2 tsp sea salt
ground black pepper
15ml/1 tbsp whole or chopped fresh chives, to garnish

1 Mix the ginger, garlic, chilli powder, coriander seeds and lemon rind in a bowl. Whisk in the lemon juice with 15ml/1 tbsp of the olive oil to make a marinade.

2 Place the trout in a shallow, non-metallic dish and cover with the marinade. Turn the fish to make sure they are well coated, cover with clear film (plastic wrap) and chill.

3 Preheat the oven to 200°C/400°F/Gas 6. Place the potatoes in a roasting pan, toss them in 30ml/2 tbsp olive oil and season with salt and pepper. Roast for 45 minutes or until tender. Remove from the oven and cool for at least 2 hours.

4 Reduce the oven to 190°C/375°F/Gas 5. Remove the trout from the marinade and place in a roasting pan. Bake for 20 minutes until cooked. Remove from the oven and leave to cool.

5 Cut the potatoes into chunks, flake the trout into bitesize pieces and toss them together in a serving dish with the remaining olive oil. Sprinkle with the chives and serve.

Cook's Tip
Look for firm pieces of fresh root ginger, with smooth skin. If bought really fresh, it will keep for up to 2 weeks in a cool place.

Garlic Baked Trout with Avocado Salad

A delectable warm salad of baked trout, roast tomatoes and avocados. Serve with lots of warm French bread.

Serves 4

6 plum tomatoes, halved
2 garlic cloves, thinly sliced
15g/½oz/½ cup fresh basil leaves
45ml/3 tbsp olive oil
4 trout fillets, each about 200g/7oz, skinned
2 avocados
juice of 1 lime
75g/3oz watercress, cress or rocket (arugula)
salt and ground black pepper
lime wedges, to garnish

1 Preheat the oven to 180°C/350°F/Gas 4. Place the tomatoes on a baking tray lined with baking parchment.

2 Sprinkle the garlic and basil over the tomatoes and season well with black pepper. Drizzle 15ml/1 tbsp of the olive oil over and bake for 25 minutes. Remove from the oven.

3 Move the tomato halves closer together, if necessary, to make room for the trout. Place the fillets on the baking tray. Return the tray to the oven for a further 15 minutes until the trout is cooked, then remove from the oven.

4 Cut the avocados in half, remove the stone (pit) and peel, then slice the flesh lengthwise into fine pieces.

5 Whisk the lime juice with the remaining olive oil. Season the dressing with salt and plenty black pepper. Divide the watercress between four individual serving plates. Top with the avocado slices. Drizzle the lime dressing over.

6 Arrange the cooked tomatoes over the salad and pour over any cooking juices accumulated on the baking parchment.

7 Flake the trout into bitesize pieces and divide between the plates, arranging it attractively amongst the salad leaves. Garnish the plates with the lime wedges and serve.

Trout & Ginger Salad

Fresh griddled and smoked trout are delicious on their own. Put them together, add a ginger dressing and you have a sensational salad that is easy to prepare.

Serves 4

15ml/1 tbsp olive oil
115g/4oz trout fillet, skinned
grated (shredded) rind and juice
of ½ lime
1 yellow (bell) pepper,
finely chopped

1 red (bell) pepper, finely chopped
1 small bunch fresh coriander
(cilantro), chopped
115g/4oz rocket (arugula)
115g/4oz smoked trout
ground black pepper

For the dressing

15ml/1 tbsp sesame oil
75ml/5 tbsp white wine vinegar
5ml/1 tsp soy sauce
2.5cm/1in piece fresh root ginger,
peeled and grated

1 Heat a griddle pan, brush with the oil, then fry the trout fillet for 5–8 minutes, until it is just cooked. Lift the fillet out of the pan and place it in a shallow bowl. Flake the trout into bitesize pieces, sprinkle with the lime rind and juice and set aside.

2 To make the dressing, mix the sesame oil, vinegar, soy sauce and grated root ginger in a small bowl. Whisk thoroughly until the dressing is combined.

3 Place the chopped yellow and red peppers, coriander and rocket in a large bowl and toss to combine. Transfer the salad to a serving dish.

4 Using kitchen scissors, cut the smoked trout into bitesize pieces. Arrange the smoked trout and griddled trout fillet on the salad. Sprinkle with black pepper. Whisk the ginger dressing again and drizzle it over the salad before serving.

> **Cook's Tip**
> This dish can easily be prepared in advance, but don't pour the dressing over the salad until the last minute.

Smoked Salmon & Rice Salad Parcels

Feta, cucumber and tomatoes give a Greek flavour to the salad in these parcels, a combination which goes well with the rice, especially if a little wild rice is added.

Serves 4

175g/6oz/scant 1 cup mixed wild
rice and basmati rice
8 slices smoked salmon, about
350g/12oz total

10cm/4in piece of cucumber,
finely diced
about 225g/8oz feta
cheese, cubed
8 cherry tomatoes, quartered
30ml/2 tbsp mayonnaise
10ml/2 tsp fresh lime juice
15ml/1 tbsp chopped
fresh chervil
salt and ground black pepper
lime slices and fresh chervil,
to garnish

1 Cook the rice according to the instructions on the packet. Drain, turn into a bowl and allow to cool.

2 Line four ramekins with clear film (plastic wrap), then line each ramekin with two slices of smoked salmon. Reserve any extra pieces of smoked salmon for the tops of the parcels.

3 Add the cucumber, feta and tomatoes to the rice, and stir in the mayonnaise, lime juice and chervil. Mix together well. Season with salt and pepper to taste.

4 Spoon the rice mixture into the salmon-lined ramekins. (Any leftover mixture can be used to make a rice salad.) Place any extra pieces of smoked salmon on top, then fold over the overlapping pieces of salmon so that the rice mixture is completely encased.

5 Chill the parcels for 30–60 minutes, then invert each parcel onto a plate, using the clear film to ease them out of the ramekins. Carefully peel off the clear film.

6 Garnish each parcel with slices of lime and a sprig of chervil.

Trout & ginger salad: Energy 177kcal/736kJ; Protein 16.1g; Carbohydrate 7.7g, of which sugars 7.2g; Fat 9.2g, of which saturates 1.1g; Cholesterol 10mg; Calcium 166mg; Fibre 5.2g; Sodium 674mg
Salmon & rice salad parcels: Energy 482kcal/2009kJ; Protein 34.9g; Carbohydrate 36.8g, of which sugars 1.8g; Fat 21.4g, of which saturates 9.3g; Cholesterol 76mg; Calcium 256mg; Fibre 0.8g; Sodium 2495mg

Salmon Tortilla Cones

Whether planning a simple midweek meal or catering for a crowd, these simple yet sophisticated wraps are just the ticket.

Serves 4

115g/4oz/½ cup soft white (farmer's) cheese
30ml/2 tbsp roughly chopped fresh dill
juice of 1 lemon

1 small red onion, finely chopped
15ml/1 tbsp drained bottled capers
30ml/2 tbsp extra-virgin olive oil
30ml/2 tbsp roughly chopped fresh flat leaf parsley
115g/4oz smoked salmon
8 small or 4 large wheat flour tortillas
salt and ground black pepper
lemon wedges, for squeezing

1 Place the soft cheese in a small bowl and mix in half the chopped dill. Add a little salt and pepper and a dash of the lemon juice to taste.

2 Add the onion, capers and olive oil to the remaining lemon juice. Add the chopped flat leaf parsley and the remaining dill and stir gently.

3 Cut the smoked salmon into short, thin strips, and add to the red onion mixture. Toss to mix. Season with plenty of pepper.

4 If using small tortillas, leave them whole, but large ones need to be cut in half. Spread a little of the soft cheese mixture on each piece of tortilla and top with the smoked salmon mixture.

5 Roll up the tortillas into cones and secure with wooden cocktail sticks (toothpicks). Arrange on a serving plate and add some lemon wedges, for squeezing. Serve immediately.

Cook's Tip
Look out for tortilla wraps in the supermarket. Thinner than traditional Mexican wheat tortillas, these come in several flavours. The spicy tomato ones would be good for this recipe.

Marinated Salmon with Avocado

Use only the freshest of salmon for this delicious salad. The marinade of lemon and dashi-konbu "cooks" the salmon, which is served with avocado, almonds and salad leaves.

Serves 4

250g/9oz very fresh salmon tail, skinned and filleted
juice of 1 lemon
10cm/4in dashi-konbu (dried kelp seaweed), wiped with a damp cloth and cut into 4 strips
1 ripe avocado

4 shiso leaves, stalks removed and cut in half lengthwise
about 115g/4oz mixed leaves such as lamb's lettuce (corn salad), frisée or rocket (arugula)
45ml/3 tbsp flaked or sliced almonds, toasted in a dry frying pan (skillet)

For the miso mayonnaise
90ml/6 tbsp good-quality mayonnaise
15ml/1 tbsp shiro miso
ground black pepper
15ml/1 tbsp lemon juice

1 Cut the first salmon fillet in half crossways at the tail end where the fillet is not wider than 4cm/1½in. Next, cut the wider part in half lengthwise. This means the fillet from one side is cut into three. Cut the other fillet into three pieces in the same way.

2 Pour the lemon juice with two of the dashi-konbu pieces into a wide shallow plastic container. Lay the salmon fillets in the base and sprinkle with the rest of the dashi-konbu.

3 Marinate the salmon fillets in a cool place for 15 minutes, then turn once and leave for 15 minutes more. Drain, reserving the marinade, and pat dry with kitchen paper.

4 Holding a very sharp knife at an angle, cut the salmon into 5mm/¼in thick slices against the grain.

5 Halve the avocado and brush the cut surface with a little of the reserved salmon marinade. Remove the avocado stone (pit) and skin, then carefully slice the flesh to the same thickness as the salmon.

6 To make the miso mayonnaise, mix the mayonnaise, shiro miso and pepper in a small bowl. Spread about 5ml/1 tsp on to the back of each of the shiso leaves, then mix the remainder with the lemon juice to loosen the mayonnaise.

7 Arrange the salad on four plates. Top with the avocado, salmon, shiso leaves and almonds. Drizzle over the remaining miso mayonnaise. Serve immediately.

Cook's Tips
• This recipe features authentic Japanese ingredients. Shiro miso, fermented soya bean paste, can be bought at Japanese food stores, as can the shiso leaves and the dried kelp seaweed.
• To slice the fish cleanly, you need a very sharp knife.
• Sprinkle the sliced avocado with lemon juice to prevent it from discolouring.

Salmon tortilla cones: Energy 374kcal/1576kJ; Protein 16.6g; Carbohydrate 53.2g, of which sugars 3g; Fat 12g, of which saturates 3.6g; Cholesterol 22mg; Calcium 128mg; Fibre 2.9g; Sodium 783mg
Marinated salmon with avocado: Energy 400kcal/1655kJ; Protein 16.6g; Carbohydrate 3.7g, of which sugars 2.9g; Fat 35.5g, of which saturates 5.4g; Cholesterol 48mg; Calcium 73mg; Fibre 2.6g; Sodium 403mg

Buckwheat Noodles with Smoked Salmon

Young pea sprouts are available for only a short time. You can substitute watercress, salad cress, young leeks or your favourite green vegetable or herb in this dish.

Serves 4
225g/8oz buckwheat or
    soba noodles

15ml/1 tbsp oyster sauce
juice of ½ lemon
30–45ml/2–3 tbsp light olive oil
115g/4oz smoked salmon, cut
    into fine strips
115g/4oz young pea sprouts
2 ripe tomatoes, peeled, seeded
    and cut into strips
15ml/1 tbsp snipped chives
ground black pepper

1 Cook the buckwheat or soba noodles in a large pan of boiling water until tender, according to the instructions on the packet. Drain the noodles, then rinse under cold running water and drain well.

2 Turn the noodles into a large bowl. Add the oyster sauce and lemon juice and season with pepper to taste. Moisten the noodles with the olive oil.

3 Add the smoked salmon, pea sprouts, tomatoes and chives. Mix well and serve immediately.

Grilled Salmon & Spring Vegetable Salad

Spring is the time to enjoy sweet, young vegetables. To make the most of their fresh flavour, toss in a simple dressing and serve with a lightly grilled salmon topped with sorrel and quail's eggs.

Serves 4
350g/12oz small new potatoes,
    scrubbed or scraped
4 quail's eggs
115g/4oz young carrots

115g/4oz baby corn on the cob
115g/4oz sugar snap peas
115g/4oz fine green beans
115g/4oz young courgettes
    (zucchini)
115g/4oz patty-pan squash
    (optional)
120ml/4fl oz/½ cup
    French dressing
4 salmon fillets, about
    150g/5oz each, skinned
115g/4oz sorrel, stems removed
salt and ground black pepper

1 Bring the potatoes to the boil in salted water and cook for about 15 minutes, until tender. Drain, cover and keep warm.

2 Cover the quail's eggs with boiling water and cook for 8 minutes. Refresh under cold water, shell and cut in half.

3 Bring a pan of salted water to the boil, add the carrots, sweetcorn, sugar snap peas, beans, courgettes and squash, if using, and cook for 2–3 minutes. Drain well. Place the hot vegetables and potatoes in a bowl, moisten with a little French dressing and allow to cool. Preheat the grill (broiler).

4 Brush the salmon fillets with some of the French dressing and grill (broil) for 6 minutes, turning once.

5 Place the sorrel in a stainless-steel or enamel pan with 30ml/2 tbsp French dressing. Cover and soften over a gentle heat for 2 minutes. Strain and cool to room temperature.

6 Divide the potatoes and vegetables among four large serving plates. Add a piece of salmon to each plate and top with a spoonful of sorrel and two pieces of quail's egg. Season.

Buckwheat noodles with smoked salmon: Energy 330kcal/1394kJ; Protein 15.1g; Carbohydrate 46.6g, of which sugars 4.6g; Fat 10.6g, of which saturates 1.1g; Cholesterol 10mg; Calcium 28mg; Fibre 2.6g; Sodium 609mg
Grilled salmon & spring vegetable salad: Energy 545kcal/2264kJ; Protein 32.3g; Carbohydrate 20.1g, of which sugars 6.3g; Fat 31g, of which saturates 6g; Cholesterol 110mg; Calcium 131mg; Fibre 4.2g; Sodium 739mg

Spiced Sardines with Grapefruit & Fennel Salad

This tasty salad is full of heady Moroccan flavours.

Serves 4–6

12 fresh sardines, gutted
1 onion, grated (shredded)
60–90ml/4–6 tbsp olive oil
5ml/1 tsp ground cinnamon
10ml/2 tsp cumin seeds, roasted and ground
10ml/2 tsp coriander seeds, roasted and ground
5ml/1 tsp paprika
5ml/1 tsp ground black pepper
1 small bunch fresh coriander
(cilantro), chopped
coarse salt
2 lemons, cut into wedges, to serve

For the salad

2 ruby grapefruits
5ml/1 tsp sea salt
1 fennel bulb, halved and sliced
2–3 spring onions (scallions), finely sliced
2.5ml/½ tsp ground roasted cumin
30–45ml/2–3 tbsp olive oil
handful of black olives

1 Rinse the sardines and pat them dry on kitchen paper, then rub inside and out with a little coarse salt.

2 In a bowl, mix the grated onion with the olive oil, cinnamon, ground roasted cumin and coriander, paprika and black pepper.

3 Make several slashes in the flesh of the sardines and smear the spice mixture all over the fish, inside and out. Leave the sardines to stand for 1 hour to allow the flavours to develop.

4 Meanwhile, make the salad. Remove the peel from the grapefruits , cutting downwards with a knife. Cut between the membranes to remove the segments. Halve the segments and put in a bowl. Sprinkle with salt. Add the fennel with the spring onions, cumin and olive oil. Toss lightly, then garnish with olives.

5 Preheat the grill (broiler). Cook the sardines for 3–4 minutes on each side, basting with any leftover marinade. Sprinkle with fresh coriander and serve immediately, with lemon wedges for squeezing over and the grapefruit and fennel salad.

Herring Salad with Beetroot & Soured Cream

Sweet, earthy beetroot and tangy soured cream team up with robustly flavoured herrings to make a salad with lots of character.

Serves 8

1 large tangy cooking apple
500g/1¼lb matjes herrings (schmaltz herrings), drained and cut into slices
2 small pickled cucumbers, diced
10ml/2 tsp caster (superfine) sugar, or to taste
10ml/2 tsp cider vinegar or white wine vinegar
300ml/½ pint/1¼ cups soured cream
2 cooked beetroot (beets)
lettuce, to serve
sprigs of fresh dill and chopped onion or onion rings, to garnish

1 Peel, core and dice the apple. Put in a bowl and add the herrings, cucumbers, sugar and cider or white wine vinegar.

2 Gently mix the ingredients, then stir in the soured cream.

3 Dice the cooked beetroot and add to the herring mixture. Chill in the refrigerator.

4 Serve the salad on a bed of lettuce leaves, garnished with fresh dill and chopped onion or onion rings.

Sardines with grapefruit & fennel: Energy 274kcal/1142kJ; Protein 18.7g; Carbohydrate 7.3g, of which sugars 6.1g; Fat 19.2g, of which saturates 3.9g; Cholesterol 0mg; Calcium 106mg; Fibre 2.3g; Sodium 109mg
Herring salad: Energy 212kcal/878kJ; Protein 9.6g; Carbohydrate 6.5g, of which sugars 6.2g; Fat 16.5g, of which saturates 4.7g; Cholesterol 51mg; Calcium 72mg; Fibre 0.6g; Sodium 266mg

Red Rice Salad Niçoise

Red rice, with its sweet nuttiness, goes well in this classic tuna salad.

Serves 6

about 675g/1½lb fresh tuna or swordfish, sliced into 2cm/¾in thick steaks
350g/12oz/1¾ cups Camargue red rice
fish or vegetable stock or water
450g/1lb green beans
450g/1lb broad (fava) beans, shelled
1 cos or romaine lettuce, leaves separated
450g/1lb cherry tomatoes, halved
30ml/2 tbsp coarsely chopped fresh coriander (cilantro)
3 hard-boiled (hard-cooked) eggs
175g/6oz/1½ cups pitted black olives
olive oil, for brushing

For the marinade

1 red onion, roughly chopped
2 garlic cloves
½ bunch fresh parsley
½ bunch fresh coriander (cilantro)
10ml/2 tsp paprika
45ml/3 tbsp olive oil
45ml/3 tbsp water
30ml/2 tbsp white wine vinegar
15ml/1 tbsp fresh lime or lemon juice
salt and ground black pepper

For the dressing

30ml/2 tbsp fresh lime or lemon juice
5ml/1 tsp Dijon mustard
½ garlic clove, crushed (optional)
60ml/4 tbsp olive oil
60ml/4 tbsp sunflower oil

1 To make the marinade, mix all the ingredients in a food processor and process them for 30–40 seconds until the vegetables and herbs are finely chopped.

2 Prick the tuna or swordfish steaks all over with a fork. Lay them side by side in a shallow dish and pour over the marinade, turning to coat. Cover with clear film (plastic wrap) and leave in a cool place for 2–4 hours.

3 Cook the rice in stock or water, according to the instructions on the packet, then drain, turn into a bowl and set aside.

4 To make the dressing, mix the citrus juice, mustard and garlic (if using) in a bowl. Whisk in the oils, then add salt and pepper to taste. Stir 60ml/4 tbsp of the dressing into the rice, then spoon the rice into the centre of a large serving dish.

5 Cook the green beans and broad beans in boiling salted water until tender. Drain, refresh under cold water and drain again. Remove the outer shell from the broad beans and add the shelled beans and green beans to the rice.

6 Add the lettuce leaves to the salad with the tomatoes and coriander. Shell the eggs and cut them into sixths. Preheat the grill (broiler).

7 Arrange the tuna or swordfish steaks on the grill pan. Brush with the marinade and a little extra olive oil. Grill (broil) for 3–4 minutes on each side, brushing with marinade, until cooked.

8 Allow the fish to cool a little, then break into large pieces. Toss into the salad with the olives and the remaining dressing. Decorate with the eggs and serve.

Fresh Tuna Salad Niçoise

Fresh tuna transforms this famous salad from the south of France into something really special.

Serves 4

4 tuna steaks, about 150g/5oz each
30ml/2 tbsp olive oil
225g/8oz fine green beans
1 small cos or romaine lettuce or 2 Little Gem (Bibb) lettuces
4 new potatoes, boiled
4 ripe tomatoes or 12 cherry tomatoes
2 red (bell) peppers, seeded and cut into thin strips
4 hard-boiled (hard-cooked) eggs, sliced
8 drained anchovy fillets in oil, halved lengthwise
16 large black olives
salt and ground black pepper
12 fresh basil leaves, to garnish

For the dressing

15ml/1 tbsp red wine vinegar
90ml/6 tbsp olive oil
1 fat garlic clove, crushed

1 Brush the tuna on both sides with a little olive oil and season with salt and pepper. Heat a ridged griddle or the grill (broiler) until very hot, then grill the tuna steaks for 1–2 minutes on each side; should still be pink and juicy in the middle. Set aside.

2 Cook the beans in a pan of lightly salted boiling water for 4–5 minutes or until just tender. Drain, refresh under cold water and drain again.

3 Separate the lettuce leaves and arrange them on four individual serving plates. Slice the potatoes and tomatoes, if large (leave cherry tomatoes whole) and divide them among the plates. Arrange the fine green beans and red pepper strips on top of them.

4 Shell the eggs and cut into thick slices. Place two slices on each plate with an anchovy fillet draped over. Scatter four olives onto each plate.

5 To make the dressing, whisk together the vinegar, olive oil and garlic and season to taste. Drizzle over the salads. Arrange the tuna steaks on top, scatter over the basil and serve.

Red rice salad Niçoise: Energy 726kcal/3041kJ; Protein 42.2g; Carbohydrate 62.3g, of which sugars 6.9g; Fat 36g, of which saturates 6.3g; Cholesterol 127mg; Calcium 142mg; Fibre 9.7g; Sodium 760mg
Fresh tuna salad Niçoise: Energy 542kcal/2260kJ; Protein 46.8g; Carbohydrate 14.3g, of which sugars 9.8g; Fat 33.7g, of which saturates 6.5g; Cholesterol 236mg; Calcium 132mg; Fibre 4.4g; Sodium 671mg

Moroccan Tuna Salad with Green Beans & Eggs

A colourful medley of fresh beans, cherry tomatoes and black olives create a mouthwatering salad.

Serves 6
6 tuna or swordfish steaks, about
  900g/2lb total weight

For the marinade
1 onion
2 garlic cloves, halved
½ bunch fresh parsley
½ bunch fresh coriander
  (cilantro)
10ml/2 tsp paprika
45ml/3 tbsp olive oil
30ml/2 tbsp white wine vinegar

15ml/1 tbsp lime or lemon juice
45ml/3 tbsp water

For the salad
450g/1lb green beans
450g/1lb broad (fava) beans
1 cos or romaine lettuce
450g/1lb cherry tomatoes, halved
30ml/2 tbsp coarsely chopped
  fresh coriander (cilantro)
3 eggs, hard-boiled (hard-cooked)
45ml/3 tbsp extra virgin olive oil
10–15ml/2–3 tsp lime or lemon
  juice
½ garlic clove, crushed
175–225g/6–8oz/1½–2 cups
  pitted black olives

1 To make the marinade, cut the onion into quarters or eighths. Place the onion, garlic, parsley, coriander, paprika, olive oil, wine vinegar and lime or lemon juice in a food processor, add the water and process for 30–40 seconds until all the ingredients are finely chopped.

2 Prick the tuna or swordfish steaks all over with a fork, place in a shallow dish that is large enough to hold them in a single layer and pour over the marinade, turning the fish so that each piece is coated. Cover and leave in a cool place for 2–4 hours, so that the flavours develop.

3 To make the salad, cook the green beans and broad beans in boiling salted water for 5–10 minutes or until tender. Drain, refresh in cold running water and drain again.

4 Discard the outer shells from the broad beans and place the bright green inner beans in a large serving bowl with the green beans. Remove the outer leaves from the lettuce and tear the inner leaves into pieces. Add to the bowl with the tomatoes and chopped coriander.

5 Shell the eggs and cut into eighths with a sharp knife.

6 To make the dressing, whisk the olive oil, citrus juice and garlic in a bowl until thoroughly combined.

7 Preheat the grill (broiler) and arrange the fish steaks on the grill pan. Brush with the marinade mixed with a little extra olive oil and grill (broil) for 5–6 minutes on each side, until the fish is tender. Brush with marinade and more olive oil when turning the fish over.

8 Allow the fish to cool a little and then break the steaks into large pieces. Toss into the salad with the olives and dressing. Add the eggs and serve immediately.

Pasta Salade Niçoise

In this fresh-tasting salad the ingredients of a classic French salade Niçoise are given a modern Italian twist.

Serves 4
115g/4oz green beans, cut into
  5cm/2in lengths
250g/9oz/2¼ cups dried penne
  rigate pasta
105ml/7 tbsp extra-virgin olive oil
2 fresh tuna steaks, 350–450g/
  12oz–1lb total weight

6 baby Italian plum tomatoes,
  quartered lengthwise
50g/2oz/½ cup pitted black
  olives, halved lengthwise
6 bottled or canned anchovies in
  olive oil, drained and chopped
30–45ml/2–3 tbsp chopped fresh
  flat leaf parsley, to taste
juice of ½–1 lemon, to taste
2 heads of chicory (Belgian
  endive), leaves separated
salt and ground black pepper
lemon wedges, to serve

1 Cook the beans in a large pan of salted boiling water for 5–6 minutes. Remove the beans with a large slotted spoon and refresh under the cold running water. Drain well.

2 Add the pasta to the pan of bean cooking water, bring back to the boil and cook according to the instructions on the packet, until *al dente*.

3 Meanwhile, heat a ridged griddle or heavy frying pan (skillet) over a low heat. Dip a wad of kitchen paper into the oil, wipe it over the surface of the pan and heat gently. Brush the tuna steaks on both sides with oil and sprinkle liberally with pepper; add to the pan and cook over a medium to high heat for 1–2 minutes on each side. Remove and set aside.

4 Drain the cooked pasta well and turn into a large bowl. Add the remaining oil, the beans, tomato quarters, black olives, anchovies, parsley, lemon juice and salt and pepper to taste. Toss well to mix, then leave to cool.

5 Break the tuna into large pieces, discarding the skin, then fold into the salad. Taste the salad for seasoning. Arrange the chicory leaves around the edge of a large shallow bowl. Spoon the pasta salad into the centre and serve with lemon wedges.

Pasta salad Niçoise: Energy 539kcal/2265kJ; Protein 31.4g; Carbohydrate 52g, of which sugars 7.5g; Fat 24.3g, of which saturates 4g; Cholesterol 27mg; Calcium 90mg; Fibre 4.6g; Sodium 514mg.
Moroccan tuna salad: Energy 402kcal/1677kJ; Protein 35.4g; Carbohydrate 14.9g, of which sugars 6.2g; Fat 22.8g, of which saturates 4.3g; Cholesterol 123mg; Calcium 134mg; Fibre 8.6g; Sodium 752mg

Tuna Carpaccio

Fillet of beef is most often used for carpaccio, but meaty fish like tuna make an unusual change. The secret is to slice the fish wafer-thin, made possible by freezing it first. This is a technique used by the Japanese for making sashimi.

Serves 4

2 fresh tuna steaks, about
  450g/1lb total weight
60ml/4 tbsp extra-virgin olive oil
15ml/1 tbsp balsamic vinegar
5ml/1 tsp caster (superfine) sugar
30ml/2 tbsp bottled green
  peppercorns or capers, drained
salt and ground black pepper
lemon wedges and green salad,
  to serve

1 Remove the skin from each tuna steak and place each steak between two sheets of clear film (plastic wrap) or non-stick baking paper. Beat with a rolling pin to flatted the steak slightly.

2 Roll up the tuna steaks as tightly as possible, then wrap tightly in clear film. Place the rolled tuna steaks in the freezer for 4 hours, or until firm.

3 Unwrap the tuna and cut crossways into the thinnest possible slices. Arrange the slices on individual serving plates.

4 Whisk together the oil, vinegar, sugar and peppercorns or capers, season with salt and pepper and pour over the tuna.

5 Cover and allow to come to room temperature for 30 minutes before serving with lemon wedges and a crisp green salad.

Cook's Tips
• Raw fish is safe to eat as long as it is very fresh, so check with your fishmonger before purchase and make and serve the carpaccio the same day. Do not buy fish that has been frozen and thawed.
• The dressing can also be served with ready-sliced smoked salmon for an instant meal.

Bean Salad with Tuna & Red Onion

This satisfying, colourful bean salad is flavoured with red onion and flaked tuna.

Serves 4

250g/9oz/1⅓ cups dried haricot
  or cannellini beans, soaked
  overnight in cold water
1 bay leaf
200–250g/7–9oz fine green
  beans
1 large red onion, very thinly sliced
45ml/3 tbsp chopped fresh flat
  leaf parsley
200–250g/7–9oz good-quality

canned tuna in olive oil, drained
200g/7oz cherry tomatoes, halved
salt and ground black pepper
fine lemon rind strips, to garnish

For the dressing
90ml/6 tbsp extra-virgin olive oil
15ml/1 tbsp tarragon vinegar
5ml/1 tsp tarragon mustard
1 garlic clove, finely chopped
5ml/1 tsp grated (shredded)
  lemon rind
a little lemon juice
pinch of caster (superfine) sugar

1 Drain the dried soaked beans and bring them to the boil in fresh water with the bay leaf added. Boil rapidly for 10 minutes, then reduce the heat and boil steadily for 1–1½ hours, until tender. The cooking time depends on the age of the beans. Drain well. Discard the bay leaf.

2 Meanwhile, to make the dressing, whisk together the oil, vinegar, mustard, garlic and lemon rind. Season to taste with salt, pepper, lemon juice and a pinch of sugar. Leave to stand.

3 Blanch the green beans in plenty of boiling water for 3–4 minutes. Drain, refresh under cold water and drain again.

4 Place both types of beans in a bowl. Add half the dressing and toss to mix. Stir in the onion and half the chopped parsley, then season to taste with salt and pepper.

5 Flake the tuna into large chunks and toss into the beans with the tomato halves. Arrange the salad on four individual plates. Drizzle the remaining dressing over the salad and scatter the remaining parsley on top. Garnish with strips of lemon rind.

Tuna carpaccio: Energy 266kcal/1112kJ; Protein 27.3g; Carbohydrate 2.3g, of which sugars 2.3g; Fat 16.6g, of which saturates 3g; Cholesterol 32mg; Calcium 40mg; Fibre 0.7g; Sodium 55mg
Bean salad: Energy 430kcal/1800kJ; Protein 28.7g; Carbohydrate 30.6g, of which sugars 4.1g; Fat 22.3g, of which saturates 3.3g; Cholesterol 25mg; Calcium 110mg; Fibre 11.5g; Sodium 175mg

Tuna Pasta Salad

An easy pasta salad, ideal for a midweek supper.

Serves 6–8

450g/1lb dried pasta shapes, such as macaroni or farfalle
60ml/4 tbsp olive oil
2 x 200g/7oz cans tuna, drained and flaked

2 x 400g/14oz cans cannellini or borlotti beans, rinsed and drained
1 small red onion, thinly sliced
2 celery sticks, thinly sliced
juice of 1 lemon
30ml/2 tbsp chopped fresh parsley
salt and ground black pepper

1 Cook the pasta in a large pan lightly salted boiling water according to the packet instructions. Drain, then rinse under cold water. Drain well and turn into a large bowl. Toss with the olive oil and set aside. Allow to cool completely.

2 Mix the tuna and the beans into the pasta. Add the onion, celery, lemon juice and parsley. Season, and let the salad stand for at least 1 hour before serving.

Quick Tuna & Bean Salad

This substantial salad makes a good light meal, and can be very quickly assembled from canned ingredients.

Serves 4–6

2 x 400g/14oz cans cannellini or borlotti beans, drained

2 x 200g/7oz cans tuna fish, drained
60ml/4 tbsp extra-virgin olive oil
30ml/2 tbsp fresh lemon juice
15ml/1 tbsp chopped fresh parsley
3 spring onions (scallions), sliced
salt and ground black pepper

1 Rinse the beans, then drain well and place in a serving dish. Break the tuna into fairly large flakes and add to the beans.

2 To make the dressing, combine the oil with the lemon juice. Season and stir in the parsley. Mix well. Pour over the beans and tuna, sprinkle with the spring onions and toss well before serving.

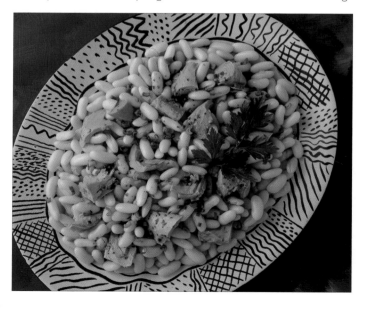

Tuscan Tuna & Bean Salad

A great store-cupboard dish, perfect for an instant supper or lunch. All you need as an accompaniment is warmed baguette.

Serves 4

400g/14oz can haricot (navy) beans
400g/14oz can kidney beans
1 red onion, finely chopped
225g/8oz canned tuna in oil, drained and lightly flaked

fresh chives and tarragon sprigs, to garnish

For the dressing

30ml/2 tbsp smooth French mustard
300ml/½ pint/1¼ cups olive oil
60ml/4 tbsp white wine vinegar
30ml/2 tbsp chopped fresh parsley
30ml/2 tbsp chopped fresh chives
30ml/2 tbsp chopped fresh tarragon or chervil
salt and ground black pepper

1 To make the dressing, whisk together the mustard, oil and vinegar in a small bowl. Whisk in the parsley, chives and tarragon or chervil and season to taste with salt and pepper.

2 Drain the haricot and kidney beans, then rinse under cold running water. Drain well and put in a serving bowl.

3 Mix the chopped onion into the beans, add the dressing and toss well together.

4 Carefully fold in the tuna. Garnish with chives and tarragon sprigs and serve.

> **Variation**
> For an alternative presentation of this dish, find some really good, ripe beef tomatoes. Using one per person, halve the tomatoes and scoop out the flesh (you can chop and mix this in with the tuna salad or discard it). Give the hollow tomato halves a good seasoning of sea salt and drizzle olive oil over before filling the cavities with the tuna and bean salad.

Tuna pasta: Energy 441kcal/1862kJ; Protein 27.4g; Carbohydrate 60.2g, of which sugars 6g; Fat 11.7g, of which saturates 1.8g; Cholesterol 25mg; Calcium 104mg; Fibre 8.2g; Sodium 543mg

Quick tuna & bean: Energy 328kcal/1378kJ; Protein 27.5g; Carbohydrate 24g, of which sugars 5g; Fat 14.2g, of which saturates 2.2g; Cholesterol 33mg; Calcium 119mg; Fibre 8.7g; Sodium 716mg

Tuscan tuna & bean: Energy 764kcal/3177kJ; Protein 28.5g; Carbohydrate 37.9g, of which sugars 8.9g; Fat 56.5g, of which saturates 8.2g; Cholesterol 25mg; Calcium 182mg; Fibre 13.2g; Sodium 1151mg

Spicy Tuna, Chickpea & Cherry Tomato Salad

A quick and easy salad using canned chickpeas and tuna, tossed in a tasty spicy tomato dressing.

Serves 6

5ml/1 tsp olive oil
1 garlic clove, crushed
5ml/1 tsp ground coriander
5ml/1 tsp garam masala
5ml/1 tsp hot chilli powder
120ml/4fl oz/½ cup tomato juice
30ml/2 tbsp balsamic vinegar
dash of Tabasco sauce

½ cucumber
675g/1½lb cherry tomatoes
1 bunch radishes
1 bunch spring onions (scallions)
50g/2oz watercress or cress
2 x 400g/14oz cans chickpeas, rinsed and drained
400g/14oz can tuna in brine or water, drained and flaked
2–3 fresh parsley sprigs, finely chopped
1 small bunch fresh chives, finely snipped
salt and ground black pepper

1 Heat the oil in a small pan, add the garlic and spices to the pan and cook gently for 1 minute, stirring constantly.

2 Stir in the tomato juice, vinegar and Tabasco sauce and heat until it bubbles gently. Remove from the heat and cool slightly.

3 Leave the skin on the cucumber, or remove it, as you prefer. Slice the cucumber into thin rounds.

4 Halve the cherry tomatoes. Trim and slice the radishes and spring onions. Remove any tough stems from the watercress and chop roughly.

5 Put the tomatoes and cucumber in a salad bowl. Add the radishes, spring onions and watercress to the salad bowl. Toss lightly to mix.

6 Stir the chickpeas, tuna and herbs into the salad. Pour the cooled tomato dressing over the salad and toss the ingredients together to mix well. Season to taste with salt and ground black pepper and serve immediately.

Mediterranean Pasta Salad

This is an ideal recipe for an easy midweek meal. Don't be tempted to chill the salad as this will only dull all the vibrant flavours.

Serves 4

225g/8oz chunky pasta shapes
175g/6oz fine green beans
2 large ripe tomatoes
50g/2oz fresh basil leaves
200g/7oz can tuna fish in oil, drained
2 hard-boiled (hard-cooked) eggs, shelled and sliced or quartered

50g/2oz can anchovy fillets, drained
capers and black olives, to taste

For the dressing

90ml/6 tbsp extra-virgin olive oil
30ml/2 tbsp white wine vinegar or lemon juice
2 garlic cloves, crushed
2.5ml/½ tsp Dijon mustard
30ml/2 tbsp chopped fresh basil
salt and ground black pepper

1 To make the dressing, whisk all the ingredients together in a small bowl. Set aside.

2 Cook the pasta in plenty of salted, boiling water according to the packet instructions, until *al dente*. Drain well and cool.

3 Blanch the beans in salted, boiling water for 3 minutes. Drain and refresh under cold running water.

4 Slice the tomatoes and arrange on the bottom of a serving bowl. Moisten with a little dressing and cover with a quarter of the basil leaves. Spoon the beans on top. Moisten with a little more dressing and cover with a third of the remaining basil.

5 Toss the pasta in a little more dressing and spoon over the vegetables. Cover with half the remaining basil and the roughly flaked tuna.

6 Arrange the sliced eggs on top of the pasta, then scatter over the anchovy fillets. Top the salad with capers and black olives to taste. Spoon over the remaining dressing and garnish with whole basil leaves. Serve the salad immediately.

Tuna, chickpea & tomato salad: Energy 186kcal/788kJ; Protein 22.7g; Carbohydrate 16.4g, of which sugars 5g; Fat 3.8g, of which saturates 0.6g; Cholesterol 34mg; Calcium 90mg; Fibre 4.9g; Sodium 381mg
Mediterranean pasta salad: Energy 552kcal/2312kJ; Protein 30.9g; Carbohydrate 44.6g, of which sugars 4.4g; Fat 29.2g, of which saturates 5.1g; Cholesterol 223mg; Calcium 105mg; Fibre 3.1g; Sodium 713mg

Tuna & Sweetcorn Salad

A family favourite, this is an excellent main course salad for an outdoor summer lunch. It travels very well, so it is good for picnics, too.

Serves 4
175g/6oz/1½ cups dried
   conchiglie pasta
175g/6oz can tuna in olive oil,
   drained and flaked
175g/6oz can sweetcorn, drained
75g/3oz bottled roasted red (bell)
   pepper, rinsed, dried and
   finely chopped
1 handful of fresh basil
   leaves, chopped
salt and ground black pepper

For the dressing
60ml/4 tbsp extra-virgin olive oil
15ml/1 tbsp balsamic vinegar
5ml/1 tsp red wine vinegar
5ml/1 tsp Dijon mustard
5–10ml/1–2 tsp honey, to taste

1 Cook the pasta in a large pan of lightly salted boiling water according to the packet instructions, with a drop of oil to prevent sticking, until al dente. Drain and rinse under cold running water. Leave to drain until cold and dry, shaking occasionally.

2 To make the dressing, put the oil in a large bowl, add the two vinegars and whisk well together until emulsified. Add the mustard, honey and salt and pepper to taste and whisk again until well combined.

3 Add the pasta to the dressing and toss well to mix, then add the tuna, sweetcorn and roasted pepper and toss again.

4 Mix in about half the chopped basil and season to taste with salt and pepper. Serve at room temperature or chilled, with the remaining basil sprinkled on top.

> **Variation**
> To save time, you could use a can of mixed sweetcorn and peppers. This is a handy item to have in your store cupboard.

Provençal Salad

Served with good French bread, this regional classic makes a wonderful summer lunch or light supper.

Serves 4–6
225g/8oz green beans
450g/1lb new potatoes, cut
   into 2.5cm/1in pieces
white wine vinegar and olive oil,
   for sprinkling
1 small romaine or round
   (butterhead) lettuce, torn into
   bitesize pieces
4 ripe plum tomatoes, quartered
1 small cucumber, peeled, seeded
   and diced
1 green or red (bell) pepper, thinly
   sliced
4 hard-boiled (hard-cooked)
eggs, quartered
24 Niçoise or black olives
225g/8oz can tuna in brine,
   drained
50g/2oz can anchovy fillets in
   olive oil, drained
basil leaves, to garnish
croûtons, to serve (optional)

For the anchovy vinaigrette
20ml/1 heaped tbsp
   Dijon mustard
50g/2oz can anchovy fillets in
   olive oil, drained
1 garlic clove, crushed
60ml/4 tbsp lemon juice or white
   wine vinegar
120ml/4fl oz/½ cup sunflower oil
120ml/4fl oz/½ cup extra-virgin
   olive oil
freshly ground black pepper

1 To make the vinaigrette, put all the ingredients except the oils in a food processor fitted with the metal blade and process to combine. With the machine running, slowly add the oils in a thin stream until the vinaigrette is thick and creamy.

2 Cook the green beans in boiling water for 3 minutes until just tender. Transfer to a colander with a slotted spoon, drain, then rinse under cold running water. Drain again and set aside.

3 Add the potatoes to the same boiling water and simmer for 10–15 minutes until just tender, then drain. Sprinkle with a little vinegar and olive oil and a spoonful of the vinaigrette.

4 Arrange the lettuce on a platter, top with the tomatoes, cucumber and pepper, then add the beans and potatoes. Arrange the eggs, olives, tuna and anchovies on top and garnish with the basil leaves. Drizzle with the remaining vinaigrette.

Hard-boiled Eggs with Tuna Sauce

A tangy tuna mayonnaise spooned over eggs makes a delicious snack.

Serves 6
200g/7oz can tuna in olive oil
3 canned anchovy fillets
15ml/1tbsp capers, drained
30ml/2 tbsp lemon juice
6 hard-boiled (hard-cooked) extra-large eggs

60ml/4 tbsp olive oil
salt and ground black pepper
capers and anchovy fillets,
    to garnish

For the mayonnaise
1 egg yolk
5ml/1 tsp Dijon mustard
5ml/1 tsp white wine vinegar or
    lemon juice
150ml/¼ pint/⅔ cup olive oil

1 To make the mayonnaise, whisk the egg yolk, mustard and vinegar or lemon juice together in a small bowl. Whisk in the oil a few drops at a time until 3–4 tablespoons have been incorporated. Whisk in the remaining oil in a slow stream.

2 Place the tuna with its oil, the anchovies, capers, lemon juice and olive oil in a blender or food processor. Process until the mixture is smooth. Fold into the mayonnaise. Season with black pepper, and salt if necessary. Chill for at least 1 hour.

3 Cut the eggs in half lengthwise. Arrange on a platter. Spoon on the mayonnaise and garnish with capers and anchovy fillets.

Cook's Tips
• *If you find that canned anchovies are too salty for your liking, you can reduce their saltiness by soaking them in milk for 20 minutes. Drain off the oil before covering with milk. After soaking, drain and rinse the anchovies in cold water.*
• *When you hard-boil eggs, prevent the greenish discolouration around the yolk by running them under cold water as soon as you take them out of the boiling water.*
• *Peel boiled eggs easily by rolling them firmly under your hand on a chopping board before attempting to take the shells off. The shells will crack evenly and should peel off in one piece.*

Anchovy & Roasted Pepper Salad

Sweet peppers, salty anchovies and plenty of garlic make a salad bursting with Mediterranean flavours. Serve with olive bread or ciabatta for a light snack or as a first course.

Serves 4
2 red, 2 orange and 2 yellow
    (bell) peppers, halved
    and seeded
50g/2oz can anchovies in olive oil
2 garlic cloves
45ml/3 tbsp balsamic vinegar
roughly torn fresh basil leaves,
    to garnish
lemon wedges, to serve
black pepper

1 Preheat the oven to 200°C/400°F/Gas 6. Place the peppers, cut side down, in a roasting pan. Roast for 30-40 minutes, until the skins are charred. Transfer the peppers to a bowl, cover with clear film (plastic wrap) and leave for 15 minutes.

2 Peel the peppers, then cut them into chunky strips. Drain the anchovies, saving the olive oil. Halve the anchovies lengthways.

3 Slice the garlic as thinly as possible and place it in a large bowl. Stir in the reserved olive oil, vinegar and a little pepper.

4 Add the pepper strips and anchovies and fold the ingredients together. Cover and chill Just before serving, sprinkle the salad with torn basil leaves and serve with lemon wedges.

Hard-boiled eggs with tuna sauce: Energy 369kcal/1529kJ; Protein 16.6g; Carbohydrate 0.1g, of which sugars 0.1g; Fat 33.8g, of which saturates 5.8g; Cholesterol 242mg; Calcium 46mg; Fibre 0g; Sodium 311mg
Anchovy & roasted pepper salad: Energy 108kcal/453kJ; Protein 6g; Carbohydrate 16.3g, of which sugars 15.5g; Fat 2.4g, of which saturates 0.5g; Cholesterol 8mg; Calcium 83mg; Fibre 4.6g; Sodium 506mg

Panzanella with Anchovies

In this lively Italian speciality, a sweet tangy blend of tomato juice, rich olive oil and red wine vinegar makes a marvellous dressing for a colourful salad.

Serves 4–6
225g/8oz ciabatta bread
150ml/¼ pint/⅔ cup extra-virgin
   olive oil
3 red (bell) peppers
3 yellow (bell) peppers
50g/2oz can anchovy fillets
675g/1½lb ripe plum tomatoes
4 garlic cloves, crushed
60ml/4 tbsp red wine vinegar
50g/2oz/⅓ cup capers, drained
115g/4oz/1 cup pitted
   black olives
salt and ground black pepper
fresh basil leaves, to garnish

1 Preheat the grill (broiler) and line the pan with foil. Also preheat the oven to 200°C/400°F/Gas 6. Cut the ciabatta into 2cm/¾in chunks and drizzle with 60ml/4 tbsp of the oil. Place on the lined grill pan and grill (broil) lightly until just golden. Set aside to cool.

2 Put the peppers on a foil-lined baking sheet and bake for about 45 minutes, turning them occasionally, until the skins begin to char. Remove from the oven, cover with a dish towel and leave to cool slightly.

3 Skin and quarter the peppers, remove the stalk and seeds. Drain and then roughly chop the anchovies. Set aside. Halve the tomatoes and scoop the seeds into a sieve (strainer) set over a bowl. Cut the tomato halves in half and set aside.

4 Using the back of a spoon, press the tomato pulp in the sieve to extract as much juice as possible. Discard the pulp and add the remaining oil, the garlic and vinegar to the juices.

5 Layer the bread croûtons, peppers, tomato pieces, anchovies, capers and olives in a salad bowl. Season the tomato dressing with salt and pepper to taste, then pour over the salad and toss lightly. Leave to stand for about 30 minutes. Serve garnished with plenty of basil leaves.

Original Caesar Salad

This much-enjoyed salad was created by Caesar Cordoni in Tijuana in 1924. Be sure to use crunchy lettuce and add the soft eggs and garlic croûtons at the last minute.

Serves 6
175ml/6fl oz/¾ cup extra-virgin
   olive oil
1 large garlic clove, crushed
115g/4oz/2 cups French or Italian
   bread, cut in 2.5cm/1in cubes
2 eggs, boiled for 1 minute
1 cos or romaine lettuce
120ml/4fl oz/½ cup lemon juice
50g/2oz/⅔ cup freshly grated
   (shredded) Parmesan cheese
6 anchovy fillets, drained and
   finely chopped (optional)
salt and ground black pepper

1 Heat 50ml/2fl oz/¼ cup of the oil in a frying pan (skillet). Add the bread and garlic and fry, stirring and turning constantly, until the cubes are golden brown. Leave to drain on kitchen paper and discard the garlic.

2 Cook the eggs in boiling water for 1 minute until soft boiled, then drain and cool under cold running water. Shell.

3 Tear large lettuce leaves into smaller pieces. Put all the lettuce in a salad bowl.

4 Add the remaining olive oil to the salad leaves and season with salt and pepper. Toss to coat well.

5 Break the soft-boiled eggs on top. Sprinkle with the lemon juice and toss to combine the ingredients. Add the grated (shredded) Parmesan cheese and anchovies, if using, then toss again. Scatter the croûtons on top of the salad and serve.

> **Cook's Tip**
> To make a tangier dressing, mix the olive oil with 30ml/2 tbsp white wine vinegar, 2.5ml/½ tsp mustard, 5ml/1 tsp sugar, and salt and pepper.

Caesar salad: Energy 236kcal/980kJ; Protein 6.2g; Carbohydrate 11.3g, of which sugars 1.1g; Fat 18.7g, of which saturates 4.1g; Cholesterol 17mg; Calcium 143mg; Fibre 0.8g; Sodium 330mg
Panzanella with anchovies: Energy 360kcal/1500kJ; Protein 8.6g; Carbohydrate 33.7g, of which sugars 14.8g; Fat 22.1g, of which saturates 3.3g; Cholesterol 5mg; Calcium 103mg; Fibre 5.2g; Sodium 977mg

Stuffed Cucumber Kimchi

This is a Korean dish that is perfectly refreshing on a hot summer's day. The spiciness of the chilli is neutralized by the succulent cucumber, with flavours that cleanse and invigorate the palate.

Serves 4
15 small pickling cucumbers
30ml/2 tbsp sea salt
1 bunch Chinese chives

For the seasoning
1 onion
4 spring onions (scallions),
   thinly sliced
75ml/5 tbsp Korean chilli powder
15ml/1 tbsp Thai fish sauce
10ml/2 tsp salt
1 garlic clove, crushed
7.5ml/1½ tsp grated fresh
   root ginger
5ml/1 tsp sugar
5ml/1 tsp sesame seeds

1 If the cucumbers are long, cut them in half widthways. Make two slits in a cross down the centre of each cucumber or cucumber half, making sure not to cut all the way to the end.

2 Coat thoroughly with the sea salt, and leave for 1 hour.

3 Cut the Chinese chives into 2.5cm/1in lengths, discarding the bulb.

4 Combine the onion and spring onions with the Chinese chives in a bowl. Add 45ml/3 tbsp of the chilli powder and add the Thai fish sauce, salt, garlic, ginger, sugar and sesame seeds.

5 Mix the ingredients thoroughly by hand, using plastic gloves to prevent the chilli powder from staining your skin.

6 Lightly rinse the cucumbers to remove the salt crystals. Coat with the remaining chilli powder, and press the seasoning into the slits.

7 Put the cucumber into an airtight container and leave at room temperature for 12 hours before serving.

8 This dish is ideal served with cold meats or poultry and a simple rice salad.

Rice Vermicelli & Salad Rolls

Hearty noodle salad wrapped in rice sheets makes a healthy change from a sandwich.

Makes 8
50g/2oz rice vermicelli, soaked in
   warm water until soft
1 large carrot, grated (shredded)
15ml/1 tbsp sugar
15–30ml/1–2 tbsp fish sauce
8 x 20cm/8in round rice sheets
8 large lettuce leaves
350g/12oz roast pork, sliced
115g/4oz beansprouts
handful of mint leaves

8 large cooked prawns (shrimp),
   peeled and halved
½ cucumber, cut into fine strips
handful coriander (cilantro) leaves

For the peanut sauce
15ml/1 tbsp vegetable oil
3 garlic cloves, finely chopped
1–2 red chillies, finely chopped
5ml/1 tsp tomato purée
120ml/4fl oz/½ cup water
15ml/1 tbsp smooth peanut butter
30ml/2 tbsp hoisin sauce
2.5ml/½ tsp sugar
juice of 1 lime
50g/2oz roasted peanuts, ground

1 Drain the noodles. Cook in boiling water for 2–3 minutes until tender. Drain, rinse in cold water, drain well. Turn into a bowl. Add the carrot and season with the sugar and fish sauce.

2 To assemble the rolls, dip a rice sheet in a bowl of warm water, then lay it flat on a surface. Place 1 lettuce leaf, 1–2 scoops of the noodle mixture, a few slices of pork, some of the beansprouts and several mint leaves on the rice sheet.

3 Start rolling up the rice sheet into a cylinder. When half the sheet has been rolled up, fold both sides of the sheet towards the centre and lay two pieces of prawn along the crease. Add a few of strips of cucumber and coriander leaves. Continue to roll up the sheet to make a tight packet. Cover with a damp dish towel while making the remaining rolls.

4 To make the sauce, heat the oil in a small pan and fry the garlic, chillies and tomato purée for 1 minute. Add the water and bring to the boil, then stir in the peanut butter, hoisin sauce, sugar and lime juice. Simmer for 3–4 minutes. Spoon the sauce into a bowl, add the peanuts and cool slightly to serve.

Rice vermicelli & salad rolls: Energy 202kcal/843kJ; Protein 15.4g; Carbohydrate 18.4g, of which sugars 2.7g; Fat 7.3g, of which saturates 1.6g; Cholesterol 52mg; Calcium 27mg; Fibre 1.1g; Sodium 66mg
Stuffed cucumber kimchi: Energy 32kcal/131kJ; Protein 2.5g; Carbohydrate 3.9g, of which sugars 3.4g; Fat 2.1g, of which saturates 0.2g; Cholesterol 0mg; Calcium 88mg; Fibre 1.4g; Sodium 2067mg

Egg Pancake Salad Wrappers

One of Indonesia's favourite snack foods. Assemble the pancakes according to taste, then dip into a spicy sauce of your choosing.

Makes 12
2 eggs
2.5ml/½ tsp salt
5ml/1 tsp vegetable oil, plus extra for frying
115g/4oz/1 cup flour
300ml/½ pint/1¼ cups water
shredded lettuce, cucumber sticks, beansprouts, shredded spring onions (scallions), cooked peeled prawns (shrimp) and coriander (cilantro) sprigs, to serve

For the filling
45ml/3 tbsp vegetable oil
1cm/½in fresh root ginger, chopped
1 garlic clove, crushed
1 small red fresh chilli, seeded and finely chopped
15ml/1 tbsp rice vinegar or white wine vinegar
10ml/2 tsp sugar
115g/4oz mooli (daikon), grated
1 carrot, grated (shredded)
115g/4oz Chinese leaves, shredded
2 shallots or 1 small red onion, thinly sliced

1 Break the eggs into a bowl and stir in the salt, vegetable oil and flour until smooth; do not over-mix. Add the water, a little at a time, and strain into a jug (pitcher). Allow the batter to stand for 15–20 minutes before use.

2 Moisten a small, non-stick frying pan (skillet) with vegetable oil and heat. Pour in enough batter just to cover the base of the pan and cook for 30 seconds until set. Turn the pancake over and cook the other side briefly. Stack the pancakes on a plate, cover and keep warm.

3 To make the filling, heat the oil in a preheated wok and add the ginger, garlic and chilli and stir-fry for 1–2 minutes. Add the vinegar, sugar, mooli, carrot, Chinese leaves or cabbage and shallots or onion. Cook for 3–4 minutes, stirring.

4 Transfer the filling to a small bowl. Place on a platter and arrange the pancakes, prawns and salad ingredients around the bowl. Serve immediately.

Thai Prawn Salad

In this salad, sweet prawns and mango are partnered with a sweet-sour garlic dressing spiced with chilli.

Serves 4–6
675g/1½lb medium raw prawns (shrimp), peeled and deveined with tails intact
finely Grated (shredded) rind of 1 lime
½ fresh red chilli, seeded and finely chopped
30ml/2 tbsp olive oil, plus extra for brushing
1 ripe but firm mango
2 carrots, cut into long thin shreds
10cm/4in piece cucumber, sliced
1 small red onion, halved and thinly sliced
a few sprigs of coriander (cilantro) and mint
45ml/3 tbsp roasted peanuts, roughly chopped
4 large shallots, thinly sliced and fried until crisp
salt and ground black pepper

For the dressing
1 large garlic clove, chopped
10–15ml/2–3 tsp caster (superfine) sugar
juice of 2 limes
15–30ml/1–2 tbsp Thai fish sauce
1 red chilli, seeded
5–10ml/1–2 tsp light rice vinegar

1 Place the prawns in a glass or china dish and add the lime rind and chilli. Season with salt and pepper and spoon the oil over them. Toss and leave to marinate for 30–40 minutes.

2 To make the dressing, place the garlic in a mortar with 10ml/2 tsp caster sugar and pound until smooth, then work in the juice of 1½ limes and 15ml/1 tbsp of the Thai fish sauce. Transfer the dressing to a bowl. Add half the chilli, chopped. Add sugar, lime juice, fish sauce and rice vinegar to taste.

3 Peel and stone (pit) the mango, then cut it into fine strips. Toss with the carrots, cucumber and onion, and half of the dressing. Arrange the salad on individual plates or in bowls.

4 Heat a heavy frying pan (skillet) until very hot. Brush with a little oil, then sear the prawns for 2–3 minutes on each side. Arrange the prawns on the salads. Sprinkle with the remaining dressing and scatter over the coriander and mint. Finely shred the remaining chilli and add with the peanuts and fried shallots.

Egg pancake salad wrappers: Energy 114kcal/474kJ; Protein 2.6g; Carbohydrate 8.9g, of which sugars 1.6g; Fat 7.8g, of which saturates 1.1g; Cholesterol 32mg; Calcium 45mg; Fibre 1.2g; Sodium 18mg
Thai prawn salad: Energy 201kcal/841kJ; Protein 22.5g; Carbohydrate 10.4g, of which sugars 8.8g; Fat 8g, of which saturates 1.3g; Cholesterol 219mg; Calcium 111mg; Fibre 1.9g; Sodium 337mg

Pomelo Salad

This cleansing fruit salad is traditionally served as part of a Thai meal to act as a foil to the other spicy dishes.

Serves 4–6
30ml/2 tbsp vegetable oil
4 shallots, finely sliced
2 garlic cloves, finely sliced
1 large pomelo
15ml/1 tbsp roasted peanuts, coarsely ground
115g/4oz cooked peeled prawns (shrimp)
115g/4oz cooked crab meat

10–12 small fresh mint leaves

For the dressing
30ml/2 tbsp Thai fish sauce
15ml/1 tbsp palm sugar (jaggery) or brown sugar
30ml/2 tbsp fresh lime juice

For the garnish
2 spring onions (scallions), thinly sliced
2 fresh red chillies, seeded and thinly sliced
fresh coriander (cilantro) leaves
shredded fresh coconut (optional)

1 To make the dressing, mix the fish sauce, sugar and lime juice in a bowl. Whisk well, then cover with clear film (plastic wrap).

2 Heat the oil in a small non-stick pan, add the shallots and garlic and cook until golden. Remove from the pan and set them aside.

3 Peel the pomelo and break the flesh into small pieces, taking care to remove any membranes. Put in a bowl with the peanuts, prawns, crab meat, mint leaves and the shallot mixture.

4 Pour the dressing over the salad, toss lightly and sprinkle with the spring onions, chillies and coriander leaves. Add the shredded coconut, if using. Serve immediately.

Cook's Tip
The pomelo is a large citrus fruit that looks rather like a grapefruit. It has pinkish-yellow flesh which is drier and sharper tasting than that of a grapefruit. Pomelos are available in many Asian markets and stores but, if you cannot find them, use a sweet, pink grapefruit or juicy oranges instead.

Grilled Prawn Salad with Peanuts & Pomelo

This refreshing Vietnamese salad makes a great addition to a barbecue.

Serves 4
16 raw tiger prawns (jumbo shrimp), peeled and deveined
1 small cucumber, peeled and cut into matchsticks
1 pomelo, separated into segments and cut into bitesize pieces
1 carrot, peeled and cut into matchsticks
1 fresh green Serrano chilli, seeded and finely sliced
30ml/2 tbsp roasted peanuts, roughly chopped

juice of half a lime
60ml/4 tbsp nuoc cham
vegetable oil, for griddling
1 small bunch fresh basil, stalks removed
1 small bunch coriander (cilantro), stalks removed
salt

For the marinade
30ml/2 tbsp nuoc mam
30ml/2 tbsp soy sauce
15ml/1 tbsp groundnut (peanut) or sesame oil
1 shallot, finely chopped
1 garlic clove, crushed
10ml/2 tsp raw cane sugar

1 Combine all the marinade ingredients in a wide bowl. Add the prawns, toss to coat well, then set aside for 30 minutes.

2 Sprinkle the cucumber matchsticks with salt and leave for 15 minutes. Rinse and drain the cucumber and mix in a large bowl with the pomelo, carrot, chilli and peanuts. Add the lime juice and nuoc cham and toss well.

3 Heat a cast-iron griddle and brush with a little oil, then cook the prawns on both sides until they turn opaque. Toss into the salad with the herbs and serve.

Cook's Tip
Nuoc cham dipping sauce and nuoc mam fish sauce are available from specialist Asian and Oriental stores.

Pomelo salad: Energy 92kcal/383kJ; Protein 7.7g; Carbohydrate 3.8g, of which sugars 3.4g; Fat 5.2g, of which saturates 0.7g; Cholesterol 51mg; Calcium 45mg; Fibre 0.4g; Sodium 143mg
Grilled prawn salad: Energy 167kcal/696kJ; Protein 11.7g; Carbohydrate 9.4g, of which sugars 8.5g; Fat 9.4g, of which saturates 1.4g; Cholesterol 98mg; Calcium 67mg; Fibre 1.7g; Sodium 635mg

Salmon Marinated with Thai Spices

This recipe is an Asian version of gravadlax, a Scandinavian speciality. Ask your fishmonger to scale the fish, split it lengthwise and remove it from the backbone in matching fillets.

Serves 4–6

tail piece of 1 salmon, weighing
  about 675g/1½lb, cleaned,
  scaled and filleted
20ml/4 tsp coarse sea salt
20ml/4 tsp sugar
2.5cm/1in piece fresh root ginger,
  peeled and grated (shredded)
2 lemon grass stalks, coarse outer
  leaves removed, thinly sliced
4 kaffir lime leaves, finely
  chopped or shredded
grated (shredded) rind of 1 lime
1 fresh red chilli, seeded and
  finely chopped
5ml/1 tsp black peppercorns,
  coarsely crushed
30ml/2 tbsp chopped fresh
  coriander (cilantro)
fresh coriander (cilantro) sprigs
  and lime wedges, to garnish

For the dressing

150ml/¼ pint/⅔ cup mayonnaise
juice of ½ lime
10ml/2 tsp chopped fresh
  coriander (cilantro)

1 Remove any remaining bones from the salmon with a pair of tweezers. Put the coarse sea salt, sugar, ginger, lemon grass, lime leaves, lime rind, chopped chilli, crushed black peppercorns and chopped coriander in a bowl and mix together.

2 Place one-quarter of the spice mixture in a shallow dish. Place one salmon fillet, skin down, on top. Spread two-thirds of the remaining mixture over, then place the remaining fillet on top, flesh-side down. Sprinkle with the rest of the spice mixture.

3 Cover with foil, then place a board on top. Add some weights, such as clean cans of fruit. Chill for 2–5 days, turning the fish daily in the spicy brine.

4 To make the dressing, mix the mayonnaise, lime juice and chopped coriander in a bowl.

5 Scrape the spices off the fish. Slice it as thinly as possible. Garnish with the herbs and lime. Serve with the lime dressing.

Hot Coconut Prawn & Papaya Salad

This colourful seafood salad is tossed in a creamy, lightly spiced coconut and lime dressing to provide a light meal, full of exotic flavours.

Serves 4–6

225g/8oz raw or cooked tiger
  prawns (jumbo shrimp), peeled
  with tails intact
2 ripe papaya
1 firm tomato
225g/8oz mixed salad leaves,
  such as cos, romaine or Little
  Gem (Bibb) lettuce, Chinese
  leaves or young spinach
3 spring onions (scallions),
  shredded
1 small bunch fresh coriander
  (cilantro), shredded
1 large fresh chilli, seeded
  and sliced

For the dressing

15ml/1 tbsp creamed coconut
30ml/2 tbsp boiling water
90ml/6 tbsp vegetable oil
juice of 1 lime
2.5ml/½ tsp hot chilli sauce
10ml/2 tsp fish sauce (optional)
5ml/1 tsp sugar

1 To make the dressing, place the creamed coconut in a screw-top jar and add the boiling water, vegetable oil, lime juice, chilli sauce, fish sauce, if using, and sugar. Shake well and set aside, but do not refrigerate.

2 If using raw prawns, place them in a pan and cover with water. Bring to the boil and simmer for 2 minutes until the prawn have turned opaque. Drain and set aside.

3 To prepare the papayas, cut each in half from top to bottom and remove the black seeds with a teaspoon. Peel away the outer skin and cut the flesh into even-sized pieces.

4 Cut the tomato in half, then remove the seeds and discard. Roughly chop the tomato flesh.

5 Place the salad leaves in a bowl. Add the prawns, papaya, tomato, spring onions, coriander and sliced chilli. Pour over the dressing and toss lightly. Serve immediately.

Salmon marinated with Thai spices: Energy 391kcal/1622kJ; Protein 23.3g; Carbohydrate 4.1g, of which sugars 4g; Fat 31.4g, of which saturates 5g; Cholesterol 75mg; Calcium 44mg; Fibre 0.4g; Sodium 166mg
Hot coconut prawn & papaya salad: Energy 201kcal/837kJ; Protein 8.1g; Carbohydrate 12.7g, of which sugars 12.6g; Fat 13.4g, of which saturates 2.9g; Cholesterol 73mg; Calcium 88mg; Fibre 3.6g; Sodium 84mg

Banana Blossom Salad with Prawns

Banana blossom doesn't actually taste of banana. Instead it is mildly tannic, similar to an unripe persimmon – a taste and texture that complements chillies, lime and fish sauce.

Serves 4

2 banana blossom hearts
juice of 1 lemon
225g/8oz cooked peeled
  prawns (shrimp)
30ml/2 tbsp roasted peanuts,
  finely chopped, fresh basil
  leaves and lime slices, to
  garnish

For the dressing

juice of 1 lime
30ml/2 tbsp white rice vinegar
60ml/4 tbsp nuoc mam or
  tuk trey
45ml/3 tbsp palm sugar
3 red Thai chillies, seeded and
  finely sliced
2 garlic cloves, peeled and
  finely chopped

1 Cut the banana blossom hearts into quarters lengthwise and then slice them very finely crossways. To prevent them discolouring, tip the slices into a bowl of cold water mixed with the lemon juice and leave to soak for about 30 minutes.

2 To make the dressing, beat the lime juice, vinegar, and nuoc mam or tuk trey with the sugar in a small bowl, until it has dissolved. Stir in the chillies and garlic and set aside.

3 Drain the sliced banana blossom and put it in a serving bowl. Add the prawns and pour over the dressing. Toss well to coat the banana blossom and prawns.

4 Garnish generously with the roasted peanuts, basil leaves and lime slices.

> ### Variation
> If you cannot find banana blossom hearts in Asian stores or supermarkets, you can always try this recipe with raw, or lightly steamed or roasted, fresh artichoke hearts.

Prawn Noodle Salad with Fragrant Herbs

A light salad with all the tangy flavour of the sea. Instead of prawns, you can also use squid, scallops, mussels or crab.

Serves 4

1/2 cucumber
115g/4oz cellophane noodles,
  soaked in hot water until soft
1 small green (bell) pepper,
  seeded and cut into strips
1 tomato, cut into strips
2 shallots, finely sliced
16 cooked peeled prawns
  (shrimp)
salt and ground black pepperfresh
  coriander (cilantro), to garnish

For the dressing

15ml/1 tbsp rice wine vinegar
30ml/2 tbsp Thai fish sauce
30ml/2 tbsp lime juice
2.5ml/1/2 tsp grated (shredded)
  fresh root ginger
1 lemon grass stalk, finely
  chopped
1 fresh red chilli, seeded and
  finely sliced
30ml/2 tbsp roughly chopped
  fresh mint
few sprigs of tarragon, roughly
  chopped
15ml/1 tbsp snipped fresh chives
pinch of salt

1 To make the dressing, combine all the ingredients in a small bowl and whisk well.

2 Peel the cucumber, then scoop out the seeds and cut the flesh into batons.

3 Drain the noodles, then plunge them in a pan of boiling water for 1 minute. Drain, rinse under cold running water and drain again well.

4 In a large bowl, combine the noodles with the green pepper, cucumber, tomato and shallots. Lightly season with salt and pepper, then toss with the dressing.

5 Spoon the noodles onto individual serving plates, arranging the prawns on top. Garnish with a few coriander leaves and serve immediately.

Banana blossom salad: Energy 103kcal/438kJ; Protein 11g; Carbohydrate 15g, of which sugars 13g; fat 0.5g, of which saturates 0.1g; Cholesterol 110mg; Calcium 54mg; fibre 0.7g; Sodium 109mg
Prawn noodle salad: Energy 156kcal/653kJ; Protein 7.4g; Carbohydrate 29.4g, of which sugars 5.4g; Fat 0.7g, of which saturates 0.1g; Cholesterol 49mg; Calcium 68mg; Fibre 2.1g; Sodium 417mg

Exotic Prawn, Fruit & Vegetable Salad

This is a variation on the famous Indonesian salad known as Gado Gado. The fruits and vegetables make an attractive centrepiece for an Indonesian or Thai meal.

Serves 6–8

115g/4oz green beans, trimmed
2 carrots, cut into batons
115g/4oz/2 cups beansprouts
1/4 head Chinese leaves, shredded
1/2 small cucumber, cut into
   thin strips
8 spring onions (scallions),
   sliced diagonally
6 cherry tomatoes or small
   tomatoes, halved
12–16 cooked tiger prawns
   (jumbo shrimp), peeled

1 small mango
1 small papaya
1 quantity lontong (compressed
   rice)
4 hard-boiled (hard-cooked)
   eggs, quartered
fresh coriander (cilantro)

For the peanut dressing

120ml/8 tbsp crunchy or smooth
   peanut butter, preferably
   unsalted
1 garlic clove, crushed
300ml/1/2 pint/1 1/4 cups
   coconut milk
15ml/1 tbsp tamarind water or
   juice of 1/2 lemon
15–30ml/1–2 tbsp light soy sauce
hot chilli sauce, to taste

1 To make the peanut dressing, place all the ingredients except the chilli sauce in a pan and heat the mixture, stirring all the time, until it is very hot and smooth. Stir in chilli sauce to taste. Keep the dressing warm, or cool and reheat before serving.

2 Cook the beans and carrots in boiling water for 3–4 minutes until just tender but still firm. Drain, then refresh under cold running water and drain again.

3 Cook the beansprouts in boiling water for 2 minutes, then drain and refresh.

4 Arrange the carrots, beans and beansprouts on a large, attractive platter, with the shredded Chinese leaves, cucumber strips, spring onions, tomatoes, and prawns.

5 Peel the mango and cut the flesh into cubes. Quarter the papaya, remove the skin and seeds, then slice the flesh. Add to the salad platter, with the lontong. Garnish with the egg quarters and fresh coriander.

6 Reheat the peanut dressing, if necessary, then pour it into a serving bowl. Place the bowl in the centre of the salad and serve. Guests help themselves, adding dressing as they wish.

Cook's Tip
To make tamarind water, soak a 2.5cm/1in cube of tamarind in 150ml/1/4 pint/2/3 cup warm water. Using your fingers, squeeze the tamarind so that the juices dissolve into the water. Strain, discarding the solid tamarind, and use as directed in the recipe. Any unused tamarind water can be kept in a container in the refrigerator for up to 1 week.

Noodles with Pineapple, Ginger & Chillies

A coconut, lime and fish sauce dressing is the perfect partner to this fruity and spicy noodle salad.

Serves 4

275g/10oz dried udon noodles
1/2 pineapple, peeled, cored and
   sliced into 4cm/1 1/2in rings
45ml/3 tbsp soft light
   brown sugar
60ml/4 tbsp lime juice
60ml/4 tbsp coconut milk

30ml/2 tbsp Thai fish sauce
30ml/2 tbsp grated (shredded)
   fresh root ginger
2 garlic cloves, finely chopped
1 ripe mango or 2 peaches,
   finely diced
ground black pepper

For the garnish

2 spring onions (scallions),
   finely sliced
2 fresh red chillies, seeded and
   finely shredded
fresh mint leaves

1 Cook the noodles in a large pan of boiling water until tender, according to the instructions on the packet. Drain, refresh under cold water and drain again.

2 Preheat the grill (broiler). Place the pineapple rings in a flameproof dish, sprinkle with 30ml/2 tbsp of the brown sugar and grill (broil) for about 5 minutes, or until golden.

3 Cool the pineapple slightly, then cut into small dice.

4 Mix the lime juice, coconut milk and fish sauce in a salad bowl. Add the remaining brown sugar with the ginger, garlic and black pepper and whisk well. Add the noodles and pineapple. Add the mango or peaches and toss. Scatter over the spring onions, chillies and mint leaves just before serving.

Variation
Add some cooked peeled prawns (shrimp) to the salad and serve with rice vermicelli noodles.

Scented Fish Salad

For a truly tropical taste, try this delicious fish salad scented with coconut, fruit and warm Thai spices.

Serves 4

350g/12oz fillet of red mullet, sea bream or snapper, cut into strips
1 cos or romaine lettuce leaves
1 papaya or mango, peeled and sliced
1 large ripe tomato, quartered
½ cucumber, peeled and cut into batons
3 spring onions (scallions), sliced
salt

For the marinade

5ml/1 tsp coriander seeds

5ml/1 tsp fennel seeds
2.5ml/½ tsp cumin seeds
5ml/1 tsp caster (superfine) sugar
2.5ml/½ tsp hot chilli sauce
30ml/2 tbsp garlic oil, made by gently cooking crushed garlic in sunflower oil

For the dressing

15ml/1 tbsp creamed coconut
45ml/3 tbsp boiling water
60ml/4 tbsp groundnut (peanut) oil
finely grated (shredded) rind and juice of 1 lime
1 fresh red chilli, seeded and finely chopped
5ml/1 tsp sugar
45ml/3 tbsp chopped fresh coriander (cilantro)

1 To make the marinade, put the coriander, fennel and cumin seeds in a mortar. Add the sugar and crush with a pestle. Stir in the chilli sauce, garlic oil, and salt to taste and mix to a paste.

2 Spread the paste over the fish, cover and leave to marinate in a cool place for at least 20 minutes.

3 To make the dressing, place the coconut and salt in a screw-top jar. Stir in the water. Add the oil, lime rind and juice, chilli, sugar and coriander. Shake well.

4 Put the lettuce in a bowl with the papaya, tomato, cucumber and spring onions. Add the dressing and toss to coat.

5 Heat a large non-stick pan, add the fish and cook for 5 minutes, turning once. Add the fish to the salad and toss lightly to coat in dressing.

Turbot Sashimi Salad with Wasabi

Eating sashimi, or raw fish, with traditional sauces disappeared when shoyu became popular in the 17th century. The use of sauces returned with the Western-inspired salad. This sauce, flavoured with wasabi, has lots of authentic flavour.

Serves 4

ice cubes
400g/14oz very fresh thick turbot or other flat fish, skinned and filleted

300g/11oz mixed salad leaves
8 radishes, thinly sliced

For the wasabi dressing

25g/1oz rocket (arugula) leaves
50g/2oz cucumber, chopped
90ml/6 tbsp rice vinegar (use brown if available)
75ml/5 tbsp olive oil
5ml/1 tsp salt
15ml/1 tbsp wasabi paste from a tube, or the same amount of wasabi powder mixed with 7.5ml/1½ tsp water

1 To make the dressing, coarsely tear the rocket leaves and process with the cucumber and rice vinegar in a food processor or blender.

2 Pour into a small bowl and add the rest of the dressing ingredients, except for the wasabi. Check the seasoning and add more salt, if required. Cover with clear film (plastic wrap) and chill until needed.

3 Chill the serving plates in the refrigerator while you prepare the fish, if you like.

4 Prepare a bowl of cold water with a few ice cubes. Using a very sharp knife, carefully cut the turbot fillet in half lengthwise, then cut into 5mm/¼in thick slices crossways. Plunge the fish slices into the ice-cold water as you slice. After 2 minutes or so, they will start to curl and become firm. Take out and drain on kitchen paper (paper towels).

5 In a large bowl, mix the fish, salad leaves and radishes. Mix the wasabi into the dressing and toss well with the fish salad.

Scented fish salad: Energy 339kcal/1410kJ; Protein 18.2g; Carbohydrate 15.7g, of which sugars 15.6g; Fat 23g, of which saturates 5.2g; Cholesterol 0mg; Calcium 119mg; Fibre 3.9g; Sodium 94mg
Turbot sashimi salad: Energy 232kcal/965kJ; Protein 18.5g; Carbohydrate 1.7g, of which sugars 1.7g; Fat 16.9g, of which saturates 2.8g; Cholesterol 0mg; Calcium 75mg; Fibre 0.9g; Sodium 72mg

Cambodian Raw Fish Salad

Sweet-fleshed freshwater fish and shellfish are often eaten raw in Cambodia. Wrapped in a lettuce leaf with extra leafy herbs, or served with noodles, this authentic salad, *koy pa*, is light and delicious.

Serves 4–6

450g/1lb white fish fillets, boned and finely sliced

juice of 4 limes
30ml/2 tbsp tuk trey
4 spring onions (scallions), finely sliced
2 garlic cloves, finely sliced
1 fresh red chilli, seeded and finely sliced
1 small bunch fresh coriander (cilantro), stalks removed
lettuce leaves, to serve

1 Place the sliced fish in a large bowl. Pour over the juice of 3 limes and toss well, making sure all the fish is coated. Cover and chill in the refrigerator for 24 hours. This will effectively "cook" the fish.

2 Drain the fish and place in a clean bowl with the juice of the remaining lime, the tuk trey, spring onions, garlic, chilli and coriander. Toss well and serve with lettuce leaves.

Cook's Tip
Tuk trey can be successfully replaced by a Thai fish sauce.

Alfalfa Crab Salad with Crispy Fried Noodles

A wonderful mix of tastes and textures, this crab and vegetable salad is divine with deliciously crisp noodles.

Serves 4–6
vegetable oil, for deep-frying
50g/2oz raw Chinese rice noodles
2 dressed crabs, or 150g/5oz frozen white crab meat, thawed
115g/4oz alfalfa sprouts
1 small iceberg or Little Gem (Bibb) lettuce
4 sprigs coriander (cilantro), roughly chopped

1 ripe tomato, skinned, seeded and diced
4 sprigs fresh mint, roughly chopped

For the sesame lime dressing
45ml/3 tbsp vegetable oil
5ml/1 tsp sesame oil
½ small fresh red chilli, seeded and finely chopped
2.5cm/1in piece stem ginger in syrup, cut into matchsticks, plus 10ml/2 tsp syrup
10ml/2 tsp soy sauce
juice of ½ lime

1 To make the dressing, combine the vegetable and sesame oils in a bowl. Add the chilli, ginger and ginger syrup, together with the soy sauce and lime juice. Stir to mix.

2 Heat the oil in a deep-fryer to 196°C/ 385°F. Fry the noodles, a handful at a time, until crisp. Drain on kitchen paper.

3 Flake the white crab meat into a bowl and toss with the alfalfa sprouts. Separate the lettuce leaves and toss with the coriander, tomato and mint.

4 Place the salad in a serving bowl and top with the crab mixture. Toss with the dressing. Serve the crab mixture immediately with the noodles.

Cook's Tip
Alfalfa sprouts are available in many supermarkets, but it is very satisfying to grow your own sprouts from seeds.

Cambodian raw fish salad: Energy 66Kcal/280kJ; Protein 14g; carbohydrate 1.2g, of which sugars 1.1g; fat 0.6g, of which saturates 0.1g; Cholesterol 35mg; Calcium 11mg; fibre 0.2g; Sodium 402mg
Alfafa crab salad: Energy 122kcal/506kJ; Protein 5.6g; Carbohydrate 10.1g, of which sugars 2.9g; Fat 6.5g, of which saturates 0.8g; Cholesterol 18mg; Calcium 44mg; Fibre 0.7g; Sodium 287mg

Gingered Seafood Stir-fry

This cornucopia of scallops, prawns and squid in an aromatic sauce makes a refreshing summer supper, served with plenty of crusty bread to mop up the juices – together with a glass of chilled dry white wine. It would also make a great dinner-party starter for four people.

Serves 2
15ml/1 tbsp sunflower oil
5ml/1 tsp sesame oil
2.5cm/1in fresh root ginger, finely chopped
1 bunch spring onions (scallions), sliced
1 red (bell) pepper, seeded and finely chopped
115g/4oz small queen scallops
8 large raw prawns (shrimp), peeled
115g/4oz squid rings
15ml/1 tbsp lime juice
15ml/1 tbsp light soy sauce
60ml/4 tbsp coconut milk
salt and ground black pepper
mixed salad leaves and lime slices, to serve

1 Heat the sunflower and sesame oils in a preheated wok or large frying pan (skillet) and cook the ginger and spring onions for 2–3 minutes, or until golden. Stir in the red pepper and cook for a further 3 minutes.

2 Add the scallops, prawns and squid rings and cook over a medium heat for about 3 minutes, until just cooked.

3 Stir in the lime juice, soy sauce and coconut milk. Simmer, uncovered, for 2 minutes, until the juices begin to thicken slightly. Season well with salt and pepper.

4 Arrange the salad leaves on two serving plates and spoon over the seafood mixture with the juices. Serve with lime slices for squeezing over the seafood.

Variation
Vary the seafood as you like and according to availability.

Fragrant Tiger Prawns with Dill

This elegant dish has a fresh, light flavour and is equally good served as a simple supper or for a dinner party. The delicate texture of fresh prawns goes really well with mild cucumber and fragrant dill, and all you need is some rice or noodles to serve.

Serves 4–6
500g/1¼lb raw tiger prawns (jumbo shrimp), peeled but with tails intact
500g/1¼lb cucumber
30ml/2 tbsp butter
15ml/1 tbsp olive oil
15ml/1 tbsp finely chopped garlic
45ml/3 tbsp chopped fresh dill
juice of 1 lemon
salt and ground black pepper
steamed rice or noodles, to serve

1 Using a small, sharp knife, carefully make a shallow slit along the back of each prawn and use the point of the knife to remove the black vein. Set the prawns aside.

2 Peel the cucumber and slice in half lengthwise. Using a small teaspoon, gently scoop out all the seeds and discard. Cut the cucumber into 4 × 1cm/1½ × ½in sticks.

3 Heat a wok over a high heat, then add the butter and oil. When the butter has melted, add the cucumber and garlic and fry over a high heat for 2–3 minutes, stirring continuously.

4 Add the prepared prawns to the wok and continue to stir-fry over a high heat for 3–4 minutes, or until the prawns turn pink and are just cooked through, then remove from the heat.

5 Add the fresh dill and lemon juice to the wok and toss to combine. Season well with salt and ground black pepper and serve immediately with steamed rice or noodles.

Cook's Tip
For the best flavour, use raw prawns for this dish. Remove the tail shells, if you prefer.

Orange Chicken Salad

Orange segments are the perfect partner for tender chicken in this tasty rice salad. To appreciate all the flavours fully, serve the salad at room temperature.

Serves 4
3 large seedless oranges
175g/6oz/scant 1 cup long
  grain rice
475ml/16fl oz/2 cups water
175ml/6fl oz/³⁄₄ cup vinaigrette
10ml/2 tsp strong Dijon mustard
2.5ml/¹⁄₂ tsp caster (superfine)
  sugar
450g/1lb cooked chicken, diced
45ml/3 tbsp chopped fresh chives
75g/3oz/³⁄₄ cup almonds or
  cashew nuts, toasted
salt and ground black pepper
mixed salad leaves, to serve

1 Pare one of the oranges thinly, removing only the zest, not the bitter white pith. Put the orange rind in a pan and add the rice. Pour in the water, add a pinch of salt and bring to the boil. Cover and cook the rice over a very low heat for about 15 minutes, or until the rice is tender and all the water has been absorbed.

2 Meanwhile, peel the oranges, removing all the white pith. Working over a plate to catch the juices, separate them into segments. Add the orange juice to the vinaigrette with the mustard and sugar, whisking to combine. Check the seasoning.

3 When the rice is cooked, remove it from the heat and discard the pieces of orange rind. Spoon the rice into a bowl, let it cool slightly, then add half the dressing. Toss well, then set aside to cool completely.

4 Add the chicken, chives, toasted nuts and orange segments to the cooled rice. Pour over the remaining dressing and toss gently to combine. Serve on a bed of mixed salad leaves.

Cook's Tip
To make a simple vinaigrette, whisk 45ml/3 tbsp wine vinegar with 120ml/8 tbsp extra-virgin olive oil and season well.

Citrus Chicken Salad

This zesty, refreshing salad is a good choice for a post-Christmas buffet, when cooked turkey can be used instead of chicken.

Serves 6
120ml/4fl oz/¹⁄₂ cup extra-virgin
  olive oil
6 boneless chicken breast
  portions, skinned
4 oranges
5ml/1 tsp Dijon mustard
15ml/3 tsp clear honey
300g/11oz/2³⁄₄ cups white
  cabbage, finely shredded
300g/11oz carrots, finely sliced
2 spring onions (scallions),
  finely sliced
2 celery sticks, cut
  into
  matchsticks
30ml/2 tbsp chopped
  fresh tarragon
2 limes
salt and ground black pepper

1 Heat 30ml/2 tbsp of the oil in a large, heavy frying pan (skillet). Add the chicken breasts to the pan and cook for 15–20 minutes, or until the chicken is cooked through and golden brown. (If your pan is too small, cook the chicken in two or three batches.) Remove the chicken from the pan and leave to cool.

2 Peel two of the oranges, cutting off all pith, then cut out the segments from between the membranes and set aside. Grate (shred) the rind and squeeze the juice from one of the remaining oranges and place in a large bowl. Stir in the Dijon mustard, 5ml/1 tsp of the honey, 60ml/4 tbsp of the oil and seasoning to taste. Mix in the cabbage, carrots, spring onions and celery, then leave to stand for 10 minutes.

3 Meanwhile, squeeze the juice from the remaining orange and mix it with the remaining honey and oil, and tarragon. Peel and segment the limes, in the same way as the oranges, and lightly mix the segments into the dressing with the reserved orange segments. Season with salt and pepper to taste.

4 Slice the cooked chicken breasts and stir into the dressed citrus fruit. Spoon the vegetable salad onto plates and add the chicken mixture, then serve at once.

Chicken & Mango Salad with Orange Rice

A modern twist to an old favourite, fusing lightly curried chicken mayonnaise with orange rice salad.

Serves 4

15ml/1 tbsp sunflower oil
1 onion, chopped
1 garlic clove, crushed
30ml/2 tbsp red curry paste
10ml/2 tsp apricot jam
30ml/2 tbsp chicken stock
about 450g/1lb cooked chicken, cut into small pieces
150ml/¼ pint/⅔ cup natural (plain) yogurt
60–75ml/4–5 tbsp mayonnaise
1 large mango, cut into 1cm/½in dice
fresh flat leaf parsley sprigs, to garnish
poppadums, to serve

For the orange rice

175g/6oz/scant 1 cup white long grain rice
225g/8oz/1⅓ cups grated (shredded) carrots
1 large orange, cut into segments
40g/1½oz/⅓ cup roasted flaked almonds

For the dressing

45ml/3 tbsp olive oil
60ml/4 tbsp sunflower oil
45ml/3 tbsp lemon juice
1 garlic clove, crushed
15ml/1 tbsp chopped mixed fresh herbs, such as tarragon, parsley, and chives
salt and ground black pepper

1 Heat the oil in a frying pan (skillet) and fry the onion and garlic for 3–4 minutes until soft.

2 Stir in the curry paste, cook for about 1 minute, then lower the heat and stir in the apricot jam and stock. Mix well, then add the chopped chicken and stir until the chicken is thoroughly coated in the paste. Spoon the mixture into a large bowl and leave to cool.

3 Meanwhile, boil the rice in plenty of lightly salted water until just tender. Drain, rinse under cold water and drain again. When cool, stir into the grated carrots and add the orange segments and flaked almonds.

4 To make the dressing, whisk all the ingredients together.

5 Stir the yogurt and mayonnaise into the cooled chicken mixture. Gently stir in the mango. Chill for about 30 minutes.

6 When ready to serve, pour the dressing into the rice salad and mix well. Spoon onto a platter and mound the cold curried chicken on top. Garnish with flat leaf parsley and serve immediately, with poppadums.

Cook's Tip

A simple way of dicing a mango is to take two thick slices from either side of the large flat stone without peeling the fruit. Make criss-cross cuts in the flesh on each slice and then turn inside out. The cubes of flesh will stand proud of the skin and can be easily cut off.

Chicken & Broccoli Salad

Gorgonzola makes a tangy dressing that goes well with both chicken and broccoli. Serve for a lunch or supper dish with ciabatta.

Serves 4

175g/6oz broccoli florets, divided into small sprigs
225g/8oz/2 cups dried farfalle pasta or other shapes
2 large cooked chicken breasts

For the dressing

90g/3½oz Gorgonzola cheese
15ml/1 tbsp white wine vinegar
60ml/4 tbsp extra-virgin olive oil
2.5–5ml/½–1tsp finely chopped fresh sage, plus extra sage sprigs to garnish
salt and ground black pepper

1 Cook the broccoli florets in a large pan of salted boiling water for 3 minutes. Remove with a slotted spoon and rinse under cold running water, then spread out on kitchen paper to drain and dry.

2 Add the pasta to the broccoli cooking water, then bring back to the boil and cook according to the packet instructions. When cooked, drain the pasta, rinse under cold running water until cold, then leave to drain and dry, shaking occasionally.

3 Remove the skin from the cooked chicken breasts and cut the meat into bitesize pieces.

4 To make the dressing, put the cheese in a large bowl and mash with a fork, then whisk in the wine vinegar followed by the oil and sage and salt and pepper to taste.

5 Add the pasta, chicken and broccoli to the dressing. Toss well, then adjust the seasoning and serve, garnished with sage.

Variation

Try adding a sprinkling of roughly chopped toasted walnuts just before serving.

Chicken & mango salad: Energy 754kcal/3141kJ; Protein 35.8g; Carbohydrate 56.6g, of which sugars 18.3g; Fat 43g, of which saturates 5.6g; Cholesterol 91mg; Calcium 162mg; Fibre 6.5g; Sodium 201mg

Chicken & broccoli salad: Energy 472kcal/1977kJ; Protein 25.3g; Carbohydrate 42.5g, of which sugars 2.5g; Fat 23.5g, of which saturates 6.8g; Cholesterol 52mg; Calcium 151mg; Fibre 2.8g; Sodium 310mg

Warm Chicken & Tomato Salad with Hazelnut Dressing

This simple, warm salad combines pan-fried chicken and spinach with a light, nutty dressing. Serve it for lunch on an autumn day.

Serves 4
45ml/3 tbsp olive oil
30ml/2 tbsp hazelnut oil
15ml/1 tbsp white wine vinegar
1 garlic clove, crushed
15ml/1 tbsp chopped fresh
    mixed herbs
225g/8oz baby spinach leaves
250g/9oz cherry tomatoes, halved
1 bunch spring onions
    (scallions), chopped
2 chicken breast fillets, cut into
    thin strips
salt and ground black pepper

1 To make the dressing, place 30ml/ 2 tbsp of the olive oil with the hazelnut oil, vinegar, garlic and chopped herbs in a small bowl and whisk together until thoroughly mixed. Set aside.

2 Trim any long stalks from the spinach leaves, then place in a large serving bowl with the tomatoes and spring onions, and toss together to mix.

3 Heat the remaining olive oil in a frying pan (skillet), and stir-fry the chicken over a high heat for 7–10 minutes until it is cooked, tender and lightly browned.

4 Arrange the cooked chicken pieces over the salad. Give the dressing a quick whisk to blend, then drizzle it over the salad. Add salt and pepper to taste, toss lightly and serve immediately.

Variations
• Use other meat or fish, such as steak, pork fillet or salmon fillet, in place of the chicken breasts. Simply stir-fry until cooked and add to the salad as described.
• Any salad leaves can be used instead of the baby spinach. Try a mix of rocket (arugula), watercress and lamb's lettuce (corn salad).

Smoked Chicken with Peach Mayonnaise in Filo Tartlets

The filling for these tartlets can be prepared a day in advance and chilled, but only fill the pastry cases when you are ready to serve.

Makes 12
25g/1oz/2 tbsp butter
3 sheets of filo pastry, each
    measuring 45 x 28cm/
    18 x 11in, thawed if frozen
2 skinless, boneless smoked
    chicken breast portions,
    finely sliced
150ml/¼ pint/⅔ cup mayonnaise
grated (shredded) rind of 1 lime
30ml/2 tbsp lime juice
2 ripe peaches, peeled, stoned
    (pitted) and chopped
salt and ground black pepper
fresh tarragon sprigs, lime slices
    and salad leaves, to garnish

1 Preheat the oven to 200°C/400°F/Gas 6. Place the butter in a small pan and heat gently until melted. Lightly brush 12 mini flan rings with a little melted butter.

2 Cut each sheet of filo pastry into 12 equal rounds large enough to line the tins and stand above the rims. Place a round of pastry in each tin and brush with a little butter, then add another round of pastry. Brush each with more butter and add a third round of pastry.

3 Bake the tartlets for 5 minutes. Leave in the tins for a few moments before transferring to a wire rack to cool. Once cool, store in a tin until ready to use.

4 Mix together the chicken, mayonnaise, lime rind, peaches and seasoning. Chill for at least 30 minutes, preferably overnight. Just before serving, spoon the chicken mixture into the filo pastry cases and garnish with tarragon, lime slices and salad leaves.

Cook's Tip
You can use small tartlet tins (mini quiche pans) if you do not have any mini flan rings.

Warm chicken & tomato salad: Energy 260kcal/1081kJ; Protein 20.7g; Carbohydrate 3.7g, of which sugars 3.6g; Fat 18.1g, of which saturates 2.6g; Cholesterol 53mg; Calcium 124mg; Fibre 2.3g; Sodium 140mg
Chicken in filo tartlets: Energy 246kcal/1021kJ; Protein 7g; Carbohydrate 6.3g, of which sugars 1.4g; Fat 21.7g, of which saturates 4.5g; Cholesterol 42mg; Calcium 13mg; Fibre 0.4g; Sodium 146mg

Chicken Maryland Salad

Grilled chicken, sweetcorn, bacon, banana and salad leaves combine in a sensational main-course salad. Serve with jacket potatoes and extra bacon, if you like.

Serves 4

4 boneless chicken breast
   portions
oil, for brushing
225g/8oz rindless unsmoked
   bacon
4 corn on the cob, husks removed
45ml/3 tbsp soft butter (optional)
4 ripe bananas, peeled
   and halved
4 firm tomatoes, halved
1 escarole or round
   (butterhead) lettuce
1 bunch watercress
salt and ground black pepper

For the dressing

75ml/5 tbsp groundnut
   (peanut) oil
15ml/1 tbsp white wine vinegar
10ml/2 tsp maple syrup
10ml/2 tsp prepared mild
   mustard

1 Preheat the grill (broiler). Season the chicken breasts with salt and pepper, brush with oil and grill (broil) for 15 minutes, turning once. Grill the bacon for 8–10 minutes, or until crisp.

2 Bring a large pan of salted water to the boil and cook the corn on the cob for 20 minutes. For extra flavour, brush the corn cobs with butter and brown under the grill.

3 Grill the bananas and tomatoes for 6–8 minutes; you can brush these with butter too if you wish.

4 To make the dressing, combine the oil, vinegar, maple syrup and mustard with 15ml/1 tbsp water in a screw-top jar and shake well to combine.

5 Separate the lettuce leaves and put into a large bowl. Pour over the dressing and toss well. Distribute the salad leaves between four individual plates.

6 Slice the chicken and arrange over the salad leaves, together with the bacon, banana, sweetcorn and tomatoes.

Chicken, Tongue & Gruyère Cheese Salad

The rich, sweet flavours of this salad marry well with the tart, peppery watercress. A minted lemon dressing freshens the overall effect. Serve with warm new potatoes.

Serves 4

2 chicken breast fillets
300ml/½ pint/1¼ cups water
½ chicken stock cube
225g/8oz ox tongue or ham,
   sliced 5mm/¼in thick
225g/8oz Gruyère cheese
1 lollo rosso lettuce
1 round (butterhead) or
   frisée lettuce
1 bunch watercress
2 green-skinned apples, cored
   and sliced
3 celery sticks, sliced
60ml/4 tbsp sesame seeds,
   toasted
salt, ground black pepper
   and freshly grated
   (shredded) nutmeg

For the dressing

75ml/5 tbsp groundnut (peanut)
   oil or sunflower oil
5ml/1 tsp sesame oil
45ml /3 tbsp lemon juice
10ml/2 tsp chopped fresh mint
3 drops Tabasco sauce

1 Place the chicken breasts in a shallow pan, cover with the water, add the ½ stock cube and bring to the boil. Put the lid on the pan and simmer for 15 minutes. Drain, saving the stock for another occasion, then cool the chicken in cold water.

2 To make the dressing, measure the oils, lemon juice, mint and Tabasco sauce into a screw-top jar and shake well. Cut the chicken, tongue or ham and cheese into fine strips. Moisten with a little dressing and set aside.

3 Combine the lettuce and watercress leaves with the apple and celery. Add the dressing and toss.

4 Divide the salad between four individual plates. Pile the chicken, tongue or ham and cheese in the centre and scatter with sesame seeds. Season with salt, pepper and freshly grated nutmeg and serve.

Chicken Maryland salad: Energy 659kcal/2768kJ; Protein 50.9g; Carbohydrate 56.4g, of which sugars 37.1g; Fat 27.1g, of which saturates 7g; Cholesterol 135mg; Calcium 51mg; Fibre 4.2g; Sodium 1319mg
Chicken, tongue & Gruyère salad: Energy 626kcal/2606kJ; Protein 46.8g; Carbohydrate 6.1g, of which sugars 6g; Fat 45.1g, of which saturates 16.2g; Cholesterol 140mg; Calcium 586mg; Fibre 3.1g; Sodium 1155mg

Dijon Chicken Salad

This attractive and classical dish is ideal to serve for a simple but tasty and elegant lunch. Serve with extra salad leaves and some warm herb and garlic bread.

Serves 4

4 chicken breast fillets
mixed salad leaves such as frisée, oakleaf lettuce, radicchio

For the marinade

30ml/2 tbsp tarragon wine vinegar
5ml/1 tsp Dijon mustard
5ml/1 tsp clear honey
90ml/6 tbsp olive oil
salt and ground black pepper

For the mustard dressing

30ml/2 tbsp Dijon mustard
3 garlic cloves, crushed
15ml/1 tbsp grated (shredded) onion
60ml/4 tbsp white wine

1 To make the marinade, mix the vinegar, mustard, honey, olive oil, salt and pepper together in a shallow glass or earthenware dish large enough to hold the chicken breasts in a single layer.

2 Add the chicken breasts to the dish, making sure they do not overlap each other. Turn the chicken over in the marinade to coat completely, cover with clear film (plastic wrap) and chill overnight.

3 Preheat the oven to 190°C/375°F/Gas 5. Transfer the chicken and the marinade into an ovenproof dish, cover with kitchen foil and bake for about 35 minutes, or until tender. Leave the chicken to cool in the liquid.

4 To make the mustard dressing, put all the ingredients into a screw-top jar and shake vigorously.

5 Using a large sharp knife, thinly slice the chicken, then transfer to individual plates, fanning out the slices.

6 Add the salad leaves to the plates. Spoon some of the dressing over the chicken and serve the rest separately.

Chicken Liver Salad

In this delicious salad, the richness of the chicken livers is complemented perfectly by the sweet tangy mustard dressing. Serve with warm crusty bread to mop up the dressing.

Serves 4

mixed salad leaves such as frisée, oakleaf lettuce, radicchio
1 avocado, diced
30ml/2 tbsp lemon juice
2 pink grapefruit

350g/12oz chicken livers
30ml/2 tbsp olive oil
1 garlic clove, crushed
salt and ground black pepper
whole fresh chives, to garnish

For the dressing

30ml/2 tbsp lemon juice
60ml/4 tbsp olive oil
2.5ml/½ tsp wholegrain mustard
2.5ml/½ tsp clear honey
15ml/1 tbsp snipped fresh chives
salt and ground black pepper

1 To make the dressing, put the lemon juice, olive oil, mustard, honey and fresh chives into a screw-top jar, and shake vigorously. Season to taste with salt and pepper.

2 Arrange the mixed salad leaves attractively on a large serving plate. Peel and dice the avocado and mix with the lemon juice to prevent browning. Add to the plate of mixed leaves.

3 Peel the grapefruit, removing as much of the white pith as possible. Split into segments and arrange with the leaves and avocado on the serving plate.

4 Dry the chicken livers on kitchen paper and remove any unwanted pieces. Using a sharp knife, cut the larger chicken livers in half. Leave the smaller ones whole.

5 Heat the oil in a large frying pan (skillet). Stir-fry the chicken livers and garlic briskly until the livers are brown all over (they should be slightly pink inside). Season to taste with salt and pepper, remove from the pan and drain on kitchen paper.

6 Place the chicken livers, while still warm, on the salad leaves and spoon over the dressing. Garnish with chives and serve.

Dijon chicken salad: Energy 344kcal/1437kJ; Protein 37g; Carbohydrate 4.7g, of which sugars 4.3g; Fat 18.8g, of which saturates 2.9g; Cholesterol 105mg; Calcium 36mg; Fibre 0.9g; Sodium 167mg
Chicken liver salad: Energy 313kcal/1299kJ; Protein 17g; Carbohydrate 8.3g, of which sugars 8g; Fat 23.7g, of which saturates 4.1g; Cholesterol 333mg; Calcium 42mg; Fibre 2.4g; Sodium 72mg

Chicken Liver, Bacon & Tomato Salad

Warm salads are especially welcome during the autumn months when the days are growing shorter and cooler. This rich salad includes sweet spinach and the bitter leaves of frisée lettuce.

Serves 4

225g/8oz young spinach, stems removed

1 frisée lettuce

105ml/7 tbsp groundnut (peanut) or sunflower oil

175g/6oz rindless unsmoked bacon, cut into strips

75g/3oz day-old bread, crusts removed and cut into short fingers

450g/1lb chicken livers

115g/4oz cherry tomatoes

salt and ground black pepper

1 Place the spinach and lettuce leaves in a salad bowl. Heat 60ml/4 tbsp of the oil in a large frying pan (skillet), add the bacon and cook for 3–4 minutes, or until crisp and brown. Remove the bacon with a slotted spoon and drain on crumpled kitchen paper.

2 To make croûtons, fry the bread in the bacon-flavoured oil, tossing until crisp and golden. Drain on kitchen paper.

3 Heat the remaining 45ml/3 tbsp oil in the frying pan, add the chicken livers and fry briskly for 2–3 minutes.

4 Turn the chicken livers out over the salad leaves and add the drained bacon and croûtons. Add the cherry tomatoes, season with salt and pepper, toss together and serve warm.

Variation

If you can't find any baby spinach leaves you can use lamb's lettuce (corn salad). Watercress would make a deliciously peppery substitute, but you should use less of it and bulk the salad out with a milder leaf so that the watercress doesn't overwhelm the other flavours.

Curried Chicken Salad

A mildly spicy sauce with tangy herbs combines brilliantly with lean chicken, pasta and fresh vegetables

Serves 4

2 cooked chicken breast portions, skinned and boned

175g/6oz green beans

350g/12oz multi-coloured penne

150ml/¼ pint/⅔ cup natural (plain) yogurt

5ml/1 tsp mild curry powder

1 garlic clove, crushed

1 fresh green chilli, seeded and finely chopped

30ml/2 tbsp chopped fresh coriander (cilantro) and leaves to garnish

4 firm ripe tomatoes, skinned, seeded and cut into strips

salt and ground black pepper

1 Cut the chicken into strips. Cut the green beans into 2.5cm/1in lengths and cook in boiling water for 5 minutes. Drain and rinse under cold water.

2 Cook the pasta in a large pan of lightly salted boiling water according to the packet instructions. Drain and rinse thoroughly.

3 To make the sauce, mix the yogurt, curry powder, garlic, chilli and chopped coriander together in a bowl. Stir in the chicken pieces and leave to stand for 30 minutes.

4 Transfer the pasta to a large serving bowl and toss with the beans and tomatoes. Add the chicken mixture. Garnish with the coriander leaves and serve.

Variations

• This salad becomes the perfect lunchbox treat, delicious, filling and healthy, if you simply toss the pasta, beans and tomato in with the chicken, so that all the ingredients have a light coating of curry sauce. It's also a good way to use up left-over roast chicken – just omit step one.

• The salad also works well with boiled and sliced waxy salad potatoes or white rice instead of the pasta. Simply add chopped red (bell) pepper for colour.

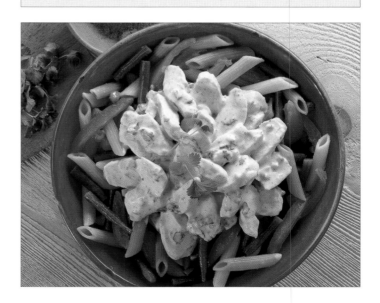

Liver & bacon salad: Energy 468kcal/1943kJ; Protein 33g; Carbohydrate 11.9g, of which sugars 3.1g; Fat 32.3g, of which saturates 6.7g; Cholesterol 457mg; Calcium 144mg; Fibre 2.2g; Sodium 1132mg

Curried chicken salad: Energy 430kcal/1828kJ; Protein 32.1g; Carbohydrate 72.5g, of which sugars 9.8g; Fat 3.4g, of which saturates 0.7g; Cholesterol 53mg; Calcium 128mg; Fibre 4.8g; Sodium 94mg

Spicy Chicken Salad

Marinate the chicken in advance for this tasty salad, which is otherwise very quick to prepare.

Serves 6
5ml/1 tsp ground cumin seeds
5ml/1 tsp paprika
5ml/1 tsp ground turmeric
1–2 garlic cloves, crushed
30ml/2 tbsp lime juice
4 skinless chicken breast fillets
225g/8oz rigatoni pasta

1 red (bell) pepper, seeded
    and chopped
2 celery sticks, thinly sliced
1 shallot or small onion,
    finely chopped
25g/1oz/¼ cup stuffed green
    olives, halved
30ml/2 tbsp clear honey
15ml/1 tbsp wholegrain mustard
15–30ml/1–2 tbsp lime juice
mixed salad leaves
salt and ground black pepper

1 Mix the cumin, paprika, turmeric, garlic and lime juice in a bowl. Season with salt and pepper. Rub this mixture over the chicken fillets. Lay these in a shallow dish, cover with clear film (plastic wrap) and leave to marinate in a cool place for about 3 hours or overnight.

2 Preheat the oven to 200°C/400°F/Gas 6. Put the chicken on a rack in a roasting pan and bake for 20 minutes. Alternatively, grill (broil) the marinated chicken fillets for 8–10 minutes on each side or until cooked through.

3 Cook the rigatoni pasta in a large pan of lightly salted, boiling water according to the packet instructions, or until *al dente*. Drain and rinse under cold water. Leave to drain thoroughly.

4 Put the red pepper, celery, shallot or small onion and olives into a large bowl with the pasta. Mix together.

5 Mix the honey, mustard and lime juice together in a small bowl and pour over the pasta mixture. Toss to coat.

6 Cut the chicken into bitesize pieces. Arrange the mixed salad leaves on a serving dish, spoon the pasta mixture into the centre and top with the spicy chicken pieces.

Warm Chicken Salad

Succulent chicken pieces, vegetables and rice in a light chilli dressing make an irresistible supper dish.

Serves 6
50g/2oz mixed salad leaves
50g/2oz baby spinach leaves
50g/2oz watercress
30ml/2 tbsp chilli sauce
30ml/2 tbsp dry sherry
15ml/1 tbsp light soy sauce
15ml/1 tbsp tomato ketchup

10ml/2 tsp olive oil
8 shallots, finely chopped
1 garlic clove, crushed
350g/12oz skinless chicken
    breast fillet, cut into thin strips
1 red (bell) pepper, seeded
    and sliced
175g/6oz mangetouts (snow
    peas), trimmed
12 baby corn on the cobs, halved
275g/10oz brown rice, cooked
salt and ground black pepper
fresh parsley sprig, to garnish

1 Arrange the salad and spinach leaves on a serving dish. Add the watercress and toss together to mix.

2 In a small bowl, mix together the chilli sauce, sherry, soy sauce and tomato ketchup. Set the sauce mixture aside.

3 Heat the oil in a large, non-stick frying pan (skillet) or wok. Add the shallots and garlic and stir-fry over a medium heat for 1 minute. Add the chicken to the pan and stir-fry for a further 3–4 minutes to brown.

4 Add the pepper, mangetouts, baby corn cobs and rice, and stir-fry for a further 2–3 minutes. Pour in the chilli sauce mixture and stir-fry for 2–3 minutes, until hot and bubbling. Season with salt and pepper to taste. Spoon the chicken mixture over the salad leaves, toss together to mix and serve, garnished with parsley.

> **Variation**
> • Use other lean meat such as turkey breast, beef or pork.
> • For a vegetarian option, substitute oyster and button mushrooms for the chicken.

Spicy chicken salad: Energy 137kcal/579kJ; Protein 24.9g; Carbohydrate 4.9g, of which sugars 3.9g; Fat 2.1g, of which saturates 0.5g; Cholesterol 70mg; Calcium 21mg; Fibre 0.8g; Sodium 236mg
Warm chicken salad: Energy 166kcal/701kJ; Protein 17.3g; Carbohydrate 18.4g, of which sugars 6g; Fat 2.4g, of which saturates 0.5g; Cholesterol 41mg; Calcium 30mg; Fibre 2g; Sodium 557mg

Corn-fed Chicken Salad
with Garlic Bread

Easy to put together, this is a great family meal. Simply serve with a tomato salad.

Serves 4

1.8kg/4lb corn-fed chicken
300ml/½ pint/1¼ cups white wine and water, mixed
24 slices French bread, 5mm/¼in thick
1 garlic clove, peeled
225g/8oz green beans
115g/4oz young spinach leaves
2 celery sticks, thinly sliced
2 sun-dried tomatoes, chopped
2 spring onions (scallions), thinly sliced
fresh chives and parsley, to garnish

For the vinaigrette

30ml/2 tbsp red wine vinegar
90ml/6 tbsp olive oil
15ml/1 tbsp wholegrain mustard
15ml/1 tbsp clear honey
30ml/2 tbsp chopped fresh mixed herbs, such as thyme, parsley, chives
10ml/2 tsp finely chopped capers
salt and ground black pepper

1 Preheat the oven to 190°C/375°F/Gas 5. Put the chicken into a casserole with the wine and water. Cook in the oven for 1½ hours, until tender. Leave to cool in the liquid. Discard the skin and bones and cut the flesh into small pieces.

2 To make the vinaigrette, put all the ingredients into a screw-top jar and shake vigorously to combine. Adjust the seasoning to taste if necessary.

3 Toast the French bread under the grill (broiler) or in the oven until dry and golden, then lightly rub with the garlic clove.

4 Cut the green beans into 5cm/2in lengths and cook in boiling water until just tender. Drain and rinse in cold water.

5 Remove the stalks from the spinach and tear into smaller pieces. Arrange on individual plates with the celery, green beans, sun-dried tomatoes, chicken and spring onions. Spoon over the vinaigrette. Arrange the toasted slices of French bread on top, garnish with fresh chives and parsley and serve immediately.

Chicken Salad
with Herbs & Lavender

A delicately scented marinade adds a delightfully fragrant flavour to this salad, which is served with golden polenta squares.

Serves 6

4 boneless chicken breast portions
900ml/1½ pints/3¾ cups light chicken stock
175g/6oz/1½ cups fine polenta
50g/2oz/¼ cup butter, plus extra for greasing
450g/1lb young spinach
175g/6oz lamb's lettuce (corn salad)
8 small tomatoes, halved
salt and ground black pepper
8 sprigs fresh lavender, to garnish

For the marinade

6 fresh lavender flowers, stripped from their stems
10ml/2 tsp finely grated (shredded) orange rind
2 garlic cloves, crushed
10ml/2 tsp clear honey
30ml/2 tbsp olive oil
10ml/2 tsp chopped fresh thyme
10ml/2 tsp chopped fresh marjoram
salt

1 To make the marinade, combine the lavender with the orange rind, garlic, honey and salt. Add the oil and herbs. Slash the chicken deeply, spread the marinade mixture over and leave to marinate in the refrigerator for 20 minutes.

2 To make the polenta, bring the chicken stock to the boil in a heavy pan. Add the polenta in a steady stream, stirring all the time until thick. Turn out onto a shallow, buttered tray. Cool.

3 Cook the chicken under the grill (broiler) for 15 minutes, basting with the marinade and turning once, until cooked.

4 Cut the polenta into 2.5cm/1in cubes using a wet knife. Heat the butter in a large pan and fry the polenta until golden.

5 Divide the spinach and lamb's lettuce between individual plates. Slice the chicken breast and arrange on the salad. Add the polenta cubes and tomato halves to each plate, season with salt and pepper and garnish with lavender.

Corn-fed chicken salad: Energy 462kcal/1939kJ; Protein 38.9g; Carbohydrate 35.4g, of which sugars 34.7g; Fat 19.3g, of which saturates 3g; Cholesterol 105mg; Calcium 119mg; Fibre 3.2g; Sodium 174mg
Chicken salad: Energy 268kcal/1121kJ; Protein 22.2g; Carbohydrate 29.5g, of which sugars 6.5g; Fat 6.6g, of which saturates 0.9g; Cholesterol 47mg; Calcium 187mg; Fibre 4.6g; Sodium 66mg

Chicken & Coriander Salad

Chicken is flavoured with the distinctive tang of fresh coriander in this sublime warm salad. Serve with roasted peppers or tomatoes and rice for a well balanced meal.

Serves 6

4 skinless chicken breast fillets
225g/8oz mangetouts
 (snow peas)
2 heads decorative lettuce such
 as lollo rosso or feuille
 de chêne
3 carrots, cut into matchsticks

175g/6oz/2⅓ cups sliced button
 (white) mushrooms
6 bacon rashers (strips), fried
 and chopped
60ml/4 tbsp fresh coriander
 (cilantro) leaves
salt and ground black pepper

For the marinade

120ml/4fl oz/½ cup lemon juice
30ml/2 tbsp wholegrain mustard
250ml/8fl oz/1 cup olive oil
75ml/2½fl oz/⅓ cup sesame oil
5ml/1 tsp coriander seeds,
 crushed

1 To make the marinade, mix all the ingredients together in a bowl. Place the chicken breast fillets in a shallow dish and pour over half the marinade. Leave to marinate overnight in the refrigerator. Chill the remaining marinade.

2 Cook the mangetouts for 2 minutes in boiling water, then refresh in cold water. Tear the lettuces into small pieces and put in a large bowl.

3 Add the mangetouts, carrots, mushrooms and bacon to the lettuce. Toss in the coriander and season with salt and pepper to taste. Arrange the salad in individual dishes.

4 Preheat the grill (broiler) to medium. Season the chicken breasts with salt and pepper, then grill (broil) for 10–15 minutes. Baste with the marinade and turn once during grilling, until cooked through.

5 Slice the chicken into thin pieces. Divide among the dishes of salad and sprinkle some of the reserved marinade over each dish. Combine quickly and serve immediately.

Chicken & Pasta Salad

This is a delicious way to use up left-over cooked chicken and, with the pasta, it makes a filling meal.

Serves 4

225g/8oz tri-coloured pasta twists
30ml/2 tbsp bottled pesto sauce
15ml/1 tbsp olive oil

1 beef tomato
12 pitted black olives
225g/8oz green beans,
 lightly cooked
350g/12oz cooked chicken, cubed
salt and ground black pepper
fresh basil, to garnish

1 Cook the pasta in a large pan of lightly salted boiling water according to the packet instructions, or until *al dente*.

2 Drain the pasta and rinse in plenty of cold running water. Put into a bowl and stir in the pesto sauce and olive oil.

3 To peel the beef tomato, cut a cross in the skin. Plunge the tomato into boiling water for about 30 seconds, then cool in cold water. The skin will now pull away easily. Cut the tomato into small cubes.

4 Add the tomato and olives to the pasta. Cut the green beans into 4cm/1½in lengths. Add the beans and chicken cubes to the pasta and season with salt and pepper to taste.

5 Toss gently, transfer to a serving dish, garnish and serve.

Cook's Tip
Although bought pesto is convenient and tasty, try making your own for a really sensational flavour. Simply crush a plump garlic clove with sea salt and add it to a blender with a bunch of destalked basil and 1oz/25g of lightly toasted pine kernels. Process until fine, then stir in 2oz/50g of finely grated fresh parmesan before bringing the mixture to a loose consistency with extra-virgin olive oil.

Chicken & coriander salad: Energy 251kcal/1045kJ; Protein 21.6g; Carbohydrate 3g, of which sugars 2.7g; Fat 17g, of which saturates 3.2g; Cholesterol 56mg; Calcium 47mg; Fibre 2g; Sodium 382mg
Chicken & pasta salad: Energy 373kcal/1575kJ; Protein 32g; Carbohydrate 44g, of which sugars 3.7g; Fat 8.9g, of which saturates 2.6g; Cholesterol 69mg; Calcium 138mg; Fibre 3.4g; Sodium 419mg

Roasted Chicken & Walnut Salad

Cook the chickens the day before, then assemble the salad at the last minute.

Serves 8
4 fresh tarragon or rosemary
  sprigs
2 x 1.8kg/4–4½lb chickens
65g/2½oz/5 tbsp softened butter
150ml/¼ pint/⅔ cup homemade
  chicken stock
150ml/¼ pint/⅔ cup white wine
115g/4oz/1 cup walnut pieces
lettuce leaves

450g/1lb seedless grapes or
  pitted cherries
1 small cantaloupe melon,
  scooped into balls or cut
  into cubes
salt and ground black pepper

For the dressing
30ml/2 tbsp tarragon vinegar
120ml/4fl oz/½ cup light olive oil
30ml/2 tbsp chopped fresh mixed
  herbs such as parsley, mint
  or tarragon

1 Preheat the oven to 200°C/400°F/Gas 6. Put the sprigs of tarragon inside the chickens and season with salt and pepper.

2 Spread the chickens with 50g/2oz/4 tbsp of the softened butter, place in a roasting pan and pour the stock around. Cover loosely with foil and roast for about 1½ hours, basting twice, until browned and the juices run clear. Remove from the roasting pan and leave to cool. Joint the chickens.

3 Add the wine to the roasting pan. Bring to the boil on the stove and cook until syrupy. Strain and leave to cool.

4 Heat the remaining butter in a frying pan (skillet) and gently fry the walnuts until lightly browned.

5 To make the dressing, whisk the vinegar and olive oil together with a little salt and pepper. Remove the fat from the chicken juices and add the juices to the dressing with the herbs. Adjust the seasoning to taste.

6 Arrange the chicken pieces on a bed of lettuce leaves, scatter over the grapes and melon, then spoon over the dressing. Sprinkle with the toasted walnuts to serve.

Duck, Avocado & Raspberry Salad

Rich duck breasts are roasted until crisp with a honey and soy glaze to serve warm with fresh raspberries and avocado. A delicious raspberry and redcurrant dressing adds a wonderful sweet-and-sour flavour as a finishing touch.

Serves 4
4 small or 2 large duck breasts,
  halved if large
15ml/1 tbsp clear honey

15ml/1 tbsp dark soy sauce
60ml/4 tbsp olive oil
15ml/1 tbsp raspberry vinegar
15ml/1 tbsp redcurrant jelly
selection of salad leaves, such as
  lamb's lettuce (corn salad), red
  chicory (Belgian endive)
  and frisée
2 avocados, stoned (pitted),
  peeled and cut into chunks
115g/4oz raspberries
salt and ground black pepper

1 Preheat the oven to 220°C/425°F/Gas 7. Prick the skin of each duck breast with a fork. Blend the honey and soy sauce together in a small bowl, then brush all over the duck skin.

2 Place the duck breasts on a rack set over a roasting pan and season with salt and pepper. Roast in the oven for 15–20 minutes, until the skin is crisp and the meat is cooked.

3 Meanwhile, to make the dressing, put the oil, vinegar and redcurrant jelly in a small bowl. Season with salt and pepper, then whisk well until evenly blended.

4 Slice the duck breasts diagonally and arrange on individual plates with the salad leaves, avocados and raspberries. Spoon over the dressing and serve immediately.

Cook's Tip
To tell if an avocado is ripe, press the pointed end and if it "gives" slightly, it is ready to eat. Always slice an avocado lengthwise, then twist the two sides in opposite directions to neatly break apart. Remove the stone (pit) with a knife.

Chicken & walnut salad: Energy 251kcal/1045kJ; Protein 21.6g; Carbohydrate 3g, of which sugars 2.7g; fat 17g, of which saturates 3.2g; Cholesterol 56mg; Calcium 47mg; fibre 2g; Sodium 382mg
Duck salad: Energy 344kcal/1429kJ; Protein 16.6g; Carbohydrate 6g, of which sugars 5.3g; Fat 29.6g, of which saturates 5.3g; Cholesterol 83mg; Calcium 36mg; Fibre 2.9g; Sodium 88mg

Duck Salad with Orange Sauce

The rich, gamey flavour of duck is enhanced by warm orange and spices, while crisp croûtons add crunch.

Serves 4

1 small orange, sliced thickly
2 boneless duck breasts
150ml/¼ pint/⅔ cup dry white wine
5ml/1 tsp ground coriander seeds
2.5ml/½ tsp ground cumin or fennel seeds
30ml/2 tbsp sugar
juice of ½ small lime or lemon
45ml/3 tbsp garlic oil
75g/3oz thickly sliced day-old bread, crusts removed and cut into short fingers
½ escarole lettuce
½ frisée lettuce
30ml/2 tbsp sunflower or groundnut (peanut) oil
salt and cayenne pepper
4 sprigs fresh coriander (cilantro), to garnish

1 Put the orange slices in a small pan. Cover with water, bring to the boil and simmer for 5 minutes to remove the bitterness. Drain the orange slices and set aside.

2 Pierce the skin of the duck breasts diagonally with a small knife. Rub the skin with salt. Heat a heavy frying pan (skillet) and cook the breasts for 20 minutes, turning once, until they are medium-rare. Transfer them to a warm plate and cover.

3 Heat the sediment in the frying pan until it begins to caramelize. Add the wine and stir to loosen the sediment. Add the coriander, cumin or fennel seeds, sugar and orange slices.

4 Boil quickly and reduce to a coating consistency. Sharpen with the lime or lemon juice and season to taste with salt and cayenne. Transfer the sauce to a bowl, cover and keep warm.

5 Heat the garlic oil in a heavy frying pan and brown the bread fingers. Season with salt, then turn out onto kitchen paper.

6 Moisten the salad leaves with oil and arrange on plates. Slice the duck breasts diagonally and divide between the plates. Spoon on the orange sauce, scatter with the croûtons and garnish with a sprig of fresh coriander. Serve warm.

Duck Breast & Pasta Salad

Tart fruit flavours act as a foil to the rich duck in this luxurious main-meal salad.

Serves 6

2 boneless duck breasts
5ml/1 tsp coriander seeds, crushed
350g/12oz dried rigatoni pasta
1 eating apple, diced
2 oranges, segmented
salt and ground black pepper
fresh chopped coriander (cilantro) and mint, to garnish

For the dressing

150ml/¼ pint/⅔ cup fresh orange juice
15ml/1 tbsp lemon juice
10ml/2 tsp clear honey
1 shallot, finely chopped
1 garlic clove, crushed
1 celery stick, chopped
75g/3oz dried cherries
45ml/3 tbsp port
15ml/1 tbsp chopped fresh mint
30ml/2 tbsp chopped fresh coriander (cilantro)

1 Preheat the grill (broiler). Remove the skin and fat from the duck breasts, season with salt and pepper and rub with the crushed coriander seeds.

2 Grill (broil) the duck breasts for 7–10 minutes. Wrap the duck breasts in foil and leave for 20 minutes.

3 Cook the pasta in a large pan of lightly salted, boiling water, until according to the packet instructions, until al dente. Drain and rinse under cold running water. Leave the pasta to cool.

4 To make the dressing, put the orange juice, lemon juice, honey, shallot, garlic, celery, cherries, port, mint and coriander into a small bowl. Whisk together and marinate for 30 minutes.

5 Unwrap the breasts from the foil and slice the duck very thinly. (It should still be slightly pink in the centre.)

6 Put the pasta into a large mixing bowl, add the dressing, diced apple and segments of orange. Toss well to coat the pasta.

7 Transfer the salad to a serving plate with the duck slices and garnish with the extra fresh coriander and mint.

Duck salad: Energy 231kcal/971kJ; Protein 17.3g; Carbohydrate 13.3g, of which sugars 4.5g; Fat 11.1g, of which saturates 1.7g; Cholesterol 83mg; Calcium 68mg; Fibre 1.5g; Sodium 185mg
Duck breast & pasta salad: Energy 312kcal/1323kJ; Protein 17.7g; Carbohydrate 53.6g, of which sugars 12.3g; Fat 4.4g, of which saturates 0.8g; Cholesterol 55mg; Calcium 50mg; Fibre 2.9g; Sodium 66mg

Warm Duck Salad with Poached Eggs

Golden duck skewers look and taste wonderful.

Serves 4

3 skinless duck breast portions, thinly sliced
30ml/2 tbsp soy sauce
30ml/2 tbsp balsamic vinegar
30ml/2 tbsp groundnut (peanut) oil
1 shallot, finely chopped
115g/4oz/1½ cups chanterelle mushrooms
4 eggs
50g/2oz mixed salad leaves
salt and ground black pepper
30ml/2 tbsp extra-virgin olive oil, to serve

1 Put the duck in a shallow dish and toss with the soy sauce and balsamic vinegar. Cover and chill for 30 minutes. Meanwhile, soak 12 bamboo skewers (about 13cm/5in long) in water to help prevent them from burning during cooking.

2 Preheat the grill (broiler). Thread the marinated duck slices onto the skewers, pleating them neatly. Place the skewers on a grill pan and cook for 3–5 minutes, then turn the skewers and cook for a further 3 minutes, or until the duck is golden brown.

3 Meanwhile, heat the groundnut oil in a frying pan (skillet) and cook the chopped shallot until softened. Add the mushrooms and cook over a high heat for 5 minutes, stirring occasionally.

4 While the chanterelles are cooking, half fill a frying pan with water, add a little salt and heat until simmering. Break the eggs one at a time into a cup, then gently tip into the water. Poach the eggs gently for about 3 minutes, or until the whites are set. Use a slotted spoon to transfer the eggs to a warm plate, pat them dry with kitchen paper, then trim off any untidy white.

5 Arrange the salad leaves on four individual plates, then add the chanterelles and skewered duck. Place the poached eggs on the plates. Drizzle the salad with olive oil, season with pepper and serve immediately.

Grilled Spiced Quail with Mixed Leaf & Mushroom Salad

This is a perfect supper dish for autumnal entertaining. Quail is at its best when the breast meat is removed from the carcass, so that it cooks quickly and can be served rare.

Serves 4

8 quail breasts
50g/2oz/¼ cup butter to cook the quail
5ml/1 tsp paprika
75g/3oz/generous 1 cup chanterelle mushrooms, sliced if large
25g/1oz/2 tbsp butter to cook the mushrooms
25g/1oz/3 tbsp walnut halves, toasted
115g/4oz mixed salad leaves

For the dressing
60ml/4 tbsp walnut oil
30ml/2 tbsp olive oil
45ml/3 tbsp balsamic vinegar
salt and ground black pepper

1 To make the dressing, whisk the oils with the balsamic vinegar, then season with salt and pepper and set aside.

2 Preheat the grill (broiler). Arrange the quail breasts on the grill rack, skin-side up. Dot with half the butter and sprinkle with half the paprika and a little salt.

3 Grill (broil) the quail breasts for 3 minutes. Turn them over and dot with the remaining butter, then sprinkle with the remaining paprika and a little salt. Grill for a further 3 minutes, or until cooked. Transfer the quail breasts to a warmed dish, cover and leave to stand while preparing the salad.

4 Heat the butter until foaming and cook the chanterelles for about 3 minutes, or until just beginning to soften. Add the walnuts and heat through. Remove from the heat.

5 Thinly slice the cooked quail breasts and arrange them on four serving plates with the warmed chanterelle mushrooms, toasted walnuts and mixed salad leaves. Drizzle the oil and balsamic vinegar dressing over the salad and and serve warm.

Warm duck salad: Energy 271kcal/1132kJ; Protein 29.2g; Carbohydrate 1.5g, of which sugars 1.1g; Fat 18.6g, of which saturates 3.9g; Cholesterol 314mg; Calcium 51mg; Fibre 0.7g; Sodium 196mg
Spiced quail salad: Energy 443Kcal/1837kJ; Protein 25.6g; Carbohydrate 0.9g, of which sugars 0.8g; fat 37.5g, of which saturates 12.3g; Cholesterol 110mg; Calcium 24mg; Fibre 0.7g; Sodium 176mg

Warm Stir-fried Salad

Warm salads are becoming increasingly popular because they are delicious and nutritious. This luscious salad of tarragon and ginger chicken on a bed of mixed leaves proves the point.

Serves 4
few large sprigs of fresh tarragon
2 skinless chicken breast fillets, about 225g/8oz each
5cm/2in fresh root ginger, peeled and finely chopped
45ml/3 tbsp light soy sauce
15ml/1 tbsp sugar
15ml/1 tbsp sunflower oil
1 Chinese lettuce
½ frisée lettuce, torn into bitesize pieces
115g/4oz/1 cup unsalted cashew nuts
2 large carrots, cut into fine strips
salt and ground black pepper

1 Strip the tarragon leaves from the stems and chop the leaves. Cut the chicken into fine strips and place in a bowl.

2 To make the marinade, mix together the tarragon, ginger, soy sauce and sugar in a bowl. Season with salt and pepper to taste and mix thoroughly.

3 Pour the marinade over the chicken strips and leave for 2–4 hours in a cool place.

4 Lift the chicken from the bowl with a slotted spoon and reserve the marinade. Heat the oil in a preheated wok. When the oil is hot, stir-fry the chicken for 3 minutes, then add the marinade and allow to bubble for 2–3 minutes.

5 Slice the Chinese lettuce and arrange on a plate with the frisée. Toss the cashews and carrots together with the chicken, pile on top of the bed of lettuce and serve immediately.

> **Cook's Tip**
> If you prefer, arrange the salad leaves on four individual plates, so that the hot stir-fry can be served quickly onto them, ensuring the lettuce remains crisp and the chicken warm.

Tangy Chicken Salad

This fresh and lively dish typifies the character of Thai cuisine. It is ideal for a starter or light lunch.

Serves 4–6
4 skinless chicken breast fillets
2 garlic cloves, crushed and roughly chopped
30ml/2 tbsp soy sauce
30ml/2 tbsp vegetable oil
120ml/4fl oz/½ cup coconut cream
30ml/2 tbsp fish sauce
juice of 1 lime
30ml/2 tbsp palm sugar (jaggery)
115g/4oz water chestnuts, sliced
50g/2oz cashew nuts, roasted
4 shallots, finely sliced
4 kaffir lime leaves, finely sliced
1 stalk lemon grass, finely sliced
5ml/1 tsp chopped galangal
1 large fresh red chilli, seeded and finely sliced
2 spring onions (scallions), finely sliced
10–12 mint leaves, torn
1 lettuce head, leaves separated
sprigs of fresh coriander (cilantro) and 2 fresh red chillies, seeded and sliced, to garnish

1 Trim the chicken breasts of any excess fat and put them in a large dish. Rub with the garlic, soy sauce and 15ml/1 tbsp of the oil. Leave to marinate for 1–2 hours.

2 Grill (broil) or pan-fry the chicken for 3–4 minutes on both sides or until cooked. Remove and set aside to cool.

3 In a small pan, heat the coconut cream, fish sauce, lime juice and palm sugar. Stir until all of the sugar has dissolved and then remove from the heat.

4 Cut the cooked chicken into strips and put in a bowl. Add the water chestnuts, cashew nuts, shallots, kaffir lime leaves, lemon grass, galangal, red chilli, spring onions and mint leaves. Stir to combine well.

5 Pour the coconut dressing over the chicken mixture, toss and mix well. Arrange the lettuce leaves on a platter, top with the chicken salad and garnish with sprigs of fresh coriander and sliced red chillies.

Warm stir-fried salad: Energy 318kcal/1322kJ; Protein 20.6g; Carbohydrate 11.6g, of which sugars 7.4g; Fat 21.3g, of which saturates 3.9g; Cholesterol 39mg; Calcium 48mg; Fibre 2.8g; Sodium 933mg
Tangy chicken salad: Energy 349kcal/1453kJ; Protein 24.3g; Carbohydrate 11.5g, of which sugars 9.8g; Fat 23.2g, of which saturates 12.3g; Cholesterol 43mg; Calcium 49mg; Fibre 1.7g; Sodium 200mg

Chicken, Vegetable & Chilli Salad

A great way to use up leftover chicken, this spicy salad is full of surprising textures and flavours. Serve as a light lunch dish or for supper with rice or noodles.

Serves 4
225g/8oz Chinese leaves
   (Chinese cabbage)
2 carrots, cut into thin strips
½ cucumber, cut into thin strips
salt
2 fresh red chillies, seeded and
   cut into thin strips
1 small onion, sliced into fine rings
4 pickled gherkins, sliced, plus
   45ml/3 tbsp of the liquid
50g/2oz/½ cup peanuts,
   lightly ground
225g/8oz cooked chicken,
   finely sliced
1 garlic clove, crushed
5ml/1 tsp sugar
30ml/2 tbsp cider or
   white vinegar

1 Finely slice the Chinese leaves and set aside with the carrot strips. Spread out the cucumber strips on a board and sprinkle with salt. Set aside for 15 minutes.

2 Turn the salted cucumber into a colander, rinse well under cold running water and pat dry.

3 Mix together the chillies and onion rings and then add the sliced gherkins and peanuts.

4 Put the Chinese leaves in a salad bowl with the carrot and cucumber strips. Add the chilli and onion mixture and chicken.

5 Mix the gherkin liquid with the garlic, sugar and vinegar. Pour over the salad, toss lightly and serve immediately.

> **Cook's Tips**
> • Add a little more cider or white wine vinegar to the dressing if a sharper taste is preferred.
> • If you want to use fresh chicken breast fillets, slice the chicken finely, then stir-fry in a little oil heated in a wok or frying pan (skillet) until tender.

Hot & Sour Chicken Salad

Tender chicken, marinated in a spicy peanut marinade, is stir-fried to succulent perfection, then served on a bed of fresh-tasting salad. Accompany with fine noodles for a complete Oriental treat.

Serves 4–6
2 skinless chicken breast fillets
1 small fresh red chilli, seeded
   and finely chopped
1cm/½in piece fresh root ginger,
   peeled and finely chopped
1 garlic clove, crushed
15ml/1 tbsp crunchy
   peanut butter
30ml/2 tbsp chopped coriander
   (cilantro) leaves
5ml/1 tsp sugar
2.5ml/½ tsp salt
15ml/1 tbsp rice or white
   wine vinegar
60ml/4 tbsp vegetable oil
10ml/2 tsp fish sauce (optional)
115g/4oz fresh beansprouts
1 head Chinese leaves (Chinese
   cabbage), shredded
2 carrots, cut into thin sticks
2 large gherkins (pickles), sliced
1 red onion, cut into fine rings,
   to garnish

1 Slice the chicken thinly, place in a shallow bowl and set aside. Grind the chilli, ginger and garlic in a mortar with a pestle. Add the peanut butter, coriander, sugar and salt.

2 Then add the vinegar, 30ml/2 tbsp of the oil and the fish sauce (if using). Combine well. Cover the chicken with the spice mixture and leave to marinate for at least 2 hours.

3 Heat the remaining oil in a wok or frying pan. Add the chicken and stir-fry for 10–12 minutes.

4 Arrange the Chinese leaves, carrots and gherkins on a serving platter, top with the chicken and garnish with the onion.

> **Cook's Tip**
> This salad is also delicious with prawns (shrimp). Allow 450g/1lb large cooked prawns to serve 4 people.

Hot & sour chicken salad: Energy 148kcal/615kJ; Protein 10g; Carbohydrate 6g, of which sugars 5.1g; Fat 9.5g, of which saturates 1.4g; Cholesterol 23mg; Calcium 44mg; Fibre 2.1g; Sodium 42mg
Chicken, vegetable & chilli salad: Energy 167kcal/700kJ; Protein 17.8g; Carbohydrate 9.1g, of which sugars 7.7g; Fat 6.9g, of which saturates 1.4g; Cholesterol 39mg; Calcium 47mg; Fibre 2.9g; Sodium 50mg

Chicken & Shredded Cabbage Salad

This spicy Oriental salad is particularly good with roasted chicken.

Serves 4–6
450g/1lb chicken, cooked and
  torn into thin strips
1 white Chinese cabbage,
  trimmed and finely
  grated (shredded)
2 carrots, finely grated (shredded)
a small bunch fresh mint, stalks
  removed, finely chopped
1 small bunch fresh coriander
  (cilantro) leaves, to garnish

For the dressing
30ml/2 tbsp vegetable or
  groundnut (peanut) oil
30ml/2 tbsp white rice vinegar
45ml/3 tbsp Thai fish sauce
juice of 2 limes
30ml/2 tbsp palm sugar
2 fresh red Thai chillies, seeded
  and finely chopped
25g/1oz fresh young root
  ginger, sliced
3 garlic cloves, crushed
2 shallots, finely chopped

1 To make the dressing, beat the oil, vinegar, fish sauce and lime juice in a bowl with the sugar, until it has dissolved.

2 Stir in the other ingredients and leave to stand for about 30 minutes to allow the flavours to develop.

3 Put the cooked chicken strips, cabbage, carrots and mint in a large bowl. Pour over the dressing and toss well. Garnish with fresh coriander leaves and serve.

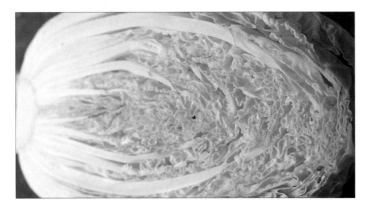

Egg Noodle Salad with Sesame Chicken

This quick and tasty salad is ideal for a midweek meal when you are short of time.

Serves 4–6
400g/14oz fresh thin egg noodles
1 carrot, cut into long fine strips
50g/2oz mangetouts (snow peas),
  topped, tailed, cut into fine
  strips and blanched
115g/4oz/1/2 cup beansprouts,
  blanched
30ml/2 tbsp olive oil
225g/8oz skinless chicken breast
  fillet, finely sliced

30ml/2 tbsp sesame
  seeds, toasted
2 spring onions (scallions), finely
  sliced diagonally, and fresh
  coriander (cilantro) leaves,
  to garnish

For the dressing
45ml/3 tbsp sherry vinegar
75ml/5 tbsp soy sauce
60ml/4 tbsp sesame oil
90ml/6 tbsp light olive oil
1 garlic clove, finely chopped
5ml/1 tsp grated (shredded) fresh
  root ginger
salt and ground black pepper

1 To make the dressing, whisk together all the ingredients in a small bowl, seasoning with salt and pepper to taste.

2 Cook the noodles in a large pan of boiling water according to the packet instructions. Be careful not to overcook them. Drain the noodles, rinse and drain well. Transfer to a bowl.

3 Add the carrot, mangetouts and beansprouts to the noodles. Pour in about half the dressing, then toss the mixture well and adjust the seasoning according to taste.

4 Heat the oil in a large frying pan. Add the chicken and stir-fry for 3 minutes, or until cooked and golden. Remove from the heat. Add the sesame seeds and drizzle in some dressing.

5 Arrange the noodle mixture on individual plates, making a nest on each plate. Spoon the chicken on top. Sprinkle with the spring onions and coriander leaves and serve any remaining dressing separately.

Chicken & cabbage salad: Energy 156kcal/656kJ; Protein 20g; Carbohydrate 8.4g, of which sugars 7.9g; Fat 4.9g, of which saturates 0.7g; Cholesterol 53mg; Calcium 73mg; Fibre 3.1g; Sodium 596mg.
Egg noodle salad: Energy 546kcal/2286kJ; Protein 19.3g; Carbohydrate 50.9g, of which sugars 3.8g; Fat 30.9g, of which saturates 5.3g; Cholesterol 46mg; Calcium 69mg; Fibre 3.2g; Sodium 860mg

Larp of Chiang Mai

The city of Chiang Mai in the north-east of Thailand is famous for its chicken salad, which was originally called "Laap" or "Larp". Duck, beef or pork can be used instead of chicken.

Serves 4–6
450g/1lb minced (ground) chicken
1 lemon grass stalk, root trimmed
3 kaffir lime leaves, finely chopped
4 fresh red chillies, seeded and chopped
60ml/4 tbsp fresh lime juice
30ml/2 tbsp Thai fish sauce
15ml/1 tbsp roasted ground rice
2 spring onions (scallions), finely chopped
30ml/2 tbsp fresh coriander (cilantro) leaves

For the garnish
thinly sliced kaffir lime leaves
mixed salad leaves
fresh mint sprigs

1 Heat a large, non-stick frying pan (skillet). Add the minced chicken and moisten with a little water. Stir constantly over a medium heat for 7–10 minutes, until it is cooked through. Remove the pan from the heat and drain off any excess fat.

2 Cut off the lower 5cm/2in of the lemon grass stalk and chop it finely.

3 Transfer the cooked chicken to a bowl and add the chopped lemon grass, lime leaves, chillies, lime juice, fish sauce, roasted ground rice, spring onions and coriander. Mix thoroughly.

4 Spoon the chicken mixture into a salad bowl. To garnish, sprinkle with sliced lime leaves, salad leaves and sprigs of mint.

Tip
...ous rice for the roasted ground rice. Put the rice in a ...n (skillet) and dry-roast it until golden brown. Grind to ...r, using a mortar and pestle or a food processor. When ...is cold, store it in a glass jar in a cool and dry place.

Sesame Duck & Noodle Salad

This salad is complete in itself and makes a lovely summer lunch, with its blend of Oriental flavours.

Serves 4
2 boneless duck breasts
15ml/1 tbsp oil
150g/5oz sugar snap peas
2 carrots, cut into 7.5cm/3in sticks
225g/8oz medium egg noodles
6 spring onions (scallions), sliced
salt
30ml/2 tbsp fresh coriander (cilantro) leaves, to garnish

For the marinade
15ml/1 tbsp sesame oil
5ml/1 tsp ground coriander
5ml/1 tsp five-spice powder

For the dressing
15ml/1 tbsp vinegar
5ml/1 tsp soft light brown sugar
5ml/1 tsp soy sauce
1 garlic clove, crushed
15ml/1 tbsp sesame seeds, toasted
45ml/3 tbsp sunflower oil
30ml/2 tbsp sesame oil
ground black pepper

1 Slice the duck breasts thinly widthways and place in a shallow dish. Mix together the ingredients for the marinade, pour over the duck and turn well to coat thoroughly. Cover and leave in a cool place for 30 minutes.

2 Heat the oil in a frying pan (skillet), add the slices of duck breast and stir-fry for 3–4 minutes, until cooked. Set aside.

3 Bring a pan of lightly salted water to the boil. Place the sugar snap peas and carrots in a steamer that will fit on top of the pan. When the water boils, add the noodles. Place the steamer on top and steam the vegetables while the noodles cook.

4 Set the steamed vegetables aside. Drain the noodles, refresh under cold water and drain again. Place in a large serving bowl.

5 To make the dressing, mix the vinegar, sugar, soy sauce, garlic and sesame seeds in a bowl. Add a generous grinding of pepper, then whisk in the oils. Pour over the noodles and mix well. Add the peas, carrots, spring onions and duck slices and toss to mix. Scatter the coriander over the top and serve.

Larp of Chiang Mai: Energy 93kcal/395kJ; Protein 18.7g; Carbohydrate 2.3g, of which sugars 0.3g; Fat 1g, of which saturates 0.2g; Cholesterol 53mg; Calcium 24mg; Fibre 0.4g; Sodium 49mg
Sesame duck & noodle salad: Energy 550kcal/2301kJ; Protein 25.3g; Carbohydrate 47g, of which sugars 4.2g; Fat 31.6g, of which saturates 5.2g; Cholesterol 99mg; Calcium 70mg; Fibre 4.5g; Sodium 192mg

Curry Fried Pork & Rice Vermicelli Salad

Fragrant pork tossed with beansprouts and fine noodles is a winning dish.

Serves 4
225g/8oz lean pork
2 garlic cloves, finely chopped
2 slices fresh root ginger, peeled and finely chopped
30–45ml/2–3 tbsp rice wine
45ml/3 tbsp vegetable oil
2 lemon grass stalks, finely chopped
10ml/2 tsp curry powder
175g/6oz/³⁄₄ cup beansprouts
225g/8oz rice vermicelli, soaked in warm water until soft then drained
¹⁄₂ lettuce, finely shredded
30ml/2 tbsp fresh mint leaves
lemon juice and Thai fish sauce, to taste
salt and ground black pepper
2 spring onions (scallions), chopped, 25g/1oz/¹⁄₄ cup toasted peanuts, chopped, to garnish

1 Cut the pork into thin strips. Place in a shallow dish with half the garlic and ginger. Season with salt and pepper, pour over 30 ml/2 tbsp rice wine and marinate for at least 1 hour.

2 Heat the oil in a frying pan (skillet). Add the remaining garlic and ginger and fry for a few seconds until fragrant. Stir in the pork, with the marinade, and add the lemon grass and curry powder.

3 Fry on a high heat until the pork is golden and cooked through, adding more rice wine if the mixture seems too dry.

4 Place the beansprouts in a sieve (strainer) and lower into a pan of boiling water for 1 minute, then drain and refresh under cold running water. Drain again. Using the same water, cook the rice vermicelli for 3–5 minutes, until tender. Drain and rinse.

5 Drain the vermicelli well and put in a large bowl. Add the beansprouts, shredded lettuce and mint leaves. Season with lemon juice and fish sauce to taste. Toss lightly.

6 Divide the vermicelli mixture between individual plates and top with the pork. Garnish with spring onions and peanuts.

Sweet Potato, Egg, Pork & Beetroot Salad

This dish is a delicious way to use up left-over roast pork. Sweet flavours balance well with the bitterness of the salad leaves.

Serve 4
900g/2lb sweet potatoes
4 chicory (Belgian endive) heads
5 hard-boiled (hard-cooked) eggs, shelled
450g/1lb pickled young beetroot (beet)
175g/6oz cold roast pork
salt

For the dressing
75ml/5 tbsp groundnut (peanut) or sunflower oil
30ml/2 tbsp white wine vinegar
10ml/2 tsp Dijon mustard
5ml/1 tsp fennel seeds, crushed

1 Peel the sweet potatoes and dice into equal-sized pieces. Add the diced sweet potatoes to a pan of boiling salted water. Bring back to the boil then simmer for 10–15 minutes, or until the potatoes are soft. Drain and allow to cool.

2 To make the dressing, combine the oil, vinegar, mustard and fennel seeds in a screw-top jar and shake vigorously to mix.

3 Separate the chicory leaves and arrange them around the edge of four individual plates.

4 Pour two-thirds of the dressing over the sweet potatoes, then stir to coat well. Spoon on top of the chicory leaves.

5 Slice the eggs and beetroot, and arrange in a circle on top of the sweet potato. Slice the pork, then cut into 4cm/1½in strips and moisten with the rest of the dressing. Pile the pork into the centre of each salad. Season with salt and serve.

> **Cook's Tip**
> To crush the fennel seeds, grind using a mortar and pestle. If you don't have these, use two dessert spoons instead.

Curry fried pork & rice vermicelli salad: Energy 409kcal/1705kJ; Protein 20.8g; Carbohydrate 48.7g, of which sugars 2.8g; Fat 14.5g, of which saturates 2.4g; Cholesterol 35mg; Calcium 68mg; Fibre 2.4g; Sodium 60mg
Sweet potato, egg, pork & beetroot salad: Energy 507kcal/2132kJ; Protein 21.9g; Carbohydrate 56.7g, of which sugars 20.9g; Fat 23.3g, of which saturates 4.4g; Cholesterol 265mg; Calcium 119mg; Fibre 7.7g; Sodium 283mg

Smoked Bacon & Tomato Salad with Pasta Twists

This tasty pasta salad is subtly flavoured with smoked bacon, which contrasts beautifully with the fresh flavour of the tomatoes and green beans.

Serves 4

350g/12oz/3 cups whole-wheat
   pasta twists
225g/8oz/1½ cups green beans
8 strips of lean smoked back
   bacon, rind and fat removed
350g/12oz cherry tomatoes,
   halved
2 bunches spring onions
   (scallions), chopped
400g/14oz can chickpeas,
   drained
90ml/6 tbsp tomato juice
30ml/2 tbsp balsamic vinegar
5ml/1 tsp ground cumin
5ml/1 tsp ground coriander
30ml/2 tbsp chopped fresh
   coriander (cilantro)
salt and ground black pepper

1 Cook the pasta in a large pan of lightly salted, boiling water according to the packet instructions, until *al dente*.

2 Meanwhile, halve the green beans and cook in boiling water for about 5 minutes, until tender. Drain and keep warm.

3 Preheat the grill (broiler) to high and cook the bacon for 2–3 minutes. Using tongs, turn the bacon over and cook for 2–3 minutes, until lightly done. Dice and add to the beans.

4 Put the tomatoes, spring onions and chickpeas in a bowl and mix together. In a small bowl, combine the tomato juice, vinegar, spices, fresh coriander and salt and pepper, then pour on top of the tomato mixture.

5 Drain the pasta well and add to the tomato mixture with the green beans and bacon. Toss to mix. Serve warm or cold.

> **Cook's Tip**
> *Always rinse canned beans and pulses before using to remove as much of the brine as possible.*

Bacon Salad with Farmhouse Cheese Dressing

Crisp lettuce topped with golden apple and bacon pieces, is dressed with a creamy Camembert dressing to create a gorgeous salad.

Serves 4

30ml/2 tbsp olive oil
50g/2oz diced streaky (fatty)
   bacon rashers (strips),
   preferably dry-cured, diced
1 eating apple, cored and
   chopped
2 small heads cos or
   romaine lettuce
squeeze of lemon juice
salt and ground black pepper
warm country bread, to serve

For the dressing

150ml/¼ pint/⅔ cup
   soured cream
15ml/1 tbsp cider
50g/2oz Camembert
   cheese, chopped
a dash of cider vinegar

1 Heat 15ml/1 tbsp of the olive oil in a large frying pan (skillet) and add the diced streaky bacon. Cook over a medium heat until crisp and golden.

2 Add the chopped apple and cook gently for 1–2 minutes until golden brown and softened.

3 Tear the lettuce into bitesize pieces. To make the dressing, heat the soured cream, cider, cheese and vinegar together in a small pan over a low heat until smooth and creamy. Remove from the heat.

4 Dress the lettuce with some of the remaining oil and the lemon juice and season with salt and pepper to taste, then divide between four individual plates. Place the warm apple and bacon on top, then drizzle over the dressing.

> **Cook's Tip**
> *For a tasty light meal, serve with a salad of sliced tomatoes and cooled, steamed green beans, tossed in a herby dressing.*

Bacon & tomato salad: Energy 582kcal/2459kJ; Protein 30.2g; Carbohydrate 87.9g, of which sugars 9.6g; Fat 14.7g, of which saturates 4.2g; Cholesterol 30mg; Calcium 136mg; Fibre 10.1g; Sodium 1155mg
Bacon salad: Energy 225kcal/931kJ; Protein 6.5g; Carbohydrate 4.7g, of which sugars 4.7g; Fat 19.8g, of which saturates 8.9g; Cholesterol 42mg; Calcium 97mg; Fibre 1.2g; Sodium 246mg

Egg, Bacon & Avocado Salad

A medley of colours, flavours and textures.

Serves 4

1 large cos or romaine lettuce
2 avocados, peeled and diced
6 hard-boiled (hard-cooked) eggs, chopped
2 beef tomatoes, peeled, seeded and chopped
175g/6oz blue cheese, crumbled
8 bacon rashers (strips), fried until crisp and crumbled

For the dressing

1 garlic clove, crushed
5ml/1 tsp sugar
7.5ml/1½ tsp lemon juice
25ml/1½ tbsp red wine vinegar
120ml/4fl oz/½ cup groundnut (peanut) oil
salt and ground black pepper

1 Slice the lettuce and arrange on a platter. Arrange the avocados, eggs, tomatoes and cheese in rows on top of the lettuce. Sprinkle the bacon over the top.

2 Combine all the dressing ingredients in a screw-top jar and shake well. Pour the dressing over the salad just before serving.

Spinach Salad with Bacon & Prawns

Serve this warm salad with plenty of crusty bread.

Serves 4

105ml/7 tbsp olive oil
30ml/2 tbsp sherry vinegar
2 garlic cloves, finely chopped
5ml/1 tsp Dijon mustard
about 115g/4oz fresh young spinach leaves
½ head oak-leaf lettuce, torn
12 cooked whole king prawns (jumbo shrimp) in the shell
115g/4oz streaky (fatty) bacon, rinded and cut into strips
salt and ground black pepper

1 To make the dressing, whisk together 90ml/6 tbsp of the olive oil with the vinegar, garlic, mustard and seasoning in a small pan. Heat gently until thickened slightly, then keep warm. Arrange the spinach and torn lettuce leaves on four plates.

2 Peel the prawns, leaving the tails intact. Set aside. Fry the bacon until golden and crisp. Add the prawns and stir-fry for a few minutes. Spoon the bacon and prawns onto the salad leaves, then pour over the hot dressing. Serve immediately.

Bacon & New Potato Salad

A rich mustard sauce gives the new potatoes added flavour and colour.

Serves 4–6

5 eggs
30–45ml/2–3 tbsp Dijon mustard
200g/7oz mayonnaise
3 celery sticks, finely chopped
115g/4oz bacon lardons
900g/2lb small new potatoes
30ml/2 tbsp chopped fresh flat leaf parsley
salt and ground black pepper

1 Place the eggs carefully into a pan of water and bring to the boil. Simmer for 5–8 minutes, drain and plunge the eggs straight into a bowl containing cold water.

2 Peel the eggs and mash three in a large bowl with a fork. Stir in the mustard, mayonnaise and celery. Season with salt and pepper. Thin down the dressing with a little water if you wish.

3 Fry the bacon pieces in a dry frying pan (skillet) until crisp and golden. Toss half of the bacon into the mayonnaise dressing. Reserve the remainder.

4 Cook the potatoes in boiling water for 20 minutes until tender. Drain and leave to cool.

5 Toss the cooled potatoes into the mayonnaise dressing and spoon onto a serving platter. Slice the remaining eggs and scatter over the salad with the reserved bacon pieces. Scatter the chopped parsley over the top and serve immediately.

Cook's Tip
Use firm salad potatoes, cut into even pieces, or use whole baby new potatoes. Cook with mint sprigs for extra flavour.

Variation
Replace the bacon with cooked peeled prawns (shrimp).

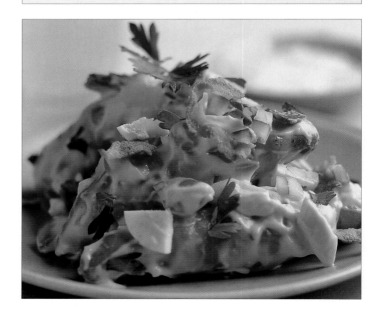

Egg, bacon & avocado salad: Energy 730kcal/3025kJ; Protein 30.8g; Carbohydrate 7.7g, of which sugars 6.7g; Fat 64.4g, of which saturates 20.2g; Cholesterol 348mg; Calcium 310mg; Fibre 4.7g; Sodium 1522mg
Spinach, bacon & prawns: Energy 305kcal/1260kJ; Protein 14.6g; Carbohydrate 1.3g, of which sugars 1.3g; Fat 26.8g, of which saturates 5.3g; Cholesterol 116mg; Calcium 104mg; Fibre 1.1g; Sodium 499mg
Bacon & new potato salad: Energy 446kcal/1854kJ; Protein 11.7g; Carbohydrate 25.3g, of which sugars 2.9g; Fat 33.9g, of which saturates 6.5g; Cholesterol 194mg; Calcium 46mg; Fibre 1.7g; Sodium 677mg

Wild Mushroom Salad with Parma Ham

An autumnal feast, this salad brings out the delicate flavour of wild mushrooms.

Serves 4
175g/6oz Parma ham,
   thickly sliced
45ml/3 tbsp butter
450g/1lb wild or cultivated
   mushrooms such as
   chanterelles, field blewits,
   oyster mushrooms, sliced
60ml/4 tbsp brandy
¹/₂ oakleaf lettuce
¹/₂ frisée lettuce

15ml/1 tbsp walnut oil
salt and ground black pepper

For the herb pancakes
45ml/3 tbsp plain
   (all-purpose) flour
75ml/5 tbsp milk
1 egg, plus 1 egg yolk
60ml/4 tbsp freshly grated
   (shredded) Parmesan cheese
45ml/3 tbsp chopped fresh mixed
   herbs such as parsley, thyme,
   tarragon, marjoram, chives
salt and ground black pepper

1 To make the pancakes, combine the flour with the milk in a measuring jug (pitcher). Beat in the egg and egg yolk with the Parmesan cheese, herbs, salt and pepper. Heat a non-stick pan and pour in enough mixture to coat the bottom of the pan.

2 When the batter has set, turn the pancake over and cook briefly on the other side. Turn the pancake out and leave to cool. Continue until you have used all the batter.

3 Roll the pancakes together and cut into 1cm/¹/₂ in ribbons. Cut the Parma ham into similar-sized ribbons and toss together.

4 Heat the butter in a non-stick pan until it begins to foam. Add the mushrooms and cook for 6–8 minutes. Add the brandy and ignite with a match. The flames will subside when the alcohol has burnt off.

5 Moisten the salad leaves with walnut oil and divide between four serving plates. Place the ham and pancake ribbons in the centre, spoon on the mushrooms, season and serve warm.

Curly Salad with Bacon

This delicious salad may also be sprinkled with chopped hard-boiled egg.

Serves 4
50g/2oz white bread
225g/8oz frisée lettuce leaves
75–90ml/5–6 tbsp extra-virgin
   olive oil

175g/6oz piece smoked bacon,
   diced, or 6 thick-cut smoked
   bacon rashers (strips), cut
   crossways into thin strips
1 small garlic clove,
   finely chopped
15ml/1 tbsp red wine vinegar
10ml/2 tsp Dijon mustard
salt and ground black pepper

1 Cut the bread into small cubes. Tear the frisée into bitesize pieces and put into a salad bowl.

2 Heat 15ml/1 tbsp of the oil in a non-stick frying pan (skillet) over a medium-low heat and add the bacon. Fry gently until well browned, stirring occasionally. Remove the bacon with a slotted spoon and drain on kitchen paper.

3 Add another 30ml/2 tbsp of the oil to the pan and fry the bread cubes over a medium-high heat, turning frequently, until evenly browned. Remove the bread cubes with a slotted spoon and drain on kitchen paper. Discard any remaining fat.

4 Stir the garlic, vinegar and mustard into the pan with the remaining oil and heat until just warm, whisking to combine.

5 Season with salt and pepper to taste, then pour the dressing over the salad and sprinkle with the fried bacon and croûtons. Serve immediately, while still warm.

Cook's Tip
To reduce the oil content, make the croûtons in the oven and do not add the 30ml/2tbsp oil at step 3. For oven-cooked croûtons, cut the bread into cubes and place in a single layer on a baking sheet. Bake in a 180°C/350°F/Gas 4 oven for 7–10 minutes or until golden, turning once.

Curly salad: Energy 226kcal/940kJ; Protein 10g; Carbohydrate 8.1g, of which sugars 1.5g; Fat 17.3g, of which saturates 3.2g; Cholesterol 14mg; Calcium 38mg; Fibre 0.8g; Sodium 721mg
Wild mushroom salad: Energy 350kcal/1460kJ; Protein 19.4g; Carbohydrate 13g, of which sugars 4.2g; Fat 21.3g, of which saturates 9.9g; Cholesterol 158mg; Calcium 241mg; Fibre 3.3g; Sodium 744mg

Salad with Omelette Strips & Bacon

Rich duck eggs produce an omelette with a lovely, delicate flavour, which combines perfectly with crispy bacon and fresh leaves in this elegant salad.

Serves 4

6 streaky (fatty) bacon rashers (strips), rinds removed and chopped

2 duck eggs
2 spring onions (scallions), chopped
few sprigs of fresh coriander (cilantro), chopped
25g/1oz/2 tbsp butter
400g/14oz bag of mixed salad leaves
60ml/4 tbsp olive oil
30ml/2 tbsp balsamic vinegar
salt and ground black pepper

1 Warm an omelette pan over a low heat and gently fry the chopped bacon until the fat runs. Increase the heat to crisp up the bacon, stirring frequently. When the bacon pieces are brown and crispy, remove from the heat and transfer to a hot dish to keep warm.

2 Beat the eggs with the spring onions and coriander and season with salt and pepper.

3 Melt the butter in the cleaned omelette pan and pour in the egg mixture. Cook for 2–3 minutes to make an unfolded omelette. Remove the omelette from the pan and set the pan aside. Carefully cut the omelette into long strips.

4 Place the salad leaves in a large salad bowl. Add the omelette strips to the salad with the bacon. Stir the oil and vinegar into the omelette pan, with salt and pepper, then heat briefly and pour over the salad. Toss well before serving.

Cook's Tip
Choose a selection of salad leaves to include some distinctively flavoured leaves that will add a bite to this salad. A combination that includes rocket (arugula), watercress or herbs would look attractive and taste good.

Asparagus & Bacon Salad

Serve this stylish salad as a light lunch or to add interest to plainly cooked chicken or fish.

Serves 4

500g/1¼lb medium asparagus spears
130g/4½oz thin-cut smoked back (lean) bacon

250g/9oz chicory (Belgian endive) leaves or other bitter-tasting leaves

For the French dressing
30ml/2 tbsp white wine vinegar
90ml/6 tbsp extra-virgin olive oil
5ml/1 tsp Dijon mustard
pinch of sugar
salt and ground black pepper

1 Trim off any tough stalk ends from the asparagus and cut the spears into three, setting the tender tips aside.

2 Heat a 1cm/½in depth of water in a frying pan (skillet) until simmering. Reserve the asparagus tips and cook the remainder of the spears for about 3 minutes, until almost tender. Add the tips and cook for 1 minute more. Drain and refresh under cold running water.

3 To make the dressing, whisk together the vinegar, oil, mustard and sugar. Season with salt and pepper to taste.

4 Dry-fry the bacon until golden and crisp and then set it aside to cool slightly. Use kitchen scissors to snip it into bitesize pieces. Place the salad leaves in a bowl and add the bacon.

5 Add the asparagus and a little black pepper to the salad leaves and bacon. Pour the dressing over and toss the salad lightly. Serve immediately.

Variation
Frisée lettuce makes a good alternative to chicory. Related to the chicory family, frisée also has a slightly bitter taste, but its leaves are feathery and curly. The leaves range in colour from yellow-white to yellow-green and look attractive in a salad.

Salad with omelette & bacon: Energy 301kcal/1246kJ; Protein 12.4g; Carbohydrate 1.8g, of which sugars 1.8g; Fat 27.3g, of which saturates 8.4g; Cholesterol 288mg; Calcium 55mg; Fibre 0.9g; Sodium 664mg
Asparagus & bacon salad: Energy 259kcal/1068kJ; Protein 9.5g; Carbohydrate 3.6g, of which sugars 3.5g; Fat 23g, of which saturates 4.6g; Cholesterol 17mg; Calcium 53mg; Fibre 2.7g; Sodium 519mg

Egg & Bacon Caesar Salad

The key elements of this popular salad are sweet lettuce, crisp croûtons and a mayonnaise-like dressing.

Serves 4–6
3 × 1cm/½in thick slices
  white bread, cubed
45ml/3 tbsp olive oil
1 large garlic clove, finely chopped
3–4 Little Gem (Bibb) lettuces or
  2 larger cos or romaine lettuces
12–18 quail's eggs

115g/4oz thinly sliced Parma,
  San Daniele or Serrano ham
40–50g/1½–2oz Parmesan
  cheese, grated (shredded)
salt and ground black pepper

For the dressing
1 large egg
1–2 garlic cloves, chopped
4 anchovy fillets in oil, drained
120ml/4fl oz/½ cup olive oil
10–15ml/2–3 tsp lemon juice or
  white wine vinegar

1 Preheat the oven to 190°C/375°F/Gas 5. Toss the bread cubes with the oil and garlic. Season to taste with salt and pepper. Turn onto a baking tray and bake for 10–14 minutes, stirring once or twice, until golden brown all over.

2 Meanwhile, to make the dressing, boil the egg for 90 seconds, then plunge into cold water. Shell and put in a food processor or blender. Add the garlic and anchovy fillets and process to mix. With the motor still running, gradually add the olive oil in a thin stream until creamy. Add the lemon juice or vinegar and season to taste with salt and pepper.

3 Separate the lettuce leaves and tear up if large. Place in a large salad bowl.

4 Put the quail's eggs in a pan, cover with cold water, then bring to the boil and boil for 2 minutes. Plunge the eggs into cold water, then part-shell them. Grill (broil) the ham for 2–3 minutes on each side, or until crisp.

5 Toss the dressing into the lettuce with 25g/1oz of the Parmesan. Add the croûtons. Cut the quail's eggs in half and add them to the salad. Crumble the ham into large pieces and scatter it over the salad with the remaining cheese.

Warm Salad of Bayonne Ham & New Potatoes

With a lightly spiced nutty dressing, this warm salad is as delicious as it is fashionable, and an excellent choice for informal entertaining.

Serves 4
225g/8oz new potatoes, halved
  if large
50g/2oz green beans
115g/4oz young spinach leaves

2 spring onions (scallions), sliced
4 eggs, hard-boiled (hard-cooked)
  and quartered
50g/2oz Bayonne ham,
  cut into strips
juice of ½ lemon
salt and ground black pepper

For the dressing
60ml/4 tbsp olive oil
5ml/1 tsp ground turmeric
5ml/1 tsp ground cumin
50g/2oz/⅓ cup shelled hazelnuts

1 Cook the potatoes in boiling salted water for 10–15 minutes, or until tender, then drain well.

2 Cook the beans in boiling water for 2 minutes, then drain.

3 Toss the potatoes and beans with the spinach and spring onions in a bowl.

4 Arrange the hard-boiled egg quarters on the salad and scatter the strips of ham over the top. Sprinkle with the lemon juice and season with plenty of salt and pepper.

5 To make the dressing, heat all the ingredients in a large frying pan (skillet) and continue to cook, stirring frequently, until the nuts have just turned golden. Pour the hot, nutty dressing over the salad. Serve immediately.

Variation
Replace the potatoes with a 400g/14oz can mixed beans and pulses. Drain and rinse the beans and pulses, then drain again. Toss lightly with the green beans and spring onions.

Egg & bacon Caesar salad: Energy 318kcal/1320kJ; Protein 13.8g; Carbohydrate 6.8g, of which sugars 0.7g; Fat 26.5g, of which saturates 5.8g; Cholesterol 180mg; Calcium 149mg; Fibre 0.3g; Sodium 546mg
Bayonne ham & new potatoes: Energy 323kcal/1341kJ; Protein 12.4g; Carbohydrate 10.9g, of which sugars 2.2g; Fat 25.8g, of which saturates 4.2g; Cholesterol 199mg; Calcium 105mg; Fibre 2.3g; Sodium 270mg

Devilled Ham & Pineapple Salad

This tasty salad, with its crunchy almond topping, can be quickly prepared using store-cupboard items.

Serves 4
225g/8oz wholewheat penne
150ml/¼ pint/⅔ cup natural
  (plain) yogurt
15ml/1 tbsp cider vinegar
5ml/1 tsp wholegrain mustard
large pinch of caster (superfine)
  sugar
30ml/2 tbsp hot mango chutney
115g/4oz cooked lean
  ham, cubed
200g/7oz can pineapple
  chunks, drained
2 celery sticks, chopped
½ green (bell) pepper, seeded
  and diced
15ml/1 tbsp toasted flaked
  almonds, chopped roughly
salt and ground black pepper
crusty bread, to serve

1 Cook the pasta in a large pan of lightly salted boiling water according to the packet instructions, until *al dente*. Drain and rinse thoroughly. Leave to cool.

2 To make the dressing, mix the yogurt, vinegar, mustard, sugar and mango chutney together. Season with salt and pepper.

3 Add the pasta to the dressing and toss lightly, then transfer it to a serving dish.

4 Add the ham, pineapple, celery and green pepper. Sprinkle toasted almonds over the top of the salad.

> **Variations**
> • Although ham and pineapple are a well known and popular combination, don't be afraid to experiment with different ingredients. For example, chicken and fresh mango would be perfect with this dressing, or use left-over roast lamb with fresh apricots.
> • Aim for soft, mellow fruits rather than apples or citrus, so that you still get the lovely juicy sweetness to contrast with the crisp nuts and celery.

Smoked Ham & Bean Salad

If you are serving this bean salad as an accompaniment, offer small portions as it is quite substantial and filling.

Serves 8
175g/6oz dried black-eyed
  beans (peas)
1 onion
1 carrot
225g/8oz smoked ham, diced
3 tomatoes, peeled, seeded
  and diced
salt and ground black pepper

For the dressing
2 garlic cloves, crushed
45ml/3 tbsp olive oil
45ml/3 tbsp red wine vinegar
30ml/2 tbsp vegetable oil
15ml/1 tbsp lemon juice
15ml/1 tbsp chopped fresh basil
15ml/1 tbsp wholegrain mustard
5ml/1 tsp soy sauce
2.5ml/½ tsp dried oregano
2.5ml/½ tsp caster (superfine)
  sugar
1.5ml/¼ tsp Worcestershire sauce
2.5ml/½ tsp chilli sauce

1 Soak the beans in cold water to cover overnight. Drain.

2 Put the beans in a large pan and add the onion and carrot. Cover with fresh cold water and bring to the boil. Lower the heat and simmer for about 1 hour, until the beans are tender.

3 Drain the beans, reserving the onion and carrot. Transfer the beans to a salad bowl.

4 Finely chop the onion and carrot. Toss with the beans. Stir in the ham and tomatoes.

5 To make the dressing, combine all the ingredients in a small bowl and whisk to mix.

6 Pour the dressing over the ham and beans. Season with salt and pepper. Toss to combine, then serve.

> **Variation**
> For speed, use drained, rinsed mixed canned pulses and beans. Cook the onion and carrot until tender and add to the beans.

Devilled ham & pineapple salad: Energy 311kcal/1319kJ; Protein 15.3g; Carbohydrate 55.5g, of which sugars 15.5g; Fat 4.7g, of which saturates 0.8g; Cholesterol 17mg; Calcium 115mg; Fibre 3.2g; Sodium 402mg
Smoked ham & bean salad: Energy 166kcal/698kJ; Protein 10.6g; Carbohydrate 12.9g, of which sugars 3.5g; Fat 8.5g, of which saturates 1.3g; Cholesterol 16mg; Calcium 34mg; Fibre 4.2g; Sodium 380mg

Peruvian Salad

This really is a spectacular salad. It could be served as a side dish or would make a delicious light lunch.

Serves 4
225g/8oz/2 cups cooked long
   grain brown or white rice
15ml/1 tbsp chopped parsley
1 red (bell) pepper, seeded
   and halved
1 small onion, sliced
olive oil, for sprinkling
115g/4oz green beans, halved
50g/2oz/½ cup baby corn on cob
4 quails' eggs, hard-boiled
   (hard-cooked)

25–50g/1–2oz Spanish ham, cut
   into thin slices (optional)
1 small avocado
lemon juice, for sprinkling
75g/3oz mixed salad leaves
15ml/1 tbsp capers
about 10 stuffed olives, halved

For the dressing
1 garlic clove, crushed
60ml/4 tbsp olive oil
45ml/3 tbsp sunflower oil
30ml/2 tbsp lemon juice
45ml/3 tbsp natural (plain) yogurt
2.5ml/½ tsp mustard
2.5ml/½ tsp sugar
salt and ground black pepper

1 To make the dressing, place all the ingredients in a bowl and whisk with a fork until smooth.

2 Put the cooked rice into a large salad bowl and spoon in half the dressing. Add the chopped parsley, stir well and set aside.

3 Preheat the grill (broiler). Place the pepper halves, cut-side down, in a small roasting pan. Add the onion rings. Sprinkle the onion with a little olive oil and grill (broil) for 5–6 minutes until the pepper chars and blisters and the onion turns golden. You may need to stir the onion once or twice so that it grills evenly.

4 Stir the onion into the rice. Put the pepper in a plastic bag, tie up and leave to cool slightly. When cool enough to handle, peel and cut the flesh into thin strips.

5 Cook the green beans in boiling water for 2 minutes, then add the corn and cook for 1–2 minutes more, until tender. Drain both vegetables, refresh them under cold water, then drain again. Place in a large mixing bowl and add the red pepper strips, quails' eggs and ham, if using.

6 Peel the avocado, remove the stone (pit), and cut the flesh into slices or chunks. Sprinkle with the lemon juice.

7 Put the salad leaves in a separate mixing bowl, add the avocado and mix lightly, being careful to keep the avocado pieces intact. Arrange the salad on top of the rice.

8 Stir about 45ml/3 tbsp of the remaining dressing into the green bean and pepper mixture. Pile this on top of the salad. Scatter the capers and stuffed olives on top and serve the salad with the remaining dressing.

> **Cook's Tip**
> *This dish looks particularly attractive if served in a deep, glass salad bowl. Guests can then see the colourful layers.*

Waldorf Ham Salad

Originally this salad consisted of apples, celery and mayonnaise, and was commonly served with duck, ham and goose. This modern-day version often includes meat and is something of a meal in itself.

Serves 4
3 apples
15ml/1 tbsp lemon juice

2 slices cooked ham, each about
   175g/6oz
2 celery sticks
150ml/¼ pint/⅔ cup good
   quality mayonnaise
1 escarole or round
   (butterhead) lettuce
1 small radicchio, finely shredded
½ bunch watercress
45ml/3 tbsp walnut or olive oil
50g/2oz/½ cup broken
   walnuts, toasted
salt and ground black pepper

1 Peel, core, slice and finely shred the apples. Moisten with lemon juice to keep them white. Cut the ham into 5cm/2in strips. Cut the celery stalks into similar-sized pieces.

2 Combine the apples, ham and celery in a bowl. Add the mayonnaise and mix thoroughly.

3 Shred all the salad leaves finely, then moisten with oil. Distribute the leaves between four individual plates. Pile the mayonnaise mixture in the centre, scatter with toasted walnuts, season with salt and pepper and serve.

Peruvian salad: Energy 415kcal/1725kJ; Protein 9.1g; Carbohydrate 52.8g, of which sugars 6.6g; Fat 18.5g, of which saturates 3.2g; Cholesterol 48mg; Calcium 77mg; Fibre 3.3g; Sodium 417mg
Waldorf ham salad: Energy 551kcal/2285kJ; Protein 19.4g; Carbohydrate 9.7g, of which sugars 9.5g; Fat 48.7g, of which saturates 7.2g; Cholesterol 79mg; Calcium 58mg; Fibre 2.6g; Sodium 1233mg

Waldorf Rice Salad

Waldorf Salad takes its name from the Waldorf Hotel in New York, where it was first made. The rice makes this salad slightly more substantial than usual. It can be served as an accompaniment, or as a main meal for two.

Serves 2–4
115g/4oz/generous ½ cup white long grain rice
1 red apple
1 green apple
60ml/4 tbsp lemon juice
3 celery sticks
2–3 slices thick cooked ham
90ml/6 tbsp good quality mayonnaise, preferably home-made
60ml/4 tbsp soured cream
generous pinch of saffron, dissolved in 15ml/1 tbsp hot water
10ml/2 tsp chopped fresh basil
15ml/1 tbsp chopped fresh parsley
several romaine or iceberg lettuce leaves
50g/2oz/½ cup walnuts, roughly chopped
salt and ground black pepper

1 Cook the rice in plenty of boiling salted water until tender. Drain and set aside in a bowl to cool.

2 Cut the apples into quarters, remove the cores and finely slice one red and one green apple quarter. Place the slices in a bowl with half the lemon juice and reserve for the garnish. Peel the remaining apple quarters and cut into fine sticks. Place in a separate bowl and toss with another 15ml/1 tbsp of the fresh lemon juice.

3 Cut the celery into thin strips. Roll up each slice of ham, slice finely and add to the apple sticks, with the celery.

4 Mix together the mayonnaise, soured cream and saffron water. Stir in salt and pepper to taste. Stir into the rice with the herbs. Add the apple and celery and the remaining lemon juice.

5 Arrange the lettuce leaves around the outside of a salad bowl and pile the rice and apple mixture into the centre. Scatter with the chopped walnuts and garnish with fans of the apple slices.

Warm Salad with Ham, Egg & Asparagus

When you think it's too hot for pasta, try serving it in a warm salad. Here it is combined with ham, eggs and asparagus, with a tangy mustard dressing made from the asparagus stems.

Serves 4
450g/1lb asparagus
450g/1lb dried tagliatelle pasta
225g/8oz cooked ham, in 5mm/¼ in thick slices, cut into fingers
2 hard-boiled (hard-cooked) eggs, sliced
50g/2oz fresh Parmesan cheese, shaved
salt and ground black pepper

For the dressing
50g/2oz cooked potato
75ml/5 tbsp extra-virgin olive oil
15ml/1 tbsp lemon juice
10ml/2 tsp Dijon mustard
120ml/4fl oz/½ cup vegetable stock

1 Trim and discard the tough woody part of the asparagus. Cut the spears in half and cook the thicker stems in boiling salted water for 12 minutes. After 6 minutes add the tips. Drain, then refresh under cold water until warm.

2 Finely chop 150g/5oz of the thick asparagus pieces. Place in a food processor with all the dressing ingredients and process until smooth.

3 Cook the pasta in a large pan of lightly salted boiling water according to the packet instructions, until *al dente*. Refresh under cold running water until just luke warm, then drain.

4 Toss the pasta with the asparagus sauce and divide between four plates. Top with the ham, boiled eggs and asparagus tips. Serve with a sprinkling of fresh Parmesan cheese shavings.

Cook's Tip
Try using thin slices of softer Italian cheese, such as Fontina.

Stir-fried Greens & Pork

This warm salad is ideal for using up a small piece of pork fillet. If you prefer, substitute the pork for chicken and the quail's eggs for baby corn cobs.

Serves 4

2 bunches spinach or 1 head Chinese leaves (Chinese cabbage) or 450g/1lb curly cale
3 garlic cloves, crushed
5cm/2in piece fresh root ginger, peeled and cut into matchsticks
15ml/1 tbsp vegetable oil
115g/4oz pork fillet (tenderloin) very finely sliced
8 quail's eggs, hard-boiled (hard-cooked) and shelled
1 fresh chilli, seeded and shredded
30–45ml/2–3 tbsp oyster sauce
15ml/1 tbsp brown sugar
10ml/2 tbsp cornflour (cornstarch), mixed with 50ml/4 tbsp cold water
salt

1 Wash the leaves well and shake them dry. Strip the tender leaves from the stems and tear them into pieces. Discard the lower, tougher part of the stems and slice the remainder evenly, with a sharp knife.

2 Fry the garlic and ginger in the hot oil, without browning, for 1 minute.

3 Add the pork to the wok and keep stirring it in the wok until the meat changes colour.

4 When the meat is cooked, add the sliced stems first and cook them quickly; then add the leaves, quail's eggs and chilli.

5 Spoon in the oyster sauce and a little boiling water, if necessary. Cover and cook for 1–2 minutes only.

6 Remove the cover, stir the mixture and add sugar and salt to taste. Stir in the cornflour and water mixture and toss thoroughly. Cook until the mixture is coated in glossy sauce.

7 Serve immediately, while the salad is still very hot and the colours are bright and jewel-like.

Frankfurter Salad with Mustard Dressing

This is a last-minute salad, ideal for a midweek meal.

Serves 4

675g/1½lb small new potatoes, scrubbed or scraped
2 eggs
350g/12oz frankfurters
1 round (butterhead) or frisée lettuce
225g/8oz young spinach leaves, stems removed
salt and ground black pepper

For the dressing

45ml/3 tbsp safflower oil
30ml/2 tbsp olive oil
15ml/1 tbsp white wine vinegar
10ml/2 tsp mustard
5ml/1 tsp caraway seeds, crushed

1 Bring the potatoes to the boil in salted water and simmer for about 15 minutes, or until tender. Drain, cover and keep warm. Hard-boil the eggs for 12 minutes. Refresh in cold water, shell and cut into quarters.

2 Score the frankfurter skins cork-screw fashion with a small knife, then cover with boiling water and simmer for about 5 minutes to heat through. Drain well, cover and keep warm.

3 To make the dressing, place all the ingredients in a screw-top jar and shake vigorously to combine.

4 Moisten the salad leaves with half of the dressing and divide between four large serving plates. Moisten the warm potatoes and frankfurters with the remainder of the dressing and scatter over the salad.

5 Finish the salad with sections of hard-boiled egg, season with salt and pepper and serve warm.

> **Cook's Tip**
> This salad has a German slant to it and calls for a sweet-and-sour German-style mustard. American mustard is similar.

Stir-fried greens & pork: Energy 111Kcal/465kJ; Protein 10.3g; Carbohydrate 8.9g, of which sugars 8.7g; fat 4g, of which saturates 0.5g; Cholesterol 20mg; Calcium 196mg; Fibre 2.5g; Sodium 358mg
Frankfurter salad: Energy 561kcal/2336kJ; Protein 20.5g; Carbohydrate 31g, of which sugars 5.9g; Fat 40.4g, of which saturates 11g; Cholesterol 162mg; Calcium 160mg; Fibre 3.9g; Sodium 1014mg

Potato Salad with Garlic Sausage

In this delicious and hearty salad, the potatoes are moistened with a little white wine before adding the vinaigrette. Great served as part of a cold spread.

Serves 4
450g/1lb small waxy potatoes
30–45ml/2–3 tbsp dry
　white wine
2 shallots, finely chopped
15ml/1 tbsp chopped
　fresh parsley
15ml/1 tbsp chopped
　fresh tarragon
175g/6oz cooked garlic sausage
fresh flat leaf parsley sprig,
　to garnish

For the vinaigrette
10ml/2 tsp Dijon mustard
15ml/1 tbsp tarragon vinegar or
　white wine vinegar
75ml/5 tbsp extra-virgin olive oil
salt and ground black pepper

1 Scrub the potatoes. Boil in salted water for 10–12 minutes, until tender. Drain and refresh under cold running water.

2 Peel the potatoes if you like, or leave in their skins, and cut into 5mm/¼ in slices. Sprinkle with the wine and shallots.

3 To make the vinaigrette, mix the mustard and vinegar in a small bowl, then whisk in the oil, 15ml/1 tbsp at a time. Season with salt and pepper and pour over the potatoes.

4 Add the chopped parsley and tarragon to the potatoes and toss until well mixed.

5 Slice the garlic sausage thinly and toss with the potatoes. Season the salad with salt and pepper to taste.

6 Serve at room temperature, garnished with a sprig of parsley.

Variation
The potatoes are also delicious served on their own, simply dressed with vinaigrette, and perhaps accompanied by marinated herrings.

Korean Chicken Salad

Hot, spicy, garlicky and a little sweet, the chicken is perfectly tempered by the mild lettuce leaves in this attractive salad.

Serves 4
900g/2lb chicken breast fillet or
　boneless thighs
2 round (butterhead) lettuces
vegetable oil
4 spring onions (scallions),
　shredded

For the marinade
60ml/4 tsp gochujang chilli paste
45ml/3 tbsp mirin or rice wine
15ml/1 tbsp dark soy sauce
4 garlic cloves, crushed
25ml/5 tsp sesame oil
15ml/1 tbsp grated (shredded)
　fresh root ginger
2 spring onions (scallions),
　finely chopped
10ml/2 tsp ground black pepper
15ml/1 tbsp lemonade

1 Combine all the marinade ingredients in a large bowl.

2 Cut the chosen chicken into bitesize pieces, add to the bowl and stir to coat it with the marinade. Transfer to an airtight container and marinate in the refrigerator for about 3 hours.

3 Remove the outer leaves from the heads of lettuce, keeping them whole. Rinse well, drain, and place on a serving dish.

4 Lightly coat a heavy griddle pan or frying pan (skillet) with vegetable oil and place it over a medium heat (the griddle can also be used over charcoal if you are barbecuing). Griddle or fry the chicken for 15 minutes, or until the meat is cooked and has turned a deep brown. Increase the heat briefly to scorch the chicken and give it a smoky flavour.

5 Serve by wrapping the chicken pieces in lettuce leaves with a few shredded spring onions.

Cook's tip
If you are unable to obtain gochujang chilli paste from your local Asian food store, substitute a regular chilli purée.

Potato salad: Energy 315kcal/1313kJ; Protein 8.3g; Carbohydrate 22.3g, of which sugars 3.1g; Fat 21.6g, of which saturates 4.4g; Cholesterol 50mg; Calcium 45mg; Fibre 2.3g; Sodium 372mg
Korean chicken salad: Energy 279Kcal/1178kJ; Protein 55g; Carbohydrate 2g, of which sugars 2g; Fat 5.7g, of which saturates 1.1g; Cholesterol 158mg; Calcium 39mg; Fibre 0.9g; Sodium 405mg

Crunchy Salad with Black Pudding

Fried until crisp, slices of black pudding are extremely good in salad, particularly with crunchy croûtons and sweet cherry tomatoes.

Serves 4

250g/9oz black pudding, sliced
1 focaccia loaf, plain or flavoured
  with sun-dried tomatoes, garlic
  and herbs, cut into chunks
45ml/3 tbsp olive oil
1 cos or romaine lettuce, torn into
  bitesize pieces
250g/9oz cherry tomatoes, halved

For the dressing
juice of 1 lemon
90ml/6 tbsp olive oil
10ml/2 tsp French mustard
15ml/1 tbsp clear honey
30ml/2 tbsp chopped fresh herbs,
salt and ground black pepper

1 Dry-fry the black pudding in a large, non-stick frying pan (skillet) for 5–10 minutes, or until browned and crisp, turning occasionally. Remove the black pudding from the pan using a slotted spoon and drain on kitchen paper.

2 Cut the focaccia into chunks. Add the oil to the juices in the frying pan and cook the focaccia cubes in two batches, turning often, until golden on all sides. Drain the focaccia on kitchen paper.

3 Mix together the focaccia, black pudding, lettuce and cherry tomatoes in a large serving bowl.

4 Whisk together the dressing ingredients, seasoning with salt and pepper. Toss the dressing into the salad and serve.

Variation
If you are unsure of black pudding, then try this recipe with spicy chorizo or Kabanos sausages instead. Cut them into thick diagonal slices before cooking. Use another crusty bread, such as ciabatta, for the croûtons, if you prefer.

Mushroom, Bean & Chorizo Salad

This combination of spicy sausage, tender, sweet beans and delicate mushrooms is quite delicious. Serve as an accompaniment to plain fish or chicken dishes, or offer with crusty bread as a hearty lunch or supper dish.

Serves 4

225g/8oz shelled broad
  (fava) beans
175g/6oz frying chorizo
60ml/4 tbsp extra-virgin olive oil
225g/8oz/3 cups brown cap
  (cremini) mushrooms, sliced
60ml/4 tbsp chopped fresh chives
salt and ground black pepper

1 Cook the broad beans in a pan of salted boiling water for 7–8 minutes. Drain and refresh under cold water.

2 Remove the skin from the sausage. If it doesn't peel off easily, score along the length of the sausage with a sharp knife first. Cut the chorizo into small chunks. Heat the oil in a small pan, add the chorizo and cook for 2–3 minutes.

3 Put the sliced mushrooms in a bowl and add the chorizo and oil. Toss to combine, then leave to cool.

4 If the beans are large, peel away the tough outer skins. Stir the beans and half the chives into the mushroom mixture, and season with salt and pepper to taste. Serve at room temperature, garnished with the remaining chives.

Cook's Tip
Although peeling the skins from broad (fava) beans can be time consuming, it is well worth it. Beans with tough, bitter skins will spoil the delicate taste and texture of this lovely salad.

Variation
If you prefer, lightly sauté the mushrooms, then add them to the drained chorizo.

Crunchy salad: Energy 702kcal/2936kJ; Protein 17.2g; Carbohydrate 67.4g, of which sugars 8.3g; Fat 42.3g, of which saturates 9.5g; Cholesterol 43mg; Calcium 204mg; Fibre 3.2g; Sodium 1132mg

Mushroom, bean & chorizo salad: Energy 283kcal/1174kJ; Protein 9.7g; Carbohydrate 11.9g, of which sugars 1.6g; Fat 22.2g, of which saturates 6.1g; Cholesterol 18mg; Calcium 56mg; Fibre 4.5g; Sodium 362mg

Warm Chorizo & Spinach Salad

Spanish chorizo sausage contributes an intense spiciness to this hearty warm salad. Spinach leaves have enough flavour to compete with the chorizo and add extra colour.

Serves 4
225g/8oz baby spinach leaves
90ml/6 tbsp extra-virgin olive oil
150g/5oz chorizo sausage, very thinly sliced
30ml/2 tbsp sherry vinegar
salt and ground black pepper

1 Discard any tough stalks from the spinach. Pour the oil into a large frying pan (skillet) and add the chorizo sausage. Cook gently for 3 minutes, until the sausage slices start to shrivel slightly and begin to colour.

2 Add the spinach leaves and remove the pan from the heat. Toss the spinach in the warm oil until it just starts to wilt.

3 Add the sherry vinegar and a little salt and pepper. Toss the ingredients briefly, then serve immediately, while still warm.

Variation
Watercress or rocket (arugula) could be used instead of the spinach, if you prefer. For an added dimension use a flavoured olive oil – rosemary, garlic or chilli oil would work perfectly.

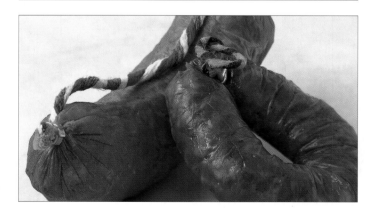

Pasta Salad with Salami

This salad is simple to make and it can be prepared in advance for a perfect starter or, served in more generous quantities, to make a satisfying main course.

Serves 4
225g/8oz dried fusilli pasta
275g/10oz jar charcoal-roasted peppers in oil
115g/4oz/1 cup pitted black olives
4 sun-dried tomatoes, quartered
115g/4oz Roquefort cheese, crumbled
10 slices peppered salami, cut into strips
115g/4oz packet mixed leaf salad
30ml/2 tbsp white wine vinegar
30ml/2 tbsp chopped fresh oregano
2 garlic cloves, crushed
salt and ground black pepper

1 Cook the pasta in a large pan of lightly salted boiling water according to the instructions on the packet, until al dente. Drain thoroughly and rinse with cold water, then drain again.

2 Drain the peppers and reserve 60ml/4 tbsp of the oil for the dressing. Cut the peppers into long, fine strips and mix them with the olives, sun-dried tomatoes and Roquefort in a large bowl. Stir in the pasta and peppered salami.

3 Divide the salad leaves between four individual bowls and spoon the pasta salad on top. Whisk the reserved oil with the wine vinegar, oregano and garlic. Season with salt and pepper to taste, then spoon over the salad and serve immediately.

Cook's Tip
Be careful not to overcook the pasta; it must still retain bite.

Variation
Use chicken instead of the salami and cubes of Brie in place of the Roquefort.

Warm chorizo & spinach salad: Energy 300kcal/1238kJ; Protein 5.6g; Carbohydrate 4.5g, of which sugars 1.4g; Fat 29g, of which saturates 7g; Cholesterol 18mg; Calcium 111mg; Fibre 1.4g; Sodium 364mg
Pasta salad: Energy 429kcal/1797kJ; Protein 17.8g; Carbohydrate 46.7g, of which sugars 6.6g; Fat 20.3g, of which saturates 8.9g; Cholesterol 37mg; Calcium 188mg; Fibre 3.9g; Sodium 1341mg

Pasta Salad with Salami & Olives

Garlic and herb dressing gives a Mediterranean flavour to a handful of ingredients from the store-cupboard and refrigerator, making this an excellent salad for winter.

Serves 4
225g/8oz/2 cups dried gnocchi or conchiglie pasta
50g/2oz/½ cup pitted black olives, quartered lengthwise

75g/3oz thinly sliced salami, skin removed, diced
½ small red onion, finely chopped
1 large handful fresh basil leaves

For the dressing
60ml/4 tbsp extra-virgin olive oil
good pinch of sugar, to taste
juice of ½ lemon
5ml/1 tsp Dijon mustard
10ml/2 tsp dried oregano
1 garlic clove, crushed
salt and ground black pepper

1 Cook the pasta in a large pan of lightly salted boiling water according to the packet instructions, until *al dente*.

2 Meanwhile, make the dressing for the pasta. Put all the ingredients for the dressing in a large bowl with a little salt and pepper to taste, and whisk well to mix.

3 Drain the pasta thoroughly, add it to the bowl of dressing and toss well to mix. Leave the pasta to cool, stirring occasionally.

4 When the pasta is cold, add the olives, salami and red onion. Add the basil leaves, adjust the seasoning, and toss to mix well.

Cook's Tip
There are many different types of Italian salami that can be used. Salame napoletano is coarse cut and peppery, while salame milanese is fine cut and mild in flavour.

Variation
Grate (shred) Parmesan into the pasta after you season it.

Beef & Sweet Potato Salad

This salad makes a good main dish for a summer buffet, especially if the beef has been cut into strips.

Serves 6–8
800g/1¾lb fillet of beef
5ml/1 tsp black peppercorns, crushed
10ml/2 tsp chopped fresh thyme
60ml/4 tbsp olive oil
450g/1lb orange-fleshed sweet potato, peeled and sliced
salt and ground black pepper

For the dressing
1 garlic clove, chopped
15g/½oz flat leaf parsley
30ml/2 tbsp chopped fresh coriander (cilantro)
15ml/1 tbsp small salted capers, rinsed
½–1 fresh green chilli, seeded and chopped
10ml/2 tsp Dijon mustard
10–15ml/2–3 tsp white wine vinegar
75ml/5 tbsp extra-virgin olive oil
2 shallots, finely chopped

1 Roll the beef fillet in the crushed peppercorns and thyme, then set aside to marinate for a few hours. Preheat the oven to 200°C/400°F/Gas 6.

2 Heat half the olive oil in a frying pan (skillet). Add the beef and brown it all over, turning frequently, to seal it. Place on a baking tray and cook in the oven for 10–15 minutes. Remove from the oven, and cover with foil, then leave to rest for 10–15 minutes.

3 Meanwhile, preheat the grill (broiler). Brush the sweet potato with the remaining olive oil, season to taste with salt and pepper, and grill (broil) for about 5–6 minutes on each side, until browned. Cut into strips and place them in a bowl. Cut the beef into slices or strips and toss with the sweet potato.

4 To make the dressing, process the garlic, parsley, coriander, capers, chilli, mustard and 10ml/2 tsp of the vinegar in a food processor until chopped. With the motor still running, gradually pour in the oil to make a smooth dressing. Season and add more vinegar, to taste. Stir in the shallots.

5 Toss the dressing into the sweet potatoes and beef and leave to stand for up to 2 hours before serving.

Marinated Beef & Potato Salad

Bresaola & Onion Salad

The beef steak needs to marinate overnight, but once that has been done, this dish is very quick to assemble and makes a substantial main meal.

Serves 6
900g/2lb sirloin steak
3 large white potatoes
1/2 red (bell) pepper, seeded and diced
1/2 green (bell) pepper, seeded and diced
1 small red onion, finely chopped

2 garlic cloves, crushed
4 spring onions (scallions), diagonally sliced
1 small cos or romaine lettuce, leaves torn
salt and ground black pepper
olive oil, to serve
Parmesan cheese shavings, to serve

For the marinade
120ml/4fl oz/1/2 cup olive oil
120ml/4fl oz/1/2 cup red wine vinegar
90ml/6 tbsp soy sauce

1 Place the beef in a large, non-metallic container. Mix together the marinade ingredients. Season with pepper and pour over the meat.

2 Cover the meat and leave to marinate for several hours, or preferably overnight.

3 Drain the marinade from the meat and pat the joint dry. Preheat the frying pan (skillet), cut the meat carefully into thin slices and fry for a few minutes until just cooked on each side, but still slightly pink. Set aside to cool.

4 Using a melon baller, scoop out rounds from each potato. Boil in lightly salted water for 5 minutes or until just tender.

5 Drain the potato and transfer to a bowl. Add the peppers, onion, garlic, spring onions and lettuce leaves. Season with salt and pepper and toss together.

6 Transfer the potato and pepper mixture to a plate with the beef. Drizzle with a little extra olive oil and serve topped with Parmesan shavings.

Bresaola is an Italian speciality. It is raw beef which has been salted in much the same way as *prosciutto di Parma*. In this salad, it is combined with sweet, juicy onions.

Serves 4
2 onions, peeled
75–90ml/5–6 tbsp olive oil
juice of 1 lemon
12 thin slices bresaola
75g/3oz rocket (arugula), washed and dried
salt and ground black pepper

1 Slice each onion into eight wedges through the root. Arrange the wedges in a single layer in a flameproof dish. Brush them with a little of the olive oil and season with salt and pepper.

2 Preheat the grill (broiler). Place the onion wedges under the hot grill and cook for about 8–10 minutes, turning once, until just beginning to soften and turn golden brown at the edges.

3 Meanwhile, to make the dressing, mix together the lemon juice and 60ml/4 tbsp of the olive oil. Add salt and black pepper to taste and whisk until thoroughly blended. Pour the lemon dressing over the hot onions, mix to coat and leave until cold.

4 Divide the bresaola slices among four individual serving plates and arrange the onions and rocket on top. Spoon over any remaining dressing and serve immediately.

Marinated beef & potato salad: Energy 296kcal/1247kJ; Protein 38g; Carbohydrate 20.1g, of which sugars 5g; Fat 7.6g, of which saturates 3.2g; Cholesterol 77mg; Calcium 40mg; Fibre 2.3g; Sodium 120mg
Bresaola & onion salad: Energy 204kcal/842kJ; Protein 7.4g; Carbohydrate 8.2g, of which sugars 5.9g; Fat 15.9g, of which saturates 2.9g; Cholesterol 15mg; Calcium 58mg; Fibre 1.8g; Sodium 45mg

Beef & Herby Pasta Salad

Lean, tender beef is marinated with ginger and garlic, then lightly grilled and served warm with a herby pasta salad.

Serves 6
450g/1lb beef fillet
450g/1lb fresh tagliatelle with
   sun-dried tomatoes and herbs
115g/4oz cherry tomatoes, halved
½ cucumber, halved lengthwise,
   seeds removed and cut into
   thin crescents

For the marinade
15ml/1 tbsp soy sauce
15ml/1 tbsp sherry
5ml/1 tsp grated (shredded)
   fresh root ginger
1 garlic clove, crushed

For the herb dressing
30–45ml/2–3 tbsp horseradish
   sauce
150ml/¼ pint/⅔ cup natural
   (plain) yogurt
1 garlic clove, crushed
30–45ml/2–3 tbsp chopped fresh
   mixed herbs such as chives,
   parsley, thyme
salt and ground black pepper

1 To make the marinade, mix all the ingredients together in a shallow dish. Add the beef fillet and turn to coat well. Cover with clear film (plastic wrap) and leave for 30 minutes.

2 Preheat the grill (broiler). Lift the fillet out of the marinade and pat it dry with kitchen paper. Place on a grill rack and cook for 8 minutes on each side, basting with the marinade.

3 Transfer the fillet to a plate, cover with foil and leave to stand for 20 minutes.

4 To make the herb dressing, put all the ingredients into a bowl and mix thoroughly.

5 Cook the pasta in a large pan of lightly salted boiling water according to the packet instructions, until *al dente*. Drain well, rinse under cold running water and leave to dry.

6 Put the pasta, tomatoes, cucumber and dressing into a mixing bowl and toss to coat. Slice the beef and arrange on individual serving plates with the pasta salad. Serve warm.

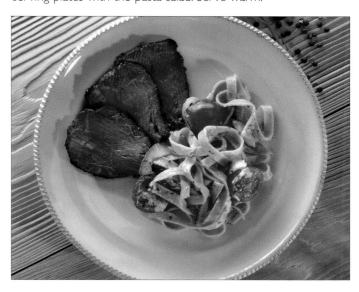

Rockburger Salad with Sesame Croûtons

This salad plays on the ingredients that make up the all-American beefburger in a sesame seed bun.

Serves 4
900g/2lb lean minced
   (ground) beef
1 egg
1 onion, finely chopped
10ml/2 tsp Dijon mustard
2.5ml/½ tsp celery salt

115g/4 oz Roquefort or other
   blue cheese
1 large sesame seed loaf
45ml/3 tbsp olive oil
1 small iceberg lettuce
50g/2oz rocket (arugula) or
   watercress leaves
120ml/4fl oz/½ cup
   French dressing
4 ripe tomatoes, quartered
4 large spring onions
   (scallions), sliced
ground black pepper

1 Place the minced beef, egg, onion, mustard, celery salt and pepper in a mixing bowl. Combine thoroughly. Divide the mixture into 16 equal portions.

2 Flatten the pieces between two sheets of polythene or waxed paper to form 13cm/5in rounds. Place 15g/½oz of the blue cheese on eight of the burgers. Sandwich with the remaining burgers and press the edges firmly. Chill, layered between sheets of waxed paper, until ready to cook.

3 To make the sesame croûtons, preheat the grill (broiler) to medium heat. Remove the sesame seed crust from the loaf, then cut the crust into short fingers. Moisten with olive oil and toast evenly for 10–15 minutes.

4 Grill (boil) the burgers for 10 minutes, turning once.

5 Toss the lettuce and rocket leaves with the French dressing, then divide between four large serving plates. Place two rockburgers in the centre of each plate and arrange the tomatoes, spring onions and sesame croûtons around the edge. Serve immediately.

Beef & herby pasta salad: Energy 419kcal/1770kJ; Protein 27.9g; Carbohydrate 59.8g, of which sugars 6.4g; Fat 9.3g, of which saturates 3.2g; Cholesterol 45mg; Calcium 83mg; Fibre 2.8g; Sodium 313mg
Rockburger salad: Energy 1259kcal/5247kJ; Protein 66.1g; Carbohydrate 69.8g, of which sugars 8.3g; Fat 74.6g, of which saturates 26.5g; Cholesterol 204mg; Calcium 359mg; Fibre 4.5g; Sodium 1528mg

"Poor Boy" Steak Salad

"Poor Boy" started life in the Italian Creole community of New Orleans, when the poor survived on sandwiches filled with scraps. Today the sandwich is filled with tender beef steak and other goodies. This is a salad version of "Poor Boy".

Serves 4
4 sirloin or rump steaks,
    each about 175g/6oz
1 escarole lettuce
1 bunch watercress
4 tomatoes, quartered
4 large gherkins, sliced
4 spring onions (scallions), sliced
4 canned artichoke hearts, halved
175g/6oz button mushrooms,
    sliced
12 green olives
120ml/4fl oz/½ cup
    French dressing
salt and ground black pepper

1 Preheat the grill (broiler). Season the steaks with black pepper. Cook under the grill for 6–8 minutes, turning once, until medium-rare. Cover and leave to rest in a warm place.

2 Combine the lettuce and watercress leaves with the tomatoes, gherkins, spring onions, artichoke hearts, mushrooms and olives and toss with the French dressing.

3 Divide the salad between four individual plates. Slice each steak diagonally and arrange over the salad. Season with salt.

Strawberry & Smoked Venison Salad

The combination of strawberries, balsamic vinegar and smoked venison creates a perfect *ménage à trois*. The tang of the vinegar sets off the sweetness of the strawberries, which must be ripe, and adds a fruity contrast to the rich, dry, smoky venison.

Serves 4
12 ripe Scottish strawberries

2.5ml/½ tsp caster (superfine)
    sugar
5ml/1 tsp balsamic vinegar
8 thin slices of smoked venison
mixed salad leaves

For the dressing
10ml/2 tsp olive oil
5ml/1 tsp balsamic vinegar
splash of strawberry wine
    (optional)
salt and ground black pepper

1 Slice the strawberries vertically into three or four pieces then place in a bowl with the sugar and balsamic vinegar. Leave for 30 minutes.

2 Meanwhile, make the dressing. Place the olive oil and balsamic vinegar in a small bowl and whisking together with the wine, if using. Add salt and ground black pepper to taste.

3 Cut the smoked venison into little strips. Mix the salad leaves together, then toss with the dressing.

4 Divide the salad between four plates and sprinkle with the strawberries and venison.

Cook's Tips
• *Suitable salad leaves include lollo rosso for colour, rocket (arugula) and lamb's lettuce (corn salad) for a peppery flavour and colour, and Little Gem (Bibb) for crunch.*
• *The sugar brings out the moisture in the strawberries, which combines with the balsamic vinegar to creates a lovely shiny coat. Do not leave them to stand for too long as they can become tired-looking – 30 minutes is about right.*

"Poor boy" steak salad: Energy 573kcal/2379kJ; Protein 43.2g; Carbohydrate 6g, of which sugars 5.8g; Fat 35.1g, of which saturates 10.4g; Cholesterol 102mg; Calcium 105mg; Fibre 3.9g; Sodium 990mg
Strawberry & smoked venison salad: Energy 116Kcal/486kJ; Protein 11.6g; Carbohydrate 3.1g, of which sugars 3.1g; fat 6.8g, of which saturates 1.2g; Cholesterol 25mg; Calcium 16mg; Fibre 0.6g; Sodium 31mg

Saeng Wa of Grilled Pork

Grilled, tender pork is tossed with a delicious sweet-sour sauce to make a marvellous warm salad.

Serves 4
30ml/2 tbsp dark soy sauce
15ml/1 tbsp clear honey
400g/14oz pork fillet (tenderloin)
6 shallots, very thinly
   sliced lengthwise
1 lemon grass stalk, thinly sliced
5 kaffir lime leaves, thinly sliced
5cm/2in piece fresh root ginger,
   peeled and sliced into fine
   shreds
½ fresh long fresh red chilli,
   seeded and sliced into fine
   shreds
small bunch fresh coriander
   (cilantro), chopped

For the dressing
30ml/2 tbsp palm sugar (jaggery)
   or light muscovado (brown)
   sugar
30ml/2 tbsp Thai fish sauce
juice of 2 limes
20ml/4 tsp thick tamarind juice,
   made by mixing tamarind paste
   with warm water

1 Preheat the grill (broiler) to medium. Mix the soy sauce with the honey in a small bowl or jug (pitcher) and stir until the honey has completely dissolved.

2 Using a sharp knife, cut the pork fillet lengthwise into quarters to make four long, thick strips.

3 Place the pork strips in a grill pan. Brush generously with the soy sauce and honey mixture, then grill (broil) for about 10–15 minutes, until cooked through and tender. Turn the strips over frequently and baste with the soy sauce and honey mixture.

4 Transfer the cooked pork strips to a board. Slice the meat across the grain, then shred it with a fork. Place in a large bowl and add the shallot slices, lemon grass, kaffir lime leaves, ginger, chilli and chopped coriander.

5 To make the dressing, place the sugar, fish sauce, lime juice and tamarind juice in a bowl. Whisk until the sugar has completely dissolved. Pour the dressing over the pork mixture and toss well to mix, then serve.

Thai Beef Salad

All the ingredients for this traditional Thai dish – known as *yam nua yang* – are widely available in larger supermarkets.

Serves 4
675g/1½lb fillet or rump steak
30ml/2 tbsp olive oil
2 small mild fresh red chillies,
   seeded and sliced
225g/8oz/3¼ cups shiitake
   mushrooms, sliced

For the dressing
3 spring onions (scallions),
finely chopped
2 garlic cloves, finely chopped
juice of 1 lime
15–30ml/1–2 tbsp fish or oyster
   sauce, to taste
5ml/1 tsp soft light brown sugar
30ml/2 tbsp chopped fresh
   coriander (cilantro)

To serve
1 cos or romaine lettuce, torn
175g/6oz cherry tomatoes, halved
5cm/2in piece cucumber, peeled,
   halved and thinly sliced
45ml/3 tbsp toasted
   sesame seeds

1 Preheat the grill (broiler) until hot, then cook the steak for 2–4 minutes on each side depending on how well done you like steak. (In Thailand, the beef is traditionally served quite rare.) Leave to cool for at least 15 minutes.

2 Use a very sharp knife to slice the meat as thinly as possible and place the slices in a bowl.

3 Heat the olive oil in a non-stick pan. Add the red chillies and mushrooms and cook for 5 minutes, stirring occasionally.

4 Turn off the heat and add the grilled steak to the pan. Stir well to coat the beef slices in the chilli and mushroom mixture.

5 Stir all the ingredients for the dressing together, then pour over the meat mixture and toss gently.

6 Arrange the salad ingredients on a serving plate. Spoon the warm steak mixture in the centre and sprinkle the sesame seeds over. Serve at once.

Saeng wa of grilled pork: Energy 190kcal/797kJ; Protein 22.9g; Carbohydrate 15.7g, of which sugars 13.9g; Fat 4.3g, of which saturates 1.4g; Cholesterol 63mg; Calcium 56mg; Fibre 1.7g; Sodium 336mg
Thai beef salad: Energy 381kcal/1591kJ; Protein 39.8g; Carbohydrate 4.1g, of which sugars 3.8g; Fat 23g, of which saturates 6.6g; Cholesterol 103mg; Calcium 105mg; Fibre 2.5g; Sodium 352mg

Thai-style Rare Beef & Mango Salad

This simplified version of Thai beef salad is especially tasty served with little bowls of fresh coriander leaves, chopped spring onions and peanuts for sprinkling at the table.

Serves 4
450g/1lb sirloin steak
45ml/3 tbsp garlic-infused olive oil
45ml/3 tbsp soy sauce
2 mangoes, peeled, stoned (pitted) and finely sliced
ground black pepper

1 Put the steak in a shallow, non-metallic dish and pour over the oil and soy sauce. Season with pepper and turn the steaks to coat in the marinade. Cover and chill for 2 hours.

2 Heat a griddle pan until hot. Remove the steak from the marinade and place on the griddle pan. Cook for 3–5 minutes on each side, moving the steak halfway through if you want a criss-cross pattern.

3 Transfer the steak to a board and leave to rest for 5–10 minutes. Meanwhile, pour the marinade into the pan and cook for a few seconds, then remove from the heat.

4 Thinly slice the steak and arrange on four serving plates with the mangoes. Drizzle over the pan juices and serve immediately.

Seared Beef Salad in a Lime Dressing

Versions of this dish are enjoyed all over South-east Asia. In this Indo-Chinese favourite, strips of seared beef are flavoured with lime and chilli, then tossed with crunchy beansprouts and fresh herbs.

Serves 4
about 7.5ml/1½ tsp vegetable oil
450g/1lb beef fillet, cut into steaks 2.5cm/1in thick
115g/4oz/½ cup beansprouts
1 bunch each fresh basil and mint, stalks removed, leaves shredded
1 lime, cut into slices, to serve

For the dressing
grated (shredded) rind and juice (about 80ml/3fl oz) of 2 limes
30ml/2 tbsp Thai fish sauce
30ml/2 tbsp raw cane sugar
2 garlic cloves, crushed
2 lemon grass stalks, finely sliced
2 fresh red Serrano chillies, seeded and finely sliced

1 To make the dressing, beat the lime rind, juice and fish sauce in a bowl with the sugar, until the sugar dissolves. Stir in the garlic, lemon grass and chillies and set aside.

2 Pour a little oil into a heavy pan and rub it over the base with a piece of kitchen paper. Heat the pan and sear the steaks for 1–2 minutes each side.

3 Transfer seared steaks to a board and leave to cool a little. Using a sharp knife, cut the meat into thin slices. Toss the slices in the dressing, cover and leave to marinate for 1–2 hours.

4 Drain the meat of any excess juice and transfer it to a wide serving bowl. Add the beansprouts and herbs and toss it all together. Serve with lime slices to squeeze over.

Cook's Tip
It is worth buying an excellent-quality piece of tender fillet steak for this recipe as the meat is only just seared.

Rare beef & mango salad: Energy 286kcal/1200kJ; Protein 27.4g; Carbohydrate 14.7g, of which sugars 14.4g; Fat 13.5g, of which saturates 3.5g; Cholesterol 57mg; Calcium 19mg; Fibre 2.6g; Sodium 615mg
Seared beef salad: Energy 233Kcal/979kJ; Protein 26g; carbohydate 12g, of which sugars 9g; Fat 9g, of which saturates 3g; Cholesterol 69mg; Calcium 74mg; Fibre 0.5g; Sodium 400mg

Bamboo Shoot Salad with Persimmon & Soy Dressing

Persimmon adds an appetizing sweetness to this beautiful salad.

Serves 1–2
200g/7oz bamboo shoots
2 shitake mushrooms, soaked in
 warm water for about 30
 minutes until softened
50g/2oz beef flank, thinly sliced
25ml/1½ tbsp vegetable oil
90g/3½oz/½ cup beansprouts
1 egg, beaten
90g/3½oz watercress or
 rocket (arugula)
salt
½ red chilli, seeded and thinly
 sliced, to garnish

For the seasoning
7.5ml/1½ tsp dark soy sauce
10g/¼oz red persimmon,
 finely chopped
½ spring onion (scallion),
 finely chopped
1 garlic clove, crushed
5ml/1 tsp sesame seeds
2.5ml/½ tsp sesame oil
ground white pepper

For the dressing
60ml/4 tbsp dark soy sauce
60ml/4 tbsp water
30ml/2 tbsp rice vinegar
40g/1½ oz red persimmon, finely
 chopped
5ml/1 tsp sesame seeds

1 When the mushrooms are soft, drain and thinly slice them, discarding the stems. Put them, with the beef slices, in a bowl. add the seasoning ingredients and mix well.

2 Stir-fry the beef and mushrooms in 15ml/1 tbsp of oil over a medium heat until cooked, then remove, cool and chill.

3 Trim the beansprouts and blanch in boiling water for 3 minutes. Drain. Do the same to the chopped bamboo shoots.

4 Combine all the dressing ingredients in a bowl and set aside.

5 Coat a frying pan (skillet) with oil, season the egg and make a thin omelette. Remove from the pan and cut into thin strips.

6 Arrange the beef on a plate with the bamboo shoots, watercress or rocket, and beansprouts. Garnish with the sliced chilli and egg strips before serving with the dressing.

Cambodian Raw Beef Salad with Peanuts

This Cambodian beef salad has a distinctive taste as it uses the flavoursome fish extract, *tuk prahoc*, and roasted peanuts. Serve with rice noodles and stir-fried vegetables for an impressive dinner party dish.

Serves 4
45ml/3 tbsp tuk prahoc
juice of 3 limes
45ml/3 tbsp palm sugar
2 lemon grass stalks, trimmed
 and finely sliced

2 shallots, peeled and finely sliced
2 garlic cloves, finely chopped
450g/1lb beef fillet, very finely
 sliced
1 fresh red chilli, seeded and
 finely sliced
50g/2oz roasted, unsalted
 peanuts, finely chopped or
 crushed
1 small bunch fresh coriander
 (cilantro), finely chopped, plus
 extra leaves, to garnish

1 In a bowl, beat 30ml/2 tbsp tuk prahoc with the juice of 2 limes and 30ml/2 tbsp of the sugar, until the sugar has dissolved. Add the lemon grass, shallots and garlic and mix well.

2 Toss the lime mixture with the slices of beef, then cover and place in the refrigerator for 1–2 hours.

3 Meanwhile, in a small bowl, beat the remaining tuk prahoc with the juice of the third lime. Stir in the remaining sugar, until it dissolves, and put aside.

4 Put the beef slices, drained of any remaining liquid, in a clean bowl. Add the chilli, peanuts and coriander. Toss with the dressing, garnish with coriander leaves and serve immediately.

Cook's Tip
Tuk prahoc *is a fish paste used in Cambodian cooking. If you cannot find it in specialist stores, use Thai fish sauce instead.*

Bamboo shoot salad: Energy 268Kcal/1115kJ; Protein 17g; Carbohydrate 9.1g, of which sugars 6.1g; Fat 18.6g, of which saturates3.6g; Cholesterol 119mg; Calcium 164mg; Fibre 3.5g; Sodium 2489mg
Cambodian raw beef salad: Energy 321Kcal/1343kJ; Protein 29g; Carbohydrate 15g, of which sugars 14g; Fat 16g, of which saturates 5g; Cholesterol 65mg; Calcium 48mg; Fibre 1.6g; Sodium 78mg

Fresh Fruit Salad

A light and refreshing fruit salad makes a healthy and nutritious end to a meal. The natural fruit sugars are kinder to the body than refined sugars.

Serves 6
2 peaches
2 oranges
2 eating apples
16–20 strawberries
30ml/2 tbsp lemon juice
15–30ml/1–2 tbsp orange
    flower water
a few fresh mint leaves,
    to decorate

1 Place the peaches in a bowl and pour over boiling water. Leave to stand for 1 minute, then lift out with a slotted spoon, peel, stone (pit) and cut the flesh into thick slices.

2 Peel the oranges with a sharp knife, removing all the white pith, and segment them, catching any juice in a bowl.

3 Peel and core the apples and cut into thin slices. Using the point of a knife, hull the strawberries and halve or quarter the fruits if they are large. Place the prepared fruit in a large dish.

4 Blend together the lemon juice, orange flower water and any reserved orange juice. Pour the mixture over the salad and toss lightly. Serve decorated with a few fresh mint leaves.

Fragrant Fruit Salad

A medley of colourful and exotic fruit, this fresh-tasting salad is the perfect dessert for a dinner party.

Serves 6
130g/4½oz/scant ¾ cup sugar
thinly pared rind and juice
    of 1 lime
150ml/¼ pint/⅔ cup water
60ml/4 tbsp brandy
5ml/1 tsp instant coffee granules
    or powder dissolved in
    30ml/2 tbsp boiling water
1 small pineapple
1 papaya
2 pomegranates
1 mango
2 passion fruit or kiwi fruit
strips of lime rind, to decorate

1 Put the sugar and lime rind in a small pan with the water. Heat gently until the sugar dissolves, then bring to the boil and simmer for 5 minutes. Leave to cool, then strain into a large serving bowl, discarding the lime rind. Stir in the lime juice, brandy and dissolved coffee.

2 Using a sharp knife, cut the plume and stalk ends from the pineapple. Cut off the peel, then remove the central core and discard. Slice the flesh into bitesize pieces and add to the bowl.

3 Halve the papaya and scoop out the seeds. Cut away the skin, then slice the papaya. Halve the pomegranates and scoop out the seeds. Add to the bowl.

4 Cut the mango lengthwise into three pieces, along each side of the stone (pit). Peel the skin off the flesh. Cut into chunks and add to the bowl.

5 Halve the passion fruit and scoop out the flesh using a teaspoon, or peel and chop the kiwi fruit. Add to the bowl and serve, decorated with lime rind.

> **Cook's Tip**
> *Allow the salad to stand at room temperature for 1 hour before serving so that the flavours can blend.*

Fresh fruit salad: Energy 29Kcal/163kJ; Protein 0.8g; Carbohydrate 9.3g, of which sugars 9.3g; Fat 0.1g, of which saturates 0g; Cholesterol 0g; Fibre 1.6g; Calcium 10mg; Sodium 0mg
Fragrant fruit salad: Energy 146kcal/620kJ; Protein 1g; Carbohydrate 33.2g, of which sugars 33.2g; Fat 0.3g, of which saturates 0g; Cholesterol 0mg; Calcium 40mg; Fibre 2.9g; Sodium 7mg

Italian Fruit Salad & Ice Cream

Fresh summer fruits are steeped in fruit juice to make a delicious Italian salad, which is delectable on its own, but can also be turned into a wickedly rich ice cream. Serve some of the fruit salad alongside the ice cream for a glorious fruity experience.

Serves 6

900g/2lb mixed summer
    fruits such as strawberries,
    raspberries, loganberries,
    redcurrants, blueberries,
    peaches, apricots, plums,
    melons and nectarines
juice of 3–4 oranges
juice of 1 lemon
15ml/1 tbsp liquid pear and
    apple concentrate
60ml/4 tbsp whipping cream
fresh mint sprigs, to decorate

1 Prepare the fruit according to type and cut into reasonably small pieces. Put the prepared fruit into a serving bowl and pour over enough orange juice to cover. Add the lemon juice and chill for 2 hours.

2 Set half the macerated fruit aside to serve as it is. Purée the remainder in a blender or food processor.

3 Gently warm the pear and apple concentrate and stir into the fruit purée. Whip the cream and fold it in.

4 Churn the mixture in an ice-cream maker. Alternatively, place in a suitable container for freezing. Freeze until ice crystals form around the edge, then beat the mixture until smooth. Repeat the process once or twice, then freeze until firm.

5 Allow to soften slightly in the refrigerator before serving, decorated with sprigs of mint.

Cook's Tip
Add 30ml/2 tbsp orange liqueur to the ice cream or the fruit salad for an added touch of luxury.

Tropical Scented Fruit Salad

With its special colour and exotic flavour, this fresh fruit salad is perfect after a rich, heavy meal. Serve the fruit salad with whipping cream flavoured with a little finely chopped drained preserved stem ginger.

Serves 4–6

6 oranges
350–400g/12–14oz/3–3½ cups
    strawberries, hulled and halved
1–2 passion fruit
120ml/4fl oz/½ cup medium dry
    or sweet white wine

1 To segment the oranges, cut a slice off the top and bottom of each orange to expose the flesh. Place on a board and remove the skin, cutting downwards. Take care to remove all the white pith. Cut between the membranes to release the segments.

2 Put the orange segments in a serving bowl with the hulled and halved strawberries. Halve the passion fruit and, using a teaspoon, scoop the flesh into the bowl.

3 Pour the wine over the fruit and toss gently. Cover and chill in the refrigerator until ready to serve.

Variation
Use three small blood oranges and three ordinary oranges.

Italian fruit salad: Energy 69kcal/289kJ; Protein 2.2g; Carbohydrate 15.2g, of which sugars 15.2g; Fat 0.2g, of which saturates 0g; Cholesterol 0mg; Calcium 38mg; Fibre 1.7g; Sodium 18mg
Tropical scented fruit salad: Energy 81kcal/342kJ; Protein 2g; Carbohydrate 15.6g, of which sugars 15.6g; Fat 0.2g, of which saturates 0g; Cholesterol 0mg; Calcium 75mg; Fibre 3g; Sodium 13mg

Iced Fruit Mountain

This dramatic display of fruit arranged on a "mountain" of ice cubes is bound to delight your guests. Cut the pieces of fruit larger than for a fruit salad and supply cocktail sticks for spearing.

Serves 6–8
1 star fruit
4 kumquats
225g/8oz large strawberries
1 apple and/or 1 Asian pear
2 large orange, peeled
1 Charentais melon and/or
  ½ watermelon
6 physalis
225g/8oz seedless black grapes
8 fresh lychees, peeled (optional)
caster (superfine) sugar, for
  dipping
wedges of kaffir lime, to decorate

1 Slice the star fruit and halve the kumquats. Leave the hulls on the strawberries. Cut the apple and/or Asian pear into wedges, and the oranges into segments. Use a melon baller for the melon or, alternatively, cut the melon into neat wedges. Chill all the fruit in the refrigerator.

2 Prepare the ice cube "mountain". Choose a wide, shallow bowl that, when turned upside down, will fit neatly on a serving platter. Fill the bowl with crushed ice cubes. Put it in the freezer with the serving platter. Leave in the freezer for at least 1 hour.

3 Remove the serving platter and bowl of ice from the freezer. Invert the serving platter on top of the bowl of ice, then turn platter and bowl over. Lift off the bowl and arrange the pieces of fruit on the ice "mountain".

4 Decorate the mountain with the kaffir lime wedges, and serve the fruit at once, handing round a bowl of sugar separately for guests with a sweet tooth.

Variation
Vary the fruit as you wish, but you need a good mix of tropical, citrus and soft fruit for the best effect.

Exotic Fruit Salad

Passion fruit makes a superb dressing for any fruit, but really brings out the flavour of exotic varieties. You can easily double the recipe, then serve the rest for the next day's breakfast.

Serves 6
1 mango
1 papaya
2 kiwi fruit
coconut or vanilla ice cream,
  to serve

For the dressing
3 passion fruit
thinly pared rind and juice of
  1 lime
5ml/1 tsp hazelnut or walnut oil
15ml/1 tbsp clear honey

1 Peel the mango, cut it into three slices, then cut the flesh into chunks and place it in a large bowl. Peel the papaya and cut it in half. Scoop out the seeds, then chop the flesh.

2 Cut both ends off each kiwi fruit, then stand them on a board. Using a small sharp knife, cut off the skin from top to bottom. Cut each kiwi fruit in half lengthwise, then cut into thick slices. Combine all the fruit in a large serving bowl.

3 To make the dressing, cut each passion fruit in half and scoop the seeds out into a strainer set over a small bowl. Press the seeds well to extract all their juices.

4 Lightly whisk the remaining dressing ingredients into the passion fruit juice, then pour the dressing over the prepared fruit in the serving bowl.

5 Mix gently to combine. Leave to chill for 1 hour before serving with scoops of coconut or vanilla ice cream.

Cook's Tip
A clear golden honey scented with orange blossom or acacia blossom would be perfect for the dressing.

Iced fruit mountain: Energy 56kcal/239kJ; Protein 1.1g; Carbohydrate 13.4g, of which sugars 13.4g; Fat 0.2g, of which saturates 0g; Cholesterol 0mg; Calcium 35mg; Fibre 1.7g; Sodium 17mg
Exotic fruit salad: Energy 66kcal/278kJ; Protein 1g; Carbohydrate 14.6g, of which sugars 14.5g; Fat 0.8g, of which saturates 0.1g; Cholesterol 0mg; Calcium 26mg; Fibre 2.9g; Sodium 7mg

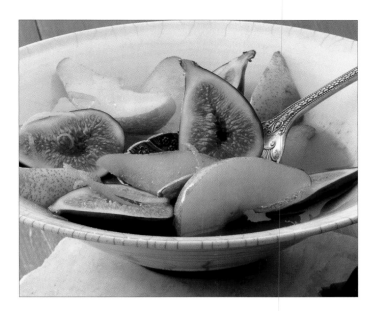

Fruit Platter with Spices

A simple fresh fruit platter sprinkled with spices makes a healthy dessert. It is low in fat and offers a range of essential vitamins and minerals that are needed for good health.

Serves 6
I pineapple
2 papayas
I small melon
juice of 2 limes
2 pomegranates
ground ginger and ground
*   nutmeg, for sprinkling*
mint sprigs, to decorate

I Peel the pineapple. Remove the core and any remaining eyes, then cut the flesh lengthwise into thin wedges.

2 Peel the papayas, cut them in half, scoop out the seeds, then cut into thin wedges. Halve the melon and remove the seeds. Cut into thin wedges and remove the skin.

3 Arrange the fruit on six individual plates and sprinkle with the lime juice.

4 Cut the pomegranates in half using a sharp knife, then scoop out the seeds, discarding any pith. Sprinkle the seeds over the fruit on the plates, then sprinkle the salad with a little ginger and nutmeg to taste. Decorate with sprigs of fresh mint and serve immediately.

Figs & Pears in Honey

A stunningly simple dessert using fresh figs and pears scented with the warm fragrances of cinnamon and cardamom and drenched in a lemon and honey syrup.

Serves 4
I lemon
90ml/6 tbsp clear honey
I cinnamon stick
I cardamom pod
350ml/12fl oz/1½ cups water
2 pears
8 fresh figs, halved

I Pare the rind from the lemon using a cannelle knife (zester). Alternatively, use a vegetable peeler to remove the rind. Cut the pared rind into very thin strips.

2 Place the lemon rind, honey, cinnamon stick, cardamom pod and the water in a heavy pan and boil, uncovered, for about 10 minutes until reduced by about half.

3 Cut the pears into eighths, discarding the cores. Place in the syrup, add the figs and simmer for about 5 minutes, or until the fruit is tender.

4 Transfer the fruit to a serving bowl. Continue cooking the liquid until syrupy, then discard the cinnamon stick and cardamom pod and pour over the figs and pears to serve.

Cook's Tips
• *Leave the skin on the pears or discard, depending on your preference. The pears should not be too ripe otherwise they will disintegrate. Choose a type with a firm texture.*
• *Figs vary in colour from pale green and yellow to dark purple. When buying, look for firm fruit without any bruises or blemishes. A ripe fig will yield gently in your hand without having to press it.*
• *It is best to use pale green or light beige cardamom pods, rather than the coarser dark brown ones. Crush the cardamom with a rolling pin to split the pod slightly.*

Fruit platter with spices: Energy 55Kcal/229kJ; Protein 1g; Carbohydrate 12.9g, of which sugars 12.9g Fat 0.3g, of which saturates 0g; Cholesterol 0g; Fibre 2.3g; Calcium 25mg; Sodium 0g
Figs & pears in honey: Energy 143kcal/606kJ; Protein 1.7g; Carbohydrate 34.4g, of which sugars 34.4g; Fat 0.7g, of which saturates 0g; Cholesterol 0mg; Calcium 109mg; Fibre 4.7g; Sodium 28mg

Fruit Salad in Orange & Lemon Juice

A really good fruit salad is always popular, and this Italian dessert is certainly a winner. The fruit is bathed in fresh orange and lemon juices to produce a truly refreshing salad.

Serves 4–6
juice of 3 large sweet oranges
juice of 1 lemon
1 banana
1–2 apples
1 ripe pear
2 peaches or nectarines
4–5 apricots or plums
²⁄₃ cup black or green grapes
²⁄₃ cup berries (summer and/or winter)
any other fruits in season
sugar, to taste (optional)
2–3 tbsp Kirsch, maraschino or other liqueur (optional)

1 Place the freshly squeezed orange and lemon juices in a large serving bowl.

2 Wash or peel the fruits as necessary. Cut them into bitesize pieces. Halve the grapes and remove any seeds. Core and slice the apples. Pit and slice soft fruits and leave small berries whole. As soon as each fruit is ready, add it to the bowl with the juices.

3 Taste the salad, adding sugar to taste. Stir in the liqueur, if using. Cover the bowl and chill for at least 2 hours. Mix well to serve.

Fruits-of-the-Tropics Salad

This is a creamy, exotic fruit salad flavoured with coconut and spices.

Serves 4–6
1 pineapple
400g/14oz can guava halves in syrup
2 bananas, sliced
1 large mango, peeled, stoned (pitted) and diced
115g/4oz stem ginger and 30ml/2 tbsp of the syrup
60ml/4 tbsp thick coconut milk
10ml/2 tsp sugar
2.5ml/½ tsp freshly grated (shredded) nutmeg
2.5ml/½ tsp ground cinnamon
strips of coconut, to decorate

1 Peel, core and cube the pineapple, then place in a serving bowl. Drain the guavas, reserving the syrup, and chop. Add the guavas to the bowl with one of the bananas and the mango.

2 Chop the stem ginger and add to the pineapple mixture.

3 Pour the 30 ml/2 tbsp of the ginger syrup and the reserved guava syrup into a blender or food processor and add the remaining banana, the coconut milk and the sugar. Blend to make a smooth, creamy purée.

4 Pour the banana and coconut purée over the fruit and add a little grated (shredded) nutmeg and a sprinkling of cinnamon on top. Serve chilled, decorated with strips of coconut.

Cook's Tip
To dice mango, slice off a piece of flesh on either side of the stone (pit). Cut a cross-hatch pattern in the flesh of the slices, bend back the skin and scrape off the diced flesh.

Variation
Add a sliced kiwi fruit or seeded papaya for extra colour.

Fruit salad in orange & lemon juice: Energy 69kcal/295kJ; Protein 1g; Carbohydrate 17g, of which sugars 16.7g; Fat 0.2g, of which saturates 0g; Cholesterol 0mg; Calcium 15mg; Fibre 1.9g; Sodium 7mg
Fruits-of-the-tropics salad: Energy 165kcal/706kJ; Protein 1.5g; Carbohydrate 41.4g, of which sugars 40.5g; Fat 0.5g, of which saturates 0.1g; Cholesterol 0mg; Calcium 46mg; Fibre 4.8g; Sodium 41mg

Cool Green Fruit Salad

Pineapple Fruit Salad

A mix of exotic fruit served up in attractive pineapple cases makes an impressive dinner party dessert.

Serves 4
75g/3oz/scant ½ cup sugar
300ml/½ pint/1¼ cups water
30ml/2 tbsp stem ginger syrup
2 pieces star anise
2.5cm/1in cinnamon stick

1 clove
juice of ½ lemon
2 fresh mint sprigs
1 mango
2 bananas, sliced
8 lychees, fresh or canned
225g/8oz/2 cups strawberries
2 pieces stem ginger, cut
  into sticks
1 pineapple

1 Place the sugar in a pan and add the water, ginger syrup, spices, lemon juice and mint. Bring to the boil and simmer for 3 minutes. Strain into a large bowl.

2 Remove both the top and bottom from the mango and remove the outer skin. Stand the mango on one end and remove the flesh in two pieces either side of the flat stone. Slice evenly and add to the syrup. Add the bananas, lychees, strawberries and ginger. Chill until ready to serve.

3 Cut the pineapple in half down the centre. Loosen the flesh with a small, serrated knife and remove to form two boat shapes. Cut the pineapple flesh into large chunks and place in the cooled syrup.

4 Spoon the fruit salad carefully into the pineapple halves and bring to the table on a large serving dish or board. There will be enough fruit salad left over to be able to offer refills for second helpings.

> **Variations**
> *A variety of fruits can be used for this salad depending on what is available. Look out for fresh mandarin oranges, star fruit, papaya, physalis and passion fruit.*

A stylish yet simple fruit salad for any time of the year. Serve with amaretti or crisp almond cookies.

1 star fruit
1 green-skinned apple
1 lime
175ml/6fl oz/¾ cup sparkling
  grape juice

Serves 6
3 Ogen or Galia melons
115g/4oz seedless green grapes
2 kiwi fruit

1 Cut the melons in half and remove the seeds. Keeping the shells intact, scoop out the flesh with a melon baller, or scoop it out with a spoon and cut into bitesize cubes. Reserve the melon shells.

2 Remove any stems from the grapes and, if they are large, cut them in half. Peel and chop the kiwi fruit. Thinly slice the star fruit. Core and thinly slice the apple. Place the grapes, kiwi fruit and apple in a mixing bowl with the melon.

3 Thinly pare the rind from the lime and cut it in fine strips. Blanch the lime strips in boiling water for 30 seconds, drain and rinse in cold water. Reserve for garnishing.

4 Squeeze the juice from the lime and toss the juice into the bowl of fruit.

5 Spoon the prepared fruit into the reserved melon shells and chill the shells until required.

6 Just before serving, spoon the sparkling grape juice over the fruit and scatter with the strips of lime rind.

> **Cook's Tip**
> *On a hot summer's day, serve the filled melon shells nestling on a platter of crushed ice to keep them beautifully cool.*

Pineapple fruit salad: Energy 82kcal/348kJ; Protein 1.2g; Carbohydrate 18.3g, of which sugars 18.1g; Fat 1g, of which saturates 0.1g; Cholesterol 0mg; Calcium 33mg; Fibre 3.7g; Sodium 9mg
Cool green fruit salad: Energy 102kcal/436kJ; Protein 1.7g; Carbohydrate 24.4g, of which sugars 24.4g; Fat 0.4g, of which saturates 0g; Cholesterol 0mg; Calcium 46mg; Fibre 1.9g; Sodium 81mg

Fresh Fig, Apple & Date Salad

Sweet Mediterranean figs and dates combine especially well with crisp dessert apples.

Serves 4
6 large apples
juice of ½ lemon
175g/6oz/generous 1 cup
   fresh dates
25g/1oz white marzipan
5ml/1 tsp orange flower water
60ml/4 tbsp natural (plain) yogurt
4 ripe green or purple figs
4 almonds, toasted

1 Core the apples. Slice thinly, then cut into fine matchsticks. Moisten with lemon juice to keep them white. Remove the stones from the dates and cut the flesh into fine strips, then combine them with the apple slices.

2 Soften the marzipan with the orange flower water and combine with the yogurt. Mix well.

3 Pile the apples and dates in the centre of four individual plates. Remove the stem from each of the figs and divide the fruit into quarters without cutting right through the base. Squeeze the base with the thumb and forefinger of each hand to open up the fig.

4 Place a fig in the centre of each fruit salad, spoon in the yogurt filling and decorate with a toasted almond.

Fruit with Yogurt & Honey

Fresh fruit most commonly follows a meal in Greece, and the addition of yogurt and honey makes it even more delicious.

Serves 4
225g/8oz/1 cup Greek (US strained plain) yogurt
45ml/3 tbsp clear honey
selection of fresh fruit for dipping, such as apples, pears, tangerines, grapes, figs and strawberries

1 Beat the yogurt, place in a dish, and stir in the honey, to leave a marbled effect.

2 Cut the fruits into wedges or bitesize pieces, or leave whole.

3 Arrange the fruits on a platter with the bowl of dip in the centre. Serve chilled.

Figs with Honey & Wine

Cooled poached figs make a salad with a difference. They are delicious served with sweetened whipped cream flavoured with vanilla extract.

Serves 6
450ml/¾ pint/scant 2 cups dry white wine
75g/3oz/⅓ cup clear honey
50g/2oz/¼ cup caster (superfine) sugar
1 small orange
8 whole cloves
450g/1lb fresh figs
1 cinnamon stick

1 Put the wine, honey and sugar in a heavy pan and heat gently until the sugar dissolves.

2 Stud the orange with the cloves and add to the syrup with the figs and cinnamon. Cover and simmer gently for 5–10 minutes until the figs are softened. Transfer to a serving dish and leave to cool completely before serving.

Fresh fig, apple & date salad: Energy 223kcal/943kJ; Protein 4.5g; Carbohydrate 43.8g, of which sugars 43.7g; Fat 4.5g, of which saturates 0.4g; Cholesterol 0mg; Calcium 170mg; Fibre 4.8g; Sodium 46mg
Fruit with yogurt & honey: Energy 131kcal/548kJ; Protein 4.7g; Carbohydrate 17.2g, of which sugars 17.2g; Fat 5.9g, of which saturates 2.9g; Cholesterol 0mg; Calcium 105mg; Fibre 1.4g; Sodium 49mg
Figs with honey & wine: Energy 316kcal/1318kJ; Protein 1.8g; Carbohydrate 29.7g, of which sugars 29.7g; Fat 18.4g, of which saturates 11.1g; Cholesterol 46mg; Calcium 101mg; Fibre 2.3g; Sodium 30mg

Pineapple with Strawberries & Lychees

The sweet, tropical flavours of pineapple and lychees combine well with richly scented strawberries to create a most refreshing salad. The pineapple shells make lovely bowls.

Serves 4

2 small pineapples
450g/1lb/4 cups strawberries
400g/14oz can lychees
45ml/3 tbsp kirsch or white rum
30ml/2 tbsp icing (confectioners') sugar

1 Remove the crowns from both pineapples by twisting sharply. Reserve the leaves for decoration.

2 Cut both pineapples in half diagonally using a large, serrated knife. Cut around the flesh inside the skin of both pineapples with a small, serrated knife, keeping the skin intact. Remove the core from the pineapple and discard. Chop the flesh and put in a freezerproof bowl. Reserve the skins.

3 Hull the strawberries and gently combine with the pineapple and lychees, taking care not to damage the fruit.

4 Mix the kirsch or rum with the icing sugar, pour over the fruit and freeze for 45 minutes.

5 Turn out the fruit into the pineapple skin shells, decorate with the reserved pineapple leaves and serve.

Cook's Tips
• A ripe pineapple will resist pressure when squeezed and will have a sweet, fragrant smell. In winter freezing conditions can cause the flesh to blacken.
• Make sure you remove all the brown "eyes" from the pineapple before cutting into pieces.
• The pineapple can be chopped finely to create almost a "crush" which will coat the other fruit.

Winter Fruit Salad

This colourful dessert is guaranteed to brighten up the winter months. It tastes luscious served with thick yogurt or cream.

Serves 6

225g/8oz can pineapple cubes in fruit juice
200ml/7fl oz/scant 1 cup freshly squeezed orange juice
200ml/7fl oz/scant 1 cup unsweetened apple juice
30ml/2 tbsp orange or apple liqueur

30ml/2 tbsp clear honey (optional)
2 oranges
2 green apples
2 pears
4 plums, stoned (pitted) and chopped
12 fresh dates, stoned (pitted) and chopped
115g/4oz/½ cup ready-to-eat dried apricots
fresh mint sprigs, to decorate

1 Drain the pineapple, reserving the juice. Put the pineapple juice, orange juice, apple juice, liqueur and honey, if using, in a large serving bowl and stir.

2 To segment the oranges, cut a slice off the top and bottom of each orange to expose the flesh. Place on a board and remove the skin, cutting downwards. Take care to remove all the white pith. Cut between the membranes to release the segments.

3 Put the orange segments and pineapple in the fruit juice mixture. Peel, core and slice the apples and pears and add to the serving bowl.

4 Stir in the chopped plums, dates and dried apricots to combine well. Cover and chill for several hours. Decorate with fresh mint sprigs to serve.

Variation
Use other unsweetened fruit juices such as pink grapefruit and pineapple juice in place of the orange and apple juice.

Pineapple with strawberries & lychees: Energy 235kcal/999kJ; Protein 2.2g; Carbohydrate 52.5g, of which sugars 52.5g; Fat 0.5g, of which saturates 0g; Cholesterol 0mg; Calcium 62mg; Fibre 4.2g; Sodium 13mg
Winter fruit salad: Energy 141kcal/603kJ; Protein 1.9g; Carbohydrate 32g, of which sugars 32g; Fat 0.4g, of which saturates 0g; Cholesterol 0mg; Calcium 60mg; Fibre 4.2g; Sodium 12mg

Citrus Fruit Flambé with Pistachio Praline

A fruit flambé makes a dramatic finale for a dinner party. Topping this refreshing citrus salad with praline makes it extra special.

Serves 4
4 oranges
2 ruby grapefruit
2 limes
50g/2oz/¼ cup butter

50g/2oz/¼ cup muscovado (brown) sugar
45ml/3 tbsp Cointreau
fresh mint sprigs, to decorate

For the praline
oil, for greasing
115g/4oz/½ cup caster (superfine) sugar
50g/2oz/¼ cup pistachio nuts

1 First, make the praline. Brush a baking sheet lightly with oil. Place the caster sugar and nuts in a small, heavy-based saucepan and cook gently, swirling the pan occasionally until the sugar has melted.

2 Continue to cook over a fairly low heat until the nuts start to pop and the sugar has turned a dark golden colour. Pour on to the oiled baking sheet and set aside to cool. Using a sharp knife, chop the praline into rough chunks.

3 Cut all the rind and pith from the citrus fruit. Holding each fruit in turn over a large bowl, cut between the membranes so that the segments fall into the bowl, with any juice.

4 Heat the butter and muscovado sugar together in a heavy-based frying pan (skillet) until the sugar has melted and the mixture is golden. Strain the citrus juices into the pan and continue to cook, stirring occasionally, until the juice has reduced and is syrupy.

5 Add the fruit segments and warm through without stirring. Pour over the Cointreau and set it alight. As soon as the flames die down, spoon the fruit flambé into serving dishes. Scatter some praline over each portion and decorate with mint.

Oranges with Caramel Wigs

The slightly bitter, caramelized orange rind and syrup has a wonderful flavour and texture that sits in perfect contrast to the sweet, juicy oranges.

Serves 6
6 oranges
120g/4oz/generous ½ cup caster (superfine) sugar
120ml/4fl oz/½ cup boiling water

1 Using a cannelle knife (zester) or vegetable peeler, pare the rind of a few of the oranges to make 12 long strips. Set aside.

2 Using a sharp knife, peel all the oranges, discarding the pith and reserving the juice that collects. Freeze the oranges separately for 30 minutes.

3 Slice the oranges evenly, then pile up the slices to reform their shape. Secure the recreated oranges with a cocktail stick (toothpick). Chill.

4 To make the wigs, simmer the 12 rind strips for about 5 minutes, then drain, rinse, and repeat. Trim with scissors.

5 Put half the sugar into a small pan and add 15ml/1 tbsp water. Heat gently until the mixture caramelizes, shaking the pan a little if one side starts to brown too fast. As soon as the mixture colours, dip the bottom of the pan into cold water. Add 30ml/2 tbsp hot water and the orange rind to the caramel, then stir until the caramel dissolves. Turn the rind onto a plate to cool.

6 To make a caramel syrup for serving, put the remaining sugar in a small pan with 15ml/1 tbsp water, and make caramel as in the previous step. When it has coloured nicely, stand well back, pour in the boiling water and stir with a wooden spoon to dissolve. Add the reserved orange juices and pour into a serving jug (pitcher).

7 To serve, arrange the orange strips in a criss-cross pattern on top of each orange. Remove the cocktail sticks and pour a little caramel syrup round the base of each orange.

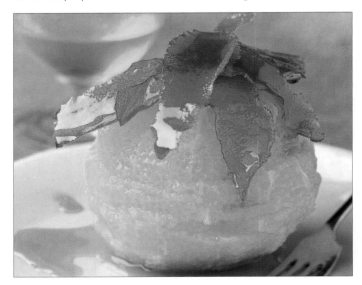

Citrus fruit flambé: Energy 446kcal/1872kJ; Protein 4.8g; Carbohydrate 65.2g, of which sugars 64.8g; Fat 17.4g, of which saturates 7.4g; Cholesterol 27mg; Calcium 127mg; Fibre 4.4g; Sodium 155mg
Oranges with caramel wigs: Energy 122kcal/521kJ; Protein 1.4g; Carbohydrate 30.8g, of which sugars 30.8g; Fat 0.1g, of which saturates 0g; Cholesterol 0mg; Calcium 66mg; Fibre 2g; Sodium 7mg

Pistachio & Rose Water Oranges

Clementines with Star Anise

This light and tangy dessert is perfect to serve after a heavy main course, such as a hearty meat stew or a leg of roast lamb. Combining three favourite Middle-Eastern ingredients, it is delightfully fragrant and refreshing. If you don't have pistachio nuts, use hazelnuts instead.

Serves 4
4 large oranges
30ml/2 tbsp rose water
30ml/2 tbsp shelled pistachio
nuts, roughly chopped

1 Slice the top and bottom off one of the oranges to expose the flesh. Using a small serrated knife, slice down between the pith and the flesh, working round the orange, to remove all the peel and pith. Slice the orange into six rounds, reserving any juice. Repeat with the remaining oranges.

2 Arrange the oranges in a shallow dish. Mix the reserved juice with the rose water and drizzle over the oranges.

3 Cover the dish with clear film (plastic wrap) and chill for about 30 minutes. Sprinkle the chopped pistachio nuts over the oranges and serve immediately.

Cook's Tips
• *Rose-scented sugar is delicious sprinkled over fresh fruit salads. Wash and thoroughly dry a handful of rose petals and place in a sealed container filled with caster (superfine) sugar for 2–3 days. Remove the petals before using the sugar.*
• *This salad is delicious served with vanilla cream. Put 150ml/¼ pint/⅔ cup double (heavy) cream in a small pan with a vanilla pod (bean). Bring almost to the boil, then leave to cool and steep for 30 minutes. Remove the vanilla pod, then transfer the cream to a bowl. Mix with another 150ml/¼ pint/⅔ cup cream and caster (superfine) sugar to taste. Whip lightly.*

A perfect choice for the festive season, this fresh-tasting salad is delicately flavoured with mulling spices. Serve with whipped cream and sweet finger biscuits for a lovely dessert to follow a turkey dish.

Serves 6
rind of 1 lime
350ml/12fl oz/1½ cups sweet
dessert wine, such as Sauternes
75g/3oz/6 tbsp caster
(superfine) sugar
6 star anise
1 cinnamon stick
1 vanilla pod (bean)
30ml/2 tbsp Cointreau or other
orange liqueur
12 clementines

1 Using a cannelle knife (zester) or vegetable peeler, thinly pare two strips of rind from the lime. Put in a pan, together with the wine, sugar, star anise and cinnamon.

2 Split the vanilla pod and add it to the pan. Bring to the boil, then lower the heat and simmer for 10 minutes.

3 Remove the pan from the heat and leave to cool, then stir in the orange-flavoured liqueur.

4 Peel the clementines. Cut some of them in half and place them all in a dish. Pour over the wine mixture and chill.

Pistachio & rose water oranges: Energy 101kcal/424kJ; Protein 3g; Carbohydrate 13.4g, of which sugars 13.2g; Fat 4.3g, of which saturates 0.6g; Cholesterol 0mg; Calcium 79mg; Fibre 3g; Sodium 47mg
Clementines with star anise: Energy 149kcal/632kJ; Protein 0.9g; Carbohydrate 24.7g, of which sugars 24.7g; Fat 0.1g, of which saturates 0g; Cholesterol 0mg; Calcium 40mg; Fibre 1g; Sodium 12mg

Jamaican Fruit Trifle

This trifle is actually based on a Caribbean fool that consists of fruit stirred into thick vanilla-flavoured cream. This is a lighter version of the original.

Serves 8

1 large sweet pineapple, peeled and cored, about 350g/12oz
300ml/½pint/1¼ cups double (heavy) cream
200ml/7fl oz/scant 1 cup crème fraîche
60ml/4 tbsp icing (confectioners') sugar, sifted
10ml/2 tsp pure vanilla extract
30ml/2 tbsp white or coconut rum
3 papayas, peeled, seeded and chopped
3 mangoes, peeled, stoned (pitted) and chopped
thinly pared rind and juice of 1 lime
25g/1oz/⅓ cup coarsely shredded or flaked coconut, toasted

1 Cut the pineapple into large chunks, place in a food processor or blender and process briefly until chopped. Turn into a sieve (strainer) placed over a bowl and leave for 5 minutes so that most of the juice drains from the fruit.

2 Whip the double cream to very soft peaks, then lightly but thoroughly fold in the crème fraîche, sifted icing sugar, vanilla extract and rum. Fold in the drained pineapple.

3 Place the papaya and mango in a large bowl and pour over the lime juice. Gently stir to mix. Shred the pared lime rind.

4 Divide the fruit mixture and the pineapple cream between eight dessert plates. Decorate with the lime shreds, toasted coconut and a few small pineapple leaves, if you like.

Cook's Tip
It is important to let the pineapple purée drain thoroughly, otherwise the pineapple cream will be watery. Don't throw away the drained pineapple juice – mix it with fizzy mineral water for a refreshing drink.

Zingy Papaya, Lime & Ginger Salad

This refreshing, fruity salad makes a lovely light breakfast, perfect for the summer months. Choose really ripe, fragrant papayas for the best flavour.

Serves 4

2 large ripe papayas
juice of 1 fresh lime
2 pieces preserved stem ginger, finely sliced

1 Cut the papaya in half lengthwise and scoop out the seeds, using a teaspoon. Using a sharp knife, cut the flesh into thin slices and arrange on a platter.

2 Squeeze the lime juice over the papaya and sprinkle with the sliced stem ginger. Serve immediately.

Cook's Tip
Ripe papayas have a yellowish skin and feel soft to the touch. Their orange-coloured flesh has an attractive, smooth texture.

Variation
This refreshing fruit salad is delicious made with other tropical fruit. Try using two ripe peeled mangoes instead of papayas.

Jamaican fruit trifle: Energy 479kcal/1995kJ; Protein 2.3g; Carbohydrate 41g, of which sugars 40.7g; Fat 34.2g, of which saturates 22.7g; Cholesterol 80mg; Calcium 79mg; Fibre 3.6g; Sodium 27mg
Zingy papaya, lime & ginger salad: Energy 55kcal/233kJ; Protein 0.8g; Carbohydrate 13.4g, of which sugars 13.4g; Fat 0.2g, of which saturates 0g; Cholesterol 0mg; Calcium 35mg; Fibre 3.3g; Sodium 8mg

Jungle Fruits in Lemon Grass Syrup

A luscious mix of exotic fruit, bathed in a delicious syrup flavoured with lemon grass, this salad would make a perfect finish to an Oriental-style meal.

Serves 6
1 firm papaya
1 small pineapple
2 small star fruit, sliced into stars
1 can preserved lychees or
   12 fresh lychees, peeled and
   stoned (pitted)

2 firm yellow or green bananas,
   peeled and cut diagonally
   into slices

For the syrup
225ml/7½fl oz/1 cup water
115g/4oz/generous ½ cup caster
   (superfine) sugar
2 lemon grass stalks, bruised

1 To make the syrup, put the water into a heavy pan with the sugar and bruised lemon grass stalks. Bring the liquid to the boil, stirring constantly until the sugar has dissolved, then reduce the heat and simmer for 10–15 minutes. Leave to cool.

2 Peel and halve the papaya, remove the seeds and slice the flesh crossways. Peel the pineapple and slice it into rounds. Remove the core and cut each round in half.

3 Put all the fruit into a bowl. Pour the syrup, including the lemon grass stalks, over the top and toss lightly to combine.

4 Cover and chill for at least 6 hours, or overnight, to allow the flavours to mingle. Remove the lemon grass stalks before serving.

> **Variations**
> This fruit salad can be made with any combination of tropical fruits – just go for a good balance of colour, flavour and texture. To give the salad a softly spiced flavour, try flavouring the syrup with a little finely chopped, peeled fresh root ginger rather than lemon grass.

Minted Pomegranate Yogurt with Grapefruit Salad

The flavourful yogurt is delicious for breakfast, but also makes a fabulous dessert when served with a delicately scented citrus fruit salad.

Serves 3–4
300ml/½ pint/1¼ cups Greek
   (US strained plain) yogurt
2–3 ripe pomegranates
1 small bunch mint,
   finely chopped

honey or sugar, to taste (optional)
handful of pomegranate seeds
   and mint leaves, to decorate

For the grapefruit salad
2 red grapefruits
2 pink grapefruits
1 white grapefruit
15–30ml/1–2 tbsp orange
   flower water

1 Put the yogurt in a bowl and beat well. Cut open the pomegranates and scoop out the seeds, removing all the bitter pith. Fold the pomegranate seeds and chopped mint into the yogurt. Sweeten with a little honey or sugar, if using, then chill.

2 Remove the peel from the grapefruits, cutting off all the pith. Cut between the membranes to remove the segments, holding the fruit over a bowl to catch the juices. Discard the membranes. Mix the fruit segments with the reserved juices.

3 Sprinkle the grapefruit segments with the orange flower water and add a little honey or sugar, if using. Stir gently then decorate with a few pomegranate seeds.

4 Decorate the chilled yogurt with a scattering of pomegranate seeds and mint leaves, and serve with the grapefruit salad.

> **Variation**
> Alternatively, you can use a mixture of oranges and blood oranges, interspersed with thin segments of lemon.

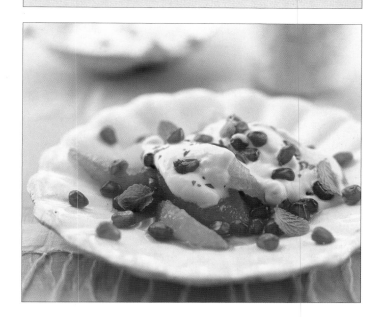

Jungle fruits in lemon grass syrup: Energy 174kcal/742kJ; Protein 1.3g; Carbohydrate 44.2g, of which sugars 43.4g; Fat 0.3g, of which saturates 0g; Cholesterol 0mg; Calcium 38mg; Fibre 2.7g; Sodium 6mg
Yogurt with salad: Energy 188kcal/784kJ; Protein 8.8g; Carbohydrate 18g, of which sugars 18g; Fat 10.5g, of which saturates 5.2g; Cholesterol 0mg; Calcium 202mg; Fibre 3.6g; Sodium 82mg

Watermelon, Ginger & Grapefruit Salad

A pretty, pink salad with the slightly tart grapefruit contrasting nicely with the sweet ginger.

Serves 4

450g/1lb/2 cups watermelon flesh
2 ruby or pink grapefruit
2 pieces stem ginger and
  30ml/2 tbsp of the syrup

1 Remove any seeds from the watermelon and cut the flesh into bitesize chunks.

2 Using a small, sharp knife, cut away all the peel and white pith from the grapefruit. Carefully remove the segments from between the membranes, catching any juice in a bowl.

3 Finely chop the ginger and place in a serving bowl with the melon cubes and grapefruit segments, adding the reserved grapefruit juice. Spoon over the ginger syrup.

4 Toss the fruits lightly to mix. Chill before serving.

Cook's Tip
Toss the fruits gently – grapefruit segments break up easily and can make the salad look unattractive.

Grapefruit Salad with Campari & Orange

The bitter-sweet flavour of Campari combines especially well with the citrus fruit to produce a refreshing salad for any time of the year.

Serves 4

150ml/¼ pint/⅔ cup water

45 ml/3 tbsp caster
  (superfine) sugar
60ml/4 tbsp Campari
30ml/2 tbsp lemon juice
4 grapefruit
5 oranges
4 fresh mint sprigs, to decorate

1 Bring the water to the boil in a small pan, add the sugar and simmer until dissolved. Transfer to a bowl, allow to cool, then add the Campari and lemon juice. Chill until ready to serve.

2 Slice the top and bottom off one of the grapefruit to expose the flesh. Using a small serrated knife, slice down between the pith and the flesh, working round the grapefruit, to remove all the peel and pith.

3 Release the segments by cutting between the flesh and the membranes, working over a bowl to catch the juices. Repeat with the remaining grapefruit and the oranges.

4 Add the grapefruit and orange segments to the bowl of Campari syrup and chill.

5 Spoon the salad into four dishes, decorate each with a sprig of fresh mint and serve.

Cook's Tips
• When buying citrus fruit, choose brightly-coloured varieties that feel heavy for their size.
• Before you discard the citrus fruit membranes, squeeze as much juice as possible from them into the bowl of juice.

Watermelon, ginger & grapefruit salad: Energy 85kcal/362kJ; Protein 1.3g; Carbohydrate 20.3g, of which sugars 20.3g; Fat 0.5g, of which saturates 0.1g; Cholesterol 0mg; Calcium 28mg; Fibre 1.2g; Sodium 25mg
Grapefruit salad: Energy 181kcal/766kJ; Protein 3g; Carbohydrate 35.4g, of which sugars 35.4g; Fat 0.3g, of which saturates 0g; Cholesterol 0mg; Calcium 113mg; Fibre 4.6g; Sodium 13mg

Fruit Kebabs with Mango & Yogurt Sauce

Enjoy these mixed fruit kebabs dipped into a refreshingly minty mango and yogurt sauce.

Serves 4

½ pineapple, peeled, cored and cubed
2 kiwi fruit, peeled and cubed
150g/5oz/scant 1 cup strawberries, hulled and cut in half lengthwise if large
½ mango, peeled, stoned (pitted) and cubed

For the sauce

120ml/4fl oz/½ cup fresh mango purée, made from 1–1½ peeled and stoned (pitted) mangoes
120ml/4fl oz/½ cup thick natural (plain) yogurt
5ml/1 tsp sugar
few drops of vanilla extract
15ml/1 tbsp finely shredded fresh mint leaves
1 fresh mint sprig, to decorate

1 To make the sauce, beat together the mango purée, yogurt, sugar and vanilla with an electric hand mixer.

2 Stir in the shredded mint. Cover the sauce and chill until required.

3 Thread the fruit on to twelve 15cm/6in wooden skewers, alternating the pineapple, kiwi fruit, strawberries and mango.

4 Transfer the mango and yogurt sauce to an attractive bowl, decorate with a mint sprig and place in the centre of a large serving platter. Surround with the kebabs and serve.

Variations

• Instead of flavouring the sauce with vanilla extract, add some finely chopped preserved stem ginger with a little of the syrup from the jar.
• For a pink sauce, replace the mango purée with strawberry or raspberry purée, sweetened with icing (confectioners') sugar.

Tropical Fruits in Cinnamon Syrup

These glistening fruits, bathed in a delicately-flavoured syrup, provide an attractive way to round off a meal. The salad is particularly good served with mango or vanilla ice cream, or thick yogurt.

Serves 6

450g/1lb/2¼ cups caster (superfine) sugar
1 cinnamon stick
1 large or 2 medium papayas (about 675g/1½lb), peeled, seeded and cut lengthwise into thin pieces
1 large or 2 medium mangoes (about 675g/1½lb) peeled, stoned (pitted) and cut lengthwise into thin pieces
1 large or 2 small star fruit (about 225g/8oz) thinly sliced

1 Sprinkle one-third of the sugar over the bottom of a large pan. Add the cinnamon stick and half of the papaya, mango and star fruit pieces.

2 Sprinkle half of the remaining sugar over the fruit pieces in the pan. Add the rest of the fruit and sugar.

3 Cover the pan and cook the fruit over medium heat for 35–45 minutes, until the sugar dissolves completely. Shake the pan occasionally, but do not stir or the fruit will collapse.

4 Uncover the pan and simmer for about 10 minutes, until the fruit begins to appear translucent. Remove the pan from the heat and allow to cool. Discard the cinnamon stick.

5 Transfer the fruit and syrup to a bowl, cover and refrigerate overnight before serving.

Cook's Tip

This salad is best prepared a day in advance to allow the flavours to develop properly.

Fruit kebabs with mango & yogurt sauce: Energy 120kcal/513kJ; Protein 3g; Carbohydrate 27.1g, of which sugars 26.9g; Fat 0.8g, of which saturates 0.2g; Cholesterol 0mg; Calcium 97mg; Fibre 3.7g; Sodium 32mg
Tropical fruits in cinnamon syrup: Energy 413kcal/1765kJ; Protein 1.8g; Carbohydrate 107.5g, of which sugars 107.1g; Fat 0.4g, of which saturates 0.1g; Cholesterol 0mg; Calcium 81mg; Fibre 6g; Sodium 13mg

Blackberry Salad with Rose Granita

In this elegant desert, a rose-flavoured granita is served over strips of white meringue and set off by a blackberry salad.

Serves 4

150g/5oz/2⁄3 cup caster
  (superfine) sugar
1 fresh red rose, petals
  finely chopped

5ml/1 tsp rose water
10ml/2 tsp lemon juice
450g/1lb/2²⁄3 cups blackberries
icing (confectioners') sugar,
  for dusting
fresh rose petals, to decorate

For the meringue

2 egg whites
115g/4oz/generous 1⁄2 cup caster
  (superfine) sugar

1 To make the granita, bring 150 ml/1⁄4 pint/2⁄3 cup water to the boil in a stainless-steel or enamel span. Add the sugar and rose petals, then simmer for 5 minutes.

2 Strain the syrup into a deep metal tray, add a further 450 ml/3⁄4 pint/scant 2 cups water, the rose water and lemon juice and leave to cool. Freeze for 3 hours, or until solid.

3 Meanwhile, preheat the oven to 140°C/275°F/Gas 1. Line a baking sheet with six layers of newspaper and cover with non-stick baking parchment.

4 To make the meringue, whisk the egg whites until they hold their weight on the whisk. Add the caster sugar a little at a time, and whisk until firm.

5 Spoon the meringue into a piping bag fitted with a 1cm/1⁄2in plain nozzle. Pipe the meringue in lengths across the paper-lined baking sheet. Dry the meringue near the bottom of the oven for 1 1⁄2–2 hours.

6 Break the meringue into 5cm/2in lengths and place three or four pieces on each of four large serving plates. Pile the blackberries next to the meringue. With a tablespoon, scrape the granita finely. Shape into ovals and place over the meringue. Dust with icing sugar, decorate with rose petals, and serve.

Blueberry, Orange & Lavender Salad

Delicate blueberries feature here in a simple salad of sharp oranges and sweet little meringues flavoured with fresh lavender.

Serves 4

6 oranges
350g/12oz/3 cups blueberries
8 fresh lavender sprigs,
  to decorate

For the meringue

2 egg whites
115g/4oz/generous 1⁄2 cup caster
  (superfine) sugar
5ml/1 tsp fresh lavender flowers

1 Preheat the oven to 140°C/275°F/Gas 1. Line a baking sheet with six layers of newspaper and cover with non-stick baking parchment.

2 To make the meringue, whisk the egg whites in a large mixing bowl until they hold their weight on the whisk. Add the sugar a little at a time, whisking thoroughly before each addition. Fold in the lavender flowers.

3 Spoon the lavender meringue into a piping bag fitted with a 5mm/1⁄4in plain nozzle. Pipe as many small buttons of meringue onto the prepared baking sheet as you can. Dry the meringues near the bottom of the oven for 1 1⁄2–2 hours.

4 To segment the oranges, remove the peel from the top, bottom and sides with a serrated knife. Loosen the segments by cutting with a paring knife between the flesh and the membranes, holding the fruit over a bowl.

5 Arrange the orange segments on four individual plates.

6 Combine the blueberries with the lavender meringues and pile in the centre of each plate. Decorate with sprigs of lavender and serve immediately.

Blackberry salad with rose granita: Energy 292kcal/1243kJ; Protein 2.1g; Carbohydrate 75g, of which sugars 75g; Fat 0.2g, of which saturates 0g; Cholesterol 0mg; Calcium 82mg; Fibre 3.5g; Sodium 22mg
Blueberry, orange & lavender salad: Energy 215kcal/915kJ; Protein 4.6g; Carbohydrate 51.5g, of which sugars 51.5g; Fat 0.4g, of which saturates 0g; Cholesterol 0mg; Calcium 146mg; Fibre 6.1g; Sodium 44mg

Raspberries with Mango Custard

This remarkable salad unites the sharp quality of fresh raspberries with a special custard made from rich, fragrant mangoes.

Serves 4
1 large mango
3 egg yolks
30ml/2 tbsp caster (superfine) sugar
10ml/2 tsp cornflour (cornstarch)
200ml/7fl oz/scant 1 cup milk
8 fresh mint sprigs, to decorate

For the raspberry sauce
450g/1lb/2⅔ cups raspberries
45ml/3 tbsp caster (superfine) sugar

1 To prepare the mango, remove the top and bottom with a serrated knife. Cut away the outer skin, then remove the flesh by cutting either side of the flat central stone. Save half of the mango flesh for decoration and roughly chop the remainder.

2 For the custard, combine the egg yolks, sugar, cornflour and 30ml/2 tbsp of the milk in a small bowl until smooth.

3 Rinse a small pan with cold water to prevent the milk from catching. Bring the rest of the milk to the boil in the pan, pour it over the ingredients in the bowl and stir evenly. Strain the mixture back into the pan, stir to simmering point and cook, stirring, until thickened.

4 Pour the custard into a food processor, add the chopped mango and blend until smooth. Allow the custard to cool.

5 To make the raspberry sauce, place 350g/12oz/2 cups of the raspberries in a stain-resistant pan. Add the sugar, soften over a gentle heat and simmer for 5 minutes. Rub the fruit through a fine nylon sieve (strainer) to remove the seeds. Allow to cool.

6 Spoon the raspberry sauce and mango custard into two pools on four individual plates. Slice the reserved mango and arrange over the raspberry sauce. Scatter the remaining raspberries over the mango custard. Decorate with mint.

Melon & Strawberry Salad

A beautiful and colourful fruit salad, this is equally suitable to serve as a refreshing appetizer or to round off a meal.

Serves 4
1 Galia melon
1 honeydew melon
½ watermelon
225g/8oz/2 cups strawberries
15ml/1 tbsp lemon juice
15ml/1 tbsp clear honey
15ml/1 tbsp chopped fresh mint
1 fresh mint sprig (optional)

1 To prepare the melons, cut them in half and discard the seeds. Use a melon baller to scoop out the flesh into balls. Alternatively, use a knife and cut the melon flesh into cubes. Place the melon in a fruit bowl.

2 Rinse and hull the strawberries, cut in half and add to the melon balls or cubes.

3 Mix together the lemon juice and honey and add about 15ml/1 tbsp water to make it easier to spoon over the fruit. Mix into the fruit gently.

4 Sprinkle the chopped mint over the top of the fruit. Serve the fruit salad decorated with the mint sprig, if wished.

Cook's Tip
Do not rinse the strawberries until just before serving, otherwise they will turn mushy. When buying in punnets, remember that a strong scent means a good flavour. Fruit in season is best.

Variation
Use whichever melons are available: replace Galia with cantaloupe or watermelon with Charentais, for example. Try to choose three melons with a variation in colour.

Raspberriess with mango custard: Energy 213kcal/903kJ; Protein 6.4g; Carbohydrate 34.7g, of which sugars 32.3g; Fat 6.5g, of which saturates 2.2g; Cholesterol 193mg; Calcium 125mg; Fibre 3.8g; Sodium 37mg
Melon & strawberry salad: Energy 204kcal/867kJ; Protein 3.9g; Carbohydrate 47.5g, of which sugars 47.5g; Fat 1.2g, of which saturates 0.3g; Cholesterol 0mg; Calcium 66mg; Fibre 2.9g; Sodium 128mg

Cantaloupe Melon with Grilled Strawberries

If strawberries are slightly underripe, sprinkling them with a little sugar and grilling them will help bring out their flavour.

Serves 4
115g/4oz/1 cup strawberries
15ml/1 tbsp icing (confectioners') sugar
½ cantaloupe melon

1 Preheat the grill (broiler) to high. Hull the strawberries and cut them in half.

2 Arrange the fruit in a single layer, cut-side up, on a baking sheet or in an ovenproof dish and dust with the icing sugar.

3 Grill (broil) the strawberries for 4–5 minutes, or until the sugar starts to bubble and turn golden.

4 Meanwhile, scoop out the seeds from the half melon using a spoon. Using a sharp knife, remove the skin, then cut the flesh into wedges and arrange on a serving plate with the grilled strawberries. Serve immediately.

Variation
Use fragrant, orange-fleshed Charentais instead of cantaloupe.

Melon Trio with Ginger Cookies

The eye-catching colours of these three different melons really make this dessert, while the crisp biscuits provide a perfect contrast in terms of texture.

Serves 4
¼ watermelon
½ honeydew melon
½ Charentais melon
60ml/4 tbsp stem ginger syrup

For the cookies
25g/1oz/2 tbsp unsalted butter
25g/1oz/2 tbsp caster (superfine) sugar
5ml/1 tsp clear honey
25g/1oz/¼ cup plain (all-purpose) flour
25g/1oz/¼ cup luxury glacé mixed fruit, finely chopped
1 1.5cm/½in piece of preserved stem ginger in syrup, drained and finely chopped
30ml/2 tbsp flaked almonds

1 Remove the seeds from the melons, then cut them into wedges and slice off the rind. Cut all the flesh into chunks and mix in a bowl. Stir in the stem ginger syrup, cover and chill until ready to serve.

2 Meanwhile, make the cookies. Preheat the oven to 180°C/350°F/Gas 4. Place the butter, sugar and honey in a pan and heat until melted. Remove from the heat and stir in the remaining ingredients.

3 Line a baking sheet with baking parchment. Space four spoonfuls of the mixture on the paper at regular intervals, leaving plenty of room to allow for the cookies spreading. Flatten the mixture slightly into rounds and bake for 15 minutes or until the tops are golden.

4 Let the cookies cool on the baking sheet for 1 minute, then lift each one in turn, using a metal spatula, and drape over a rolling pin to cool and harden. Repeat with the remaining ginger mixture to make eight curved cookies in all.

5 Transfer the melon chunks and syrup to a large serving dish or individual glasses and serve accompanied by the crisp ginger cookies.

Cantaloupe melon with strawberries: Energy 53kcal/223kJ; Protein 0.9g; Carbohydrate 12.7g, of which sugars 12.7g; Fat 0.2g, of which saturates 0g; Cholesterol 0mg; Calcium 23mg; Fibre 0.8g; Sodium 41mg
Melon trio with ginger cookies: Energy 350kcal/1479kJ; Protein 4.8g; Carbohydrate 65g, of which sugars 60.1g; Fat 9.7g, of which saturates 3.8g; Cholesterol 13mg; Calcium 74mg; Fibre 2.5g; Sodium 167mg

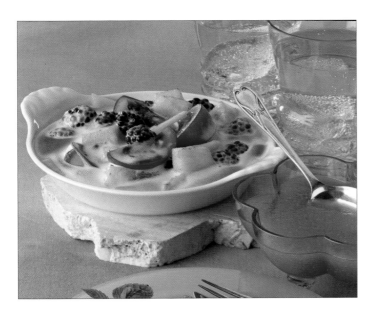

Tropical Fruit Gratin

This out-of-the-ordinary gratin is strictly for grown-ups. A colourful combination of fruit is topped with a simple sabayon before being flashed under the grill.

Serves 4
2 tamarillos
½ sweet pineapple
1 ripe mango
175g/6oz/1½ cups blackberries
120ml/4fl oz/½ cup sparkling white wine
115g/4oz/½ cup caster (superfine) sugar
6 egg yolks

1 Cut each tamarillo in half lengthwise and then into thick slices. Cut the rind and core from the pineapple and take spiral slices off the outside to remove the eyes. Cut the flesh into regular chunks. Peel the mango, cut it in half and slice the flesh from the stone.

2 Divide all the fruit, including the blackberries, among four 14cm/5½in gratin dishes set on a baking sheet and set aside. Heat the wine and sugar in a pan until the sugar has dissolved. Bring to the boil and cook for 5 minutes.

3 Put the egg yolks in a large heatproof bowl. Place the bowl over a pan of simmering water and whisk until pale. Slowly pour on the hot sugar syrup, whisking all the time, until the mixture thickens. Preheat the grill (broiler).

4 Spoon the mixture over the fruit. Place the baking sheet holding the dishes on a low shelf under the hot grill until the topping is golden. Serve immediately.

> **Cook's Tip**
> Blackberries are widely cultivated from late spring to autumn and are usually large, plump and sweet. The finest wild blackberries have a bitter edge and a strong depth of flavour – best appreciated with a sprinkling of sugar.

Banana & Mascarpone

If you are a fan of cold banana custard, you'll love this recipe. It is a grown-up version of an old favourite. No one will guess that the secret is ready-made custard sauce.

Serves 4–6
250g/9oz/generous 1 cup
  mascarpone cheese
300ml/½ pint/1¼ cups fresh

ready-made custard sauce
150ml/¼ pint/⅔ cup Greek
  (US strained plain) yogurt
4 bananas
juice of 1 lime
50g/2oz/½ cup pecan nuts,
  coarsely chopped
120ml/4fl oz/½ cup maple syrup

1 Combine the mascarpone, custard sauce and yogurt in a large bowl and beat together until smooth. Make this mixture up to several hours ahead, if you like. Cover and chill, then stir before using.

2 Slice the bananas diagonally and place in a separate bowl. Pour over the lime juice and toss together until the bananas are coated in the juice.

3 Divide half the custard mixture between four to six dessert glasses and top each portion with a generous spoonful of the banana mixture.

4 Spoon the remaining custard mixture into the glasses and top with the rest of the bananas. Scatter the nuts over the top. Drizzle maple syrup over each dessert and chill for 30 minutes before serving.

> **Cook's Tip**
> • *Fresh custard sauce is now readily available from the chilled sections of supermarkets. Canned can be used if necessary.*
> • *If pecans are not available, use roughly chopped toasted walnuts or flaked (sliced) almonds.*

Dressed Strawberries

Fragrant strawberries release their finest flavour when moistened with a sauce of fresh raspberries and scented passion fruit.

Serves 4
350g/12oz/2 cups raspberries,
  fresh or frozen
45ml/3 tbsp caster (superfine)
  sugar
1 passion fruit
675g/1½lb/6 cups
  small strawberries
8 plain finger biscuits, to serve

1 Place the raspberries and sugar in a stain-resistant pan and soften over a gentle heat to release the juices. Simmer gently for 5 minutes. Allow to cool.

2 Halve the passion fruit and, using a teaspoon, carefully scoop out the seeds and juice.

3 Turn the raspberries into a food processor or blender, add the passion fruit and blend until well combined.

4 Pass the blended fruit sauce through a fine nylon sieve (strainer) to remove the seeds.

5 Fold the strawberries into the sauce, then spoon into four stemmed glasses. Serve with plain finger biscuits.

Banana & mascarpone: Energy 222kcal/931kJ; Protein 5.6g; Carbohydrate 27.8g, of which sugars 25.5g; Fat 10.4g, of which saturates 3.8g; Cholesterol 12mg; Calcium 64mg; Fibre 0.8g; Sodium 62mg
Dressed strawberries: Energy 113kcal/481kJ; Protein 2.7g; Carbohydrate 26.1g, of which sugars 26.1g; Fat 0.5g, of which saturates 0.1g; Cholesterol 0mg; Calcium 55mg; Fibre 4.2g; Sodium 14mg

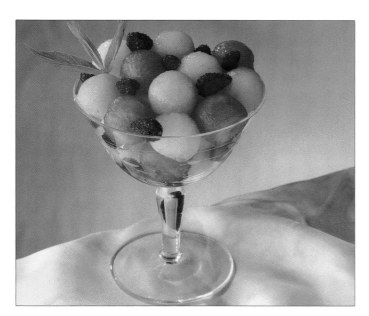

Mixed Melon Salad with Wild Strawberries

Ice-cold melon is a delicious way to end a meal. Here, several varieties are combined with strongly flavoured wild or woodland strawberries.

Serves 4
1 cantaloupe or Charentais melon
1 Galia melon
900g/2lb watermelon
175g/6oz/1 1/2 cups wild
  strawberries
4 fresh mint sprigs, to decorate

Using a large, sharp knife, cut all the melons in half. Remove the seeds from the cantaloupe and Galia melons with a spoon.

2 With a melon baller, scoop out as many melon balls as you can from all three melons. Transfer to a large bowl, mix gently together and chill.

3 Add the wild strawberries and turn out into four stemmed glass dishes. Decorate with sprigs of fresh mint and serve.

Cook's Tip
If the tiny wild strawberries are not available, you can use ordinary strawberries, cut in half.

Muscat Grape Frappé

The flavour and perfume of the Muscat grape is wonderful in this ice-cool, sophisticated salad.

Serves 4
1/2 bottle Muscat wine
150ml/1/4 pint/2/3 cup water
450g/1lb Muscat grapes

1 Pour the wine into a stainless-steel or enamel tray, add the water, place in the freezer and freeze for 3 hours, or until the wine is completely solid.

2 Remove the seeds from the grapes with a pair of tweezers. If you have time, you can also peel the grapes. Scrape across the frozen wine with a tablespoon to make a fine ice. Combine the grapes with the ice, spoon into four shallow glasses and serve.

Apricots in Marsala

Apricots gently poached in Marsala and served chilled make a versatile dessert. Serve with sweetened whipped cream mixed with yogurt and flavoured with ground cinnamon.

Serves 4
12 apricots
50g/2oz/4tbsp caster (superfine)
  sugar
300ml/1/2 pint/1 1/4 cups Marsala
2 strips pared orange rind
1 vanilla pod (bean), split
250ml/8fl oz/1 cup water

1 Halve and stone (pit) the apricots, then place in a bowl of boiling water for about 30 seconds. Drain, then slip off the skins.

2 Place the sugar, Marsala, orange rind, vanilla pod and water in a pan. Heat gently until the sugar dissolves. Bring to the boil, without stirring, then simmer for 2–3 minutes.

3 Add the apricot halves and poach for 5–6 minutes, or until just tender. Using a slotted spoon, transfer to a serving dish. Boil the syrup rapidly until reduced by half, then pour over the apricots and leave to cool. Cover and chill. Remove the orange rind and vanilla pod before serving.

Mixed melon salad: Energy 154kcal/655kJ; Protein 3g; Carbohydrate 35.4g, of which sugars 35.4g; Fat 1g, of which saturates 0.2g; Cholesterol 0mg; Calcium 62mg; Fibre 1.9g; Sodium 100mg
Muscat grape frappe: Energy 150kcal/634kJ; Protein 0.6g; Carbohydrate 22.5g, of which sugars 22.5g; Fat 0.1g, of which saturates 0g; Cholesterol 0mg; Calcium 27mg; Fibre 0.8g; Sodium 14mg
Apricots in marsala: Energy 159kcal/673kJ; Protein 1.3g; Carbohydrate 26.5g, of which sugars 26.5g; Fat 0.1g, of which saturates 0g; Cholesterol 0mg; Calcium 36mg; Fibre 2.1g; Sodium 13mg

Fresh Fruit with Mango Sauce

Fruit coulis, became trendy in the 1970s with nouvelle cuisine. It makes a simple fruit dish special.

Serves 6
1 large ripe mango, peeled, stoned (pitted) and chopped
rind of 1 unwaxed orange
juice of 3 oranges
caster (superfine) sugar, to taste
2 peaches

2 nectarines
1 small mango, peeled
2 plums
1 pear or ½ small melon
25–50g/1–2oz/2 heaped tbsp wild strawberries (optional)
25–50g/1–2oz/2 heaped tbsp raspberries
25–50g/1–2oz/2 heaped tbsp blueberries
juice of 1 lemon
small mint sprigs, to decorate

1 In a food processor fitted with the metal blade, process the large mango until smooth. Add the orange rind, juice and sugar to taste and process again until very smooth. Press through a sieve (strainer) into a bowl and chill the sauce.

2 Peel the peaches, if you like, then slice and stone (pit) the peaches, nectarines, small mango and plums. Quarter and core the pear, or if using, slice the melon thinly and remove the peel.

3 Place the sliced fruits on a large plate, sprinkle the fruits with the lemon juice and chill, covered with clear film (plastic wrap), for up to 3 hours before serving.

4 To serve, arrange the sliced fruits on serving plates, spoon the berries on top, drizzle with a little mango sauce and decorate with mint sprigs. Serve the remaining sauce separately.

Variation
Use a raspberry coulis instead of a mango one: purée raspberries with a little lemon juice and icing (confectioners') sugar to taste, then pass through a sieve (strainer) to remove the pips. You can use frozen raspberries for this, so it can be made at any time of year.

Bananas with Lime & Cardamom Sauce

Cardamom and bananas go together perfectly, and this luxurious dessert makes an original treat.

Serves 4
6 small bananas
50g/2oz/¼ cup butter
seeds from 4 cardamom pods, crushed

50g/2oz/½ cup flaked (sliced) almonds
thinly pared rind and juice of 2 limes
50g/2oz/⅓ cup light muscovado (brown) sugar
30ml/2 tbsp dark rum
ice cream, to serve

1 Peel the bananas and cut them in half lengthwise. Heat half the butter in a large frying pan. Add half the bananas, and cook until the undersides are golden. Turn carefully, using a metal spatula. Cook until golden all over.

2 Once cooked, transfer the bananas to a heatproof serving dish. Cook the remaining bananas in the same way.

3 Melt the remaining butter, then add the cardamom seeds and almonds. Cook, stirring until the almonds are golden.

4 Stir in the lime rind and juice, then the sugar. Cook, stirring, until the mixture is smooth, bubbling and slightly reduced. Stir in the rum. Pour the sauce over the bananas and serve with vanilla or coconut ice cream.

Cook's Tip
Use green cardamom pods. Split them open and scape out the black seeds, then crush to help release the aromatic flavour.

Variation
If serving to children, replace the rum with orange juice.

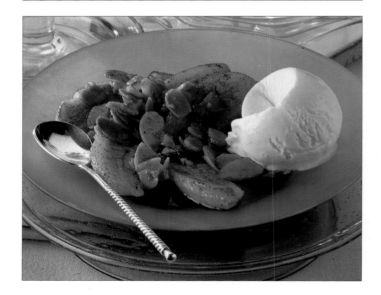

Papayas in Jasmine Flower Syrup

The fragrant syrup can be prepared in advance, using fresh jasmine flowers from a house plant or the garden. It tastes fabulous with papayas, but it is also good with other tropical fruits, such as lychees or mangoes.

Serves 2
105ml/7 tbsp water
45ml/3 tbsp palm sugar (jaggery) or light muscovado (brown) sugar
20–30 jasmine flowers, plus a few extra, to decorate (optional)
2 ripe papayas
juice of 1 lime

1 Place the water and sugar in a small pan. Heat gently, stirring occasionally, until the sugar has dissolved, then simmer, without stirring, over a low heat for 4 minutes.

2 Pour into a bowl, leave to cool slightly, then add the jasmine flowers. Leave to steep for at least 20 minutes.

3 Peel the papayas and slice in half lengthwise. Scoop out and discard the seeds. Plate the papayas and squeeze lime over.

4 Strain the syrup into a clean bowl, discarding the flowers. Spoon the syrup over the papayas.

5 Serve at once, decorated with a few fresh jasmine flowers.

> **Cook's Tip**
> *Although scented white jasmine flowers are perfectly safe to eat, it is important to be sure that they have not been sprayed with pesticides or other harmful chemicals. Washing them may not remove all the residue.*

> **Variation**
> *Spoon the warm syrup over a tall glass of ice cream to create a quick but stylish dessert.*

Indian Fruit Salad

This lightly spiced salad is ideal after a heavy meal.

Serves 6
115g/4oz seedless green and black grapes
225g/8oz canned mandarin segments, drained
2 navel oranges, peeled and segmented
225g/8oz canned grapefruit segments, drained
1 honeydew melon and ½ watermelon, flesh cut into balls
1 fresh mango, peeled, stoned (pitted) and sliced
juice of 1 lemon
2.5ml/½ tsp sugar
1.5ml/¼ tsp ground cumin seeds
salt and ground black pepper

1 Place all the fruit in a large serving bowl and add the lemon juice. Gently toss to prevent damaging the fruit.

2 Mix together the remaining ingredients and sprinkle over the fruit. Gently toss, chill thoroughly and serve.

Chinese Fruit Salad

An unusual fruit salad with an Oriental flavour, ideal for rounding off a spicy meal.

Serves 4
115g/4oz/½ cup caster (superfine) sugar
300ml/½ pint/1¼ cups water
thinly pared rind and juice of 1 lime
400g/14oz can lychees in syrup
1 ripe mango, peeled and sliced
1 eating apple, cored and sliced
2 bananas, chopped
1 star fruit, sliced (optional)
5ml/1 tsp sesame seeds, toasted

1 Place the sugar in a pan with the water and the lime rind. Heat gently until the sugar dissolves, then increase the heat and boil gently for about 7–8 minutes. Set aside to cool.

2 Drain the lychees and reserve the juice. Pour the juice into the cooled lime syrup with the lime juice. Place all the prepared fruit in a bowl and pour on the lime and lychee syrup. Chill for about 1 hour. Just before serving, sprinkle with sesame seeds.

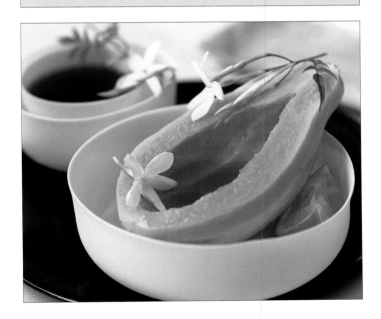

Indian fruit salad: Energy 120kcal/512kJ; Protein 2.6g; Carbohydrate 28.6g, of which sugars 28.5g; Fat 0.3g, of which saturates 0g; Cholesterol 0mg; Calcium 67mg; Fibre 3.5g; Sodium 61mg
Chinese fruit salad: Energy 264kcal/1123kJ; Protein 1.7g; Carbohydrate 66.1g, of which sugars 64.9g; Fat 1g, of which saturates 0.2g; Cholesterol 0mg; Calcium 36mg; Fibre 2.4g; Sodium 6mg
Papayas in jasmine flower syrup: Energy 197kcal/837kJ; Protein 1.6g; Carbohydrate 49.9g, of which sugars 49.9g; Fat 0.3g, of which saturates 0g; Cholesterol 0mg; Calcium 81mg; Fibre 6.6g; Sodium 17mg

Index